D1432254

THE MAKING OF MODERN PROPERTY

In this original intellectual history, Anna di Robilant traces the history of one of the most influential legal, political, and intellectual projects of modernity: the appropriation of Roman property law by liberal nineteenth-century jurists to fit the purposes of modern Europe. Drawing from a wealth of primary sources, many of which have never been translated into English, di Robilant outlines how a broad network of European jurists reinvented the classical Roman concept of property to support the process of modernization. By placing this intellectual project within its historical context, she shows how changing class relations, economic policies, and developing ideologies converged to produce the basis of modern property law. Bringing these developments to the twentieth century, this book demonstrates how this largely fabricated version of Roman property law shaped and continues to shape debates concerning economic growth, sustainability, and democratic participation.

ANNA DI ROBILANT is Professor of Law at Boston University. A legal scholar trained in Europe and in the United States, she has published extensively on the history and theory of modern property law. She is the chair of the property section of the "Common Core of European Private Law," a project that brings together more than 200 legal scholars and practitioners to analyze and map the connections and underlying similarities in contract, property, and torts laws across Europe.

THE MAKING OF MODERN PROPERTY

Reinventing Roman Law in Europe and Its Peripheries
1789–1950

ANNA DI ROBILANT

Boston University

CAMBRIDGE
UNIVERSITY PRESS

Shaftesbury Road, Cambridge CB2 8EA, United Kingdom

One Liberty Plaza, 20th Floor, New York, NY 10006, USA

477 Williamstown Road, Port Melbourne, VIC 3207, Australia

314–321, 3rd Floor, Plot 3, Splendor Forum, Jasola District Centre, New Delhi – 110025, India

103 Penang Road, #05-06/07, Visioncrest Commercial, Singapore 238467

Cambridge University Press is part of Cambridge University Press & Assessment, a department of the University of Cambridge.

We share the University's mission to contribute to society through the pursuit of education, learning and research at the highest international levels of excellence.

www.cambridge.org
Information on this title: www.cambridge.org/9781108494779
DOI: 10.1017/9781108859844

First published 2023

A catalogue record for this publication is available from the British Library.

Library of Congress Cataloging-in-Publication Data
Names: Di Robilant, Anna, author.
Title: The making of modern property : reinventing Roman Law in Europe and its peripheries 1789-1950 / Anna di Robilant, Boston University.
Description: Cambridge, United Kingdom ; New York, NY : Cambridge University Press, 2023. | Includes bibliographical references and index.
Identifiers: LCCN 2022056970 (print) | LCCN 2022056971 (ebook) | ISBN 9781108494779 (hardback) | ISBN 9781108796934 (paperback) | ISBN 9781108859844 (epub)
Subjects: LCSH: Property–History. | Property (Roman law) | Property–Latin America. | Property–Europe. | Roman law–Influence.
Classification: LCC K720 .D57 2023 (print) | LCC K720 (ebook) | DDC 346.04–dc23/eng/20230403
LC record available at https://lccn.loc.gov/2022056970
LC ebook record available at https://lccn.loc.gov/2022056971

ISBN 978-1-108-49477-9 Hardback

A Benno e Milo con tanto amore

CONTENTS

ACKNOWLEDGMENTS

I could have never written a book of this scope without the invaluable help and guidance of many friends and colleagues, to whom I am deeply indebted.

My academic mentors, Charlie Donahue, Duncan Kennedy, Mitch Lasser, and Ugo Mattei, have guided, supported, and inspired me, starting from my very first steps on the academic path in Europe and at every subsequent stage of my intellectual development. Their mentorship is an immense gift for which I will be forever grateful.

My debt toward Greg Alexander, Hanoch Dagan, Joe Singer, and Laura Underkuffler is also immensurable. When I moved to the United States, they welcomed me with great generosity in their "Progressive Property" group. Their work changed my thinking about property and indelibly shaped my research agenda, and their constant support and patient guidance helped me progress through the various steps of my academic career as an émigré.

Talha Syed and Roni Mann have given me the invaluable gift of deep friendship, vigorous intellectual exchange, and political comradery. Talha taught me analytical clarity and conceptual creativity. His deep passion for ideas and politics inspires me every day. Throughout the years, reading the work of Oren Bracha, David Grewal, Nien-He Hsieh, Sam Moyn, and Jed Purdy, has been a source of great inspiration, and for this I thank them. At Boston University, my friends Daniela Caruso, Kris Collins, Pnina Lahav, Gary Lawson, Gerry Leonard, David Seipp, and Robert Tsai have generously read and provided feedback on many, many drafts over the years.

This book was inspired and shaped by a number of towering scholars in European legal and intellectual history whose work I admire immensely, some of whom I had the fortune of meeting and others whom I have never had the pleasure to know personally: Clifford Ando, Robert Brenner, Luigi Capogrossi Colognesi, Paul du Plessis, Thomas Duve, Antonio Gambaro, James Gordley, Paolo Grossi, Dick Helmholz, Ellen Meiksins Wood, Pierre

Rosanvallon, Aldo Schiavone, Alessandro Somma, Bernardo Sordi, James Whitman and Reinhard Zimmermann.

Many friends and colleagues in Europe and in the United States have generously contributed in different ways, reading and giving feedback on drafts of chapters, inviting me to workshops, or simply engaging with my work: Bram Akkermans, Luisa Antoniolli, Bernadette Atuahene, Frederic Audren, Marietta Auer, Shyam Balganesh, Paulo Barrozo, Betahny Berger, Jane Bestor, Rafe Blaufarb, Bob Bone, Richard Buxbaum, Hannah Buxbaum, Eric Claeys, Jens Dammann, David Dana, Sannoy Das, Nestor Davidson, Ben Depoorter, Rashmi Dyal-Chand, Jorge Esquirol, Willy Forbath, Oliver Gerstenberg, Tom Ginsburg, Maeve Glass, Betta Grande, Michele Graziadei, Christophe Jamin, Emily Kadens, Amalia Kessler, Jeremy Kessler, Andrew Kull, Martin Hesselink, Bob Hockett, Maxi Langer, Adrian Lanni, Katarina Linos, John Lovett, Maria Rosaria Marella, Giovanni Marini, Ajay Mehrotra, Tom Merrill, Naomi Metzger, Ralph Michaels, Thomas Mitchell, Hanri Mostart, PG Monateri, Francesco Parisi, Eduardo Penalver, Katarina Pistor, Andrea Pradi, Mathias Reimann, Ezra Rosser, Maria Salah, Alvaro Santos, Hani Sayed, Kim Scheppele, Chris Serkin, Amr Shalakany, Dan Sharfstein, Nadav Shoked, Jed Shugerman, Henry Smith, Holger Spamann, Philomila Tsoukala, and Lua Yulle. Special gratitude goes to the late Andre van der Walt, whose wonderful conversations and thoughtful feedback I deeply miss.

At Boston University, many dear friends have inspired and generously supported me throughout the years: Aziza Ahmed, Susan Akram, Jack Beermann, Julie Dahlstrom, Stacey Dogan, Jon Feingold, Alan Feld, Jim Fleming, Wendy Gordon, Michael Harper, Scott Hirst, Naomi Mann, Steve Marks, Linda McClain, Mike Meurer, Nancy Moore, Karen Pita Loor, Sadiq Reza, Sarah Sherman-Stokes, Kate Silbaugh, Jessica Silbey, Rob Sloane, Fred Tung, David Walker, David Webber, Jay Wexler, and Kathy Zeiler.

I am immensely grateful to my dean, Angela Onwuachi-Willig, who has generously supported and inspired me in so many ways. My deeply felt gratitude also goes to my colleagues in the Boston University leadership team who have been so patient with me as I was completing this book and serving as in leadership capacities: Jill Collins, Ellen Frentzen, Alissa Leonard, Gerry Muir, Emily Robichaud, Aida Ten, and Jeremy Thompson.

But my greatest debt is to three colleagues without whose help I would have never finished this book. My friend Charlie Bartlett devoted countless hours of invaluably helpful research and editing. Charlie also provided translations of Greek and Latin passages and assisted with the translation of German texts. Stephanie Weigmann, associate director for research of the Boston University Law Pappas-Fineman Libraries, and Ron Wheeler, director of the Boston University Law Pappas-Fineman Libraries, worked tirelessly to expand and reorganize the bibliography. Working with the Pappas-Fineman library has been a wonderful experience. Each and every librarian at the Pappas and Fineman Libraries has generously offered their expertise, time, and passion. Special gratitude goes to Katharine Haldeman, Kelly Johnson, and Amelia Landenberger, who have tirelessly helped me over the years with great skill, immense patience, and graciousness. At Cambridge University Press, Finola O' Sullivan, Marianne Nield, and Rachel Imrie believed in this project and guided me with great patience.

My husband, Arnulf Becker Lorca, has been a loving and patient source of support throughout the long process of writing this book and has read and commented on innumerable drafts. Our two boys, Benno and Milo, are the light of my life. My mother, Costanza di Robilant, and my late father, Enrico di Robilant, instilled in me the passion for ideas and encouraged me to pursue an academic career. My brother, Manfredo di Robilant, has always been my rock and my greatest source of inspiration. Sara Toomey has given me the wonderful gift of her friendship. Kattia Wilson made it possible for me to raise two boys while also pursuing tenure and writing a book.

Introduction

The Romanist-Bourgeois Property Culture: *Dominium*, the Social Function, and Resources

The idea of property structures virtually every aspect of our lives. It informs our views about the market and our understanding of the role of the state; it also shapes how we conceive of the physical space we inhabit and how we relate to each other. In contemporary liberal democracies, lawyers and nonexperts alike understand property as a set of robust legal entitlements that give the owner broad control over a resource, while also recognizing that these entitlements are shaped to reflect the characteristics of different resources and limited to protect the interests of others and of the public in relation to specific resources. This contemporary idea of property is often seen as arising from Anglo-American political and legal thought. In this view, the emphasis on the owner's power is rooted in Lockean liberalism and epitomized by the notion of "sole and despotic dominion" made famous by the eighteenth-century English jurist William Blackstone;[1] the realization of the necessarily limited character of ownership entitlements is the product of twentieth-century sociological jurisprudence and American Legal Realism.[2]

This book challenges this conventional wisdom by tracing the evolution of the contemporary idea of property to Roman law and its creative reinvention in continental Europe, and its informal imperial periphery, over the course of the nineteenth and early twentieth centuries. I endeavor to show that our understanding of property is deeply indebted

---

[1] David B. Schorr, "How Blackstone Became a Blackstonian" (2009) 10 *Theoretical Inquiries in Law* 16; Robert P. Burns, "Blackstone's Theory of the 'Absolute; Rights of Property'" (1985) 54 *University of Cincinnati Law Review* 67; Carol M. Rose, "Canons of Property Talk, or Blackstone's Anxiety" (1998) 108 *Yale Law Journal* 601.

[2] Felix Cohen, "Dialogue on Private Property" (1954) 9 *Rutgers Law Review* 357; Morris R. Cohen, "Property and Sovereignty" (1927) 13 *Cornell Law Quarterly* 8; Hanoch Dagan, "The Real Legacy of American Legal Realism" (2018) 38 *Oxford Journal of Legal Studies* 123.

1

to the legal concepts developed by a global network of jurists, located in France, Germany, Italy, and later in Latin America, who shared a training in Roman law and the ambition to "modernize" their countries' property law. I call the property tradition explored in this book "Romanist-bourgeois" because the jurists, in their effort to modernize property, turned to Roman antiquity, selectively appropriating doctrines developed by the Roman jurists and creatively reshaping them to meet the needs of nineteenth-century economies and bourgeois societies.[3]

Beginning in late eighteenth-century France, jurists embarked on a project that would have momentous economic and cultural consequences: developing a new concept of property and a new body of property doctrines for modern, liberal, industrializing society. As European countries started on the long and tortuous path toward liberalism and capitalism, their property systems were still, largely, based on forms of limited and hierarchical landholding that smacked of feudalism and seemed inimical to productive enterprise. Property needed a dramatic transformation and a clear break with anything "feudal." Working in relative isolation from parallel intellectual developments in the Anglo-American world, jurists in continental Europe and its peripheries "invented" a modern concept of property inspired by a largely fictitious idea of Roman *dominum*. *La proprietà, la propriété, Eigentum, la propiedad*, despite their differences, were all molded on the blueprint of *dominium*. By the 1850s, the quest for modern property had spread to the informal periphery of Europe, and the discourse of property modernization continued, albeit in different terms, well into the twentieth century.

The making of modern property is a project that unfolded over two centuries, during which, successive generations of metropolitan and peripheral jurists trained in Roman law engaged in a dialogue over the structure and the scope of property, as well as its justification. They devoted their legal creativity and their intellectual and political energy to what they saw as a shared, and to some degree global, project. To be sure, not all was new. The conceptual foundations of the new concept of

---

[3] I owe the concept of "Romanist-bourgeois" law to the path-breaking work of Aldo Schiavone: among his many works, see *Alle origini del diritto romano borghese. Hegel contro Savigny* (Rome: Laterza, 1984); *La storia spezzata. Roma antica e Occidente moderno* (Rome: Laterza, 1996); Margery H. Schneider (trans.), *The End of the Past: Ancient Rome and The Modern West* (Cambridge, MA: Harvard University Press, 2000); Jeremy Carden and Antony Shugar (transs.), *The Invention of Law in the West* (Cambridge, MA: Harvard University Press, 2011).

property were already solidly in place. The canon lawyers of the twelfth through fourteenth centuries and the Spanish Scholastics of the sixteenth century had firmly established the idea that made Romanist-bourgeois property possible: the idea that property is a subjective natural right, a right or power of the individual grounded in the law of nature and in reason. However, while historians have extensively explored the medieval and early modern foundations of modern property,[4] a comprehensive account of the invention of Romanist-bourgeois property has yet to be written.[5]

The Romanist-bourgeois property tradition is more complex and capacious than the now dominant Anglo-American property culture. It includes the idea, allegedly Roman, and purely aspirational, that property consists of "absolute" *dominium*, but it also foregrounds the notion that property has a "social function," a notion to which jurists have attributed widely differing scope and content, depending on their moral and ideological commitments. However, the truly distinctive, and largely forgotten, contribution of this alternative property tradition is that its focal point is the "things," or resources, that are the object of property rights. Jurists trained in the Romanist tradition sought to mediate the apparently intractable tension between the owner's "absolute" *dominium* and property's "social function" by focusing on the "thing," on the specific interests and values implicated by the different resources that can be the object of property. One of the most prominent property scholars in the United States recently described property as "the law of things."[6] Roman

---

[4] The bibliography on the early modern origins of property is extensive. See Michel Villey, *Le droit et les droits de l'homme* (Paris: Presses Universitaires de France, 1983); Id., La formation de la pensee juridique moderne, 4th ed. (Paris: Montchretien, 1975); Brian Tierney, The Idea of Natural Rights (Atlanta: Scholars Press, 1997); Charles Donahue Jr., "Ius in the Subjective Sense in Roman Law: Reflections on Villey and Tierney," in Domenico Maffei, Italo Birocchi, Mario Caravale, Emanuele Conte, and Ugo Petronio (eds.), *A Ennio Cortese* (Rome: Il Cigno Edizioni, 2001), 1:506–535; James R. Gordley, "Suárez and Natural Law," in Benjamin Hill and Henrik Lagerlund (eds.), *The Philosophy of Francisco Suárez* (Oxford University Press, 2012), 209–229; Annabel Brett, "Individual and Community in the 'Second Scholastic': Subjective Rights in Domingo de Soto and Francisco Suárez," in Constance Blackwell and Sachiko Kusukawa (eds.), *Philosophy in the Sixteenth and Seventeenth Centuries: Conversations with Aristotle* (London: Routledge, 1999), 146–168.

[5] For a wonderful analysis of the legacy of Roman law and the ambitions of the Roman law professoriate in eighteenth- and nineteenth-century Germany, see James Q. Whitman, *The Legacy of Roman Law in the German Romantic Era* (Princeton, NJ: Princeton University Press, 2014 [1990]).

[6] Henry E. Smith, "Property as the Law of Things" (2012) 125 *Harvard Law Review* 1691.

property law was quintessentially a "law of things." The Roman jurists classified the *res* (things) that can be owned according to their physical characteristics, social and economic value, and cultural and religious meaning, and they shaped ownership entitlements to reflect these features. In Roman law, a special set of rules applied to objects used for the cult of a deity, to tombs or burial grounds, and to the wall and gates of the city; air, running water, the sea and the seashore were treated differently than roads, rivers, and harbors; land situated in Italy, enslaved individuals, or four-footed animals were subject to special rules that did not apply to all other things. Building on the insights of their Roman predecessors, nineteenth-century jurists understood that the dilemmas of property law, that is, the tension between the owner's entitlements and the interests of neighbors or the public, can be eased only through a practical, contextualist analysis of the unique characteristics of resources as different as water, minerals, agricultural land, housing, or commercial property. Conflicts between ownership prerogatives and the public interest as well as tensions between the multiple goals that property aims at facilitating, which include autonomy, self-authorship, equality, and efficiency, remain an ineluctable challenge of any property system to this day. The focus on resources as key to mediating these conflicts is a critical intuition, now accepted by economists and by the most sophisticated property theorists, but one that has remained marginal to Anglo-American property until relatively recently.[7]

For over two centuries, this Romanist-bourgeois notion of property – with all its complexities and tensions, the aspiration to absolute *dominium*, the realization that property has an ineludible social dimension, and the pragmatic focus on "things" – has occupied a central place in the imaginary of modern Europe. Starting in eighteenth-century France, property quickly became synonymous with modernity. It was hailed as the cornerstone of the new political structure of modern Europe, the horizontal order of politically equal citizens and free owners that replaced the vertical feudal hierarchy. This modern notion of property was also the foundation of the new economy that was slowly moving toward capitalism. Because of these manifold aspects of significance, a

---

[7] Elinor Ostrom, "How Types of Goods and Property Rights Jointly Affect Collective Action" (2003) 15(3) *Journal of Theoretical Politics* 239–270; Hanoch Dagan, *Property: Values and Interests* (Oxford: Oxford University Press, 2011); Gregory S. Alexander, "Pluralism and Property" (2011) 80 *Fordham Law Review* 1017; Nestor M. Davidson, "Standardization and Pluralism in Property Law" (2008) 61 *Vanderbilt Law Review* 1597.

numerous and diverse cohort of writers and scholars claimed an expertise in property. Philosophers and political theorists discussed the reasons and goals that justify giving individual private property rights. Economists investigated its relation to economic growth and proposed a variety of recommendations for reform. The agronomists of the many "Agricultural Societies" that flourished in eighteenth- and nineteenth-century Europe had their own theories on the relation between property and agricultural improvement. And pamphleteers of all stripes debated the virtues and vices of property. But the ones who did the actual work of shaping and operationalizing modern property were the jurists, academic and practicing. The jurists were the architects of the modern law of property and the movers and shakers in the real-world life of property. Yet, their work is largely underappreciated. Historians of property have delved deep into the more rousing writings of publicists and the normatively ambitious theories of philosophers and economists but have left the technicalities of property law to the competence of doctrinal lawyers. This book retrieves the work of the jurists from the narrow purview of doctrinal studies and restores it to its central place in the global intellectual history of modernity. The making of Romanist-bourgeois property is a fascinating story of economic and political struggle, professional power and scholarly devotion. It is also a story about the circulation and coproduction of specialized knowledge across geographic and imperial boundaries through global intellectual networks.

Modernizing Property

The jurists who are the main characters of this book belonged to a generation of legal academics who began in the early nineteenth century to share, albeit with varying acuity and commitment, the consciousness of living in a new, "modern" era. Enlightenment ideas about progress, the complex legacy of the revolutionary upheavals, the development of agrarian capitalism in England, and, later, the shock of industrialization and the shifting configurations of class struggle were among the transformations that engendered and solidified the experience of modernity.[8] The jurists experienced a sense of unprecedented and seemingly

---

[8] Marshall Berman, *All That Is Solid Melts into Air: The Experience of Modernity* (New York: Penguin, 1982); C. A. Bayly, *The Birth of the Modern World 1780–1914* (Malden, MA: Blackwell, 2004); Aldo Schiavone, *Progresso* (Bologna: Il Mulino, 2020). (English translation: Ann Goldstein, trans., *What Is Progress* [Rome: Europa Editions, 2021]).

incessant change that demanded an overhaul of the legal system. Because of property's centrality to questions of constitutional political economy, the reform of property law appeared particularly urgent. Property was one of the central institutions of the new modern age and the jurists set out to modernize the law of property. Yet, their understandings of what modernization entailed differed dramatically and changed over time.

In the late eighteenth century and well into the nineteenth century, modernizing property meant dismantling the vestiges of feudal property that still existed throughout continental Europe and creating a new property law infrastructure, capable of supporting the development of a more advanced and productive agricultural economy and of facilitating investment in land by a rising entrepreneurial middle-class. The development of agrarian capitalism in England made an impression on the reformist elites of the Continent, inspiring ambitious disciplinary reform agendas focused on agricultural improvement, from the political economy of the Physiocrats to the science of public administration advocated by the German "Cameralists." A strident anti-feudal rhetoric inspired these reform agendas and a robust and secure notion of private property was their centerpiece. Yet, in large sections of the European continent, land was still held in a dizzying variety of limited and divided ownership forms that were, essentially, feudal. While European feudalism was internally diverse, feudal property was, by and large, "divided property" (*dominium divisum*) with ownership entitlements effectively split between two owners, an owner with *dominium directum*, that is, title, and an owner with *dominium utile*, that is, use rights and a set of varying, but often burdensome, duties. This split and limited feudal landholding regime had, obviously, changed over time. By the eighteenth century, holders of *dominium utile* had acquired broader rights to use and transfer and had been relieved of many of their duties. Nonetheless, these old property forms appeared antithetical to the new liberal and reformist ideas. They tied up superior and inferior owners in rigid status hierarchies and contravened the new imperatives of improvement and enhanced productivity by limiting the ability of direct users to manage the land.

Inspired by the ideas of liberal philosophers and political theorists and guided by the experts' recommendations about agricultural improvement, the jurists who made it their mission to modernize property sought to wipe out any feudal remnants and to introduce a modern concept of free and full property. Modern property, reformers argued, would not allow for hierarchies between a superior and an inferior owner or for different property gradations, as between full property and property that is less than full. Modern property would be the one and only right of its kind, a broad and secure right that gives the owner a full set of robust entitlements. To craft this modern concept of property, nineteenth-century jurists turned to Roman law. From the rich inventory of Roman property concepts, they selected those that conferred on owners the broadest control over the resources they owned. Through this selective reading, they recast Roman *dominium* as an "absolute" and "exclusive" right. Of course, absolute ownership, free from restrictions, is impossible in any organized society and Roman property was far from absolute. Yet "absolute" became the jurists' mantra, a catchphrase signaling that property is a right unique in kind, broad in content, and robust vis-à-vis others and the state. Having effectively invented this idea of Roman "absolute" *dominium*, the jurists proposed it as the blueprint for the property law of modern European nation-states. This Roman-inspired, modern concept of *dominium* held two promises. It promised to establish the foundations for liberal constitutionalism, for a horizontal political order of equal citizens endowed with free, full, and secure property rights; and it promised to facilitate the transition from a pre-capitalist agrarian economy to increasingly capitalist relations of production. Feudal "superior" owners extracted profit from dependent, "inferior" owners through direct, extra-economic coercion, in the form of military, political, or juridical power.[9] By contrast, with modern *dominium* firmly in place, land would be held by owners who, secure in their property rights, would seek to extract maximum profit from legally free wage laborers by purely economic means.[10]

The transition to a capitalist economy in continental Europe would eventually prove more uneven, slower, and more difficult than the proponents of absolute property had anticipated. Residual semi-feudal powers and privileges proved difficult to eradicate. In France and in Germany, the absolutist state afforded the propertied classes new modes of appropriating profits through political coercion rather than through purely economic coercion. And, in the short term, the new concept of property strengthened the rights of small peasant owners and prevented the rise of a class of large capitalist landowners comparable to the English one. Absolute property would deliver its promises only in the long term,

---

[9] Ellen Meiksins Wood, *The Origin of Capitalism: A Longer View* (London: Verso, 2017).
[10] Robert Brenner, "Agrarian Class Structure and Economic Development in Pre-Industrial Europe" (1976) 70(1) *Past & Present* 30–75; Id., "The Agrarian Roots of European Capitalism" (1982) 97(1) *Past & Present* 16–113; Wood, *The Origin of Capitalism*.

in conjunction with changes in the nature of the state, the development of an integrated national market, and the pressure of an increasingly international capitalist system.

When, later in the nineteenth century, the discourse of property modernization as the establishment of a new, Romanist absolute *dominium* reached the informal periphery of Europe, the agenda of the modernizers was more complex and multifaceted. Absolute property lent itself to the diverse concerns of the local modernizing elites. Latin America is a case in point. Economic development was a priority for the modernizers of the newly independent republics of Latin America. While, in the nineteenth century, Spanish America was well integrated into the metropolitan-dominated world market, the prevailing relations of production were still pre-capitalist. Property forms such as the *hacienda* or the *inquilinaje* differed from the old world, but they could still be called "feudal" as they were based on extra-economic coercion of unfree, servile labor. The expansion of the world market, far from acting as a disintegrating force on feudalism, actually consolidated feudalism, strengthening these forms of servile coercion to increase production.[11] Between the 1840s and the 1870s, republican legislatures in Mexico, Chile, and Colombia came to see absolute *dominium* as key to establishing and expanding a "modern" sector of the economy, moved by the constant desire for growth that would come by way of improving the labor productivity of a workforce of free wage laborers, largely of indigenous descent. Modern *dominium* developed in conjunction with racial schemas that defined the modern, rational, productive economic actor as white, European, or *creole*. This definition justified the dispossession of indigenous populations who were portrayed as lacking the moral virtues and ethos of productivity required to be owners. Dispossessed of their individual and communal lands, indigenous direct producers formed a large class of propertyless wage laborers vulnerable to the economic coercion of the landed *creole* elites. Yet, in the identity-creation discourse of the newly independent republics, the racialized nature of modern *dominium* was conveniently played down and the attention centered

---

[11] Andre Gunder Frank, *Capitalism and Underdevelopment in Latin America: Historical Studies of Chile and Brazil* (New York: Monthly Review Press, 1967); Ernesto Laclau(h), "Feudalism and Capitalism in Latin America" (May–June, 1971) I(67) *New Left Review* 19–38; Kyle Steenland, "Notes on Feudalism and Capitalism in Latin America" (1975) 2 (1) *Latin American Perspectives* 49–58.

instead on the image of the abstract, raceless, citizen-owner endowed with free and full *dominium* that formally admits no hierarchies.

However, by the late nineteenth century, the jurists' ideas about modernizing property changed. European nations faced increasing social interdependence, the negative spillover effects of industrialization, the "social question," and the mounting antagonism of the working classes. The public conversation about property and its role in modern society had already started changing decades earlier. In 1840, Pierre-Joseph Proudhon published his incendiary attack on private property as theft and a practical impossibility, because if it existed "society would devour itself."[12] And in the 1840s, Karl Marx outlined the fundamentals of his own critique of the exploitative nature of private property.[13] By the 1850s, a heated debate about the nature of private property pitted the many and diverse strands of socialism that were blossoming in Europe against the liberal elites who had forged modern Romanist *dominium*.[14] However, the juristic conceptualization of property only started shifting when a new generation of jurists, inspired by the themes of this impassioned public debate on property, but also committed to a new, purpose-oriented method of legal analysis, took a more realistic approach to property.

Starting in the closing decades of the nineteenth century, as France was experiencing a radical social and economic transformation, a new generation of *jurists inquiets* called for methodological renewal in the study of private law, prompting jurists like Emmanuel Lévy (1871–1944), Léon Duguit (1859–1928), and Louis Josserand (1868–1941) to denounce the growing gap between the purely abstract concept of absolute *dominium* and the life of property law on the ground, in which constantly evolving legislation limited proprietary entitlements and burdened owners with

---

[12] Pierre-Joseph Proudhon, *Qu'est-ce que la propriété?* (1840) (English translation: Donald R. Kelley and Bonnie G. Smith, eds. and transs., *Proudhon: What Is Property?* (Cambridge: Cambridge University Press, 1994); Id., *Théorie de la propriété* (1862).

[13] Karl Marx, *Einleitung* (1857); Id., *Zur Kritik der politischen Okonomie* (1859) (English translation: Maurice Dobb, ed., and S. W. Ryazanskaya, trans., *A Contribution to the Critique of Political Economy* [Moscow: Progress, 1970]); Karl Max and Friedrich Engels, *Manifest der Kommunistischen Partei* (1848) (English translation: *Manifesto of the Communist Party: By Karl Marx and Frederick Engels. Authorized English Translation: Edited and Annotated by Frederick Engels* [Chicago: Charles H. Kerr & Company, 1888]).

[14] Donald R. Kelley and Bonnie G. Smith, "What Was Property? Legal Dimensions of the Social Question in France (1789–1848)" (1984) 128(3) *Proceedings of the American Philosophical Society* 200–230.

new duties.[15] In Germany, between the 1860s and the first decade of the twentieth century, a methodological and epistemological reorientation also encouraged a new approach to property. Rudolf von Jhering (1818–1892) led the revolt against philosophical abstraction and conceptualism in German jurisprudence, shifting the focus of legal analysis from the question of the formal definition of property to the question of its function.[16] Further, in 1904, Austro-Marxist Karl Renner (1870–1950) published his famous *The Institutions of Private Law and Their Social Functions*, in which he analyzed how property, without changing its form, had changed its function. In the stage of simple commodity production, property could still be simplistically portrayed as a comprehensive and self-sufficient legal institution concerned with owners and their "things." By contrast, with the development of industrial capitalism, property shifted its concern to the relations between capital and labor and necessarily required supplementary institutions, such as the employment contract and company law.[17] More generally, society and the economy came to be understood in pluralistic rather than individualistic terms, as constituted not by individuals but by collective organizations representing them, such as trade unions or collectives of homeowners and tenants. This new framework undermined the very idea of a coherent property law system unified by the normative commitment to protecting the will of the individual. Further, throughout Europe, the war economy of the First World War led to resource-specific emergency

---

[15] Marie Claire Belleau, "Les Juristes Inquiets" (1999) 40 *Les Cahiers de Droit* 507; Andres-Jean Arnaud, *Les jurists face a la societe du XIX siècle a nos jours* (Paris: Presses Universitaires de France, 1975); Paul Cuche, *A la recherche du fondement du droit: y a-t-il un romantisme juridique?* Extrait de la Revue trimestrielle de droit civil 2 (Paris: Librairie du Recueil Sirey, 1929); Julien Bonnecase, *Science du droit et romantisme: le conflit des conceptions juridiques en France de 1880 à l'heure actuelle* (Paris: Librairie du Recueil Sirey, 1928); Nader Hakim, "Socialisation du droit et romantisme juridique: autour d'une controverse entre Julien Bonnecase et Paul Cuche," in Bernard Gallinato-Contino and Nader Hakim (eds.), *De la terre à l'usine: des hommes et du droit. Mélanges offerts à Gérard Aubin* (Bordeaux: Presses Universitaires de Bordeaux, 2014), 139–173.

[16] Rudolf von Jhering, *Der Kampf ums Recht* (Vienna: Manz'sche Buchhandlung, 1872) (English translation: John J. Lalor, trans., and Albert Kocourek, *The Struggle for Law* [Chicago: Callaghan and Company, 1915]); Id., *Der Zweck im Recht*, vol. 1 (Leipzig: Breitkopf und Härtel, 1877) (English translation: Isaac Huisk, trans., *Law as a Means to an End* [Boston: The Boston Book Company, 1913]).

[17] Karl Renner, *Die Rechtsinstitute des Privatrechts und ihre sozial Function: Ein Beitrag zur Kritik des bürgerlichen Rechts* (Tübingen: J. C. B. Mohr, 1929) (English translation: Agnes Zchwarzschild, trans., *The Institutions of Private Law and Their Social Functions* [London: Routledge, 1949]).

and social legislation, with the long-term effect of redesigning entire subfields of private law.[18] For instance, the state enacted legislation addressing housing shortages and took control of much of extractive industry. Consequently, property law specialized into separate subdomains governed by ideas such as individuals' social obligations and duties with regard to housing or mineral wealth.

The social critics differed in their ideological commitments. Utopian socialists and revolutionary communists challenged the very idea of property as a natural right, denouncing first appropriation as an act of violence and property as an arbitrary creation of the state and demanding a collectivist property system. Still others were inspired by "solidarism," a strand of left-republicanism that emerged in the late nineteenth century and claimed that property rests on the modern division of labor and hence is "common wealth" to be divided into individual and public shares. The social critics attacked modern absolute *dominium* as descriptively inaccurate and normatively undesirable. They recognized that property cannot be absolute and they exposed the negative, real-world outcomes of "absolute" proprietary entitlements. The recent economic and social transformations, the critics argued, required shifting the focus of property debates from owners' freedom to neighbors' security from harm, from absolute *dominium* to the notion that property is, and should be, regulated. The liberal architects of absolute *dominium* were preoccupied with enabling the freedom of productive owners. By contrast, their critics attempted to lessen the negative effects of industrial uses of property and to grant limited protection to nonowners seeking to use or access critical resources such as agricultural land or urban housing. Truly modern property was now seen as having a "social function" and modernizing property now meant limiting and regulating ownership entitlements.[19] To be sure, this transformation in the juristic project of property modernization was by no means clear-cut: modern absolute *dominium* lingered and would never disappear. Yet the questions the jurists raised in their essays and monographs changed and so did the larger public conversation about the place of property in modern society.

---

[18] Léon Duguit, "Changes of Principle in the Field of Liberty, Contract, Liability and Property," in *The Progress of Continental Law in the Nineteenth Century*, The Continental Legal History Series, vol. 11 (Boston: Little, Brown, and Company, 1918), 65–146; Natalino Irti, *L'età della decodificazione* (Milan: Giuffrè, 1999).

[19] Léon Duguit, *Le droit social, le droit individuel et la transformation de l'État: conférences faites à l'École des hautes études sociale* (Paris: F. Alcan, 1908).

The social jurists' attack on modern, Romanist *dominium* started in the core countries of continental Europe, but it was escalated by jurists in the periphery, particularly in Latin America, in the first decades of the twentieth century. Throughout Latin America and the Caribbean, arguments and priorities in the debates about property law modernization had also changed. Earlier in the nineteenth century, the legislatures of the newly independent republics had incorporated absolute *dominium* in their recently enacted codes in the belief that it would facilitate the transition from an incipient market economy to a capitalist system connected to the international markets. However, by the end of the century, it was clear that modern *dominium* had failed to deliver on its promises. Traditional and indigenous property forms had been eliminated almost everywhere, and yet, land was concentrated in the hands of *latifundia* owners, who were not capitalists but rather employed a variety of disguised forms of servile labor and extra-economic coercion. The struggle over land between the landed elites and the dispossessed peasants resulted in endemic rural violence. In the last quarter of the nineteenth century, in several Latin American nations, liberals returned to power, armed with a new approach to social policy inspired by scientific positivism and the social sciences. By the dawn of the new century, nurtured in this intellectual milieu, the idea of property's "social function" was rapidly gaining steam and academic jurists and legislators reshaped, and often radically expanded, the "social function" doctrine in light of local struggles and demands.[20] Again, as with Romanist *dominium*, "social property" became an integral part of racialized identity-building efforts. "Social property" proved a key concept in the struggle between the liberal elites and a variety of emergent social movements, including the politically active middle and working classes and the indigenous communities, over the scope of republicanism and democratic innovation. In Chile, the moderate liberals of the Club de la Reforma embraced the idea that property ought to serve the common good and presented the Chilean republic as the ideal terrain where the (European) idea of modernity – inspired by Roman law and based on the

---

[20] M. C. Mirow, "Origins of the Social Function of Property in Chile" (2011) 80 *Fordham Law Review* 1183; Id., "Léon Duguit and the Social Function of Property in Argentina," in Paul Babie and Jessica Viven-Wilksch (eds.), *Léon Duguit and the Social Obligation Norm of Property: A Translation and Global Exploration* (Singapore: Springer Singapore Pte., 2019), 267–285; Alexandre dos Santos Cunha, "The Social Function of Property in Brazilian Law" (2011) 80 *Fordham Law Review* 1171.

greatest extension of liberty and property to its ostensibly raceless citizenry – could flourish. By contrast, radicals such as Francisco Bilbao (1823–1865) and Santiago Arcos (1822–1874), founders of the Sociedad de la Igualdad, envisioned a distinctively Latin American modernity built on equitable access to property and inclusive of the urban artisanal class and of indigenous populations of the southern region of Araucania.[21] The idea of social property found its most expansive formulation in the debates surrounding the adoption of the Mexican Codigo Civil of 1928, and particularly in the work of Francisco H. Ruiz (1872–1958). Close to the global network of scholars known as *socialismo jurídico*, Ruiz conceived of the code as *codigo privado-social*, which would "extend the sphere of law from the rich to the poor, from the owner to the worker," and of property law as a tool for empowerment rather than for the domination of one class over the other.[22]

The appropriation and expansion of modern "social property" by peripheral jurists was by no means limited to Latin America. In Egypt, between the 1930s and the 1950s, the "social function" of property was embraced by the moderate legal reformers who sought to shape a modern Arab civil law.[23] In an Egyptian monarchical society polarized between rich and poor, urban and rural, reformers shunned ideas of agrarian reform and instead hoped to promote "social solidarity" by emphasizing the social limits of absolute property. And after the Nasserite revolution of 1952, the "social function" of property was dramatically expanded and radicalized, becoming a critical aspect of Arab Socialism.

The counterattack on social property was just as powerful as the social critics' assault. In Europe and in Latin America, conservative liberal jurists denounced the idea that modern property varies in scope and that it leaves ample room for affirmative social obligations as a return to the oppressive system of limited and divided property dominant before the liberal revolutions or the struggles for independence. The powerful

---

[21] James E. Sanders, *The Vanguard of the Atlantic World: Creating Modernity, Nation and Democracy in Nineteenth-Century Latin America* (Durham, NC: Duke University Press, 2014); Miguel A. Centeno and Agustin E. Ferraro, "Republics of the Possible: State Building in Latin America and Spain," in Miguel A. Centeno and Agustin E Ferraro (eds.), *State and Nation Making in Latin America and Spain: Republics of the Possible* (Cambridge: Cambridge University Press, 2013), 3–24.

[22] Francisco H. Ruiz, "La Socialization del derecho privado y el codigo civil de 1928" (July-September 1946) 8(31) *Revista de la Escuela Nacional de Jurisprudencia* 45–88.

[23] Guy Bechor, *The Sanhuri Code and the Emergence of Modern Arab Civil Law (1932 to 1949)* (Leiden: Brill, 2008).

anti-feudal rhetoric used to support the introduction of modern Romanist *dominium* into the legal systems of European and Latin American nations was revamped, and allusions to the return of feudal property dotted the introductions to property law monographs, newspaper articles, and political pamphlets.

Despite the virulence of the social critics' attack, "social" property never ousted modern absolute *dominium*. These two ideas about the nature of modern property and the differing objectives of the property modernization agendas coexisted uneasily well into the twentieth century. The concept of *dominium* and the idea of "social function" became the two foundational pillars of a capacious and contradictory Romanist-bourgeois property culture. And ever since, jurists, courts, and legislatures have struggled to navigate the tension between these two central ideas.

Why Rome? The Modern, Bourgeois Revival of Roman *Dominium*

In their effort to craft a new concept of "absolute" property for modern Europe, nineteenth-century jurists turned to Roman antiquity. Their choice may appear baffling. In Roman law, property was by no means "absolute," in the sense of free from restrictions. In fact, Roman law imposed a set of limits on owners that looked very much like those of a modern legal system. Nor was Roman property unitary in the sense that it knew only one form of ownership. Alongside *dominium*, the form of ownership reserved to Roman citizens, there existed a wealth of more limited forms of "owning" resources, a plurality of resource-specific and variable packages of property entitlements. Not only was Roman property neither absolute nor unitary, Roman law did not even provide a definition of *dominium*. Yet, modern jurists' turn to Rome is hardly surprising.

Neo-Romanism was not new. It had long been an irresistible temptation for lawyers in continental Europe. There had been two previous waves of pronounced neo-Roman initiative, each with distinctive characteristics. In the thirteenth and fourteenth centuries, the jurists in the recently founded law schools had reappropriated the texts of Justinian's *Corpus Iuris Civlis* to craft a new, supra national *ius commune* for Europe. Later, the Humanists of the fifteenth and sixteenth centuries sought to restore the philological purity of the Roman materials and to reorganize them in a more logical order. But the third wave of neo-

Romanism, in the eighteenth and nineteenth centuries, was remarkable in its sheer creativity and scope, extending well beyond private law.[24]

Roman law provided jurists and legislatures with a rich inventory of property doctrines that could be repurposed to fit modern needs. However, what most attracted the nineteenth-century jurists was the fact that Roman law, along with doctrinal blueprints, also offered a method of analysis, a *science* of property law. Developed by jurists outside of their time, this science of law could be presented as far remote from the pressure and immediacy of political and economic conflicts. The science to which modern jurists looked was the so-called classical Roman science. The jurists of the late Republic (133–31 BC) had transformed law into a "science" by importing from Greek philosophy a logical method of classification that organized concepts and sub-concepts according to a general-specific relation. The jurists of the classical era (roughly 30 BC to AD 240) further perfected this method, refining the taxonomy sketched by the republican jurists. The resulting mode of legal analysis combined formalism and practical reason. Legal concepts were divided, subdivided, organized into a logical system, and then applied to concrete cases, real or imaginary. The modern jurists saw a fundamental affinity between this mode of reasoning and what they regarded as the canons of an objective and rigorous science. Roman legal science provided a sophisticated property "syntax,"[25] a system of fundamental concepts that could be used to govern property relations in modern societies with the appearance of impartiality. The result was a new method of legal reasoning that casuistically explored the contours of legal ideas and their relations and organized them systematically.

In Rome, along with a scientific mode of reasoning, the modern jurists also found a powerful professional role model: a prestigious professional class of jurists uniquely qualified to play a preeminent role in governing property relations by virtue of their technical expertise and ethos of neutrality. Starting around the middle of the second century BC, the Roman jurists asserted themselves as the experts who would develop a stable, technical, and neutral framework of legal concepts to secure citizens' property rights and structure their interactions, gaining in return

---

[24] For the continuing importance of Roman law well into the twentieth century, see the contributions in Kaius Tuori and Heta Björklund (eds.), *Roman Law and the Idea of Europe* (London: Bloomsbury, 2019).

[25] On the idea of a legal "syntax," see Duncan Kennedy, "A Semiotics of Critique" (1991) 42 *Syracuse Law Review* 75.

professional power and unprecedented intellectual prestige.[26] By presenting themselves as the heirs of the Roman jurists, the nineteenth-century jurists made more persuasive their claim to the role of architects of modern property, further consolidating their position vis-à-vis the courts and the political process, as well as the other specialists asserting an expertise in property.

But turning to Roman law was an obvious choice also because it accorded with the larger cultural and political sensibility of the late eighteenth and nineteenth century. In France, the myth of republican Rome was ubiquitous in the arts, the letters, the language, and fashions of the revolutionary period.[27] In the history and institutions of republican Rome, the revolutionaries found an ideology of opposition, an idealized notion of liberty, a fully fledged republican vocabulary and blueprints for political and legal institutions. Roman antiquity was also used to justify revolutionary violence.[28] The bloodshed that led to the foundation of the Roman republic also provided an illustration and rationalization of the sacrifices expected of republican founders and citizens. In the Napoleonic era, the cult of antiquity was particularly germane to law, with Napoleon presented as the new Justinian and the *Code Napoléon* as the new *Corpus Iuris Civilis*.[29]

In the German-speaking world, Roman law, private and public, had also long been considered a beacon of justice and an unrivaled expression of fine juristic craftsmanship. In 1816, an incredible discovery further boosted the prestige of Roman private law. As he was parsing through the collections of the library of the cathedral of Verona in search of Saint Jerome's *Epistles*, German scholar Barthold Georg Niebuhr (1776–1831) found a manuscript of an entirely different kind: a legal text. Niebuhr knew he was on to something momentous and he alerted his friend

---

[26] Bruce W. Frier, *The Rise of the Roman Jurists* (Princeton, NJ: Princeton University Press, 1985).

[27] Wilfried Nippel, *Antike oder moderne Freiheit? Die Begründung der Demokratie in Athen und in der Neuzeit* (Frankfurt: Fischer, 2008) (English translation: Keith Tribe, trans., *Ancient and Modern Democracy: Two Concepts of Liberty?* [Cambridge: Cambridge University Press, 2015]); Thomas Chaimowicz, *Antiquity as the Source of Modernity: Freedom and Balance in the Thought of Montesquieu and Burke* (Piscataway, NJ: Transaction, 2008); Catherine Steel, "Introduction: The Legacy of the Roman Republican Senate" (2015) 79(1) *Classical Receptions Journal* 1–10.

[28] Jesse Goldhammer, *The Headless Republic: Sacrificial Violence in Modern French Thought* (Ithaca: Cornell University Press, 2005).

[29] Donald R. Kelley, *The Historians and the Law in Post-Revolutionary France* (Princeton, NJ: Princeton University Press, 1984).

Friedrich Karl von Savigny (1779–1861), one of the greatest Roman law scholars. "My dear Savigny," Niebuhr wrote, "here lies a treasure waiting for your hands to dig it up; a bait that shall lure you over the Alps to us, or will you persuade someone else to come?"[30] Savigny did not travel to Verona but the Royal Academy of Berlin sent a delegation to reproduce the manuscript in its entirety. The manuscript turned out to contain nothing other than the *Institutiones*, the textbook authored by the celebrated Roman jurist Gaius (AD 130–180) long thought to be lost. The discovery of Gaius' textbook generated an outburst of enthusiasm throughout Europe and sparked even greater interest in Roman law science.[31] No less influential than private law was Roman public law, which had long pervaded debates about political freedom and constitutionalism in the German states. In the sixteenth century, Roman freedom and Roman law were critical to the "Public Peace Movement," a treaty-based arbitral system that sought to pacify conflicts between cities or princes in the absence of a central state with the monopoly of legitimate force.[32] And, in the Romantic era, the Roman constitution of the time of the Nerva-Antonine Dynasty, was celebrated as a model of harmony that could nurture the new German anti-absolutist constitutionalism.[33]

Because Roman antiquity had so much to offer, Neo-Romanism remained a critical feature of the discourse of modern property well into the twentieth century. For jurists and legislators, "Roman" property and its putative opposite, "medieval" or "feudal" property, became two powerful archetypes used to describe starkly different visions of the economy and society. For most of the nineteenth century, the former almost invariably alluded to a variety of desirable goals: a scientific method, impartiality, individual autonomy. The latter, with rare exceptions, had a pejorative flavor, signifying conceptual confusion, political oppression, economic exploitation, and personal servitude. Toward the

---

[30] "Letter 213," in the Chevalier Bunsen and Professors Brandis and Lorbell, *The Life and Letters of Barthold George Niebuhr: With Essays on His Character and Influence* (New York: Harper and Brothers, 1852), 319–321 (German original: *Lebensnachrichten uiber Barthold Georg Niebuhr, aus Briefen desselben und aus erinnerungen einiger seiner nächsten Freunde* [Hamburg: Perthes, 1838]).

[31] Donald R. Kelley, "Gaius Noster. Substructures of Western Social Thought" (1979) 84(3) *The American Historical Review* 619–648. Similarly, the rediscovery of a different Roman law text, namely the *Digest*, in the late eleventh century set off the first wave of interest in neo-Romanism mentioned above; the jurist Irnerius was instrumental at the beginning of this wave of juristic activity.

[32] Whitman, *The Legacy of Roman Law in the German Romantic Era*, 10–12, 15, 19, 23.

[33] Schiavone, *The End of the Past*, 16–22.

very end of the nineteenth century – as a variety of socialist utopias flourished in Europe and Latin America – in insular circles of socialist reformist jurists, "medieval" property lost its negative connotation and came to suggest an organized cooperative economy and an interdependent and cohesive society.

Two Conceptual Models of Property: Absolute *Dominium* and Social Property

Pretending to revive a Roman concept of absolute *dominium* that hardly existed in the first place, early nineteenth-century jurists shaped a concept of property with a number of critical features, all of which evinced the absolute character of the owner's right. To begin with, modern *dominium* was described as an *exclusive relation between a person and a thing*. It denoted how one person, the owner, relates directly and exclusively to a resource and exercises broad control over it. Today, the idea that property is a social relation, that property signifies how two or more persons are related with respect to a resource, is widely accepted among property scholars.[34] And, it is difficult even for an observer with no legal training to fathom how others – non-owners who nonetheless have an interest in the property – could fall out of sight: others who have a duty to stay off the owner's land, neighbors who interfere with the owner's quiet enjoyment of the land, members of community who have to suffer the consequences of the owner's use. Yet, effacing the social and relational nature of property was the foundational conceptual move of the architects of modern *dominium*, the move that, in turn, determined, all its other features.

This exclusive relation between the owner and the thing was structured as a *unified aggregate* of *absolute entitlements*. To be sure, the owner has discrete entitlements that our jurists, in their treatises, analyzed separately for analytical purposes: the *ius utendi, fruendi,* and *abutendi*. However, these entitlements were seen as being tightly packaged to form a monolithic right that gives the owner virtually absolute control over a resource. Single entitlements may not be eliminated by the government and owners who wish to parcel out single entitlements

---

[34] Joseph W. Singer, "Property as the Law of Democracy" (2014) 63 *Duke Law Journal* 1287; Stephen R. Munzer, *A Theory of Property* (Cambridge: Cambridge University Press, 1990); John Christman, *The Myth of Property: Toward an Egalitarian Theory of Ownership* (Oxford: Oxford University Press, 1994).

through private bargaining may only choose among a limited number of predetermined forms.[35] In other words, each of these entitlements needs to be present for the relation between the owner and the thing to be characterized as property.

Owners' apparently limited ability to transfer single entitlements is a particularly puzzling feature of modern *dominium* and one that exposes a fundamental tension at its core. On the one hand, our jurists were committed to developing a property law system that would facilitate the goals of a modern economy. One of the ways owners derive value from their property and accomplish their economic plans is precisely by parceling out entitlements. For this purpose, Roman law recognized a sizable menu of *iura in re aliena*, literally "rights over a thing owned by another." Owners could grant easements and servitudes, split ownership between the owner of a building and the owner of the subjacent land, transfer broad use rights for life to another through a usufruct, or cede a form of control akin to ownership for a long term through an *emphyteusis*. On the other hand, these "rights over a thing owned by another" threatened the very idea of absolute property because they burdened or, when broad in scope, potentially emptied the owner's property rights. In other words, the needs of a modern economy were at odds with our jurists' desire to preserve the conceptual coherence of their idea of absolute property. Easing this tension required a good dose of conceptual creativity, and the jurists' solution was to distinguish between varying degrees of property's "absoluteness" or "perfection" and to emphasize that property is flexible. *Dominium* is, in principle, "perfect" but, because of its inherent flexibility, it could become, temporarily, "imperfect" or "very imperfect" if entitlements are parceled out to others.

Not only were ownership entitlements indivisible, they were also *invariable*. The shape of each individual entitlement – which activities or uses it covers, how it is enforced, who and how many should enjoy it – is fixed, that is, not subject to variation. This notion of property as invariable could only be maintained by eclipsing the relational nature of property. Only by neglecting the fact that each of the owner's entitlement imposes a correlative burden or dis-entitlement on others – that if the owner has the right to exclude from the land, others have a duty to

---

[35] On the numerus clausus principle, see Bram Akkermans, "The Numerus Clausus of Property Rights," in Michele Graziadei and Lionel Smith (eds.), *Comparative Property Law: Global Perspectives* (Cheltenham: Edward Elgar, 2017), 100–120.

stay off – could the architects of Roman-bourgeois *dominium* evade the question of whether the owner's entitlements should be qualified to protect the interest of others and the community at large. Because they did not attend to the relational nature of property, the architects of Romanist-bourgeois property could present it as the owner's ample *sphere* of *negative liberty*. The image of property as a "sphere" of absolute sovereignty over a thing, free from the coercive interference of either the state or other private individuals, was a common trope in the writings of our jurists, from Savigny to the Italian Pietro Bonfante (1864–1932). And so was the idea that property law's task is merely to coordinate the seamless coexistence of these independent spheres of sovereignty to make sure they never come into conflict.

Critical among the entitlements that constituted modern *dominium* was the owner's *right to destroy* the thing owned. The status of the right to destroy one's property in Roman law was at best uncertain. A passage from the jurist Ulpian (AD 170–228?) did include the phrase *re sua se abuti* but, in all likelihood, *abuti* meant "to be consumed" rather than destroyed.[36] However, in the treatises of the nineteenth-century jurists, the *ius abutendi* took on new meaning, becoming a critical feature of ownership, the most striking example of the owner's absolute sovereignty. Today, courts and property scholars are reluctant to recognize that the owner has a right to destroy valuable property, but the few who do cite a wealth of expressive and social welfare reasons.[37] In this contemporary view, the right to destroy allows the owner to express deeply felt values, protects privacy, and furthers innovation and creativity. While the architects of modern absolute *dominium* poured rivers of ink to emphasize the importance of the right to destroy, their normative justifications always and unmistakably appealed to an abstract concept of negative liberty.

Monolithic and invariable, modern *dominium* was therefore also *insensitive to context* and resource type. The owner has the full aggregate of absolute entitlements, regardless of the resource owned. This lack of nuance and contextualization is the feature of modern *dominium* that

---

[36] Digest 5.3.25.11. See also F. Piccinelli, "Studi e ricerche intorno alla definizione 'Dominium est ius utendi et abutendi res sua, quatenus iuris ratio patitur'" (Firenze: rist. anast., 1886; reprint. Naples: Jovene, 1980)

[37] Gregory S. Alexander, *Property and Human Flourishing* (Oxford: Oxford University Press, 2018), 231–266; Lior Strahilewitz, "The Right to Destroy" (2005) 114 *Yale Law Journal* 781.

was most un-Roman. The Roman jurists foregrounded the *res*, the things, their unique features, their meaning, value, and use. In their treatises and textbooks, the nineteenth-century jurists did offer long and detailed accounts of the Roman classification of things, often in the manner of an introductory section. However, by and large, this introductory classification read as an antiquarian conceptual exercise, with hardly any bearing on the discussion of the content of ownership entitlements that followed.

Modern Romanist *dominium* was also *broad* in *space* and *perpetual* in *time*. Our jurists solemnly invoked the maxim *cuius est solum, eius est usque ad coelum et ad inferos*, attributed to the medieval Italian jurist Accursius (ca. 1182–1263) and declared that the owner's rights extend upwards to the heavens and downward to the center of the earth.[38] These confident and serious statements about the spatial reach of property were largely unsupported by the Roman sources, but this did not prevent our jurists from insisting on the broad spatial scope of ownership rights. Time was another critical dimension of Romanist-bourgeois property. The owner's entitlements were perpetual and not subject to temporal terms or conditions. While some acknowledged that no Roman text supported this statement, our jurists were content to declare that the perpetual nature of property was logically implied by its absolute character.

Abstract and aspirational, the concept of absolute *dominium* dominated property debates for most of the nineteenth century until, in the 1880s, the social jurists launched their attack. The social critics engaged the proponents of modern *dominium* in a heated contest over the definition and the scope of modern property and proposed an alternative conceptual model of property that placed front and center the social interdependence that characterized the developing modern industrial economy. This contest over the nature and the scope of property was also a contest over the nature of Roman property law. In the academic discipline of law, no matter how influential the new sociological and positivist theories proved, Neo-Romanism remained the intellectual currency of the day. Hence, just like the jurists who had crafted Romanist absolute *dominium*, the social critics also felt the need to legitimate the doctrines they proposed by emphasizing their Roman origin. However,

---

[38] For a discussion of the importance of legal maxims within Roman law both in antiquity and later, see Peter Stein, *Regulae Iuris: From Juristic Rules to Legal Maxims* (Edinburgh: Edinburgh University Press, 1966).

the social jurists projected a starkly different image of the legal past: in their hands, Roman property became limited and remarkably pluralistic. The social critics' first move was to show that the Roman law of property was far from absolute and was more than mere *dominium*. "Absolute" *dominium* was only one of the several ownership forms that Roman property law made available. Alongside *dominium*, the critics argued, there was a multiplicity of more limited forms not technically called "property" but rather designated with formulas such as *possidere* or *habere, possidere, frui*. These forms granted their holders relatively robust sets of use entitlements that effectively resembled ownership and yet were far from absolute, being subject to a variety of limitations with regard to enforcement and transfer.

Another important move of the critics was to emphasize the relational nature of property. To the idea of *dominium* as the relation between the owner and a thing, the social jurists contraposed the notion that property is a web of relations between the owner and others with respect to the thing. The critics zeroed in on the structure of the property relation, showing how, for each of the owner's entitlements, there is a corresponding disentitlement for another. In other words, private property, always and necessarily, entails a degree of coercion. This awareness led the critics to raise the question of which entitlements, and of what scope, owners should be granted. It predisposed them to accept the elimination or limitation of single entitlements when the correlative burden imposed on others was not justifiable. It also encouraged them to retrieve the ostensibly Roman notion of "abuse of rights," by which the owner has a duty to exercise her entitlements reasonably. The relational and coercive nature of ownership entitlements is usually considered a relatively recent intuition that contemporary property theory credits to the American jurist Wesley Newcomb Hohfeld (1879–1918) and to representatives of the loose intellectual movement known as Legal Realism, such as Felix Cohen (1907–1953) and Robert Hale (1884–1969). Only rarely are we reminded that the most sophisticated property scholars in the Roman law world had long been keenly aware that property is a web of social relations that, by necessity, involves disentitlements and coercion. These scholars were particularly alert to the relational and coercive nature of property because of their familiarity with the living law of the many medieval forms of divided *dominium*, which predisposed them to identify the power relations between the multiple "owners" and users.

While the social critics agreed that the relational and coercive nature of property calls for limiting owners' entitlements, they had sharp disagreements about how significant these limitations had to be. Moderate reformers continued to justify the need for robust property entitlements with natural law arguments about labor or autonomy. For these moderates, the relational structure of property only requires mitigating the negative spillover effects of the exercise of ownership entitlements and balancing the owner's exclusion rights and the public's right of access. By contrast, jurists animated by socialist or solidaristic ideas took a more radical approach, arguing that property has a "social function" and that owners, in addition to entitlements, also have positive duties, the scope of which was yet another reason for disagreement among jurists who embraced different variants of the social ideology.

The notion that property also carries a social obligation was doubtlessly an important insight and one that has remained relatively marginal in the Anglo-American property tradition. Yet it also presented its proponents with an apparently intractable challenge. Unless given clear and specific content, the social obligation would remain a hopelessly vague nod to the new methodological and ideological ideas, with hardly any practical effect. However, if given precise content, it would clash with the aspiration to a robust core of proprietary entitlements, an aspiration that had remained powerful – in both lay and expert circles – despite the new ideas. This tension became especially critical as the twentieth century progressed and the threat of fascism and authoritarianism loomed large. In the face of authoritarianism, the aspiration to a robust, autonomy-enhancing core of entitlements acquired new meaning and urgency, and so did the fear that the social function could be used to justify an assault on individual rights in service of the objectives of the fascist state.

It was in response to this challenge that the social jurists began to explore the ramifications of what I consider the most intriguing insight at their disposal: the idea that the shape and scope of the owner's entitlements vary depending on the resource owned. For once, this insight was truly Roman. The Roman "law of things" was not the only acknowledgment in antiquity of the resource-specific nature of property. The Roman jurists also made available a variety of standardized bundles of ownership entitlements tailored to the unique characteristics of specific resources, such as public land (*ager publicus*) or provincial land, that is, land located in the provinces of the Roman Empire. Both types of land were of critical economic and geo-political importance, and ownership entitlements were shaped to promote the relevant interests. For instance, in Roman Egypt, the Roman government, seeking to promote and monitor the production of agricultural commodities for the Mediterranean market, shaped property entitlements with varying degrees of security and different fiscal benefits, depending on the type of land (royal land, private land, or temple land) and on the geographical location.[39] Similarly, the *ius Italicum*, a special set of entitlements for provincial land that was fictionally declared to be Italian soil, was used to reward and "Romanize" municipalities in the provinces.[40]

The Roman "law of things," and the more general resource-specific nature of Roman property, provided the social jurists with the key to the puzzle. The social obligation was neither a vague and empty notion nor a far-reaching authoritarian inroad into the owner's sphere of autonomy. Rather, its content and scope depended on the "thing" owned. The obligations and limits it entailed could be broader for resources that implicated a fundamental public interest, such as mines, water, and artistic and historic treasures; accurately geared toward goals of access and productivity for critical economic resources, such as agrarian land or industrial property; fine-grained for necessary resources such as rental housing; and minimal for rental commercial real estate. The Italian jurist Salvatore Pugliatti (1903–1976) nicely captured this focus on resources in the image of property as a tree with a trunk and many branches.[41] The trunk comprised a core of entitlements that characterize all forms of ownership, most importantly, the right to use resources for beneficial purposes. The branches described the variously shaped sets of entitlements conferred to owners of specific resources such as urban housing, agricultural land, or mineral resources.

Another powerful Roman law-inspired tool of the social jurists, largely forgotten today but incendiary in the nineteenth century, was the *lex agraria* (agrarian law). In the imaginary of the nineteenth-century elites, steeped in the classics, the *lex agraria* was associated with the land reform enacted by the mythical Gracchi brothers, the populist political leaders who sought to address the problems of Rome's poor. Over time, much of the public land (*ager publicus*), which the Roman state assigned to private

---

[39] Andrew Monson, *From the Ptolemies to the Romans: Political and Economic Change in Egypt* (Cambridge: Cambridge University Press, 2012), 142–153 and 162–172; Dennis Kehoe, *Law and the Rural Economy of the Roman Empire* (Ann Arbor: University of Michigan Press, 2007), 60–61, 93–97, 163–164, and 190–194.

[40] Peter Garnsey and Richard Saller, *The Roman Empire: Economy, Society and Culture* (Oakland: University of California Press, 2014), 36–54; A. N. Sherwin-White, *The Roman Citizenship* (Oxford: Clarendon Press, 1973), 316–322.

[41] Salvatore Pugliatti, *La Proprietà nel Nuovo Diritto* (Milan: Giuffrè, 1954).

users for cultivation, had come to be held by a relatively small number of large landholders who produced for the growing urban market. In 133 BC, Tiberius Gracchus, who, a year earlier, had been elected to the office of tribune of the people (*tribunus plebis*), proposed a law that sought to improve the situation of the impoverished small farmers by distributing to the poor and the landless any public lands possessed by private holders in excess of a specified cap. The Gracchan agrarian law was limited in scope, applying exclusively to public lands, and many of its details are uncertain and hotly debated.[42] Yet, its retrieval in the eighteenth, nineteenth, and twentieth centuries fueled extreme passions. It galvanized political radicals, providing them with a comprehensive blueprint for land reform, and it terrified property owners and the liberal elites who raised the specter of massive confiscations and redistribution of private lands accompanied by ruthless violence.[43]

These two competing concepts of property, absolute *dominium* and the relational, variable, and resource-specific idea of property proposed by the critics, have dominated property debates for the last two centuries. The relation between the two is more complicated than a simple pendulum-swing, where *dominium* dominates for most of the nineteenth century, dies out toward the end of the century, and is replaced by the relational and variable concept of property. Rather, the two have coexisted uneasily. The law of property as we know it today is the product of the constant tension, and attempts at creative mediation, between these two concepts of property.

Why Was the Idea of *Dominium* so Powerful?

The social critics crafted a concept of relational property, consisting of varying entitlements and duties that, if interpreted expansively and fully implemented, had the potential to make social and economic relations more equitable and democratic. Yet, for all the zeal of their attack on absolute *dominium*, the social critics were never able to undermine its powerful and long-lasting appeal. The Romanist-bourgeois idea of *dominium* as an absolute and exclusive right that promotes individuals' autonomy anchors their personhood and provides the foundation for a

---

[42] Saskia T. Roselaar, *Public Land in the Roman Republic* (Oxford: Oxford University Press: 2010).

[43] R. B. Rose, "The Red Scare of the 1790s: The French Revolution and the Agrarian Law" (1984) 103(1) *Past & Present* 113–130.

liberal polity shaped the social imaginary of the next two centuries. Obviously, on the ground and in the courts, the outcomes of conflicts over access to and use of privately owned resources were often very different than the concept of absolute *dominium* would allow. And yet this is not a reason to discount the relevance of the jurists' persistent and enthusiastic call for a robust modern concept of *dominium* throughout the nineteenth century, well into the twentieth century, and even up to this day. This pervasive and lasting influence has long puzzled property scholars. If "absolute" property is impossible in any organized society, how to explain this unrealistic and aspirational idea of *dominium*? This book argues that key to the success of this robust Roman-inspired idea of property was the combination of material interests and a powerful nexus of ideological beliefs. The need of rising capitalist elites to extract profit played an obvious role in entrenching modern *dominium*, but *dominium* would hardly have had such a profound and enduring impact had the jurists not articulated and promoted a wide-ranging set of arguments justifying *dominium* that appealed to ideologically diverse segments of the politically active elites.

Historians have long argued that the revival of Romanist absolute *dominium* in Europe was a response to the interests of the rising commercial and manufacturing bourgeoisie and paved the way for capitalism. Perry Anderson captured the gist of this view in one crisp sentence: "The classical past awoke again within the feudal present to assist the arrival of the capitalist future, both unimaginably more distant and strangely nearer to it."[44] This view certainly overstates the influence of Romanist property, making the rise of capitalism appear almost inevitable. And yet, the reinvention of *dominium* in nineteenth-century continental Europe did play a critical, albeit indirect, role in the rise of capitalist economies.[45] The law of modern *dominium* conceptualized in legal terms the emergent capitalist "social-property relations," that is, the relations by which owners of capital extract surplus value from direct producers. While the shift toward capitalist social-property relations was primarily

---

[44] Perry Anderson, *Lineages of the Absolutist State* (London: Verso, 2013), 422.

[45] Brenner, "Agrarian Class Structure and Economic Development in Pre-industrial Europe"; Id., "The Agrarian Roots of European Capitalism," in T. H. Aston and C. H. E. Philpin (eds.), *The Brenner Debate: Agrarian Class Structure and Economic Development in Pre-Industrial Europe* (Cambridge: Cambridge University Press, 1985), 323–327; Id., "Bourgeois Revolution and Transition to Capitalism," in A. L. Beier et al. (eds.), *The First Modern Society: Essays in English History in Honour of Lawrence Stone* (Cambridge: Cambridge University Press, 1989), 271–304.

determined by class conflict on the ground between landlords and laborers and by the changing nature and role of the state, the doctrines of modern Romanist property law structured, legitimated, and further solidified the emergent capitalist class structure. This is not to say that the relationship between modern Romanist *dominium*, the conscious aims of the entrepreneurial bourgeoisie, and the effective establishment of capitalism was direct or immediate; rather, it was slow and indirect and varied dramatically by region.

In France, despite the fact that the revolution and the Napoleonic state had ushered in modern absolute *dominium* and created many of the formal preconditions for capitalist development, the rise of an entrepreneurial bourgeoisie and of industrial capitalism was delayed. The persistence of large *rentier* landownership alongside small peasant ownership – and the continued importance of the bureaucratic state dominated by a powerful class of office-holders – freed proprietors, peasants, and the state from the relentless competitive pressure to intensify labor productivity, which is typical of capitalism. Large owners and the state continued to extract profits through rents and taxation, that is, through the use of political rather than economic levers. Only well into the nineteenth century – with the growing economic competition with England, state development policies, and the unification of the internal market – did the legal doctrines of modern *dominium* actually start facilitating capitalist growth. The same is true for Germany, where, despite reforms aimed at abolishing feudal divided *dominium* and establishing "absolute" *dominium*, the continued hegemony of the landed aristocracy, the political backwardness of the liberal bourgeoisie, and the power of the absolutist bureaucratic state delayed the rise of capitalism. A truly capitalist economy only developed with Bismarck's "revolution from above." Similarly, virtually all the republics of Latin America passed civil codes that enshrined absolute *dominium*, but the agrarian and extractive economy remained pre-capitalist, with large landowners maximizing their profits by increasing semi-feudal servile exactions on the peasantry, well into the twentieth century.

Despite its delayed and circuitous relation to capitalist interests and growth, the newly reinvented Romanist absolute *dominium* rapidly gained traction and became such a powerful and persistent concept because jurists and legislatures justified it with a variety of arguments that appealed to broad, ideologically diverse segments of the intellectual and political elite. In other words, the ideological foundations of Romanist-bourgeois *dominium* are richer and more diverse than is often assumed and cannot be reduced to a thin liberal individualism or a simplistic bourgeois ethos. In the prefaces to their treatises and monographs, jurists were eager to rise above the technical, disciplinary discourse of property and to engage in larger public conversations about the role of property in society. They presented modern Romanist absolute *dominium* as intimately related to two cardinal ideas of modernity: freedom and equality. Neither relation was without complications. Modern *dominium* was constitutive of freedom because it placed an external thing at the disposal of an individual, as a means to set and pursue her or his ends. And yet, by laying a duty not to disturb the owner on all others, property also encroached on others' freedom, imposing on all others a duty of noninterference. The relationship between *dominium* and equality was even more complicated, since inequalities in property ownership could corrode the very fabric of modern political equality.

As the architects of modern *dominium* sought to clarify its relation to freedom and explain away the tensions with equality, their audience and their temporal horizon extended beyond their own time. When they dealt with the technicalities of the science of property law, the jurists engaged their contemporary fellow professional jurists in Europe and beyond; but, when they discussed the relation between property, freedom, and equality, they spoke to the citizens of modernity, stretching into the future. The prefaces and forewords to the jurists' treatises and textbooks were suffused with a high-sounding, optimistic liberal universalism. Addressing present and future "moderns," the jurists justified Romanist *dominium* with a variety of arguments, old and new and not necessarily consistent or coherent. For instance, in eighteenth-century France, arguments drawn from the discipline of political economy, then relatively new, emphasized the relation between property, social wealth, and civic virtue and lured a vast audience. Robust and exclusive property rights, political economists argued, encouraged owners to make autonomous and socially responsible choices about what uses of their resources would bolster and expand the nation's economy.[46] Similarly, in the German principalities of the early nineteenth century, Romanist absolute *dominium* dovetailed with the teachings of cameralism, the

---

[46] John Shovlin, *The Political Economy of Virtue: Luxury, Patriotism and the Origins of the French Revolution* (Ithaca, NY: Cornell University Press, 2009); Liana Vardi, *The Physiocrats and the World of the Enlightenment* (Cambridge: Cambridge University Press, 2012); Steven L. Kaplan and Sophus A. Reinert (eds.), *The Economic Turn: Recasting Political Economy in Enlightenment Europe* (London: Anthem Press, 2019).

science of public administration that sought to increase the prince's income, promote economic development, and create a prosperous and well-ordered society.[47]

Arguments about democratic equality were also marshalled in support of modern *dominium*. Modern *dominium*, its egalitarian supporters asserted, would lead to greater *equality of autonomy* because it freed *all* politically equal citizens and owners from the many restraints that the Old Regime had imposed for the benefit of the seigneurial elite and the Church, giving them equal autonomy to manage their property. Those making these egalitarian and democratic arguments were well aware that, in the long run, modern Romanist *dominium* might facilitate the accumulation of private wealth, resulting in the corrosion of political equality and the establishment of new political oligarchies. Even so, their optimistic egalitarian liberalism made them believe that the free circulation of property in the market would effectively prevent excessive wealth inequalities; liberal egalitarians also hoped that the quality of the social bond, that is, citizens' sentiment of fraternity and moral equality, would serve as a corrective to economic inequality. The idea of equality of this optimistic liberalism was imaginary and thin: equality was understood not so much as a measure of the distribution of wealth but rather as a relation, namely that between like human beings, autonomous individuals, and equal citizens. And yet it proved powerful because it was deeply germane to the spirit of the post-revolutionary generation in France and throughout the continent.[48]

Of course, not all was novel in the jurists' writings. Alongside these newly reworked ideas, the jurists marshalled arguments from the medieval and early modern natural law tradition that appealed to classical liberals. For example, they justified *dominium* by invoking a strictly formal conception of freedom, devoid of content and independent of context or circumstance. In this view, *dominium* is the positive law affirmation of a pre-political, natural right of property, based on the

---

[47] David F. Lindenfeld, *The Practical Imagination: The German Sciences of the State in the Nineteenth Century* (Chicago: University of Chicago Press, 1997); Marten Seppel and Keith Tribe (eds.), *Cameralism in Practice: State Administration and Economy in Early Modern Europe* (Woodbridge: Boydel & Brewer, 2017); Andre Wakefield, *The Disordered Police State: German Cameralism as Science and Practice* (Chicago: University of Chicago Press, 2009).

[48] Pierre Rosanvallon and Arthur Goldhammer (trans.), *The Society of Equals* (Cambridge, MA: Harvard University Press, 2013).

universal law of freedom, a right to have a thing at one's disposal in pursuing one's own ends, consistent with the freedom of others. To be sure, those who held this view had to explain away the tension between property and the universal law of freedom, to explain how the first occupant of a thing can constrain the freedom of all others by imposing upon them an obligation to stay away from the thing that they would not otherwise have had. Generations of scholars, from the medieval canonists to the Spanish Scholastics, to Christian Wolff and Immanuel Kant had struggled with this tension. The jurists rehashed the arguments of these natural law writers about a "permissive" principle within the law of nature that could authorize an act that would otherwise be forbidden. Echoing their sources, the jurists claimed that this "permissive natural law" authorized the owner to put all others under an obligation of noninterference which they would not otherwise have.[49]

As skilled rhetoricians – conversant with the different discourses of modernity that coexisted in eighteenth- and nineteenth-century France, Germany, Italy, and South America – the jurists effectively built a broad and long-lasting consensus on the desirability of modern, absolute *dominium*. Key to the success of Romanist-bourgeois property was also the jurists' ability to present themselves as the true *scientists* of property.[50] The aspiration to scientific inquiry – to habits of mind conducive to an organized, universally valid, and testable body of knowledge about phenomena – was a pervasive one in nineteenth-century Europe. The high status of science was largely the result of a political and social transformation that was happening, at different paces, throughout Europe: the gradual rise to power of a commercially active bourgeoisie and a technically trained, bureaucratic personnel who valued science, expertise, and talent. Obviously, the specific sciences held in high esteem varied by time and place. For instance, physiology and Hippocratic medicine were highly influential in late eighteenth- and early nineteenth-century France, while romantic *Naturphilosophie* and

---

[49] Brian Tierney, *Liberty and Law: The Idea of Permissive Natural Law, 1100–1800*. Studies in Medieval and Early Modern Canon Law 12 (Washington, DC: Catholic University of America Press, 2014).

[50] Hans-Peter Haferkamp, "The Science of Private Law and the State in Nineteenth Century Germany" (2008) 56(3) *The American Journal of Comparative Law* 667–689; Christian Joerges, "The Science of Private Law and the Nation State = Die Wissenschaft vom Privatrecht und der Nationalstaat," EUI working paper. LAW; no. 98/4. San Domenico (FI) Italy: European University Institute, 1998.

Leibnizian geometry held sway in Germany.[51] And toward the end of the nineteenth century, references to organic biology punctuated law professors' monographs throughout the continent. Regardless of the type of science they looked up to, jurists sought to transfer methodologies and practices from the study of the natural world into the study of legal institutions.

The aspiration to scientific modes of inquiry permeated the study of law in general, but it surfaced in property law debates in particularly striking terms because of property law's inherent distributive and public dimension. Property law governed the distribution of resources that were key to nineteenth-century economies, such as land and water. The development of large-scale commercial agriculture and industrial manufacturing involved major conflicts over access and use between owners, non-owners, and the larger surrounding community, as well as conflicts between existing uses and new, highly profitable uses of property. The jurists claimed the ability to manage these conflicts through a science that, like geometry, mathematics, or physics, had its own internal principles and requirements. By characterizing property law as a science, nineteenth-century property scholars insulated property from overtly political discussion. On the ground, courts and lawyers almost systematically resolved these distributive conflicts in favor of owners rather than users or possessors and in favor of dynamic, productive uses of property rather than long-established communal uses. Yet, they always pretended that they were merely applying the doctrines of an age-old property science.

Were property scholars consciously strategic in their appeals to science? Obviously, the jurists were not engaging in actual science, in truly disinterested and unprejudiced inquiry. Rather, their property science was a form of scientism, a prejudiced analysis that assumes the most appropriate way of investigating property and indeed the outcomes. Nevertheless, the idea of a consciously strategic and disingenuous appropriation of scientific methods does not fully capture the Romanists' unique combination of sincere scholarly devotion to their discipline and instinctive adherence to a larger discourse of science, visible across disciplines as well as in the spirit of the age.

---

[51] Richard G. Olson, *Science and Scientism in Nineteenth-Century Europe* (Urbana: University of Illinois Press, 2008).

Romanist-Bourgeois Property as a Professional Project

The jurists' appropriation of scientific methods and practices not only sheds light on the deep and lasting influence of the idea of *dominium*, but it also opens up new vistas on the jurists as a professional group, replete with very mundane interests and internal power struggles. Modernizing the law of property was a complex effort that required different types of specialized knowledge. Political economists, agronomists, political theorists, and moral philosophers were among the experts who sought to play a role in the modernization of property. Shaping a modern property law was not only a matter of fine legal craftsmanship; it also required a grasp of institutional realities and a sensitivity to political and economic needs. Further, modern property had to appeal to the larger intellectual and ideological movements of the time. Professors of private law and Roman law could plausibly claim to have familiarity with all these dimensions. They were technicians with a solid command of the law and intellectuals steeped in the larger conversations of the moment. Their prestigious academic jobs and, often, judicial appointments brought them close to the levers of institutional and political power without putting them on the forefront of partisan politics. The prolific property law literature penned by the jurists provides a unique perspective on how academic jurists navigated these multiple roles.

The ambition to be the movers and shakers who would effectively redesign a critical institution like property was not the jurists' only motivation. Jurists also yearned for intellectual recognition by their academic colleagues and aspired to play the role of the gatekeepers of legal academia that was and is granted to those who have achieved intellectual prestige. Law, as with all academic disciplines, was the locus of a struggle for "academic capital," a contest to determine the criteria of legitimate membership and hierarchy in the field.[52] Declarations about property theory and doctrine were also social strategies through which professional power was affirmed and claimed. Leadership of the most influential specialized law journals, chairs, appointments, and promotions were very much present in the mind of property scholars as they wrote their textbooks and monographs and intervened in property debates.

---

[52] Pierre Bourdieu and Peter Collier (trans.), *Homo Academicus* (Stanford: Stanford University Press, 1988).

The antagonism between the champions of absolute *dominium* and the advocates of the "social function" of property intersected in complex ways with larger power struggles within law schools. Undeniably relevant was the friction between the legal disciplines that could stake a claim to property expertise, the prestigious and time-honored disciplines of private law and Roman law, and "younger," but burgeoning, disciplines, such as landlord/tenant law, labor law, agrarian law, and mining law. Property had traditionally been seen as the central pillar of the private law system, the core of modern civil codes, and, therefore, the exclusive domain of scholars of private law and Roman law. However, between the 1850s and the 1920s, rapid industrialization, the agrarian crisis, the social question, and World War I dramatically transformed property, throwing into sharp relief the relevance of "special" legislation and the salience of larger public interests in property matters. These transformations made property pertinent to the newer disciplines. The Romanists, whose power and status in law faculties was becoming precarious for a variety of reasons, were particularly eager to defend their position in the field of property.

Also relevant to the debate about the scope and shape of modern property was the conflict between the "mandarins" of private law, the established and methodologically more conservative scholars who were the gatekeepers of legal academia and controlled promotions, and the up-and-coming, more iconoclastic property writers. The vitriole of the attacks and counterattacks launched by the proponents of absolute *dominium* and their social critics is surprising for contemporary readers and can only be understood against the background of this larger struggle for reputation. Jurists who aspired to emerge as innovators who would shatter the dogmas of property law challenged their colleagues who sought the prestige of solid, timeless property craftsmanship. No less relevant was the feud between the "locals," that is, jurists who were fully immersed in their own domestic academic scene, and the "cosmopolitans," who sought to build cross-national alliances to promote their ideas about property. For instance, many of the French or Italian jurists who identified with the movement known as "legal socialism" felt marginalized in their own national academies and restlessly promoted their political agenda and their work abroad.

A Global Network of Jurists

Dominium and social property, the two central ideas of the Romanist-bourgeois property culture, were neither a product of Europe conceived as a homogenous legal space, with its own values and traditions, nor a product of any territorially defined legal space. Rather, *dominium* and social property were both shaped by a loose network of jurists, located both in continental Europe as well as in its informal periphery, who shared a training based on Roman law, a commitment to modernization, and common methodological beliefs. For the jurists who were part of this network, Europe was a cultural reference point, a reference used strategically by some and critically by others. Many jurists in the "core" countries of Europe, that is, France, Germany, Italy, and the Netherlands, saw modern *dominium* as the most distinctive product of "European modernity" and the embodiment of the unique values of modern European liberalism. These jurists' efforts to export their theories of modern *dominium* to the formerly colonial peripheries fit into a larger imperial design to disseminate the political and legal culture of European liberal capitalism. Their imperial endeavor was successful, and modern Romanist *dominium* found its way into the civil codes of virtually all newly independent nations from Haiti (1825), to Chile (1855), to Mexico (1870), and Egypt (1949).

However, outside of Europe, jurists' references to European legal modernity and its concept of property were far more ambiguous. To be sure, throughout the nineteenth century, a brand of Europhile cultural modernity was dominant among peripheral elites, from Latin America to the Caribbean to Egypt. Many of the most influential political and legal thinkers believed that Europe was *the* locus of modern law and progress and that its peripheries inevitably lagged behind and ought to chase this distant European modernity. And yet, particularly, but not exclusively, in Latin America, critical and denunciatory references to European modern liberal legalism were far from uncommon. A cadre of Latin American jurists reversed the imperial gaze, judging and criticizing the empty promises of Europhile legal modernity. This critique of European modernity and its concept of property was rooted in the belief that an alternative, non-European modernity, based on norms of republicanism and democracy, was taking shape in Spanish America.[53] The champions of this authentic, republican Latin American modernity shared an optimistic liberalism similar to the one that decades earlier had animated broad segments of the European elite in the wake of the French Revolution. Energized by this optimism, radical liberal jurists,

---

[53] Sanders, *The Vanguard of the Atlantic World.*

throughout Latin America, believed that this authentic modernity was not merely about safeguarding abstract political and personal rights of privileged individuals. Rather, they viewed modernity as a broader and inclusive political project supported by the popular masses and infused with both a democratic challenge and assertions of social and economic rights. These jurists went well beyond launching a passionate attack on modern *dominium*, and they sought to dramatically expand the core doctrines of "social property," such as abuse of rights and the promotion of the *lex agraria*.

Modern *dominium* and "social property" moved across legal and geographical boundaries through mechanisms of colonial imposition and informal power but also through the work of "cultural intermediaries."[54] Cosmopolitan intellectuals and energetic academic impresarios, these cultural intermediaries operated at the boundaries between different legal cultures and established connections, creating competing global networks of jurists who shared political sympathies, methodological commitments, and, often, professional power ambitions. Some of these "cultural intermediaries" were highly prominent legal academics who acquired worldwide notoriety. Léon Duguit (1859–1928), a professor of constitutional law and the most visible and active proponent of the idea of property's "social function," epitomizes the entrepreneurial and successful global networker. A native of Bordeaux, Duguit rose swiftly to academic prominence, gaining both high intellectual reputation and considerable professional power, eventually becoming the dean of the law faculty at the University of Bordeaux. In a series of lectures delivered at the University of Buenos Aires, Duguit captured the gist of his theory of property in a catch line that made an impression around the globe: the opposition between the old *propriété-droit* (property-as-right) and the new *propriété-fonction* (property-as-function). Duguit was a cosmopolitan academic promoter with a restless schedule of international academic travel that took him from Buenos Aires, to Bucharest, to New York, to Cairo. A skillful cultural intermediary, Duguit bridged the divisions between different cultural and legal traditions. He flattered

---

[54] Samuel Moyn and Andrew Sartori, "Approaches to Global Intellectual History," in Samuel Moyn and Andrew Sartori (eds.), *Global Intellectual History* (New York: Columbia University Press, 2013), 3–30; Vanessa Smith, "Joseph Banks's Intermediaries: Rethinking Global Cultural Exchange," in Samuel Moyn and Andrew Sartori (eds.), *Global Intellectual History* (New York: Columbia University Press, 2013), 82–84.

his audiences in the periphery with remarks about a universalist and inclusive modernity and about a shared agenda of legal progress.[55] Over decades of travels, Duguit established connections with other anti-formalist jurists who shared an interest in sociology and scientific positivism and successfully disseminated his *propriété-fonction* around the globe.

Among the jurists who expanded and radicalized Duguit's theory about property's *fonction sociale* was another cosmopolitan cultural intermediary, Francesco Cosentini. A native of Torino, Italy, Cosentini was an eclectic legal intellectual who restlessly promoted his "socialist" agenda among widely diverse academic cohorts around the world. He remained a marginal figure in the prolific Italian *socialismo giuridico* movement but achieved notoriety in Belgium, Switzerland, and Latin America. A visiting professor at the National University of Mexico in the late 1920s, Cosentini had the ear of two of the most influential jurists of the law faculty, Francisco H. Ruiz and Ignacio García Téllez, who were also members of the *comisión redactora* charged with drafting the new Código Civil. Cosentini and Garcia Tellez discussed the idea of a new type of civil code, a *codice privato sociale* (private social code), vocally advocated by Italian socialist jurists like Enrico Cimbali and Giuseppe Vadalà Papale. The draft code, enacted in 1928, reflected these exchanges; it was an ambitious *código privado social* that incorporated many of the property doctrines proposed by the social jurists.[56]

Graduate students from the periphery also played a critical role as cultural intermediaries. Wang Shije, who obtained his doctorate in law from the University of Paris in 1920, helped make Duguit's work known in China. Doctor Wang went on to a successful career between academia and government and was eventually instrumental in drafting the Land Expropriation Law of 1928, which was certainly consistent with Duguit's theory of property, even though not directly influenced by it. Another foreign graduate student in France who was a critical figure in the global "social property" network was Abd al-Razzaq al-Sanhuri. Like most Egyptian law students in France, Sanhuri studied at the University of Lyon where he was part of the circle that gathered around Professor Edouard Lambert, a leading anti-formalist and social critic. Sanhuri was

---

[55] Mirow, "Léon Duguit and the Social Function of Property in Argentina," 269.
[56] José Ramón Narváez Hernández, "El Código Privado-Social: Influencia de Francesco Cosentini en el Código Civil mexicano de 1928" (2004) 16 *Anuario Mexicano de Historia del Derecho* 201–226.

destined for a brilliant academic career in the law faculty of the University of Cairo and in the legislative committee charged with drafting the new Egyptian Civil Code (1949). Sanhuri's agenda for the Code was to introduce moderate legal reform in the spirit of European social legal thought. Convinced that, in Monarchist Egypt, where the existing social order was founded on land and property laws, social change would be secured primarily through property law, Sanhuri envisioned a law of property that would help increase social solidarity. Accordingly, Sanhuri's draft Code reflected both *propriété-droit* and *propriété-fonction*. Romanist-bourgeois property remained the central pillar of the code, but it was to be qualified with an explicit reference to property's "social function."

Property ideas traveled outside of continental Europe via these networks of jurists who shared a similar agenda for property reform and exchanged letters, translated each other's monographs, and held visiting positions at each other's universities. European and non-European members of the network presented themselves as equal participants in the project of modernizing property law. Was peer collaboration a mere pretension concealing actual hierarchies of power and prestige, in which non-European jurists occupied a subordinate position? More specifically, was the creation of property knowledge a simple process of diffusion and acceptance, or was there an active reconfiguration of concepts and doctrines by peripheral jurists, a true intercultural constitution of legal knowledge? The answer is, obviously, complicated. The academic profession is a highly stratified one, organized around a plurality of rival principles of hierarchization, and a quick glance at preambles, forewords, letters, and conference programs reveals ubiquitous traces of non-European jurists' asymmetric and unequal position. Yet, in important ways, the creation of modern property was a coproduction.

French, German, and Italian property concepts were often creatively reshaped and expanded by jurists and legislatures outside of Europe and eventually brought back to bear on European debates. The theory of the "social function" of property is a case in point. Duguit's theory of the social function was narrowly circumscribed. The Bordeaux jurist cautiously framed his theory as descriptive and was reluctant to explicitly draw normative conclusions. For Duguit, the observation of property's new nature evinced the need for doctrines that would qualify and limit the owner's entitlements but not the need for more radical redistributive measures. It was the Latin American members of the network who dramatically expanded Duguit's theory, giving it an openly normative flavor. In their treatises, as well as in the debates of the legislative committees they joined, Chilean, Brazilian, and Mexican jurists explicitly linked the "social function" to broader arguments about a new economic structure that secures to each individual what is necessary for his or her material security and human flourishing. This expanded notion of the "social function" justified an ambitious redistributive agenda that included the expropriation of large landed estates, uncultivated lands, and unproductive factories. From Latin America, this expansive reformulation of the "social function" theory traveled back to Europe in the second half of the twentieth century. It now informs the work of scholars and activists engaged in a variety of reform projects, from the "urban commons" to the movement for equitable access to water utilities.

Creativity also marked the introduction of the "social function" theory in Egypt. While Sanhuri's initial formulation of the theory was a moderate's attempt to introduce mild social reforms acceptable to the monarchist regime, in the aftermath of the Nasserite Revolution of 1952, the "social function" became the vehicle for introducing the principles of Arab Socialism into Egyptian property law. In this new socialist reading, the "social function" enabled a redistributive agenda that included greater equality in the distribution of income as well as the encouragement and protection of small ownership. Sanhuri read the "social function" in conjunction with Islamic principles and proposed highly original solutions in various areas, including housing law. One of the most original innovations was the new regime regulating multi-apartment buildings, which the revolutionary regime considered critical to the goals of alleviating the housing crisis in overcrowded cities and increasing homeownership among the middle-class. Informed by the idea of "social function" and by the principles of *al-uluww wal-sufl*, the new regime encouraged cooperation between owners of the lower floor and the upper floors, imposing on each specific obligations with regard to maintenance, and established building management committees based on egalitarian and democratic principles.

1

What Roman Antiquity Had to Offer

A Scientific Method and a Vast Inventory of
Property Concepts

The Legend of Roman Absolute Dominium

Roman property is enveloped in a mist of mythology. In his 1885 lectures
at the University of Rome, Professor Vittorio Scialoja (1856–1933), one
of the most prominent Italian Roman law scholars of the time, introduced the topic by warning students that "the Roman theory of property
has inspired the strangest legends not only among the populace but also,
sometimes, among the educated."[57] Scialoja was onto something. Roman
property has long struck the imagination not only of lawyers but also of
historians, economists, and philosophers because of its supposedly "absolute," "individualistic," "unitary," "extremely concentrated" nature.
A quick glance at modern Roman law textbooks reveals the ubiquitous
presence of the idea that Roman property is absolute. "The Roman law of
classical times" – a leading textbook reads – "is dominated by what is
commonly called the absolute conception of ownership," which is
defined as "the unrestricted right of control over a physical thing."[58]
This unrestricted right of control includes the right to use (*ius utendi*),
the right to draw fruit (*ius fruendi*), and the right to abuse (*ius
abutendi*).[59] The owner, we also learn, has very limited ability to parcel
out to other individuals these three entitlements, in the way, in the
Anglo-American common law, an owner can, for example, divide up
ownership of land between a tenant for life and a reversioner. This

---

[57] Vittorio Scialoja, *Teoria della proprietà nel diritto romano*, vol. 1 (Rome: Sampaolesi, 1928), 242.
[58] H. F. Jolowicz and Barry Nicholas, *Historical Introduction to the Study of Roman Law* (Cambridge: Cambridge University Press, 2008 [1972]), 140.
[59] Barry Nicholas, *An Introduction to Roman Law* (Oxford: Oxford University Press, 1995 [1962]), 154.

limited ability in Roman law makes property a "unitary" or "concentrated" right.[60]

Such assertions of absoluteness and individualism come with either scathing criticism or impassioned praise. Critics denounce the ruthless individualism of Roman property as both dangerous and lacking realism. For example, Otto von Gierke (1841–1921), who opposed the idea of a "Romanist" private law for Germany, championing instead an indigenous German private law, was blunt in his criticism of Roman property. The Roman concept of absolute property, which had been adopted in the first draft of the German Civil Code, was a fantasy, and a dangerous one, because it encouraged the assumption that property rights are unrestricted and it ignored the limits required by ethics and public law.[61] Another critic, Sir Frederick Pollock (1845–1937), could not resist teasing his fellow jurists for embracing a Romanist concept of absolute property that "has no being for English lawyers except when they are trying to pose as economists."[62] As to how Roman property came to be so strongly individualistic, a bewildered Pollock noted that "we are not aware of any answer to this, or even of any clue. Roman law makes its first historical appearance with its leading ideas already full blown."[63] Others, however, acclaimed Roman absolute property as a sound model that we should strive to revive. In his book *In Defense of Property*, Gottfried Dietze

---

[60] See also W. W. Buckland and Arnold D. McNair, *Roman Law and Common Law: A Comparison in Outline* (Cambridge: Cambridge University Press, 1965 [1936]), 81–82, for this direct comparison with the common law:

> The classical [Roman] jurists had an extremely concentrated notion of ownership, that is to say, although they recognised that various people could own the same thing in common at the same time, they did not attempt any division of ownership as such. This excluded for instance anything in the nature of feudal tenure, under which the ownership of land could be split up between landlord and tenant: even in respect of leases, the landlord was full owner, and the tenant had only the benefit of an obligation. Similarly it excluded anything in the nature of a doctrine of estates, whereby the ownership of land could be divided in respect of time .... Finally there could be no distinction between the legal and equitable estate. In other words, one could not dissociate the owner's powers of management from his rights of enjoyment, and vest the former in a trustee, and the latter in a beneficiary.

[61] Otto von Gierke, *Die soziale Aufgabe des Privatrechts* (Berlin: Springer, 1889), 17–20.

[62] Frederick Pollock, "Review of *Property, Its Duties and Rights Historically, Philosophically and Religiously Regarded: Essays by Various Writers, with an Introduction by the Bishop of Oxford*" (1914) 117 *The Law Quarterly Review* 111–112.

[63] Id., 111.

(1922–2006), a German-born American political theorist of anarcho-conservatist leaning, lauded Roman law for being "the most individual-istic and property-conscious of all legal systems."[64] Writing at a time when America was suffering the consequences of a "growing disregard for property," Dietze praised the Roman jurists for realizing that "the liberal principle demanded that ownership should be as unrestricted as possible and that the greatest possible latitude should be given to indi-vidual action and initiative."[65]

Despite its pervasiveness, the idea that, in Roman law, property was an absolute right is, as Scialoja put it, a legend, concocted by Roman law and property law scholars in the nineteenth century. The actual Roman law of property was complex, diverse, and transformed significantly over time, spanning as it did a period of a thousand years, from the Twelve Tables (451–450 BC), an early statute that restated the rules of traditional customary law, to the *Corpus Iuris Civilis*, the wholesale compilation of Roman law carried out by the Emperor Justinian primarily in the second quarter of the sixth century AD.[66] These thousand years saw the succes-sion of radically different constitutional regimes: from the early Republic, where power was shared between a handful of magistrates, the senate, and the citizens' assemblies; to the Principate, in which powers were concentrated in the hands of the Emperor, who shared legislative author-ity with the senate; to the Dominate, where the *Princeps* became a sort of Hellenistic monarch, first in Rome and then in Constantinople.[67] These thousand years also saw drastic changes in Rome's economic structure and class relations.[68] From a small city-state based on agriculture and a

---

[64] Gottfried Diezte, *In Defense of Property* (Baltimore: The Johns Hopkins Press, 1963), 13.

[65] Id., 14.

[66] For an overview of the sources of Roman law from the Twelve Tables to Justinian's compilation, see Hans Julius Wolff, *Roman Law: An Historical Introduction* (Norman: University of Oklahoma Press, 1951), 27–84; Nicholas, *An Introduction to Roman Law*, 14–17 and 38–42; Paul Du Plessis, *Borkowski's Textbook on Roman Law*, 4th ed. (Oxford: Oxford University Press, 2010), 27–62.

[67] For an overview of the constitutional background of Rome, see Nicholas, *An Introduction to Roman Law*, 3–12; Du Plessis, *Borkowski's Textbook on Roman Law*, 1–23; Wolfgang Kunkel, *An Introduction to Roman Legal and Constitutional History*, 2nd ed. (J. M. Kelly, trans.) (Oxford: Oxford University Press, 1973). For analyses of aspects of Roman law before 451 BC, see the contributions to Sinclair W. Bell and Paul Du Plessis (eds.), *Roman Law before the Twelve Tables: An Interdisciplinary Approach* (Edinburgh: Edinburgh University Press, 2020).

[68] For an overview of the social and economic conditions at various points in Rome's history, see T. J. Cornell, *The Beginnings of Rome* (London: Routledge, 1995); Luigi Capogrossi Colognesi, *Law and Power in the Making of the Roman Commonwealth*

relatively strong free peasantry; to the progressive concentration of land in aristocratic hands; to the huge territorial expansion of the later Republican era and the beginning of the Empire, with the concomitant accumulation of vast private fortunes by means of exploitation, corruption, and plunder; to the economic integration and growth of the early Empire; to the eventual solidification of social and economic identities starting in the third century AD; and to the economic turbulence and social fragmentation attending the fall of the Western Empire. Finally, these thousand years witnessed a rich and changing cultural landscape: from the appropriation and modification, to the point of originality, of Greek philosophy and political theory; to the "invention" of law as a specific form of social regulation; to the birth of Roman Christianity and the development of a systematic Christian theology.[69] These political, economic, and cultural/ideological transformations were inevitably reflected in the intellectual development of property law; through their logical and systematic methodology, the Roman jurists developed a rich conceptual vocabulary of property, that is, a set of concepts, organizational schemes, and doctrines to describe and solve the constantly changing legal questions posed by property.

When they set out to develop modern property, the nineteenth-century jurists approached the juristic texts of Roman antiquity with a combination of sincere scholarly devotion and instrumental spirit. They regarded the writings of the Roman jurists as highly authoritative and deserving of rigorous historical and philological study. Yet they approached these writings with their own practical questions, ideological views, methodological queries, and professional ambitions. Hence, they

(Laura Copp, trans.) (Cambridge: Cambridge University Press, 2014); Harriet I. Flower, *Roman Republics* (Princeton, NJ: Princeton University Press, 2010); Peter Garnsey and Richard Saller, *The Roman Empire: Economy, Society and Culture*, 2nd ed. (Oakland: University of California Press, 2015); Peter Sarris, "The Eastern Empire from Constantine to Heraclius (306–641)," in Cyril Mango (ed.), *The Oxford History of Byzantium* (Oxford: Oxford University Press, 2002), 19–70; Andrea Giardina, "The Transition to Late Antiquity," in Walter Scheidel, Ian Morris, and Richard P. Saller (eds.), *The Cambridge Economic History of the Greco-Roman World* (Cambridge: Cambridge University Press, 2007), 743–768.

[69] See Aldo Schiavone, *The Invention of Law in the West* (Jeremy Carden and Antony Shugaar, transs.) (Cambridge, MA: Harvard University Press, 2012); Claudia Moatti, *The Birth of Critical Thinking in Republican Rome* (Janet Lloyd, trans.) (Cambridge: Cambridge University Press, 2015); Duncan MacRae, *Legible Religion: Books, Gods, and Rituals in Roman Culture* (Cambridge, MA: Harvard University Press, 2016); Jed W. Atkins, *Roman Political Thought* (Cambridge: Cambridge University Press, 2018).

selectively borrowed from the vast and diverse conceptual vocabulary of property developed over the centuries by the Roman jurists only the ideas and doctrines that spoke to the absolute character of property rights, overlooking all else. Readers accustomed to the legend of absolute *dominium* that pervades the nonspecialist literature on Roman property will be surprised at how much richer and more varied the Roman conceptual vocabulary of property actually was. Lost in the legend of absolute *dominium* is all that was pluralistic, amenable to being disaggregated, relative, and limited in Roman property law.

The literature that explores the complexity of Roman property law is wide and ambitious, and scholars have offered remarkably different narratives of Roman property's development.[70] The objective of this chapter is not to provide an exhaustive and detailed account of Roman property law but rather to offer an inevitably simplified overview of Roman property that will serve as a preamble to the story of the invention of Romanist-bourgeois property. In the pages that follow, we will look into the features of Roman law that attracted the nineteenth-century property modernizers: a scientific method and an inventory of concepts and doctrines that could easily be repurposed.

A Powerful Professional Role Model: The Roman Jurists and the Promise of an Impartial Legal Science

Who were the Roman jurists who captivated the imagination of their nineteenth-century heirs and shaped their professional ambitions? And what were the reasons for, and the scope of, their promise of a neutral

---

[70] Of the vast literature, see (in English): Herbert Hausmaninger and Richard Gamauf (eds.), *A Casebook on Roman Property Law* (George A. Sheets, trans.) (Oxford: Oxford University Press, 2012); Peter Birks (ed.), *New Perspectives in the Roman Law of Property. Essays for Barry Nicholas* (Oxford: Oxford University Press, 1989); M. I. Finley (ed.), *Studies in Roman Property by the Cambridge University Seminar in Ancient History* (Cambridge: Cambridge University Press, 1976); De Plessis, *Borkowski's Textbook on Roman Law*, 151–204; Alan Rodger, *Owners and Neighbours in Roman Law* (Oxford: Clarendon Press, 1972); Fritz Schulz, *Classical Roman Law* (Oxford: Clarendon Press, 1951); Alan Watson, *The Law of Property in the Later Roman Republic* (Oxford: Clarendon Press, 1968). See also Ennio Cortese (ed.), *La proprietà e le proprietà: Pontignano, 30 settembre–3 ottobre 1985* (Milan: Giuffrè, 1988); Luigi Capogrossi Colognesi, s.v. Proprietà (dir. rom.), in *Enciclopedia del diritto* (Milan: Giuffrè, 1988), 37; Max Kaser, *Das römische Privatrecht* (Munich: C. H. Beck, 1955); Otto Karlowa, *Römische Rechtsgeschichte*, 2 (Leipzig: Metzger and Wittig, 1901); Scialoja, *Teoria della proprietà nel diritto romano*.

property science? To fully understand what exactly the Roman jurists had to offer their nineteenth-century successors, we have to look back to the early days of Rome.

The jurists' demand for recognition as a distinct professional class grew out of the fascinating development of the nature of their work, from religious rituality to scientific reason.[71] In early Rome, law was the domain of a specific priestly circle, the *pontifices*, who were the guardians of the *mos maiorum*, the religious and social custom of the ancestors. The *pontifices* were not priests in the sense of spiritual figures. Rather, they were men of patrician social standing who, because of their economic privilege, could undertake public duties without pecuniary remuneration. Their prescriptive pronouncements took the form of "responses" (*responsa*) to questions of the *patres* (the living male patriarchs of the community), who wanted to know what ritual should be used when performing specific operations of daily life, such as claiming power over a thing, conveying property, or entering into marriage.[72] The *pontifices'* responses combined formalism and practical rationality, prescribing times, words, gestures, and the use of ritual objects, such as the wand, the piece of bronze, and the scales, to address practical questions of everyday life. As Aldo Schiavone has noted, the combination of formalistic ritualism and practical reason that we find in this early priestly jurisprudence would, in time, develop into a critical feature of legal science, both Roman and modern.[73] This ability for both abstraction and case-based practical knowledge would be the basis of the jurists' assertion of expertise and their claim to power.

Between the end of the fourth and the beginning of the third century BC, the locus of power shifted from religion toward politics and giving *responsa* became an aristocratic prerogative, rather than a priestly one.[74] *Responsa* were now produced by experts drawn from the new "aristocracy of government," which included not only the patrician elite but also the most important plebeian families.[75] These aristocratic legal experts were not yet "jurists" in the modern understanding of the term, and their work was not yet "science" in the sense of constructing abstract concepts;

---

[71] Schiavone, *The Invention of Law in the West*, 70–79 and 201.
[72] Id., 76–80; Fritz Schulz, *History of Roman Legal Science* (Oxford: Clarendon Press, 1946), 6–20.
[73] Schiavone, *The Invention of Law in the West*, 79.
[74] Capogrossi Colognesi, *Law and Power in the Making of the Roman Commonwealth*, 108.
[75] Id., 63–67. It is no coincidence that Tiberius Coruncanius, the first person to give *responsa* in public, was also the first plebeian *pontifex maximus*.

rather, they engaged in practical legal analysis with the aim of solving individual cases.[76] The "revolution" that transformed legal knowledge into a science and the jurists into a highly influential professional class of their own happened around the middle of the second century BC. The only surviving narrative account of the rise of Roman legal science is a short passage from the *Enchiridion*, a treatise written around AD 130–140 by the jurist Sextus Pomponius. Pomponius believes that three men, M. Manilius, M. Junus Brutus, and P. Mucius Scaevola, "established the civil law" and that "Quintus Mucius, son of Publius and *pontifex maximus*, was the first to set the civil law in order by arranging it *generatim* [by genera] into eighteen books."[77]

Pomponius' account is laconic and sheds no light on the reasons that led to the "establishment" of a science of law nor on the specific contributions of this new science. In his book *The Rise of the Roman Jurists*, Bruce Frier identifies the origins of Roman legal science in the "tacit bargain" between the newly emergent socioeconomic elite of the Late Republic, who, at a time of political instability and social ferment, demanded greater security of property and contract rules, and the jurists, eager to be recognized as a powerful professional class. The new elite included the established "equestrian" class of well-off citizens – who owned less property than did members of the senatorial class, often derived their income from their estates and from trade, and in many cases performed roles that were crucial to the functioning of the state – as well as a heterogeneous group of upwardly mobile municipal notables, shippers, and merchants. Largely comprising self-made men, this group had individualistic social values and was more rule-oriented in its understanding of private law than were the old citizens who had greater familiarity with Roman private law;[78] consistent with this interest in private law as it developed from the middle of the second century BC is the fact that the equestrian class would produce some of the most influential of the Roman jurists. The rules of property and contract appeared to this new elite increasingly more unstable for a variety of reasons. Among these reasons were the significant increase in the number of disputes following the expansion of Roman citizenship after

[76] Bruce W. Frier, *The Rise of the Roman Jurists: Studies in Cicero's* Pro Caecina (Princeton, NJ: Princeton University Press, 1985), 140.
[77] Id., 156; Schiavone, *The Invention of Law in the West*, 156–158. For the two quoted passages, see Digest 1.2.2.39 and 1.2.2.41.
[78] Frier, *The Rise of the Roman Jurists*, 256–259.

the Social War of 91–88 BC and the earlier introduction of a new procedural system, the formulary procedure, which gave the *praetor*, the magistrate who controlled the granting of remedies, more discretion to fashion legal actions and, hence, to shape new law. The jurists' response to the new elite's demand for greater stability in private law was to turn law into a written science with its own concepts and modes of reasoning, seemingly insulated from transient political changes.[79] What was the essence of this new science? All Pomponius tells us is that Quintus Mucius Scaevola (140–82 BC) was the first to organize the civil law *generatim*, that is, by *genera*, or "categories." Generations of historians from the nineteenth century to the present have identified the systematic organization of legal concepts as the unique contribution of this new science and hailed Quintus Mucius, and his colleague Servius Sulpicius Rufus (ca. 105–43 BC), as close contenders for the role of the father of Roman, and modern, legal science.[80] Whether the Roman jurists themselves understood systematic legal analysis to be the essence of the science of Quintus Mucius and Servius is unclear, but certainly this seems to be the view of Cicero. Cicero, who, as a former student of Quintus Mucius and a friend of Servius, was close to both men, praised Quintus Mucius as the exemplary Roman hero and credited him with making good practical use of the law while also lauding Servius for transforming law into an *ars* of *iuris scientia*.

> Scaevola was the most eloquent of those learned in the law .... But perhaps [Servius] preferred that which he achieved, to be the foremost expert, not only among men of his own time, but even relative to those who came before him, in knowledge of the civil law .... Scaevola and others had great practical command of the civil law, but only Servius made it an art. He could never have done this by knowledge of the law alone, not without first acquiring *that* art which instructs one to divide the whole into its constituent parts, to uncover the latent elements by defining them, to explain the obscure through interpreting; to see first the ambiguities and then to distinguish; and finally to keep a method by which are judged truths and falsehoods, and what conclusions follow from what premises and what do not ... the greatest of all arts ... dialectic.[81]

The supposedly systematic approach of Quintus Mucius and Servius was part of a larger intellectual movement to improve the organization of

---

[79] Schiavone, *The Invention of Law in the West*, 162.
[80] Id., 318; Schulz, *History of Roman Legal Science*, 68–69.
[81] Cicero, *Brutus*, 39.145–42.153.

knowledge in different domains, from law to grammar, to eloquence, to architecture.[82] As Cicero described it in his *De Oratore*:

> All the things that are now included in the arts, were once scattered and disordered; as in music, meter, tones and measure; in geometry, lines, forms, spaces and magnitudes; in astronomy, the revolution of the sky, the rising, setting, and movement of the stars; in philology, the study of the poets, the learning of histories, the interpretation of words, the sound in delivery; and finally in this very system of speaking, to devise, to embellish, to arrange, to memorize, to deliver, once seemed unknown and quite separate to everyone. A certain extrinsic art was therefore applied from another particular sphere, which philosophers claim entirely for themselves, so that it might bind together things that had been disconnected and divided and hold them together in some system. Let this therefore be the purpose of the civil law: the preservation of justice, stemming from law and custom, in the matters and concerns of citizens.[83]

That the Roman jurists' "scientific revolution" consisted of binding together into a system legal concepts that had been loose and divided, as Cicero nicely captured it, was also the understanding of one of the most prominent Romanists of nineteenth-century Germany, Georg Puchta (1798–1846). Puchta played a critical role in popularizing the legend of Quintus Mucius as a virtuous statesman and the father of the systematic approach to legal analysis. To be sure, Puchta may well have been anachronistically attributing to Quintus Mucius his own methodological creed, which focused on the task of system-building.

The truth is that while the legend of Quintus Mucius continues to thrive, we know very little about the actual nature of his work. None of his writings have survived intact, and we are left with sparse traces of his thought in later works, almost always in the form of quotations by later jurists.[84] These later quotes can only give us a superficial sense of what Quintus Mucius' systematic classifications may have looked like. For example, Gaius recounts that Quintus Mucius identified five types of tutorship:

---

[82] Moatti, *The Birth of Critical Thinking in Republican Rome.*

[83] Cicero, *De Oratore*, 1.187–188.

[84] The three passages in the Digest attributed to Quintus Mucius – 41.1.64; 50.16.241; and 50.17.73 – do not allow us much understanding of his contribution. Quotations of Quintus Mucius by later jurists are found throughout the Digest; for a list of these quotations, see Kaius Tuori, "The Myth of Quintus Mucius Scaevola: Founding Father of Legal Science?" (2004) 72 *Tijdschrift voor Rechtsgeschiedenis* 243–262, at 251. Quintus Mucius was also quoted by writers who were not jurists.

It suffices to remind that some, such as Quintus Mucius, have said that there are five *genera*, others, such as Servius Sulpicius, three, others, such as Labeo, two, while others still have maintained that there are as many *genera* as there are *species*.[85]

Similarly, we learn from the jurist Paulus, active during the reign of the Emperors Septimius Severus and Caracalla, that Quintus Mucius' classified possession into distinct types, or *genera possessionis*, although Paulus was not persuaded by this schema:

> Quintus Mucius was quite wrong to include among the *genera* of possession those cases in which we possess a thing by order of a magistrate so as to preserve that thing: for the magistrate who renders a creditor in possession so as to preserve the thing, either because a remedy has not been provided due to threatened damage or in the name of an unborn child, does not grant possession but custody and control of the property.[86]

The method of classifying larger concepts into kinds that we see applied in these brief surviving quotes was not Quintus Mucius' own invention; he borrowed it from Greek philosophy. *Diairesis* was a method of reaching a definition through the logical division of kinds (*genera* and *species*). This classification into kinds would then lead to the discovery of the principles governing the kinds and explaining individual cases. The diairetic method was first developed in Plato's dialogues and later became a method for classification used in the Aristotelian and Stoic schools.[87] Quintus Mucius was familiar with *diairesis* because it was a part of the intellectual culture of the Roman aristocracy.[88] Quintus Mucius' appropriation of *diairesis* for the purpose of legal analysis was the fundamental move that transformed law into a "science," in the sense in which the term is used by Plato and Aristotle, and introduced Roman jurisprudence into the circle of the Hellenistic professional sciences.[89] Through the diairetic method, law achieved what was required from a science: the logical classification of elements, their systematic integration, and the definition of their governing principles.

The methodology supposedly developed by Quintus Mucius would influence the nineteenth-century craftsmen of Romanist-bourgeois property

---

[85] Gaius, *Institutes*, 1.188.
[86] Digest 41.2.3.23.
[87] Donald R. Kelly, "Gaius Noster: Substructures of Western Social Thought" (1979) 84(3) *American Historical Review* 619–648.
[88] Schiavone, *The Invention of Law in the West*, 185.
[89] Id., 184–186; Schulz, *Roman Legal Science*, 62–65.

in two critical ways. To begin with, the diairetic method combined two intellectual processes – formalistic abstraction and practical case-oriented analysis – which the modern jurists would continue to see as the essence of legal science and of their unique expertise.[90] To analyze the facts of social life, such as belongings, exchanges, and obligations, into *genera* and *species*, the Roman jurists needed both a good grasp of the living reality they were studying as well as the ability to organize this living material in abstract concepts. In property, this meant organizing the myriad different types of "things" (*res*) that can be the object of owner- ship according both to their physical characteristics and to the interests and values they implicate; it also meant classifying the many possible ways in which something "belongs" to someone within the abstract concepts of *dominium*, bonitary ownership, possession, and a number of lesser real rights. This ability for abstraction and practical reasoning was sharpened by the use of *diairesis* but, as we have seen, it was already present in the early days of the priestly jurists who prescribed formal rituals for everyday legal acts.

Another aspect of Roman legal science would influence the creators of modern Romanist-bourgeois property. From Quintus Mucius onward, the Roman jurists saw their abstract concepts not merely as useful categories of thought but as real entities, as objective things that legal science would study and analyze but that had a life of their own, separate from, and preexistent to, the intellectual activity of the jurists.[91] As Aldo Schiavone notes, it is difficult to determine whether Platonic or Aristotelian ideas directly influenced the jurists' belief in the objective existence of legal concepts, but certainly this epistemic commitment to the objectivity of legal concepts owes a lot to Greek philosophy and would feature prominently in nineteenth-century property science.[92]

Historians like Franz Wieacker have doubted that either Quintus Mucius or Servius could have developed anything like a systematic organization of the law since both were still inevitably hamstrung by the jumbled and casuistic framework of the Twelve Tables, the earliest

---

[90] Schiavone, *The Invention of Law in the West*, 199; Peter Stein, *Roman Law in European History* (Cambridge: Cambridge University Press, 1999), 119–127.

[91] Friedrich Karl von Saigny, *Vom Beruf unserer Zeit für Gesetzgebung und Rechtswissenschaft* (Heidelberg: Mohr und Zimmer, 1814), ch. 1, sec. 4, n. 17. As Schiavone indicates (*The Invention of Law in the West*, 202), the implications of the insight of this passage were not immediately realized.

[92] Schiavone, *The Invention of Law in the West*, 202.

and most influential compilation of Roman laws.[93] The story of Quintus Mucius and Servius may well be yet another modern legend concocted by nineteenth-century Roman law scholars eager to bolster their own professional power.[94] Yet its influence is still with us today. Just as the legend of absolute *dominium* lent prodigious power to the modern robustly individualistic idea of property, so too the legend of Quintus Mucius' systematic science conferred tremendous strength on the abstract formalistic approach that enabled the fiction of absolute property.

The Elements of the Roman Conceptual Vocabulary of Property

To be sure, *dominium ex iure Quiritium*, that is, the right that gave Roman citizens exclusive and ample legal power over the things that, under the law, could be privately owned, was an important concept of Roman property law. However, the Roman conceptual vocabulary of property comprised a variety of doctrines and concepts that made property plural, flexible, and limited. These elements of pluralism and variability include: (1) a classification of the different things (*res*) that could be the object of property rights and the correspondent variety of *res*-specific property regimes; (2) a wide menu of lesser forms of "ownership," conflated under the label of "*possession*," that existed alongside full *dominium*; (3) a menu of lesser property rights over things owned by another (*iura in re aliena*) that allowed owners to parcel out entitlements and achieve a variety of social and economic goals; (4) a complex

---

[93] Franz Wieacker, "Über das Verhältnis der römishen Fachjurisprudenz zur griechisch-hellenistischen Theorie" (1969) 20 *Iura* 448–477; Id., "Cicero und die Fachjurisprudenz seiner Zeit" (1978) 3 *Ciceroniana* 69–77; Antonio Carcaterra, *Le definizioni dei giuristi romani: metodo, mezzi e fini* (Naples: Jovene, 1966); Bruno Schmidlin, *Die römischen Rechtsregeln* (Cologne: Böhlau, 1970); Id., "Horoi, pithana und regulae – Zum Einkluß der Rhetorik und Dialektik auf die juristische Regelbildung," in Hildegard Temporini (ed.), *Aufstieg und Niedergang der römischen Welt 2.15: Recht (Methoden, Schulen, Einzelne Juristen)* (Berlin; New York: de Gruyter, 1976), 101–130. Remo Martini, *Le definizioni dei giuristi romani* (Milan: Giuffrè, 1966).

[94] See Tuori, "The Myth of Quintus Mucius Scaevola," as well as Alan Watson, "The Birth of the Legal Profession" (1987) 85 *Michigan Law Review* 1071. The interest, on the part of scholars of Roman law, in how Roman jurists worked within and advanced their profession extends to the schools to which Roman jurists of the early Empire belonged. Much ink has been spilt over the supposed differences – methodological, doctrinal, and political – between the two schools, called the Proculians and the Sabinians, but this discussion too often reflects contemporary academic and political debates, rather than ancient realities. On this topic, see Charles Bartlett and Anna di Robilant, "Labeo Noster: The Proculians and the Sabinians in legal and political history" (forthcoming).

regulatory regime that limited owners' entitlements and the broad catch-all concept of "abuse of rights"; and (5) the notion of *lex agraria*, a blueprint for a comprehensive plan to correct patterns of inequitable access to fundamental resources. In the pages that follow, we will focus on these five features of Roman property both because they present a stark contrast with the legend that Roman property was absolute and unitary, and because these five features would have pride of place in the making and remaking of modern property. Each of these features would be retrieved by subsequent generations of modern jurists who would draw inspiration from them while fiercely disagreeing over their meaning and applicability.

The Roman Law of Things: The Classification of the Various Types of *"Res"*

A reader searching for *the* definition of property in the Roman sources would be disappointed. After all we have said about the legends surrounding Roman "absolute" *dominium*, the absence of *the* definition, or of any definition, comes as a surprise. But offering one, univocal definition of property, good for all purposes, is not how Romans thought about property or law more generally.[95] As noted by Pietro Bonfante (1864–1932), one of the most eminent Italian Romanists, "the attempt to define property is typical of modern jurisprudence. In the Roman sources, there is no trace of a definition. There are, indeed, many definitions that pass as textual and Roman, or at least as inspired by Roman texts. But this is an illusion of the exegetic fetishism of modern times."[96]

Roman law textbooks, from Gaius' *Institutes* to modern textbooks, begin their exposition of the law of property not with a definition of the concept of property but with a classification of the various types of *res*. For our purposes, we will translate *res* as "thing," although the Roman meaning of *res* is broader and is the object of significant controversy

---

[95] The famous definition of law as "the art of the good and the equitable" (Digest 1.1.1.pr.) by the jurist Celsus is unusual and hardly overly-specific.

[96] Pietro Bonfante, *Corso di diritto romano: Vol. II, La Proprietà* (Milan: Giuffrè, 1966 [1926]), part 1, 233. See also K. Kagan, "Res corporalis and res incorporalis – A Comparison of Roman and English Law of Interests of Life" (1945–1946) 20 *Tulane Law Review* 98.

among Roman law scholars.[97] The idea that property is a "law of things" is a popular one today, nicely captured in the title of a highly-cited recent article by US property scholar Henry Smith.[98] Roman property law was, quintessentially, a "law of things." Before delving into a more detailed exploration of how the Roman jurists classified things, we need to pause and consider the fundamental relevance of "the law of things." While obscured in the modern legend of Roman absolute *dominium*, this pragmatic focus on things is the single most important legacy of Roman property. The Roman classification of things is interesting intrinsically, as a mode of legal analysis, as well as for the influence it had on modern jurists.

As a mode of legal reasoning, the Roman "law of things" is a good example of the Roman jurists' talent for combining practical reasoning and formal categorization. The Roman jurists did not base their classification of things on some abstract and intuitive understanding of the different types of things. Rather, they brought into play specific frames of positive or normative analysis, external to law and drawn, to a considerable extent, from religion and philosophy. This pragmatic, positive, and extralegal cognizance of things was then organized into formal, legal categories. The significance of the Roman "law of things" for modern property thinking is momentous albeit largely overlooked. Contrary to the legend of a monolithic and absolute *dominium*, the Roman classification of things speaks to the pluralism of property values and the consequent variability of property entitlements. As Pietro Bonfante noted, the Romans had the intuition that "property is not, and cannot be, a uniform, monolithic block; property is subject to varying limits and regulations, so that it assumed radically different configurations depending on the object that is owned."[99] In the hands of modern jurists,

---

[97] Bernhard Windscheid, a leading figure of the German nineteenth-century Pandectist School of legal thought, which sought to "actualize" Roman law, argues that the term *res* denotes any material thing or right or obligation that is part of one's patrimony. See Bernardo Windscheid, *Diritto delle Pandette: con note e riferimenti al diritto civile italiano*, vol. I (Carlo Fadda and Paolo Emilio Bensa, transs.) (Turin: UTET, 1930 [1902]), 478, n. 3. By contrast, Vittorio Scialoja suggested that *res* has an even broader meaning, independent from the concept of patrimony. Scialoja's argument rests on a passage from Ulpian that calls *res* (*incorporales*) legal relations, which in Roman law were not part of the patrimony in the way that was the inheritance (which became part of one's patrimony only after it was acquired), or the tutelage that a former patron had over a freed female slave (*liberta*); see Scialoja, *Teoria della proprietà nel diritto romano*.
[98] Henry E. Smith, "Property as the Law of Things" (2012) 125 *Harvard Law Review* 1691.
[99] Bonfante, *Corso di diritto romano: Vol. II, La Proprietà*, part 1, 211.

this intuition about the pluralism and variability of property would be a fertile source of theoretical and practical innovation.

Let's now take a look at some of the specific ways in which the Roman jurists classified things, which is maddeningly complicated to our modern eyes. In modern property law, the most familiar and fundamental distinctions are that between movables and immovables, or real property and personal property, and between private property and public property. While some of the Roman distinctions mirror modern ones, much of the Roman world is opaque to us and we must guard against anachronism in our effort to understand its legal system. To understand the Roman classification of things we have to shed these familiar distinctions and look at Roman law and Roman society with fresh eyes.

The first and fundamental distinction between the various *res*, fundamental because it marks the very boundaries of the realm of property, is that between "corporeal things" (*res corporales*) and "incorporeal things" (*res incorporales*). This origin of this distinction is philosophical.[100] The Roman jurists borrowed it from Roman philosophers who, in turn, got it from Aristotle. We can find a neat example of this slippage from the language of philosophy to that of law in Cicero's *Topica*. Cicero starts by providing a philosophical definition of corporeal and incorporeal things but then draws his examples from law.

> I say things "exist" when they are able to be seen and touched, as for example a farm, a house, a wall, rain water, a slave, cattle, furniture, food, and so on; certain things of this class you must define at times. On the other hand, I say things "do not exist" that are not able to be touched or indicated, but still can be discerned by the mind and understood, for example if you were to explain *usucapio*, guardianship, the familial clan, or agnatic relation, none of which has an underlying physical substance, there is nevertheless a certain form distinguished and impressed on the intellect, which I call a "notion." Often in argumentation, this notion must be explicated by definition.[101]

The transition from philosophical debates to legal textbooks seems to be complete by the time of Gaius, the jurist of the second century AD, who, in his *Institutes*, discusses the distinction between corporeal and incorporeal things in a manner that closely tracks Cicero's and that would be

---

[100] See Raymond Monier, "La date d'apparition du 'dominium' et de la distinction juridique des 'res' en 'corporales' et 'incorporales,'" in *Studi in onore di Siro Solozzi* (Naples: Jovene, 1948), 357–374, at 360.

[101] Cicero, *Topica*, 5.27.

literally reproduced in Justinian's *Institutes*.[102] For Gaius, corporeal things are the material, tangible things that are the object of property, while the term "incorporeal things" has the broader sense of "legal relations." In other words, the distinction between corporeal and incorporeal things seems to have the same meaning of another distinction that is recurrent in the sources, that between *corpora* and *iura*, that is, material, tangible things and rights. Both ways of distinguishing demarcate property as the realm of tangible things.

Another distinction that was central to the Roman social and legal imagination is that between *res in commercio* and *res extra commercium*. The former were things that could be privately owned and freely exchanged in the market; the latter were exempt from private property and market transactions because of either their religious significance (*res divini iuris*) or their public import (*res humani iuris*). Among the things that involved religious interests were the objects and buildings used to honor the gods (*res sacrae*), to remember the dead – such as graves and burying sites –(*res religiosae*), and the walls that encircled the city of Rome and its gates (*res sanctae*). Two aspects of this classification are fascinating for the modern reader. First, this distinction does not map neatly onto our familiar modern distinction between private property and public property. As Yan Thomas has suggested, by classifying things into *res in commercio* and *res extra commercium*, the Romans marked off a separate realm – the sacred – from that of the public, while using terms that indicated their contiguity and close relation.[103] This fuzziness of the line that separates the sacred and the public is for us largely unfathomable, as it confounds our ideas about the separation between human and divine, state and church, law and religion.

A second aspect of this distinction that deserves mention is its constitutive role. By ascribing things to different classes, Roman law did not

---

[102] "Moreover, some things are corporeal, others incorporeal. Corporeal things are those that can be touched, such as a farm, a slave, clothing, gold, silver, and in fact innumerable other things. Those things that cannot be touched are incorporeal, and they are such that they exist only in law, for example inheritance, usufruct, and obligations contracted by whatever means. And it does not matter that things included in an inheritance are corporeal, or that fruits, which are obtained from a farm (subject to a usufruct), are corporeal, and that what we owe under an obligation is usually corporeal, such as a farm, a slave, or money; for the right of succession, in itself, and the right of usufruct, in itself, and the right of an obligation, in itself, are all incorporeal" (Gaius, *Institutes*, 2.12–14).

[103] Yan Thomas, "Le valeur des choses: Le droit romain hors la religion" (2002) 57(6) *Annales: Histoire, Sciences Sociales* 1431–1462.

simply recognize and ratify the existing, shared, and plain cultural, social, or economic value of a thing. It also constituted new things, giving them new status, meaning and value.[104] Take the case of "sacred things" (*res sacrae*), that is, the things used to honor the gods. A building or an object would become "sacred," and hence exempt from private ownership and market transactions, through a procedure. *Res sacrae* were consecrated to the gods in a solemn ceremony. After previous authorization of the Roman people (through a *lex*, a *plebiscitum*, or later a *senatusconsultum*), a magistrate representing the Roman people transferred ownership of the *res sacra* to the gods, represented by the *pontifex*.[105] Occasionally, the consecration of property to the gods could become a highly controversial affair involving fierce political rivalries and acts of retaliation, as happened in a case involving Cicero. During Cicero's exile, his enemy P. Clodius Pulcher, consecrated Cicero's house on the Palatine Hill to the goddess *Libertas*. Clodius' consecration was clearly an act of political aggression against a rival. In a highly emotional speech entitled *De Domo Sua*, Cicero fiercely disputed the validity of the consecration and, ultimately, prevailed. Cicero's speech deserves attention not only because it gives us a sense of the procedural requirements of the ritual of consecration, but also because it illuminates the constitutive role of the Roman classification of things. Through the legal and religious ritual of consecration, Cicero's house, privately owned, was constituted into something different, a *res sacra*, thereby changing its status and value. A distressed and mystified Cicero decries the cruel and vengeful use of the legal category of *res sacra*:

> What? In a dedication do we not ask who dedicates, and what he dedicates, and in what way? Or do you so confound and disturb these principles that it is possible for whoever wishes to do so to dedicate whatever he wants and however he likes? Who were you, the dedicator? By what right? What law? What precedent? What authority? When did the Roman people entrust this to you? For I see that there is an old tribunician law which prohibits a building, land, or an altar being consecrated without the order of the people; and at that time Quintus Papirius, who proposed this law, did not think, nor did he suspect, that there would be any danger that the homes or possessions of citizens, who had not been condemned, would be consecrated . . . . If you interpret the terms of the legislation to pertain to our houses and lands, I do not contest it; but I ask

---

[104] Giorgio Agamben, "Introduction," in Michele Spano (ed.), *Yan Thomas: Il valore delle cose* (Macerata: Quodlibet, 2015).
[105] Bonfante, *Corso di diritto romano: Vol. II, La Proprietà*, part 1, 20–21.

what law was passed that you should consecrate my house, from where
this authority was given to you, by what right you acted. And here I am
not discussing religion but in fact the property of us all, not pontifical
rights, but public rights. The Lex Papiria prohibits a building being
consecrated without the order of the people. Let it be understood clearly
that this refers to our buildings and not to public temples. Show me even a
single word having to do with consecration in your law, if it actually is a
law at all, and not the expression of your evil and cruel nature.[106]

Moving to distinctions that are more familiar to the modern reader,
Roman law's treatment of the distinction between private and public
property deserves close attention. Things that were exempt from private
property and market transactions because of the public interest were
subdivided into "common things" (res communes), "public things" (res
publicae), and "things belonging to the municipality" (res universitatis).
The concept of "common things" has inspired the moral and legal
imagination of generations of modern jurists in Europe and beyond,
who have framed legal claims about access to natural resources, water,
or artistic and historic treasures in the language of "common things."
Despite its modern appeal, the notion of res communes is controversial
among Romanists because, while it appears in Justinian's Institutes, it is
absent from Gaius, whose Institutes inspired Justinian's, and from virtually every other classical source. The only exception is Marcianus, a jurist
of the time of the Severi, who wrote that:

> Indeed by natural law these things are common for everyone: air, flowing
> water, and the sea, and through this the shores of the sea.[107]

Roman law scholars, from Mommsen to Bonfante, have dismissed the
significance of this passage. For some, Marcianus was sloppy in his use of
language, and by res communes he really meant res publicae.[108] Others
assert that Marcianus was simply translating in legalese what was, in fact,
a philosophical concept.[109] Once again, as in the case of corporeal and
incorporeal things, the legal category of "common things" seems to be
directly informed by philosophical ideas. In a passage of his moral
treatise De Beneficiis, Seneca explains the philosophical concept of

---

[106] Cicero, De Domo Sua, 49.127–50.128.
[107] Digest 1.8.2.1.
[108] Theodor Mommsen, "I. Sopra una iscrizione scoperta in Frisia, II. Nuovo esemplare
dell'editto 'de accusationibus' di Costantino" (1889) 2(3–5) Bullettino dell'Istituto di
Diritto Romano 129–135, at 131.
[109] Bonfante, Corso di diritto romano: Vol. II, La Proprietà, part 1, 55.

"common things" as the gifts that the gods have bestowed on all humans, regardless of merit, such as the sun, the alternation of seasons, natural fonts, and regularly blowing winds.[110] Over time, "common things" became a legal concept that applies to the air, the flowing water, the sea and the sea shores, as well rivers and river banks. In Justinian's *Institutes*, the idea of an essential, innate gift from which no one can be excluded is no less vivid than in Seneca but is associated with a specific legal regime, the core element of which is that the public has the temporary and shared right to access and use common things.[111]

[110] "The gods too," he said, "bestow much upon the ungrateful. But they had prepared those things for the good; still, the bad also partake of them, because they cannot be separated from the good. It is better then, to aid also the bad for the sake of the good, than to neglect the good for the sake of the bad. So those things you note – the day, the sun, the sequence of winter and summer and the moderate seasons of spring and autumn between them, rains and fonts for drinking, the fixed blowings of the winds – the gods invented for all; they could not except individuals. A king gives honors to the worthy, but largess to the unworthy as well. The thief, the perjurer, and the adulterer all receive public grain, as does everyone, who has been registered, without distinction of *mores*; whatever else he is, a man receives public grain, not because he is good, but because he is a citizen, and the good and the bad obtain the same. God has also given certain gifts to the entire human race, from which no one is shut out. For, while it was a common good that the commerce of the sea lie open and the domain of mankind expand, it was impossible for the same wind to favorable to good men and contrary to bad; and law was not able to govern the falling rains, so that they would not fall upon the fields of the bad and the wicked. Certain things are placed in common. Cities are founded for the good and no less for the bad; publication broadcasts works of genius even if they will pass to the unworthy; medicine shows its power even to criminals; no one has suppressed the compounding of salutary remedies, so that the unworthy will not be healed." Seneca, *De Beneficiis*, 4.28.1–4.

[111] "By natural law certain things are common to all . . .. And indeed the things that by natural law are common to all are these: the air, and flowing water, and the sea, and through this the shores of the sea. Therefore no one is to be prohibited from going to the shore of the sea, but nevertheless he should keep away from houses, monuments, and buildings, because these things are not subject to the law of all peoples (*ius gentium*), as is the sea. Rivers are common property and ports are state property: the right to fish in ports and rivers is common to all. The shore of the sea exists as far as the highest winter tide runs. Use of the banks is public and subject to the law of all peoples (*ius gentium*), just as is use of the river itself: everyone is free to moor their boats on them, to fasten ropes from the trees growing there, to unload some cargo on them, just as to navigate the river. But ownership of the banks belongs to those who own the adjacent fields; for this reason, the trees growing on the banks are also their property. Similarly, use of the sea-shores is public and subject to the law of all peoples (*ius gentium*), just as is use of the sea itself. And so anyone is free to erect a shack there, in which he can take shelter, just as he can dry his nets and pull his boat ashore. Ownership of these shores belongs to no one, but they are subject to the same law that also governs the sea and the land or sand that lies under the sea." Justinian, *Institutes*, 2.1; 2.1.1–2.1.5.

Turning to things that belonged to the realm of private property and market transactions, the fundamental modern distinction between real property and personal property exists in the Roman sources, but its actual relevance is unclear, at least in the classical period. For one thing, this distinction seems to be absent in the terminology of the classical jurists, who, instead of "real property," used more specific expressions such as *fundus* (parcel of land), *praedium* (farm), or *fundus et aedes* (land and buildings). For another, the supposed differences in the way classical Roman law treated real property and personal property (employing different terms for *usucapio*/prescription, recognizing different remedies to protect possession, and indicating differences in the modalities for conveyance by *traditio*) are less meaningful than they appear.[112]

Regardless of the merit of these arguments, Roman law scholars seem to agree that, in the classical period, the distinction between real property and personal property is obscured by another, more fundamental, distinction: that between *res mancipi* and *res nec mancipi*.[113] This latter way of classifying things is foreign to the modern way of thinking. It is rooted in the peculiar ritualistic formalism that characterized early Roman legal thought and it refers to the different modes of conveyance required for these two classes of things. *Res mancipi* could only be conveyed by *mancipatio* or *in iure cessio*. A simple delivery would not suffice. *Mancipatio* was a ritual ceremony involving a fictitious sale, described in detail by Gaius:

> Now *mancipatio*, as we have said already, is a sort of fictitious sale; it too is a legal institution unique to Roman citizens. This is how it is performed: in the presence of no less than five witnesses who are Roman citizens of full age, and also of another with the same status who holds a bronze scale, and is therefore called the *libripens* (scale-holder), the party who is accepting by *mancipatio*, while holding a piece of bronze, says the following: "I declare that this man is mine by quiritary right, and let him be purchased by me with this bronze and bronze scale." Then he strikes the scale with the piece of bronze, and he gives the piece of bronze

---

[112] Bonfante, *Corso di diritto romano: Vol. II, La Proprietà*, part 1, 217–218.

[113] Bonfante, "Forme primitive ed evoluzione della proprietà romana (*Res mancipi e res nec mancipi*)," in *Scritti giuridici varii: Vol. II, Proprietà e servitù* (Turin: UTET, 1918), 1–326. See also Bonfante, *Corso di diritto romano: Vol. II, La Proprietà*, part 1, 170 ff.; Id., *Istituzioni di diritto romano* (Turin: G. Giappichelli, 1946), 246 f.; Fernand de Visscher, *Mancipium et res mancipi* (Rome: Apollinaris, 1936), 263 ff.; Id., *Nouvelles études de droit romain: public et privé* (Milan: Giuffrè, 1949), 193 ff.; Max Kaser, *Das römische Privatrecht*, vol. I (Munich: Beck, 1955), 44 f.; Id., *Eigentum und Besitz im älteren römischen Recht*, vol. II (Cologne: Böhlau, 1956), 388.

to the party from whom he accepts by *mancipatio* symbolically instead of paying a price.[114]

As Gaius' passage suggests, *mancipatio* as a mode of conveyance was not available to just anyone. The limited availability of *mancipatio* reflected the inequities of the Roman law of persons. *Mancipatio* was initially limited to Roman citizens and only subsequently extended to Latins, both *coloniarii* (inhabitants of the colonies) and *Iuniani* (informally manumitted slaves). And women could perform *mancipatio* only with the authorization of their guardian. The other way for transferring ownership of *res mancipi*, *in iure cessio*, was no less formal or cumbersome. It simulated the action asserting ownership (*vindicatio*) and it required appearing before the *praetor*.

Ceremonies aside, what types of things were *res mancipi*, and how is this distinction related to that between movables and immovables? Pseudo-Ulpian informs us that:

> All things are either *res mancipi* or *res nec mancipi*. *Res mancipi* include estates on Italian soil, whether rural, such as a farm, or urban, such as a house; also rights attached to rural estates, such as driving paths, walking paths, herding paths, or the right to draw water; also slaves, and quadrupeds that are broken by the saddle or the yoke, for example cattle, mules, horses, and donkeys. Other things are *res nec mancipi*. Elephants and camels, although they may be broken by the yoke or the saddle, are *res nec mancipi*, because they are among the number of wild animals.[115]

The nature of the things on Pseudo-Ulpian's list suggests that *res mancipi* were the resources that had significant value in the early Roman agricultural economy. In other words, the distinction between *res mancipi* and *res nec mancipi* was based on their socioeconomic significance.[116] The distinction partially overlaps with that between real property and personal property because most items on Ulpian's list happen to be land or rights related to land. And the rationale of the two distinctions seems to be similar: certainty and publicity. Because of their socioeconomic significance, the transfer of ownership of *res mancipi* required specific, highly ritualized modalities capable of ensuring certainty in economic transactions. By the time of Diocletian (AD 284–305), the distinction

---

[114] Gaius, *Institutes*, 1.119.

[115] Pseudo-Ulpian, *Liber singularis regularum*, 19.1.

[116] Filippo Gallo, *Studi sulla distinzione fra "res mancipi" e "res nec mancipi"* (Turin: G. Giappichelli, 1958), 13. Similarly, Bonfante, "Forme primitive ed evoluzione della proprietà romana," 217.

between *res mancipi* and *res nec mancipi* had lost relevance and it was eventually abolished by Justinian. As the distinction between *res mancipi* and *res nec mancipi* declined in importance, that between movables and immovables gained more relevance.

Real property was the object of further classifications that reflected either the economic use of the resource or its location. Immovables were divided into *rustici* and *urbani*. The former were land and buildings used for agricultural purposes, the latter for residential purposes. The economic use, not the location, was the basis for the distinction, so that there was rustic real property in the city and urban real property outside the city. The location of the land was, at least initially, the basis for another distinction, that between Italic land, located in Italy, and provincial land. The distinction was a critical one: Italian land could be owned in *dominium*, that is, the full ownership reserved to Roman citizens. By contrast, as Gaius explains:

> In the provinces it is generally accepted that land cannot become *religiosum*, because *dominium* in these areas is held either by the Roman people or by Caesar, and we individuals seem to have only possession or usufruct. But still, although it is not *religiosum*, it is treated as such. Similarly, something in the provinces that is consecrated not under the authority of the Roman People is not strictly *sacrum*, but it is treated as such.[117]

Because it belonged to the Roman people, provincial land could not be the object of *dominium*. It was owned by the Roman state and granted to private individuals who had entitlements similar to those of an owner but who were subject to an annual tax. These provincial landholders were not formally owners and were designated with formulas such as *habere possidere* or *frui licere*. However, as time passed, the distinction lost its initial connection with the location of the land and came to be based merely on the legal regime the land was subject to. Italic land came to designate any land subject to the *ius Italicum*, even if actually located outside of Italy. Hence, the *ius Italicum* is yet another example of how the Roman classification of things actually created or constituted new "things" with new value and legal meaning. The *ius Italicum* was a legal fiction, a privilege granted to certain communities in the Roman provinces whose land was treated as if it were in Italy. Lands that had the privilege of the *ius Italicum* were governed by Roman private law and

---

[117] Gaius, *Institutes*, 2.7–7a.

could be the object of *dominium*.[118] The legal fiction of the *ius Italicum* may have been an important tool to negotiate the political complexities of Roman imperial expansion. This new, imperially minded use of the *ius Italicum* was formulated in the first years of Vespasian's Principate, when Vespasian, pressed by the urgent need for new revenue, reorganized imperial finances, significantly raising taxes. The grant of the *ius Italicum* was a way to exempt from the highly unpopular tax reforms colonies established by Italians, who were overwhelmingly legionary veterans.[119] The distinction between Italic land and provincial land lost relevance with time and was eventually abolished by Justinian.

Finally, another set of classifications hinged on the physical nature of the thing itself. Roman law distinguished between fungible and non-fungible things. The former (*res quae in genere suo functionem recipiunt*) are things whose individual units are capable of mutual substitution, such as wine, olive oil, or grain of the same quality. Non-fungible things are unique in their individuality. A bemused Bonfante illustrates this distinction between fungible and non-fungible things with an anecdote. Today, Bonfante notes, we think of works of art as non-fungible. This was not the case for the Romans. Apparently, at the time of the conquest and sack of Corinth (146 BC), which entailed one of the largest hauls of artistic treasures in Rome's history, the general Lucius Mummius had the shippers who brought back the bronzes to Rome promise that, if the bronzes were lost in transit, they would replace them with new ones.[120] Probably, Bonfante took too seriously a joke about Mummius' lack of sophistication that was popular among Mummius' rivals.

---

[118] On the *ius Italicum* see: Jochen Bleicken, "'In provinciali solo dominium populi Romani est vel Caesaris.' Zur Kolonisationspolitik der ausgehenden Republik und frühen Kaiserzeit" (1974) 4 *Chiron* 4 359–414; Thomas H. Watkins, "Vespasian and the Italic Right" (1988) 84(2) *The Classical Journal* 117–136. Valeriu Şotropa, *Le droit romain en Dacie* (Amsterdam: J. C. Gieben, 1990); Giuseppe Luzzatto, *Sul regime del suolo nelle province romane: spunti critici e problematica.* Excerpted from *Atti del Convegno Internationale sul tema: "I diritti locali nelle province romane con particolare riguardo alle condizioni giuridiche del suolo"* (Roma, 26–28 ottobre 1971) (Rome: Accademia Nazionale dei Lincei, 1974), 2; Mario Talamanca, "Gli ordinamenti provinciali nella prospettiva dei giuristi tardoclassici," in G .G. Archi (ed.) *Istituzioni giuridiche e realtà politiche nel tardo impero (III–V sec. d.C.)* (Milan: Giuffrè, 1976), 95–246, at n. 322 (217–219) and n. 379 240–241).

[119] Watkins, "Vespasian and the Italic Right," 120–125.

[120] Bonfante, *Corso di diritto romano: Vol. II, La Proprietà*, part 1, 107–108. For the ancient assertion of Mummius's lack of sophistication, see Velleius Paterculus, *Compendium of Roman History*, 1.13.3–4.

Roman Jurists also distinguished between things that can be consumed and things that cannot. The distinction was legally relevant mainly because the former could not be the object of a usufruct, that is, the right to use another's property and to take its fruits, without impairing its substance. Another distinction, one that is partially opaque to us because rooted in Stoic physics, is that between "single things" (*res unitae*), "composite things" (*res compositae*), and "totalities of things" (*universitates rerum*). Let us hear Pomponius' explanation:

> There are three types of things: the first, that which is comprised of one spirit, called in Greek "unitary," as for example a slave, a piece of timber, a rock, and similar things; another, that which arises out of things connected to each other, that is from multiple things joined together among themselves, which [in Greek] is called "constructed," such as a building, a ship, or a cabinet; the third, that which consists of discrete entities, not as many bodies separated, but placed under one name, such as the people, a legion, a flock.[121]

Pomponius describes "unitary" as characterized by the fact that they contain one single spirit. His explanation is informed by the Stoic understanding of nature. For the Stoics, material things of the world hold together because of an internal flow of either one *pneuma* or numerous *pneumata*, the breath(es) of life, that produces cohesion, called *hexis*, in the matter.[122] Hence, a log or a seashell is held together by the "dynamic process" of *hexis*, which, in the case of a unitary thing, consists in one *pneuma*, translated by Pomponius as "spirit."[123] In property law, whether a thing is single or composite or a *universitas rerum* mattered mostly for the purpose of acquisition by *usucapio* (adverse possession). Does the adverse possessor of a composite thing acquire the whole, or are the distinct things that become part of composite thing acquired separately? Pomponius explains that:

> There is no question that the first kind [single things] should be subject to *usucapio*, but it is less clear with the other two [composite things and totalities of things]. Labeo, in his books of epistles, says that if someone, who needs ten days to finish *usucapio* of roof tiles or columns, installs them in a building, he will complete *usucapio* just the same, provided that

[121] Digest 41.3.30.pr.

[122] On Stoic physics see Samuel Samburski, *Physics of the Stoics* (Princeton, NJ: Princeton University Press, 2014 [1959]) pp. 21–48; Bernard Besnier, "La conception stoïcienne de la matière" (2003) 37(1) *Revue de métaphysique et de morale* 51–64.

[123] Samburski, *Physics of the Stoics*, 21–22.

he possesses the building. So what about things that do not become fixed in the earth, but continue to be removable, such as a gemstone in a ring? In this case it is true that both the gold and the gemstone may be possessed and usucapted, as long as each one remains intact.[124]

While intricate and, at times, opaque, the significance of the Roman classification of the various kinds of *res* cannot be overstated because it impacts the very conceptual structure of property. Where the modern reader, familiar with the legend of Roman unitary and absolute *dominium*, expects to find a general, all-encompassing definition of property, we find instead a pluralistic structure, consisting of many *res*-specific property regimes.

A Critical Conceptual Pair: Absolute *Dominium* and Possession

The pluralism of the Roman classification of things did not guide the creative activities of nineteenth-century jurists, who, instead, embarked on the quest for *the* definition of property. They projected their own agendas and concerns on the few, short ancient passages that could suggest a definition of property, at times going so far as to drastically change or even invert what they found in the works of their Roman predecessors.

As it happens, the Roman jurists themselves had little to say about the concept of property. To begin with, the terminology varies and one would be tempted to conclude that, in the early and classical period, the Romans did not even have a term that unequivocally meant "property." In fact, the words used for property seem to have had broader meanings. *Mancipium*, which seems to be the earliest term for property, also designated the authority of the king, of a magistrate, or of the *pater familias* over the members of his family. *Dominium* was often used in the wider sense of a "subjective right," and *dominus* had the broader meaning of "right-holder," not only the holder of property rights (*dominus proprietatis*) but also the holder of a usufruct (*dominus usufructus*) or the heir (*domimus hereditatis*).[125] Only the word *proprietas*, which became

---

[124] Digest 41.3.30.pr.–1.
[125] Monier, "La date d'apparition du 'dominium,'" 358, who notes that the early references to *dominium* (for example, in the *De Re Rustica* of Varro [116–27 BC]), which some Roman law scholars have interpreted as referring to the abstract idea of property, in fact were more specific.

more widely used in the later imperial era, seems univocally to have meant "property."[126]

No less puzzling is the fact that, while Romanists have identified in the sources several "definitions" of property, all of which emphasize the broad scope of the owner's powers, at closer inspection, none of these supposed definitions is really about property. Rather, these definitions are extrapolated from texts that discuss specific legal questions that bear only a loose relation to property. A first definition takes the form of a maxim inferred from a rescript of the Emperor Constantine.[127] It reads "every man is the ruler and arbiter of his own property according to the *ius civile*." The precise Latin wording of this definition is not found in any ancient text but is rather a product of later juristic reformulation.[128] Neither this definition nor the rescript, however, includes the word *dominus*. Further, in order to construe the meaning of "one in complete control of his property," the maxim had to take the opposite of the meaning of the relevant sentence of the rescript, which says explicitly that the "ruler and arbiter" cannot do as he pleases with regard to his property in all instances. So this first definition can be ruled out.

Another supposed definition that made an impression on the nineteenth-century jurists for its absolutist tone is that property is "the right to use and abuse one's thing (*ius utendi et abutendi re sua*)." It is drawn from a passage of Ulpian on the claim for inheritance:

> The senate has been mindful of the interests of good faith possessors, so that they are not brought into complete ruin, but may be held liable only to the extent to which they were enriched. Therefore whatever outlay from an inheritance they make, if they cause something to deteriorate or to be lost, although they think that they were consuming their own property, they will not be responsible for it. If they have made a gift, they will not be considered to have been enriched, even though they have of course obligated someone to return the favor by giving them a gift. Clearly, if they received return-gifts, it must be said that they were

---

[126] Bonfante, *Corso di diritto romano: Vol. II, La Proprietà*, part 2, 229–233; Scialoja, *Teoria della proprietà nel diritto romano*, 255.

[127] The rescript in question is: "In a case of mandate, there is a risk not only in terms of money, which is certainly the object of the action of mandate, but also to reputation. For whoever is the ruler and arbiter of his own property does not conduct all his dealings, but rather most of them, according to his own design. But the affairs of others must be managed with exacting care, and nothing in their administration that is neglected or done unsuitably is free from blame." Code 4.35.21.

[128] See Konrad Summenhart, *De contractibus* (Hagenaw: Heinrich Gran and Johannes Rynman, 1500), *quaestio* 57 for one instance of this maxim.

made richer to the extent of what they received: because this would be a kind of bartering.[129]

The reader will wonder what this passage has to do with property. The text addresses the problem related to a possessor in good faith of an inheritance, only indirectly casting some light on the question of the powers of an owner. Because the good faith possessors of the inheritance here believed that they were owners and hence were entitled to "abuse" their property, they should not be held liable for the acts listed, including "squandering" and "causing waste." Nineteenth-century property writers would tirelessly play up these words as suggesting that Ulpian conceived of property as the absolute right to use and abuse one's thing. However, the matter is more complicated since, as the translation suggests, the word *abuti* is closer in meaning to "consuming" than to "abusing."[130] In other words, the *ius utendi* and *abutendi re sua* suggests that the owner has the right to use the thing and to fully consume it to the point of exhausting it, rather than the right to abuse, waste, or capriciously destroy the thing.

A third famous "absolutist" definition *of dominium* says that "it is the right of complete disposal over a corporeal thing, as long as it is not prohibited by law."[131] But this definition is not Roman. Its author is the medieval jurist Bartolus de Saxoferrato (1313–1357), who coined it in his comment on a passage of Ulpian that explains the difference between ownership and possession but says nothing about an owner's absolute right over a thing.[132] Yet another supposed definition of property, one that would serve as a template for many of the modern civil codes, is taken from Florentinus, a jurist of the second century. Florentinus tells us that:

> Liberty is the natural capability of a person to do what he likes, except for what is prohibited either by force or by law.[133]

---

[129] Digest 5.3.25.11.
[130] Bonfante, *Corso di diritto romano: Vol. II, La Proprietà*, part 2, 233.
[131] Bartolus ad Digest 41.2.17.1. See Bartolus de Saxoferrato, *In Primam Digesti Novi Partem* (Venice: Giunti, 1585), 84v.
[132] The passage of Ulpian on which Bartolus comments is: "The difference between *dominium* and *possessio* is this, that *dominium* remains even when the owner does not wish to be such, but *possessio* lapses when the possessor decides he does not wish to possess. Therefore, if someone has transferred *possessio* with a mind that it would be returned to him later, he ceases to possess" (Digest 41.2.17.1).
[133] Digest 1.5.4.pr.

This sentiment, here concisely and powerfully expressed, would be critical to modern political and legal theory, that is, in the idea of negative freedom and its limits, but, once again, it is not about property.

The terminological and definitional vagueness that surrounds Roman property leaves us wondering whether the Roman jurists actually intended to be "absolute" and "unitary," as the nineteenth-century architects of Roman-bourgeois property wanted us to believe. The answer is far from straightforward. Undoubtedly *dominium ex iure Quiritium* had unique features. It was the broadest form of ownership, reserved to the *Quirites*, the ancient Roman citizens, intrinsically connected to the (Roman) land and therefore charged with high political and symbolic meaning. As Pietro Bonfante argued, *dominium* was a right akin to territorial sovereignty and it belonged to its owner, the quiritary citizen and *pater familias*, "not only for the economic purpose of utilization, but also for the political purpose of preservation and defense."[134]

Because of its social and political relevance, *dominium* was highly symbolic and its unique features were staged through elaborate rituals. Its intrinsic connection with sovereignty over land was performed through the ritual of *limitatio*. In this solemn ceremony, the boundaries of land owned by a Roman citizen were marked with *termini*, that is, posts of wood or stone. A free space, five-feet wide, was left to separate neighboring parcels. This free space, called the *limes*, was devoted to public use, ingress and egress, and ploughing. The *limitatio* could be of one of two types: *centuriatio*, which divided the land in square or rectangular parcels forming a regular grid, and *scamnatio*, which divided the land in rectangular plots irregularly arranged. A fascinating example of legal geography, the *limitatio* shaped the appearance of the physical landscape and determined the legal and social relations of its inhabitants.[135] It marked, physically and symbolically, an enclosed space within which the sovereignty of the owner extended above and below the surface, was purportedly immune from the interference of neighbors and of the state, and was perpetual.[136] In other words, the function of

---

[134] Bonfante, "Forme primitive ed evoluzione della proprietà romana," 19.

[135] On "legal geography," see Jane Holden and Carolyn Harrison (eds.), *Law and Geography* (Oxford: Oxford University Press, 2003). On the physical landscape of Roman property, see Éva Jakab, "Property Rights in Ancient Rome," in Paul Erdkamp, Koenraad Verboven, and Arjan Zuiderhoek (eds.), *Ownership and Exploitation of Land and Natural Resources in the Roman World* (Oxford: Oxford University Press, 2015), 107–131.

[136] Bonfante, *Corso di diritto romano: Vol. II, La Proprietà*, part 2, 243 and 327.

the *limitatio* was to eliminate, symbolically, from the property the reality of the inevitable conflicts and interrelations between neighbors by relegating these conflicts into a dedicated public buffer zone. The nineteenth-century architects of Roman-bourgeois property would successfully popularize it, making it a central image of the modern liberal legal and political imaginary. But the real authors of the image of property as separate spheres of absolute sovereignty are the Roman *pontifices* and jurists, who, through their ritualism, inscribed it, however unrealistically, onto the landscape of property.

Rituals aside, in what way was the *dominus'* sphere of "sovereignty" truly absolute? The *dominus'* partial immunity from state power was achieved by exempting the *dominus* from real estate taxes. The *dominus* paid taxes, of course, but personal taxes, not property taxes. *Dominium* was absolute also in another way: it was protected through a special action, the *rei vindicatio*. The *rei vindicatio* was an assertion of absolute title. It was the only action of this type. The dispossessed *dominus* sued the possessor of the thing for its recovery, asserting *"ex iure Quiritium meum esse aio"* (I claim this under quiritary law).[137] The ability to make this assertion of title in a *rei vindicatio* was the essential feature of *dominium*. It was so essential that the jurist Celsus, not without some circularity, tells us that:

> What is mine is whatever remains of my property over which I have the right of vindication.[138]

But, practically, the *rei vindicatio* was hardly a convenient remedy. If the defendant denied the plaintiff's ownership, the plaintiff had to prove that he had acquired *dominium* over the thing from its previous *dominus*, who in turn had acquired it from the *dominus* before him. Proving the entire chain of title back until the first owner's original acquisition must have been, in many cases, almost impossible. The possessory interdicts available for the protection of possession were a much more efficient option. Ritualism suggesting full sovereignty over a thing also characterized the transfer of *dominium*. For *dominium* to be successfully transferred, the parties had to use one of two specific forms, *mancipatio* or *in iure cessio*. *Mancipatio*, we have already learned, consisted in the

---

[137] Pietro Bonfante, *Corso di diritto romano: Vol. II, La Proprietà* (Milan: Giuffrè, 1968 [1926]), 395–418. Because the titles of the volumes in Bonfante's *Corso* are similar, this part will be denoted as "*Corso di diritto romano: Vol. II, La Proprietà* (1968)."
[138] Digest 6.1.49.1.

transferee's declaration that "this is mine" accompanied by a ritual with bronze and scales in the presence of five Roman citizens as witnesses. *In iure cessio*, as we have seen, also involved a resolute claim of ownership in the context of a fictitious dispute in which the transferee acted as a dispossessed owner.[139]

Despite these many rituals and formalities asserting the "absolute" character of *dominium*, *dominium* was, obviously, not absolute. It was certainly not absolute in the sense that the *dominus* had full enjoyment of the thing, free of any restrictions. Obviously, equal, unrestricted enjoyment for all owners is hardly conceivable. For an owner to have unfettered entitlements against all persons with respect to a thing would mean that others have no legitimate interests, meriting legal protection, in their things or in their person that may conflict with the owner's exercise of his rights. Even the crudest legal system restricts the owner's enjoyment to allow the similar enjoyment of other owners and to protect, even if minimally, the public interest. As we will see shortly, Roman law imposed a set of limits on owners that look very much like those of a modern legal system. The transformation from a small agrarian economy to an imperial market economy, the empire's growing demand for revenue, and the increasing pressure for redistributive policies left their mark on the law of property. By Justinian's time, the public policy limitations on property did not differ too much from the modern regime of limited property entitlements we are familiar with. *Dominium* could also have been absolute in the sense that the *dominus* was immune from losing ownership without his consent. But this was not the case in Roman law, which knew various forms of prescription (*usucapio, longi temporis praescriptio, praescriptio quadriginta annorum*), by which an owner could lose title to a possessor in good faith by the simple lapse of time.[140]

Finally, as Barry Nicholas suggests, *dominium* may have been absolute in the sense that it was the best, ultimate right and the only of its kind because there was no other formal *right* to "own" a thing. In other words, one was either a *dominus* or a mere de facto possessor. However, *dominium* was not the only right of its kind. There were two modes of owning that were, in substance, equivalent to *dominium*. The first was the case of the "bonitary owner," the transferee who had received a *res mancipi* by mere conveyance (*traditio*) rather than through the prescribed forms. The second was the person whose title was defective

---

[139] Bonfante, *Corso di diritto romano: Vol. II, La Proprietà* (1968), 181–198.
[140] Nicholas, *An Introduction to Roman Law*, 156.

because he or she had received the thing, in good faith, from someone who was not the owner. Technically, both the "bonitary owner" and the *good faith* possessor had no better title than a mere possessor, entitled to the limited remedy of the interdicts. However, in the late Republic, the *praetor* granted both protection equivalent to that of an owner (*dominus*), de facto creating two other forms of ownership that came to be known as "praetorian ownership" and differed from *dominium* only in name.[141] After a certain *praetor*, called Publicius, made available to the "bonitary owner" the *Actio Publiciana*, which was essentially a *vindicatio* in which the necessary lapse of time for *usucapio* was fictitiously presumed, the "bonitary owner" was protected against everyone, including the owner *ex iure Quiritium*, and hence was, for nearly all practical purposes, in the position of an owner. But the Romans, Nicholas notes, could not bring themselves to call the "bonitary owner" *dominus* and opted for the convoluted formula "*in bonis esse*," which means "to have something in one's estate."[142] The modern jurist can only be baffled. Someone who is not an owner merely because he failed to perform an old cumbersome ritual is put in the same exact position of an owner, through a legal fiction, and yet denied the name "owner" and designated instead with a clumsy circumlocution. Preserving the symbolic and conceptual uniqueness of *dominium* required as much.

To conclude, the answer to the question of whether *dominium* was *truly* absolute is both no and yes. *Dominium* was not absolute in its actual daily operation. It was not the ultimate and unique right, as the owner was not entitled to unfettered enjoyment and was not wholly immune from loss. But *dominium* was absolute in the formalities and rituals it involved. The most important moments in the life of *dominium* – from the tracing of the physical boundaries of the parcel, to the transfer of ownership, to its protection – were marked by resolute assertions of absolute ownership. The echoes of such assertions would resonate in the overblown rhetoric of the treatises and monographs of the nineteenth-century architects of Roman-bourgeois property.

Dominium also had a twin concept, possession (*possessio*). Today, possession has largely slipped out of legal scholars' sight, and it is often dismissed by Anglo-American jurists as "the vaguest of all vague terms."[143] Yet, possession was a critical concept in Roman law and, in

---

[141] Id., 155–156.
[142] Id., 128, 157.
[143] Reg. v Smith 1855 6 Co C C 554, 556; see also Burke Shartel, "Meanings of Possession" (1931) 16 *Minnesota Law Review* 611.

turn, in Romanist-bourgeois property law. *Dominium* and possession were twins because, in very simplified terms, *dominium* was a *right* while possession was a *fact*. In other words, the *dominus* was *entitled* to have a thing while the possessor *actually had* a thing, meaning that the possessor exercised actual physical control over a thing and intended to exercise such control, albeit without having a formal legal entitlement.[144]

However, the notion that, in Roman law, possession is merely a fact and not a right is misleading and needs clarification. There were two situations in which the fact of possession did have legal consequences, regardless of formal title. The first was *usucapio*, that is, the acquisition of *dominium* by continuous possession. Present certain requirements, the person who possessed a thing for a protracted period of time became its owner. In other words, *usucapio* operated similarly to a familiar institution of Anglo-American property law that puzzles every first-year law student, that is, adverse possession. The second case in which possession had legal consequences is less familiar but truly fascinating. While the possessor had no formal entitlement over the thing, she or he still received some degree of protection from the law through remedies known as "possessory interdicts." Interdicts were orders issued by the *praetor* at the request of the claimant and aimed at quickly solving the controversy. Through these interdicts, the possessor could restrain others from interfering with his possession and recover possession from anyone who had dispossessed him. Different types of interdicts applied to specific types of property and circumstances. The *interdictum utrubi* applied to movables while the *interdictum uti possidetis* was available for immovables; the *interdictum de vi* covered cases of dispossession through physical force and the *interdictum de vi armata* cases of dispossession with the assistance of armed persons.[145] To enjoy the protection of the interdicts, the possessor had to hold the thing in the manner of an owner, that is, to have both sufficient physical control of the thing, either directly or through another person, and the intention to possess like an owner.[146]

---

[144] Nicholas, *An Introduction to Roman Law*, 107.

[145] Watson, *The Law of Property in the Later Roman Republic*, 86–89.

[146] This meant that someone who held the thing in pursuance of a contract with the owner, for example, a lessee, was not considered a possessor protected by the interdicts. A lessee could, of course, proceed *in personam* against the lessor but could not avail himself of the interdicts. For the same reason, the interdicts were unavailable to anyone who held the thing in the exercise of one of the more limited real rights; see Nicholas, *An Introduction to Roman Law*, 107–108.

Why the law would protect a possessor who is acting with no right was a question that fascinated the nineteenth-century architects of modern Romanist property law. In 1803, the German jurist Friedrich Karl von Savigny published a treatise *On Possession* that proved immensely influential and sparked a vivacious, and at times violently polemical, debate among jurists throughout Europe.[147] For Savigny, Roman possession was a matter of protecting the peace and order of society against force and lawlessness; for others, possession was about protecting the will of the possessor, actualized in the exercise of control over a thing; still others stressed that safeguarding possession was an indirect and imperfect means of affording effective and temporary protection without the need to prove chain of title.

The Limits of Roman Property

The nineteenth-century proponents of modern, Romanist *dominium* were eager to emphasize that the very idea of limits was foreign to the way the Romans thought about property. As Bonfante put it:

> From what we said about the origins and the concept of Roman property, it appears that limits were not an original characteristic of property: the primigenial structure of *dominium ex iure Quiritium* does not allow for real limits, or at least limits are few and dissimulated.[148]

Yet, there are good reasons to question Bonfante's statement. Limits to property entitlements may have been "few and dissimulated" in the early days of Rome but, as Roman society developed and the Roman economy grew, the number, if not the nature, of the regulatory limits to private property came to resemble modern property law. For religious as well as public health reasons, owners were prohibited from burying the dead on their land within the city walls. In case of land located outside the city, when a holder of the *ius sepulchri* was not also owner of the land, the latter had a duty to grant the former access to the land for the purposes of mourning and honoring the deceased. If flooding prevented the use of a public road, neighboring owners had a duty to grant a temporary public right of passage over their land. By late imperial times, limitations were imposed on owners' rights over the subsurface of their land.[149]

---

[147] Friedrich Carl von Savigny, *Das Recht des Besitzes. Eine civilistische Abhandlung* (Baden-Baden: Nomos Verlagsgesellschaft, 2011 [Giessen: Heyer, 1803]).

[148] Bonfante, *Corso di diritto romano: Vol. II, La Proprietà*, part 2, 277.

[149] The maxim *cuius est solum, eius est usque ad coelum et ad inferos* is at times thought to apply to conditions during the classical period of Roman law, but here again we have a medieval maxim posing as an ancient rule. See p. 278.

A constitution of the Emperors Gratian, Valentinian, and Theodosius on quarries prescribed the division of the materials excavated between the owner, the person who excavates and the state:

> If any persons with laborious digging follow a vein of stone through lands belonging to private individuals, they are to pay a tenth to the fiscus and a tenth to the owner of the land, and what remains they may vindicate according to their wishes.[150]

Detailed regulations also limited the ability of owners to develop and build on their land, whether urban or rural. Conservation regulations, aimed at securing the stability and the aesthetic value of buildings in the city, prohibited owners from separating valuable materials, for example, marbles, from buildings for the purpose of selling them. And a senatorial decree during the reign of the Emperor Claudius prohibited altogether the sale of buildings when the object of the transaction was not the building itself but rather its materials. Further, legislation in the imperial period began to prescribe the minimum distance between buildings and to regulate the height of buildings and the width of party walls, reflecting a concern present in modern legal systems as well. Also, under the Emperors Leo and Zeno the regulation of relations among neighbors made a qualitative and quantitative leap, becoming a comprehensive, detailed body of rules. A constitution issued by Zeno for the city of Constantinople gives us a good sense of what the new regulatory regime looked like. In addition to the new limits as to height and distance, Zeno introduced easements (δουλεία, in the Greek text of the constitution) for light and air and for the view of the sea. Another important limitation, this one originating in the Twelve Tables, was the *actio aquae pluviae arcendae*, an action given against the owner of neighboring land for having constructed improvements that changed the natural flow of rainwater such that it damaged the plaintiff's property. By Justinian's time, juristic debate over the *actio aquae pluviae arcendae* had expanded to cover interferences that resulted in a diminution of the natural flow of a source of water.

It was a common contention among the nineteenth-century proponents of modern *dominium* not only that limits to property entitlements were "few and dissimulated" but also that the Roman state had no eminent domain power to take private property for public use. Proponents of this view pointed to the absence of any legislative or

---

[150] Theodosian Code 10.19.10.

juristic text expressly recognizing the principle and to a variety of texts from which it can, supposedly, be inferred that no such principle existed. For example, in his speech *De Lege Agraria*, Cicero, criticizing the demagogic and unrealistic nature of proposal of the tribune P. Servius Tullius that the state buy privately owned parcels of land and redistribute them to the landless, notes:

> Now observe the unbounded and unacceptable license of all the provisions. Money has been collected to buy lands; further, they will not be bought from those who are unwilling to sell. If the owners agree not to sell, what will happen?[151]

What Cicero is describing is the classic holdout problem, traditionally offered as a justification for eminent domain: when private owners refuse to sell their land, which the government needs for a public purpose, the government takes it by eminent domain and pays just compensation. Cicero's ironic interrogation – "what will happen if owners refuse to sell?" – is taken to suggest that the Roman state had no power to take property in the case of holdouts. Further evidence of the absence of eminent domain in Rome was found in an anecdote recounted by the historian Livy (64 or 59 BC–AD 12 or 17). During their term of office (179–174 BC), the censors M. Aemilius Lepidus and M. Fulvius Nobilior, Livy tells us, had planned to build an aqueduct, but the realization of the project was frustrated by the opposition of one single owner, M. Licinius Crassus, who refused to sell his land.[152] However, this story does not prove much; it may speak more to the power of one man than to the question of eminent domain. Crassus was a member of one of the prominent families in Rome, the *gens Licinia*, and it is possible that he would have succeeded in his opposition even if eminent domain existed.

Were the Roman law scholars who, in the nineteenth and twentieth centuries, argued for the existence of eminent domain in Roman law all socialistic ideologues anxious to redeem Roman property from the accusation of being excessively individualistic and anti-social, as Bonfante seemed to believe? Certainly not. While the absence of explicit statements and discussion of eminent domain is surprising, there is an abundance of texts from which such a general principle can be inferred. The Romans may not have felt the need to articulate such a general principle, or to develop a full-fledge theory of takings, but they were

---

[151] Cicero, *De Lege Agraria*, 1.5.15.
[152] Livy, *Ab Urbe Condita*, 40.51.7.

certainly familiar with the state taking property for public purposes. To begin with, citizens' property could be taken for religious reasons if it interfered with the Roman people's relation with the supernatural. We have seen how entangled the public and the sacred were, and indeed Roman property can hardly be understood if one forgets their interrelation. Cicero tells a story that gives a sense of how religion could justify a loss of property:

> For example, when the augurs were preparing to make observations from the citadel and they ordered Tiberius Claudius Centumalus, who owned a house on the Caelian Hill, to demolish the parts of the structure that blocked the taking of the auspices because of their height. Claudius advertised the block for sale, and Publius Calpurnius Lanarius bought it. The augurs ordered him to do the very same thing.[153]

The *augures* were a college of high priests whose distinct prerogative was to ritualistically interpret the auspices, which meant observing certain natural phenomena to determine whether or not the gods approved of an important public action about to be launched. What is not clear from this passage is whether the mandate to destroy Claudius' house gave rise to any claim for compensation.

But the most significant traces of eminent domain in the Roman law of property can be found in the literature on aqueducts. Our informant is Frontinus, not a jurist but a high-ranking public official who was appointed water commissioner for the city of Rome in AD 97. In his *De Aquis Urbis Romae*, a treatise about the administration of the Roman aqueducts, Frontinus explained the process of planning and building an aqueduct. In the section devoted to the tracing of the aqueduct's path, Frontinus cited a decree of the senate imposing a variety of limits on private owners whose land was located on the aqueduct's route. Further, Frontinus described, as an example of admirable balancing of private and public interests, what to our modern eyes seems a typical case of taking with payment of just compensation:

> The consuls Quintus Aelius Tubero and Paulus Fabius Maximus made a report that the courses the aqueducts, which come into the city, are encumbered with monuments and buildings and planted with trees, and upon putting the matter to the senate for decision, it has been resolved: because, in order to repair channels and conduits (the blockages and encumbrances must be cleared) by which public infrastructure is

---

[153] Cicero, *De Officiis*, 3.16.66.

damaged, it is decreed that around the fountains, arches, and walls a space of fifteen feet is to be left clear on each side; and that around the channels that are underground and the conduits both within the city and within buildings adjacent to the city, a space of five feet is to remain clear on each side, and it is not permitted to build a monument or a building, nor to plant trees, in these places after this time; if there are now trees within this space, they will be extirpated unless they are connected to a house or enclosed in buildings . . . .. This resolution of the senate would seem quite just, even if these areas were claimed only for the sake of public utility. But our ancestors, with much more admirable justice, did not take from private citizens even those areas that were integral to the public project, but, when they were building aqueducts, if a proprietor made a fuss about selling a part, they bought the whole field, and, after the necessary expanse was determined, they sold the field again, so that, within their own boundaries, the state and private citizens should have their own right.[154]

This brief glance at Roman property's limits leaves us with a puzzle: if the regulations limiting owners' entitlements were vast and detailed, and the texts alluding to the state's power of eminent domain are numerous, what justifies the idea that Roman property suffered no limit? Roman law scholars who are proponents of this idea have one last arrow in their quiver: the absence of a general principle prohibiting *aemulatio* or "abuse of rights," that is, the owner's abusive exercise of her rights. The principle was included in several of the nineteenth- and twentieth-century civil codes and was the object of enthusiastic endorsements and heated polemics in the debates between the proponents of modern absolute *dominium* and their social critics. The former sought to show that a general principle of "abuse of rights" was nowhere to be found in the Roman sources, while the latter were eager to affirm the Roman character of the doctrine of "abuse of rights." As with eminent domain, the proponents of "abuse of rights" could not point to a text explicitly articulating a general principle but found numerous sparse allusions to the doctrine. Most of these were allusions to a prohibition of a spiteful, malicious, or purposeless exercise of one's right in connection to a specific resource, namely water. For example, a passage from Ulpian seems to suggest a consensus among jurists that acts done with the intent to harm, *animus nocendi*, and not for useful purposes, are not within the scope of the owner's right:

---

[154] Frontinus, *De Aquis Urbis Romae*, 2.127–128.

The same authorities (Sabinus and Cassius) say that everyone can retain rainwater on his own property or can lead surface rainwater from his neighbor's property onto his own property, as long as work is not done on another's property, and that no one is to be held liable for this, because no person is prohibited from enriching himself as long as he does not harm anyone while he does it. Next, Marcellus writes that against someone who, while digging on his own property, diverts a water source of his neighbor, no action can be brought, not even the action for fraud. And certainly the neighbor should not have an action, if that someone did this not with a mind to harm his neighbor, but to make his land better.[155]

Another allusion to malice, considered important by Roman law scholars because it does not concern waters but rather seems a more general statement of a principle is contained in a passage from Celsus, a jurist of the classical era. Celsus, while discussing the rights of the good faith possessor who makes improvements on the owner's land, states:

There must be no allowance for malice. If, for instance, you want to scrape away plaster, which you have applied, and destroy pictures, you will accomplish nothing but to be obnoxious.[156]

Bonfante may have been right that the Roman jurists aptly disguised the limits to property. They made it easy for their modern counterparts to downplay the relevance of these limits and to focus instead on the absence of general principles regarding eminent domain or the prohibition of abuse of rights. Yet, these limits were neither few nor insignificant.

Public Land and Provincial Land: The Lesser Forms of Resource-Specific "Ownership"

Dominium was the supreme property form but, alongside *dominium* and the two equivalent forms of "praetorian ownership," there were other forms of "ownership." These other forms were not called "property" but were rather designated with formulas such as *possidere, uti, frui,* or *habere possidere frui,* all of which evoke the idea of a full enjoyment of the thing. And, in fact, the scope of the owner's entitlements was so broad as to make these forms hardly distinguishable from "property" as we think of it today. The existence of these lesser "properties" is one of the most important features of Roman property that the nineteenth-century

---

[155] Digest 39.3.1.11–12.
[156] Digest 6.1.38.

legend of *dominium* has virtually erased. One aspect of these lesser forms of "ownership" is worth noting. These "properties" were, to a large extent, resource-specific. They were tailored to the specific interests and needs implicated by different types of land that were key to the Roman economy or to Roman geo-political designs, such as public land and provincial land. By variously tweaking the entitlements comprised in these lesser forms of ownership, the Roman state was able to effectively pursue a variety of political and economic goals with regards to public and provincial lands.

Not all land in Italy was held as private property by *domini*. Large swathes of land were public land, known as the *ager publicus populi Romani*.[157] Public land, which the Roman state acquired by confiscation from defeated enemies, was owned by the state but was made available to private citizens through a variety of forms that closely resembled ownership. Initially, not all private citizens had access to public land. The sources for the early Republic suggest that plebeians, the lower class, were originally excluded from public land.[158] The tenure regime for public land was, initially, very informal. Public land, to the extent it was not used by the state, could be freely "occupied" (*ager occupatorius*) by users who wished to work it. A passage by Appian of Alexandria, a Roman historian of Greek origin who wrote in the second century AD, gives us a good sense of the informality characterizing this early "ownership" regime for public land:

> As the Romans subdued Italy piece by piece in war, they would take a part of land and make new cities there, or they would enlist colonists of their own to settle in cities that already existed. They intended to use these cities in place of garrisons, and whenever they took land in war, what was being cultivated they would immediately distribute, sell, or lease to the colonists. But as they did not have the time to divide the land that was

---

[157] On Roman public lands, see Alberto Burdese, *Studi sull'ager publicus* (Turin: G. Giappichelli, 1952); Luigi Capogrossi Colognesi, "Alcuni problemi di storia romana arcaica: 'ager publicus', 'gentes' e clienti (1980) 83 *Bullettino dell'Istituto di Diritto Romano "Vittorio Scialoja"* 29–65; Saskia Roselaar, *Public Land in the Roman Republic: A Social and Economic History of Ager Publicus in Italy, 396–89 BC* (Oxford: Oxford University Press, 2010); Dominic W. Rathbone, "The Control and Exploitation of *ager publicus* in Italy under the Roman Republic," in Jean-Jacques Aubert (ed.), *Tâches publiques en enterprise privée dans le monde romain* (Neuchâtel: University of Neuchâtel, 2003), 135–178.

[158] Luigi Capogrossi Colognesi, "Ager publicus e ager privatus dall'età arcaica al compromesso patrizio-plebeo," in Jaime Roset (ed.), *Estudios en homenaje al Profesor Juan Iglesias* (Madrid: Universidad Complutense de Madrid, 1988), Vol. II, 639–650.

then lying fallow because of the war, which was the majority usually, they would auction it in the interim to anyone who wanted to work it for a tax on the annual harvest, a tenth of what was sown, and a fifth of what was planted. A tax was imposed also on those keeping livestock, whether larger or smaller animals.[159]

In this early stage, occupiers' use rights were highly unsecure. Users held the land without a legal title and the state could take away the land from the occupier whenever it was needed, without any duty to pay compensation. How much public land users could occupy and who was allowed to occupy are highly contentious questions. From the *agrimensores*, the professional surveyors who codified the Roman land system, we gather that, at an earlier time, "each man did not occupy as much land as he could then cultivate, but he sought to gain as much as he had the hope of cultivating."[160] It also appears that in 367 BC, the *Lex Licinia de modo agrorum* capped the amount of land that could be occupied by one individual to 500 *iugera*. This limit, however, seems to have remained dead letter.

From the third century BC on, these informal use rights evolved into more stable and secure forms of "ownership" in response to larger structural changes in the Roman economy as well as in the Roman class structure. Over the course of the third century, what some historians have called a Roman market economy started taking shape.[161] As Rome

---

[159] Appian, *Bellum Civile*, 1.7.26–27.

[160] *Commentum*, 50.28–30.

[161] Scholars passionately disagree on whether Rome had a market economy, that is, an economy where many resources are allocated by prices that are free to move in response to changes in underlying conditions. Ancient historian Moses Finley maintained that Rome's economy was qualitatively different from a modern market economy and argued that, in the Roman "ancient economy," an ideology of agricultural self-sufficiency as well as status considerations acted as brakes on the development of factor markets, technology, trade, and profit maximization. See M. I. Finley, *The Ancient Economy* (Foreword by Ian Morris) (Berkeley: University of California Press, 1999). However, in recent decades, a variety of new methodological approaches to the Roman economy have cast light on the relevance, the size, and the actual operation of the Roman, and larger Mediterranean, market. Peter Temin has devoted a great deal of effort to showing that the economy of the early Roman Empire was primarily a market economy. Building on abundant evidence and extensive earlier studies of the wheat market and prices, Temin makes two claims: that many individual actions and interactions in the Roman world are best seen as market transactions and that there were enough market transactions to constitute a market economy. Further, Temin suggests that, while local markets were not tied together as tightly as they are today, they were still interconnected and functioned as part of a comprehensive Mediterranean market. This Mediterranean market promoted regional specialization and exploited the comparative advantage of different parts of the

rapidly grew into a Mediterranean empire, the acquisition of new territory and the influx of money and slaves made larger commercial agricultural production possible. Commercial agriculture required a significant
investment in the forms of equipment, slaves, wages for free laborers,
livestock, seeds or plants and transportation, but insecurity of tenure
under this informal form of occupation made commercial farmers reluctant to invest. Under the pressure of this expanding economy, the inflex-
ibility of a property system that offered either absolute *dominium* or
informal, unsecure use rights became apparent, and new types of "ownership" were developed whereby land remained the property of the state
but users were granted an official title, broad entitlements, and security
of tenure.

The earliest of these new "ownerships" concerned public lands known
as *ager quaestorius*.[162] This form of tenure derived its name from the fact
that it was "sold" in fifty-*iugera* blocks at an auction, presumably at
market rates, by the *quaestores*, elected officials who supervised the
treasury and the finances of the state. The sources use the word *vendere*,
which means to sell, but what was "sold" was, technically, use rights, not
the land itself, which remained the property of the state. However, the
"owners" had broad entitlements that made their position similar to
ownership. Use rights over the parcels gave the "owner" full control over
the use and management of the land, were freely transferable, and could

Mediterranean. See Peter Temin, *The Roman Market Economy* (Princeton, NJ: Princeton
University Press, 2013). See also Philip Kay, *Rome's Economic Revolution* (Oxford:
Oxford University Press, 2014); Alan Bowman and Andrew Wilson (eds.), *Quantifying
the Roman Economy* (Oxford: Oxford University Press, 2009); Walter Scheidel (ed.), *The
Cambridge Companion to the Roman Economy* (Cambridge: Cambridge University
Press, 2012); André Tchernia, *The Romans and Trade* (Oxford: Oxford University
Press, 2016); Cameron Hawkins, *Roman Artisans and the Urban Economy*
(Cambridge: Cambridge University Press, 2016). Scholars adhering to the "New
Institutional Economics" approach have also focused on the existence and operation
of markets in the Roman world. The picture these scholars present is a more complicated
one. The Roman economy was a mixed system, whereby a price-setting market coexisted
with public supply channels and the government was heavily involved in some areas of
resource exploitation, such as mining. The market and public supply supported each
other in various ways and promoted efficient outcomes, either outcomes that were
efficient economically or in other social respects, especially in regard to religion or
politics. See Arjan Zuiderhoek, "Introduction: Land and Natural Resources in the
Roman World in Historiographical and Theoretical Perspective," in Paul Erdkamp,
Koenraad Verboven, and Arjan Zuiderhoek (eds.), *Ownership and Exploitation of
Land and Natural Resources in the Roman World* (Oxford: Oxford University Press,
2015) 1–18, at 11–16.
[162] Roselaar, *Public Land in the Roman Republic*, 121–127.

be bequeathed to heirs. In the "law in the books," "owners" had a duty to pay rent, but there is reason to doubt that, in practice, collection actually happened. As to security of tenure, it appears from the sources that the protection of "owners" against dispossession by third parties was gradually reinforced by making available the possessory interdicts. What is not clear is whether the state could take back the land. Some scholars have argued that the parcels could be bought back by the state only at the initiative of the "owner." In any event, regardless of what the status of the "owner" vis-à-vis the state was formally, it seems that, in practice, tenure was made relatively secure by the fact that supervising, administering, and, possibly, taking back public lands was costly and complicated for the state.[163]

Another form of "ownership" for public lands, called *ager in trientalibus*, was developed as a way to finance the Second Punic War.[164] Private citizens gave their gold, silver, and jewelry to the treasury for the purpose of financing the war effort, with the agreement that they would be paid back in three money installments. However, in 200, when the time came for the second payment and no money was available, the senate decided to repay citizens by granting use of parcels of the *ager publicus*. As Livy recounts,

> As the private citizens made a fair request, and nevertheless the republic could not repay the loan, the senate decreed something that was mid-way between fair and pragmatic, namely that, because a large part of these citizens said that lands were generally for sale and that they needed to buy some, the public land that was within fifty miles should be available to them: the consuls were to appraise the land and impose a tax of an *as* per *iugerum* for the sake of maintaining that the land was public, so that if anyone, when the state was solvent, wanted to have money instead of land, he could restore the land to the people. Happily the private citizens accepted this proposition; this land was called "*trientabulum*," because it had been given to satisfy one third of the debt.[165]

Rich farmers interested in commercial agriculture found this compromise very attractive. The fact that the land was situated within a fifty-mile radius from Rome meant that it was in high demand among those wishing to produce for the market in the city. As in the case of the *ager quaestorius*, "owners" of the *ager in trientalibus* had the entitlements of

---

[163] Id., 123–124.
[164] Id., 127–128.
[165] Livy, *Ab Urbe Condita*, 31.13.5–9.

an owner and virtually complete security of tenure. Land could only be taken back by the state at the initiative of the "owner" who preferred cash, and there is no evidence that anyone exchanged land for money. The *ager in trientalibus* was mentioned as a category of land in the *lex agraria* of 111 BC and, by this time, its "owners" had held their parcels undisturbed for almost ninety years.[166]

Yet another special "ownership" form was developed for public lands known as *ager censorius* because these were leased out by the *censor*, a high Roman magistrate, with an arrangement that resembled a long lease rather than ownership.[167] However, in the sources, the recipients of such lands were at times called *redemptores* (buyers), which suggests that, in practice, their entitlements were not too different from those of an owner.[168] Although the prevailing opinion was that recipients of *ager censorius* were lessees rather than owners, the potential perpetuity of the lease and the ability to transfer the land to one's heirs made them de facto owners.

Public lands were a critical resource in the economic, social, and political life of the Roman Republic, and the Roman state made available these lesser forms of "ownership" for a number of reasons. Chief among these was the policy of supporting the material prosperity and, in turn, the demographic growth of Roman farmers as well as of Latin and Italian farmers, who were not Roman citizens but who provided manpower critical to Rome's wars of expansion. These various forms of private "ownership" of public lands also made it possible for the state to finance its war efforts and to promote economic initiatives, such as the development of commercial farming.

Public land was not the only type of land for which the Roman state made available a smaller, customized form of "ownership." Provincial land (*solum provinciale*) was exempt from Roman property rules and from *dominium*. However, because the majority of the inhabitants of the empire lived in the provinces, a type of "provincial ownership" had to be developed. As with the various "ownership" forms available for public lands, provincial ownership was not technically ownershi, but rather was described, in the classical sources, as *possessio* or *usufructus*. Roman jurists always treated provincial ownership as an exception. They emphasized the rules and doctrines that did not apply to it: ownership of

---

[166] Roselaar, *Public Land in the Roman Republic*, 128.
[167] Id., 128–133.
[168] Id., 129.

provincial land could not be transferred through *mancipatio* or *in iure cessio* and it was exempted from acquisition by *usucapio*.[169] As a result, we know very little about the positive regime of provincial ownership, beyond the fact that it was subject to a yearly tax and that it was protected through a *vindicatio*, not a *rei vindicatio*, which was reserved to *dominium*, but a *vindicatio* based on *aequitas*, that is, on considerations of equity. In recent years, historians of Rome have started exploring in greater depth provincial ownership but, because of the scant evidence, have found it difficult to develop a detailed schema of provincial land-ownership that is consistent across provinces. The picture these scholars trace is one of significant legal pluralism. As a general principle, Rome respected the local legal systems in the provinces and only intervened to clarify or supplement local property regimes.[170] However, on the ground, a spectrum of different ownership bundles developed out of the inter-action of the competing claims of different actors: local elites, local peasants, Romans in the provinces, and Rome's political elite.[171]

Egypt is the one province for which we have good evidence based on a rich stream of source material and hence has been the focus of this recent scholarship.[172] In Egypt, a variety of land regimes coexisted. To begin with, a special form of ownership was made available for provincial state land. In Egypt, Rome inherited a long tradition of state ownership of land and, under Roman rule, all land for which taxes had previously been paid directly to the Ptolemaic monarchs continued to be treated as public land. This was the case for formerly royal land and portions of the lands formerly belonging to temples. This public land was assigned to state farmers whose entitlements comprised use rights, a positive duty to cultivate the land, a duty to pay a yearly tax, the right to transfer or "sublet" their cultivation rights, and the right to pass their rights and duties to their successors.[173] Other land was treated as "private," including land already recognized as private under the Ptolemies, but also some

---

[169] Lisa Pilar Eberle, "Law, Empire, and the Making of Roman Estates in the Provinces during the Late Republic" (2016) 3(1) *Critical Analysis of Law* 50–69.

[170] Andrea Jördens, Julian Wagstaff, and Dennis P. Kehoe, "Possession and Provincial Practice," in Paul J. du Plessis, Clifford Ando, and Kaius Touri (eds.), *The Oxford Handbook of Roman Law and Society* (Oxford: Oxford University Press, 2016), 553–568.

[171] Eberle, "Law, Empire, and the Making of Roman Estates in the Provinces during the Late Republic," 67; Andrew Monson, Communal Agriculture in the Ptolemaic and Roman Fayyum, Princeton/Stanford Working Papers in Classics Paper No. 100703 (2007).

[172] Jördens, Wagstaff, and Kehoe, "Possession and Provincial Practice," 554.

[173] Id., 558.

temple land, the land of the Ptolemaic military settlers, and former state lands that had been privately cultivated for generations. "Owners" of this private land had a different set of ownership entitlements and duties. They had a duty to pay a tax, called the *artabeia*, which was, on average, only a third of the rate of the tax applied to public land. Also, because this land was originally public, transfer of this land could not take the form of a true sale but rather required special modalities. Yet another type of "ownership" characterized temple estates, where priesthoods administered the many economic functions – including farming, manufacturing, and grain distribution – that had made each estate "a system unto itself" since pharaonic times.[174] These holdings could be inherited by successors, leased and pledged as security.

By recognizing these types of "ownership" with different scope and shape, the Roman state sought to achieve both economic and fiscal goals with regard to the province of Egypt.[175] The Roman government promoted the free alienability of privately owned land and protected security of tenure in order to unleash private investment in large productive estates. With sufficient financial outlay, highly remunerative, but capital-intensive, forms of agriculture, such as viticulture, could be further developed. In fact, there is much evidence that, during the course of Roman rule, Egypt saw the creation of large commercial estates that had not existed before.[176] Another reason for the state to retain direct control of land in Egypt was the desire to manage the productive targets for the province's economy, deciding what crops would be planted and, for example, subsidizing the production of wheat by leasing wheat land on favorable terms.[177] From a fiscal perspective, through these forms of private tenure, the Roman state could do much to ensure that revenues, which largely depended on the rents extracted from the production of small farmers on state lands, were stable over the long term. This stability

---

[174] J. G. Manning, *The Last Pharaohs: Egypt under the Ptolemies, 305–30 BC* (Princeton, NJ: Princeton University Press, 2009), 83.

[175] Dennis P. Kehoe, "Property Rights over Land and Economic Growth in the Roman Empire," in Paul Erdkamp, Koenraad Verboven, and Arjan Zuiderhoek (eds.), *Ownership and Exploitation of Land and Natural Resources in the Roman World* (Oxford: Oxford University Press, 2015), 88–106, at 90–91; Id., *Law and Rural Economy in the Roman Empire* (Ann Arbor: The University of Michigan Press, 2007).

[176] Dominic Rathbone, *Economic Rationalism and Rural Society in Third-Century A.D. Egypt: The Heroninos Archive and the Appianus Estate* (Cambridge: Cambridge University Press, 1991).

[177] Kehoe, "Property Rights over Land and Economic Growth in the Roman Empire," 101.

was crucial not only to the governance of Egypt but to the administration of the entire empire.

The *Iura in Re Aliena* and the Disaggregation of Property Entitlements

The supposed "indivisibility" of Roman property is a recurrent theme in Roman law and comparative law scholarship. As we have seen, the classical jurists, we are told, "had an extremely concentrated notion of ownership"[178] and were generally uncomfortable with the idea that the entitlements comprised in the owner's "absolute sovereignty" could be split up between different subjects. Hence, Roman law knew no doctrine of estates, whereby ownership of land could be divided in time between a present owner and a future owner to whom the property would, at some point, "revert."[179] This unitary character of Roman property also precluded anything in the nature of a trust, whereby property interests could be split between a trustee, who would have the power to manage the property, and a beneficiary, who would have the right to enjoy the profits.[180]

This supposed indivisibility is hard to fathom for contemporary property lawyers. Our property culture is permeated by the idea that property is a legal device to create, capture, and retain certain kinds of economic value, of utility. Divisibility, that is, the ability to split up ownership entitlements, is critical to creating and capturing economic value. In modern property systems, owners have the ability to create and maximize property value by disaggregating property entitlements.[181] How could it have been that Roman property law, which was the central institution through which the Roman elite extracted value, did not permit divisibility?

Indivisibility may well be yet another aspect of the "legend" of Roman property law. In reality, Roman law offered owners a number of ways to parcel out single entitlements through a sizable menu of "rights over a thing owned by another" (*iura in re aliena*). It is worth taking a closer look at the list of available rights not only to get a sense of the type of

---

[178] Buckland and McNair, *Roman Law and Common Law*, 81.
[179] Id., 81–82.
[180] Id., 82.
[181] Abraham Bell and Gideon Parchomovsky, "Reconfiguring Property in Three Dimensions" (2008) 75 *University of Chicago Law Review* 1015.

social and economic goals owners were able to achieve by creating and parceling out these lesser real rights but also to gain insight into the conceptual dilemmas that these rights posed to the jurists. Servitudes were the oldest of the *iura in re aliena*, and the only ones that can safely be said to exist already in classical law. A servitude is the right of a person other than the owner to make a certain use of that owner's land, for example by using a road for ingress and egress or drawing water for irrigation purposes; such a person was usually the owner of a neighboring piece of land. Max Kaser argued that servitudes were sharply distinguished from ownership and classified as "rights in a thing owned by another" only at a later time and were initially conceived as functionally divided ownership. The person entitled to the servitude was considered as the owner of that part of the land over which the road or the watercourse passed. But this ownership was confined to the function or purpose of the servitude, and the owner of the servient estate was owner for all other intents and purposes.[182]

As compared with contemporary servitudes, the Roman law of servitudes limited what the parties could achieve in two important ways. First, in classical Roman law, the concept of servitudes likely included only servitudes that benefited land and not servitudes that benefited a person. Personal servitudes were a later development that stirred up the passions of nineteenth-century Romanists. With his usual sharpness, Pietro Bonfante noted that so called personal servitudes have little in common with "praedial" servitudes and that the assimilation of the two categories was a product of the conceptual confusion and ignorance of the "Byzantine" jurists.[183] A second significant limitation came from the rule that a servitude could not impose on the owner of the servient estate an affirmative duty to do something, with the sole exception of support rights, that is, the right to have one's structure or building supported by the neighbor's land. As this passage from book 17 of Ulpian's *Libri ad Edictum* shows, even this narrow exception stirred disagreement among Roman jurists:

---

[182] Max Kaser, *Das römische Privatrecht* (Munich: C. H. Beck, 1959) 2.178–180. On the *iura in re aliena* and their role in the emergence of *dominium*, see Charles Bartlett, "The Development of *dominium*: Ownership Rights and the Creation of an Institution," in Charles Bartlett and Michael Leese (eds.), *Law, Institutions, and Economic Performance in Classical Antiquity* (Ann Arbor: University of Michigan Press)

[183] Pietro Bonfante, *Corso di diritto romano: Vol. III, Diritti Reali* (Milan: Giuffrè, 1972 [1933]), 19, 23–24.

So concerning a servitude, which has been imposed for the purpose of providing support, we have a right of action to ensure that the servient owner both provide the support and repair his structures in the way that was envisioned when the servitude was created. Gallus thinks a servitude cannot be imposed in such a way, with the result that someone is forced to do something, but rather only so that he cannot prohibit me from doing something: for in all servitudes repair is the duty of he who benefits from the servitude, not of he whose property is servient. But the view of Servius has won, so that in this specific case, someone can defend his claim that he is able to force his opponent to repair a wall so that it can bear the load. Labeo, however, writes that this servitude does not oblige the person, but rather the property, and so the owner is able to abandon the property.[184]

Servitudes were subdivided by Roman jurists into two subcategories: rustic and urban. Because the former were critical to the Roman agrarian economy, they were treated as *res mancipi*, created through the ritual of *mancipatio* to ensure certainty and publicity about their existence and scope. The rustic servitudes included three types of right of way: *iter* (passage foot or horse), *actus* (passage of herds and agricultural equipment), and *via* (the use of a traced path with the predetermined width of eight feet in straight sections and sixteen feet at turns). Other rustic servitudes included a variety of *iura aquarium* – rights to draw water for irrigation or drinking, or rights to expel run-off surface waters – the right to dig sand, to take clay, to burn lime, to graze cattle and to gather acorns. Urban servitudes included three big clusters of rights, namely rights to expel rainwater and sewage, rights relating to the construction and support of buildings and rights to view, light, and air.

This quick glance at the list of servitudes raises the question of whether the list was a closed one. In other words, could the parties create their own custom-made servitudes, or were they limited to the standard servitudes we have just examined? This question is an important one. A system with a closed menu of forms guarantees predictability and low information costs. Individuals who wish to acquire property entitlements know what options are available and what they can expect.[185] By contrast, free customization resonates with liberal values and promotes individuals' ability of self-authorship by allowing them to freely acquire and exchange resources and entitlements and to enlist one another in the

---

[184] Digest 8.5.6.2.

[185] Thomas W. Merrill, Henry E. Smith, "Optimal Standardization in the Law of Property: The Numerus Clausus Principle" (2000) 110 *Yale Law Journal* 1.

pursuit of private goals and purposes.[186] As we will see over the course of our journey through modern property, from the nineteenth century to the present, property lawyers on both sides of this debate have drawn arguments from Roman law, emphasizing either the supposed "closure" or the alleged flexibility of its property system.[187] However, once again, the truth is that we know very little about the possibility to customize servitudes in Roman law. The classical sources are silent on this point, but sparse references to the parties' ability to create new servitudes appear in Justinian's legislation.[188] Further, some Romanists suggest that even in classical times, the parties had the ability to modify and reshape by agreement the servitudes recognized by the law.[189]

Another way of dividing up property entitlements was for the owner to grant an usufruct, which the Roman jurist Paulus defined as "the right to use and enjoy the fruits of another's property without impairing the substance of the thing."[190] How to properly conceptualize the usufruct was a question that generations of nineteenth-century Roman law scholars debated with passion. Once the post-classical jurists, in all likelihood, invented the concept of personal servitudes, usufruct seemed to fit easily into the new category. However, Bonfante, who, as we have seen, had doubts about the very category of personal servitudes and explained its creation as stemming from the lack of a solid conceptual grasp on the part of the Byzantine jurists, was not convinced. The classical jurists, with their conceptual acumen, Bonfante argued, had understood that servitude and usufruct are radically different concepts. A servitude is a mere limitation on the *dominium* of the servient owner, who has to tolerate the dominant owner's exercise of a narrow entitlement, say passage by foot or horse, but is not deprived of the enjoyment of the land. By contrast, the effect of the usufruct is to transfer to the holder of the usufruct a portion of the owner's *dominium*, specifically, the right to use the land and to appropriate its revenue, for a period of time that cannot exceed the latter's life. In other words, the usufruct does not merely limit *dominium* but actually carves out a portion of *dominium*.[191]

---

[186] Hanoch Dagan, "Markets for Self-Authorship" (2018) 27 *Cornell Journal of Law and Public Policy* 577.

[187] Silvio Perozzi, *Sulla struttura tipica delle servitù prediali in diritto romano* (Rome: Forzani, 1888).

[188] Bonfante, *Corso di diritto romano: Vol. III, Diritti Reali*, 40.

[189] Id., 41.

[190] Digest 7.1.1.

[191] Bonfante, *Corso di diritto romano: Vol. III, Diritti Reali*, 23, 65–73.

And yet even defining the usufruct as a portion of *dominium* seemed hardly satisfactory, because the transferred portion came with one important limitation: the holder of the usufruct could not allow the thing to deteriorate or diminish or change its current productive use. Ulpian provides us with a wealth of examples:

> A usufructuary cannot make the condition of the property worse, but he can make it better. If the usufruct of an estate is left by a legacy, then the usufructuary cannot cut down fruit trees or bring down farm structures or do anything to the detriment of the property. And if by chance the estate is for pleasure, having verdant gardens or drives or walking paths shaded pleasantly with trees that do not bear fruit, the usufructuary cannot cut them down, so that he may plant vegetable beds or something similar, with an eye to profit.[192]

In other words, Bonfante explained, the holder of the usufruct had a right over the thing in its current form or quality (*species rei*), not a right over the "substance of the thing" (*substantia rei*), which remained with the owner. As the non-agricultural sectors of the Roman economy expanded and the state became more involved in the extraction of raw materials and minerals, the limits on the ability of the usufructuary to change the use of the land were further relaxed. By Justinian's time, the prerogatives of the usufructuary were broadened, allowing for change in the use of the land. The subsequent passage in the Digest from Ulpian was likely interpolated to provide an explicit rule for mining.[193] The rule omitted any reference to the substance of the property and instead allowed the usufructuary to engage in the most productive use of the land:

> The question is whether the usufructuary himself can open stone quarries or chalk pits or sand pits? I think he is indeed able to open them, as long as he does not occupy a part of the land necessary for something else while doing this. And so, he can indeed search for veins of stones and of metals so obtained: therefore, he is able either to work the mines of gold, silver, sulfur, copper, iron or other minerals that were opened by the *pater familias*, or to open such mines himself, as long as this does not bring any harm to the cultivation of the land. And if by chance more profit should be returned from a mine that he opened than from the vineyards, or the plantations, or olive groves which were there beforehand, perhaps he will be able to cut these down, since he is able to improve the property.[194]

---

[192] Digest 7.1.13.4.
[193] For a discussion of the likelihood of interpoliation, see Bonfante, *Corso di diritto romano: Vol. III, Diritti Reali*, 78–79.
[194] Digest 7.1.13.5.

This expansion of the entitlements of the holder of the usufruct made the usufruct look even more like *dominium* and less like a personal servitude. Throughout the nineteenth century, scholars of Roman law and private law continued to question the fuzzy line between *dominium* and usufruct and to see usufruct as a lesser form of "ownership" that existed uneasily alongside *dominium*.

Similar to the usufruct but more limited in scope was the right of *usus*, which entitled its holder to use another's property but not to appropriate the revenue or fruits of the thing. If no use of the thing was possible other than taking the fruits, for example, in the case of an orchard, the right holder could use the fruits for himself but not sell them. A particular variant of the right of *usus* was the right of *habitatio*, that is, the right to use another's house for dwelling. Two other "rights over a thing owned by another" that were fully developed only at a later time were the right of *superficies* and the right of *emphyteusis*. The former was developed in the context of increasing urban intensification and land oligopoly in the city of Rome, as land came to be owned by a relatively small number of corporations and private owners. The right of *superficies* was a way of slicing the land. It made it possible for the developer who built on land owned by another to acquire a perpetual and hereditary right to use the surface of the land by paying an annual "rent" called *solarium*.[195]

Emphyteusis was yet another hybrid form that presented classificatory problems similar to the ones posed by the right of usufruct. Land was transferred to an emphyteutical possessor over very long periods of time, or even in perpetuity, in exchange for payment of an annual rent.[196] *Emphyteusis* shared characteristics with both a contract of lease, which transferred possession for a term, and a sale, which transferred full ownership. A constitution of the Emperor Zeno clarified that emphyteusis could not be assimilated to either a sale or a lease but rather was a distinct form giving rise to a set of entitlements that was unique in kind:

> The right of *emphyteusis* should not be related to those of lease or alienation, but it has been determined that this right is of a third type, separate from both of those contracts mentioned, and without connection or likeness to them; that it has its own composition and definition; and that it is a just and valid contract, by which all things, which were agreed upon by both contracting parties, ought, in all cases, even those that happen by chance, if put in writing, to be kept as firm and unalterable

---

[195] Bonfante, *Corso di diritto romano: Vol. III, Diritti Reali*, 165–166.
[196] Id., 161 and 165.

through a perpetual stability in all ways: so that, if those things that occur by accident were not figured as part of the pact when the agreement was made, and if indeed some calamity comes to pass, which brings to utter ruin the very property which was subject to the *emphyteusis*, this loss will not redound to the *emphyteucarius*, who was left with nothing, but to the *dominus* of the property, who, because it resulted from fate, must be held responsible, as there was nothing about the other party's liability in the contract. But if some specific or otherwise light damage occurs, by which the substance of the property was not deeply harmed, the *emphyteucarius* should not hesitate to assume this as his charge.[197]

Zeno's constitution settled the matter only temporarily, and the question of the real nature and appropriate classification of *emphyteusis* would periodically resurface. While the duty to pay rent put the *emphytecarius* in the position of a lessee, the *emphytecarius* had full and secure use entitlements analogous to those of an owner and could sell, bequeath, or otherwise alienate his or her rights to others. *The emphytecarius* could only lose his or her rights for non-payment of the rent for three consecutive years.

To conclude, while these lesser real rights, or "rights over a thing owned by another," differed in shape and scope, each speaks to the pluralism and variability of Roman property. By appropriately combining these smaller rights, owners were able to achieve a wide range of social and economic outcomes. They could multiply the number of subjects who benefited from the resource, design with relative precision the scope of each user's entitlements, disaggregate control and management of the resource at any particular time, and slice up the resource into different assets. Further, over time, as the rules regulating these lesser rights were relaxed, owners acquired greater ability to customize forms and outcomes. Finally, the broadest of these rights, usufruct and emphyteusis, granted the right-holder entitlements comparable to those of an owner. They were, effectively, more limited forms of "ownership" that added to the already striking variety of modes of owning that we have explored in the previous sections.

Property Law and Redistribution: The *Lex Agraria*

The *Lex Sempronia agraria* was a law proposed by the tribune Tiberius Gracchus in 133 BC, and re-proposed by his brother Gaius Gracchus in

[197] Code 4.66.1.

123, that sought to limit the maximum amount of public land individuals could possess and to redistribute the land possessed in excess of this limit to the indigent.[198] Although hastily dismissed by the proponents of modern *dominium* as a radical and arbitrary political act, a redistributive *lex agraria*, as shown by the recurring fascination and legislative energy it has engendered, is nevertheless a critical element of the conceptual vocabulary of Roman property, one that figured prominently in the discourse of eighteenth-century revolutionaries and of the nineteenth-century social reformers. In fact, among the Roman property concepts, the *lex agraria* may be second only to *dominium* in the lasting and vivid impression it has made on generations of historians, politicians, and activists. The *lex agraria* has provided modern reformers with a vocabulary to discuss questions of land redistribution, a blueprint for reform, and a set of powerful rhetorical arguments about the relationship between property, equality, and freedom.

While the *lex agraria* became a centerpiece of modern reformers' discourse about distributive justice, the social and economic situation that led to its proposal, the aims of the Gracchi, and the actual content of the law remain the object of controversy among historians of Rome. Throughout the eighteenth and nineteenth centuries, there was sustained debate as to whether the *lex agraria* applied to private as well as to public land, but scholars now agree that it only concerned the *ager publicus*. In the conventional narrative, told by Appian and Plutarch and by generations of modern historians, the *lex agraria* was proposed to address the accumulation of public land by the wealthy and the consequent proletarianization of the free Roman citizen.[199] Plutarch describes this process of proletarianization and its consequences with great clarity:

> Of the territory of their neighbors that the Romans won in war, some they sold and some they made common, and gave it to the poor and needy of the citizens to possess, once they paid a small tax to the public treasury. And when the rich began to offer higher taxes and expelled the poor, a law was passed that no one person could hold more than five hundred *iugera*

---

[198] For admirably clear discussions of the various *leges agrariae* in Roman history, see Roselaar, *Public Land in the Roman Republic*.

[199] Gianfranco Tibiletti, "Il possesso dell'*ager publicus* e le norme *de modo agrorum* sino ai Gracchi" (1948) 26 *Athenaeum* 173–236; and (1949) 27 *Athenaeum* 3–41; Arnold Toynbee, *Hannibal's Legacy: The Hannibalic War's Effects on Roman Life* (Oxford: Oxford University Press, 1965); Keith Hopkins, *Conquerors and Slaves* (Cambridge: Cambridge University Press, 1978); David Stockton, *The Gracchi* (Oxford: Oxford University Press, 1979).

of land. For a short time, this legislation checked the greediness of the rich, and it aided the poor in remaining on the land according to how it had been rented and in maintaining the allotments which each had held from the outset. But later, the rich neighbors, by means of false identities, transferred these leases to themselves, and finally possessed most of the land blatantly in their own names. The poor, who had been forced off, did not appear eager any longer for military campaigns, and had no care for the rearing of children, with the result that soon all Italy perceived the shortage of freemen, and was full of fettered gangs of foreign slaves, through whom the rich, as they had expelled the citizens, cultivated their estates.[200]

The story Plutarch tells is one of greedy accumulation of land by the rich and related proletarianization of the small farmer. More recently, historians have revised elements of this narrative, contesting the idea of a demographic decline and downplaying the causal relevance of the accumulation of public lands in the hands of the elite.[201] In this revised account, the Gracchian *lex agraria* was passed to tamp down the growing demand for the limited stock of land caused by technological and economic developments in central Italy.

Paradoxically, for a law that has fueled so much political controversy over the centuries, what we know about the actual content of the *Lex Sempronia agraria* is largely speculative and is in fact inferred from a subsequent agrarian law, passed in 111 BC. One thing about the law seems clear: the *Lex Sempronia agraria* marked a fundamental turning point. Limits on the amount of public land individuals could occupy (passed through *leges de modo agrorum*) were not new, but violators had seldom been fined and their excess possessions were left undisturbed. The *Lex Sempronia agraria*, for the first time, took back the land owned in excess of the limit. During the second century BC, "owners" of the *ager publicus* had treated their land as private property, even though they had no formal guarantees of secure tenure: they had sold it, mortgaged it and bequeathed it. Naturally, dispossession caused great mayhem. Appian tells us that:

> Standing together, they complained each in turn and put forward to the poor that their farms and plantations and buildings were ancient. Some asked if they would lose the money paid to their neighbors along with the land, some said that their ancestral tombs were on the land and that they

[200] Plutarch, *Vitae Parallelae: Tiberius Gracchus*, 8.1–3.
[201] Roselaar, *Public Land in the Roman Republic*, 150–219, 290, 297.

had made divisions into inheritances as if it were hereditary, others stated that their wives' dowries had been invested in these lands or that the land had been given as a dowry to their daughters, and moneylenders could show debts contracted on this security. In short, there was disorderly lamentation and vexation.[202]

Whether dispossessed "owners" received compensation is unclear. It seems that, initially, Tiberius Gracchus intended to buy back the excess land from the owners but that the final version of the bill did not provide for any compensation. Tiberius apparently argued that, for the rich, acquiring secure tenure over their remaining, legitimate holdings of public land was itself just compensation for the loss of the excess land. The actual limit set by the *Lex Sempronia agraria* is a debated issue. From Appian, we learn that the limit was 500 *iugera* plus an additional amount for the main occupant's children;[203] from Livy, we hear that the limit was 1,000 *iugera*.[204] Most Roman law scholars side with Appian, reasoning that, in order to make its passage more likely, Tiberius would have wanted to present his law as a mere repetition of earlier laws – as reinforcing the *mos maiorum* – rather than as a radical innovation, and that he would hardly have been able to do so if the limit proposed had been twice that of the earlier legislation. It is also unclear how much of the excess land repossessed by the state each of the indigent beneficiaries received. Based on a passage from the *lex agraria* of 111, it is often suggested that the lots amounted to thirty *iugera*.[205] However, some scholars cast doubt on this figure, noting that the amount seems large compared to the amount granted to colonists in earlier colonization programs.[206] Also, if each beneficiary were assigned thirty *iugera*, only a relatively small number of people would have benefited from the *Lex Sempronia agraria*.[207] Another aspect of the *Lex Sempronia agraria* that has not been fully elucidated is the nature and scope of the beneficiaries' entitlements. Historians agree that the recipients of the land had a duty to pay a rent (*vectigal*) and no right to sell the land. These two basic facts

---

[202] Appian, *Bellum Civile*, 1.10.39.
[203] Appian, *Bellum Civile*, 1.9.37.
[204] Livy, *Periochae*, 58.1.
[205] Jérôme Carcopino, *Autour des Gracques: etudes critiques* (Paris: Les Belles Lettres, 1967); Ernst Badian, "Tiberius Gracchus and the Beginning of the Roman Revolution" (1972) 1 *Aufstieg und Niedergang des römischen Welt* 668–731.
[206] Roselaar, *Public Land in the Roman Republic*, 231.
[207] Id., 231.

raise the question of whether the land became the private property of the beneficiaries or remained in the public domain.

An alternative possibility is that the land given to beneficiaries by the *Lex Sempronia agraria* was in fact private property but of a more limited nature. This may be yet further evidence of the fact that, in Roman property law, alongside full *dominium*, there was a variety of lesser forms of ownership. In a somewhat anachronistic fashion, one could say that Tiberius appears to have shaped the entitlements of this limited form of private ownership to maximize the likelihood that the law would achieve the goal of improving the economic condition of the recipients in the long term. Owners' inability to sell was designed to prevent them from transferring their smaller holdings to large landowners who would have been eager to purchase them; such sales had played a central role in swelling the landless urban population, which the *lex Sempronia agraria* was meant to aid by returning such citizens to the land. The possible solution that Tiberius had crafted with this limited ownership form designed to protect the long-term security of the beneficiaries, if this was what he devised, was not to last, as the *lex agraria* of 111 made the land distributed under the *Lex Sempronia agraria* fully private.[208]

The Gracchan reform program involved more than the distribution of public lands. One of the reasons that the Gracchi have been hailed as visionaries by modern progressive reformers is that the *lex agraria* and the related measures could be seen, with contemporary eyes, as establishing a comprehensive set of welfare entitlements. The limited private property entitlements over the parcels of land were complemented by other entitlements. We know from Plutarch that Tiberius intended to grant the new owners a sum of money to stock their small farms. Further, when Caius Gracchus re-proposed the *lex agraria* ten years after the death of his brother, he also advocated that the government supply grain at half the market price to indigent Roman citizens who applied. This marked a radical departure in policy.[209] The Roman government had previously resorted to similar measures in years of crop failure and famine, but the grain law was the first permanent relief measure. The elites saw the passage of the law as a populist measure, an attempt to win the support of the proletariat. But they still took advantage of it. Cicero tells the story of Lucius Calpurnius Piso Frugi, a wealthy consul who

---

[208] Id., 236.

[209] Edwin W. Bowen, "The Relief Problem of Ancient Rome" *The Classical Journal* 37, 1942, 407–420, 414–416.

opposed the grain law but was then found in line to get his share of grain.[210] The story has also been taken to suggest that the law as actually enacted did not include a need-test for beneficiaries. Practically, the grain law failed: it was financially unsustainable and it defeated the very purposes of the agrarian law, namely benefiting small farmers in Italy, by putting enslaved labor in the grain-rich provinces in competition with the free laborers of Italy.

The *lex agraria* acquired a legendary status among modern reformers and revolutionaries and was hailed as the first comprehensive social reform designed to endow citizens with a minimum of fundamental material resources. If we pierce the veil of legend that envelopes the Gracchan reforms, the *lex agraria* appears as a much more complex effort to strengthen the Roman Republic – socially, politically, and economically – by expanding democratic participation, managing social tensions, and promoting a sense of belonging, and bolstering military power.

Conclusion

As this brief excursion through the intricacies of Roman property law suggests, Roman property was not "absolute." *Dominium* was robust and its claim to be the supreme form of ownership was staged daily through elaborate rituals. But alongside *dominium*, Roman property law offered a rich set of forms and doctrines that made it pluralistic and variable. The unique feature of Roman property – and its enduring legacy to modern property – is not its alleged absolute character but its "law of things," its focus on resources. Rather than offering abstract definitions of *dominium*, the Roman jurists pragmatically looked at the special characteristics of different resources and relied on external frameworks, drawn from philosophy or religion, to examine the distinct values and interests different resources implicated. The result was a plurality of variable and limited resource-specific property forms that facilitated and balanced different, and often conflicting, normative considerations.

Further, despite the Roman jurists' promise of an autonomous property science, Roman property law was actually at the center of a complex governance project. The conceptual vocabulary of property developed by the jurists was key to sustaining a highly unequal class structure, in which

---

[210] Cicero, *Tusculanae Disputationes*, 3.20.48.

a small social and economic elite derived its wealth and power from the exploitation of a widening social base of Roman, Italian, and provincial small landholders, urban poor, and slaves.[211] As the various iterations of the *lex agraria* show, when the social tensions generated by this highly unequal class structure threatened to destroy Rome's political institutions, adjustments in the legal regime of property mitigated class conflict by achieving some realignment of Rome's political structure with its social base.

In addition to supporting an unequal class structure, Roman property law also supported the needs of a complex Mediterranean economy. Property forms and doctrines buttressed the economic policies of the Roman state. As we have seen, by making available several forms of private "ownership" for public land, the government promoted the expansion of large-scale, capital-intensive commercial agriculture on estates that produced for the Mediterranean market. While important for a full understanding of Roman property, this renewed focus on the operation of market forces and on trade in the Roman world should not obfuscate the fundamental differences between the Roman economy and the capitalist mode of production that the nineteenth-century jurists were seeking to support through Romanist-bourgeois property law. The Roman conceptual vocabulary of property supported an economic order of owners of land and slaves and of merchants, not of producers. Rome knew commerce and markets but not capitalism. The Roman economy was an overwhelmingly slave-based economy in which private property seldom met free, wage labor. As Aldo Schiavone puts it, this contact between property and wage labor is the authentic crucible of modernity, one that never materialized in Rome.[212]

Finally, the Roman conceptual vocabulary of property needs to be understood against the background of the Roman project of imperial expansion. Rome's control of territory was only partly due to its military

---

[211] Capogrossi Colognesi, *Law and Power in the Making of the Roman Commonwealth*, 54–63, 108–120.

[212] Aldo Schiavone, *The End of the Past: Ancient Rome and the Modern West* (Margery J. Schneider, trans.) (Cambridge, MA: Harvard University Press, 2000), 165–174. In contrast to this view, Peter Temin has argued that "free hired labor was widespread and that ancient slavery was part of a unified labor force in the early Roman empire." See Peter Temin, "The Labor Market of the Early Roman Empire" (Spring 2004) 24(4) *Journal of Interdisciplinary History* 513–538, at 515. Temin sees substantially more contact between free and slave labor than did, e.g., Finley, who characterized free hired labor as "casual and seasonal." See Finley, *The Ancient Economy*, 185–186.

might. It owed as much to a complex set of policies, including a land policy, to govern the territories over which it had extended its hegemony.[213] Imperial stability, Clifford Ando has shown, required consensus regarding Rome's right to govern and to establish a normative political culture. Land policy and property law were part of the official discourse of Rome's imperial government, a discourse that turned on Rome's ability to elicit its subjects' obedience and their self-justifications for participating in their own subjugation.[214] Rome's pluralistic system of provincial property allowed the Roman state to balance two conflicting goals: building consensus among its provincial subjects by leaving largely intact preexisting local property systems, while also facilitating the plainly imperialistic exploitation of the provinces. War and territorial expansion had become Rome's largest form of investment, generating colossal economic returns for the Roman governing class.

---

[213] Capogrossi Colognesi, *Law and Power in the Making of the Roman* Commonwealth, 98.
[214] Clifford Ando, *Imperial Ideology and Provincial Loyalty in the Roman Empire* (Berkeley: University California Press, 2000). Id., *Law, Language and Empire in the Roman Tradition* (Philadelphia: University of Pennsylvania Press, 2011).

2

The Foundations of Romanist-Bourgeois Property

Robert Joseph Pothier and the Transition from Medieval "Divided *Dominium*" to Modern Absolute *Dominium*

A Conceptual Conundrum

The nineteenth-century jurists who set out to develop a modern law of property inspired by Roman *dominium* faced a fundamental conceptual and practical conundrum. The Romanist concept of property they developed in their treatises and sought to enshrine in the new national civil codes described property as unitary and "absolute." Yet, throughout Europe, the life of property law on the ground presented a stark contrast to the jurists' descriptions. In its daily life, property was still an intricate web of land tenure forms with entitlements that were not only limited but also split between different subjects. These landholding forms had originated in medieval times. Some were feudal in nature, while others had developed from late-Roman property forms. The combination of these various feudal and non-feudal land tenure forms created a property landscape in which multiple "owners" had limited entitlement over the same parcel of land, prompting the medieval jurists to conceptualize these forms as "divided *dominium*" (*dominium divisum*).

The challenge for the property modernizers of the early nineteenth century was to reconcile their new concept of modern "absolute" *dominium* with the existing property landscape in which forms of divided *dominium* survived and thrived. Solving this conundrum required both conceptual creativity and ideological innovation. The new concept of property had to be superimposed on the living law of divided *dominium* without appearing artificially forced upon it. At the level of ideology, the jurists had to explain the reasons for, and the benefits of, the transition from divided *dominium* to unitary and absolute *dominium*. The jurists' task was made easier by the work done by earlier generations of sixteenth- and seventeenth-century legal scholars and constitutional theorists, who had effectively laid the conceptual and ideological foundations for modern property. This chapter will focus on these precursors and will reconstruct the foundational moment in the invention of Romanist-bourgeois property in France. Robert Joseph Pothier (1699–1772), a professor of law at the University of Orleans, whose life, his biographer writes, was "the most ordinary and uneventful, the only events being his major scholarly works,"[215] effectively, if unintentionally, changed the course of property law in the West. In his *Traité du droit du domaine de propriété*, Pothier guided the reader through a seamless conceptual journey from divided *dominium* to full, modern, Romanist *dominium*. The constitutional theory to explain the new concept of property was readily available in the writings of Charles Loyseau (1564–1627), a lawyer in the local and seigneurial courts and eventually in the Parliament of Paris, the highest royal court in Paris. In his *Traité de seigneuries* (1608), Loyseau laid the constitutional foundations of modern absolute *dominium* by clarifying the distinction between private property and public sovereignty, which were inextricably entangled in the world of divided *dominium*. Finally, the economists of the Physiocratic school and of the many societies for "agricultural improvement" active in eighteenth-century France explained how a robust and unitary concept of property would enhance the land's productivity for profit. These seventeenth- and eighteenth-century precursors were not committed to any conscious and coherent project of property modernization. They developed their ideas about property at different times and in discrete and unrelated contexts, and they came to property with disparate motivations, moved by scholarly zeal, political interest and policy-making ambitions. They had a practical intuition that property forms were changing, or would have to change, but could not presage the transformation that the nineteenth century would witness. Yet, their legal-analytical, constitutional, and economic theories opened the way for modern property.

The Concept of "Divided *Dominium*"

To fully appreciate the complexity of the path from divided *dominium* to modern absolute *dominium*, we need to take a closer look at the medieval concept of divided *dominium* and at the social and political changes that

---

[215] A. F. M. Frémont, *Recherches Historiques et Biographiques sur Pothier: Publiées à l'Occasion de l'Érection de sa Statue* (Orleans: Gatineau, 1859), 2.

had engendered it. The background for divided *dominium* is the disintegration of the Roman Empire and the transition to feudal society. In the
Roman world, as we have seen in Chapter 1, the distinction between
dominium, that is, robust and exclusive private property, and *imperium*,
that is, public sovereignty, was neat. Roman society was organized
around these two poles: private property and a mode of imperial sovereignty that allowed for a substantial degree of local self-government. Both
of these institutions had the potential to lead to considerable fragmentation of power and, with the collapse of the Roman Empire, these tenden-
cies toward fragmentation finally prevailed.[216] Historians passionately
disagree on whether this process was sudden or gradual. Some argue
that, around the millennium, a "feudal revolution" swept away private
property, free peasants, and public sovereignty and replaced them with
local lordships and serfdom;[217] others place greater emphasis on continu-
ities, as well as on regional variation, both in property forms and in
administrative structures, between the late Roman period and the "medieval" period.[218]

Regardless of its pace, this transformation reshaped the institution of
property in terms of both its operation on the ground and the way
lawyers conceptualized it. The landowning aristocracy appropriated
important aspects of public power, with the result that property and
sovereignty became inextricably entangled.[219] Further, these hybrid pro-
prietary/sovereign entitlements were vertically split between lords and
vassals. The *Libri Feudorum*, an immensely influential compilation of
legal texts assembled in Lombardy between 1150 and 1180, produced a
legal vocabulary to describe this new property landscape.[220] This new

---

[216] Ellen Meiksins Wood, *Liberty and Property: A Social History of Western Political Thought from the Renaissance to Enlightenment* (London: Verso, 2012), 5.

[217] Thomas N. Bisson, "The Feudal Revolution" (1994) 142 *Past & Present* 6–42; Georges Duby, *La Société aux XIe et XIIe Siècles dans la Région Mâconnaise* (Paris: Éditions de l'EHESS, 1955); Pierre Bonnassie, "La Catalogne du Milieu du Xe à la fin du XIe Siècle: Croissance et Mutations d'une Société" (1982) 98 *Cahier de Civilisation Médiévale* 143–147; J.-P. Poly, E. Bournazel, *La Mutation Féodale, Xe–XIIe Siècles* (Paris: PUF, 1980) (Caroline Higgitt, trans., *The Feudal Transformation, 900–1200* (Teaneck, NJ: Holmes & Meier, 1991); Guy Bois, *La Mutation de l'An Mil: Lournand, Village Mâconnais de l'Antiquité au Féodalisme* (Paris: Fayard, 1989).

[218] Dominique Barthélemy and Stephen D. White, "The Feudal Revolution. Response" (1996) 152 *Past & Present* 196–223; Timothy Reuter and Chris Wickham, "The Feudal Revolution, Response" (1997) 155 *Past & Present* 177–208.

[219] Perry Anderson, *Passages from Antiquity to Feudalism* (London: Verso, 1974), 148.

[220] An edition of the *Libri Feudorum* can be found in Karl Lehman, *Das Langobardische Landrecht* (Gottingen, 1896). See also Attilio Stella, "Bringing the Feudal Law Back

feudal vocabulary came to be used by lawyers throughout Europe and, in turn, further facilitated the spread of tenure forms called "fiefs."[221] The Bolognese jurist Jacobus de Belviso (c. 1270–1335), one of the many jurists who, throughout the thirteenth and fourteenth centuries, appropriated and honed the vocabulary of feudal property found in the *Libri Feudorum*, offered a definition of the *fief* as involving a split of entitlements that is remarkable for its clarity:

> Therefore first it must be seen what a fief is, which is described in two ways. In one way thus: a fief is the granting of a thing made in return for homage; this description is asserted in *Liber extra* 2.26.17. And homage is properly said to differ from the right of emphyteusis in that there is a concession on account of some yearly fealty. See Justinian's Code 4.66.2.1 and Institutes 3.24.3. In the second way it is described thus: a fief is the granting of a thing made with the handing over of *dominium utlie* for use and enjoyment and with the performance of some honorable service. Use and enjoyment is so called for the reason, that the fief-holder has use and usufruct. And so indeed an honorable service is specified, because there is no obligation arising from a shameful act. See Digest 45.1.26 and 17.1.6.3.[222]

Jacobus' definition pinned down the essence of feudal land tenure: the lord had what in today's parlance we would describe as "title" as well as a variety of accessory rights and duties, while the fief-holder had *uti* and *frui*, that is, the effective right to use and enjoy the land, along with multiple duties of a pecuniary, military, or religious nature. Well before Jacobus, another innovative Italian jurist, Pillius da Medicina (d. ca. 1212), had dared to explicitly suggest that both the lord and the fief-holder were, in fact, owners, the former having *dominium directum*

Home: Social Practice and the Law of Fiefs in Italy and Provence (1100–1250)" (2020) 46 (4) *Journal of Medieval History* 396–418; Maria Di Renzi Villata, "La Formazione dei Libri Feudorum, tra Pratica di Giudici e Scienza di Dottori," in *Il Feudalesimo nell'Alto Medioevo* (Spoleto: Centro italiano di studi sull'alto medioevo, 2000), 651–721; Peter Weimar, "Die Handschriften des Liber Feudorum und seiner Glossen" (1990) 1 *Rivista Intenrazionale di Diritto Comune* 31–98.

[221] Susan Reynolds, "Fiefs and Vassals: Fiefs and Vassals after Twelve Years," in Sverre Bagge, Michael H Gelting, and Thomas Lindkvist (eds.), *Feudalism: New Landscapes of Debate* (2011); Emanuele Conte, *Framing the Feudal Bond* (Leiden: Tijdschrift voor Rechtsgeschiedenis, 2012).

[222] Jacobus de Belviso, *Apparatus in Usus & Consuetudines Feudorum* (Heidelberg: Hans Kohl, 1559), 1v–2r.

and the latter *dominium utile*.[223] *Dominium utile* was undoubtedly a bold invention but Pillius did ostensibly base it in Roman law.[224] In one of his *glossae* (comments) to the *Libri Feudorum*, Pillius reasoned that, since Roman law extended to tenants in long-term or perpetual leases the action available to owners – the *rei vinidcatio*, calling it a *rei vindicatio utilis* – the same action should be granted to the holder of the fief who is in a similar position:

> And it is no wonder, that since the *rei vindicatio utilis* is available also to him who leased a farm perpetually or for a time not specified, as in Digest 6.3.1.1, and it is given to the *superficiarius*, as in Digest 13.7.16.2 . . . that therefore it is customary to grant even more to the fief-holder.[225]

The fief was not the only form of split ownership. Alongside fiefs, a variety of other forms that separated effective use and enjoyment from title proliferated in medieval society. For instance, forms developed during the high or late Roman Empire, such as the right of *emphyteusis*, the right of *superficies*, or the grant of a *precarium*, but also distinctively medieval forms like the contract of *livello*, became convenient tools for large owners, including abbeys and monasteries, to put their land to productive use by granting others use and enjoyment entitlements similar to those of an owner while retaining ultimate title. To describe these many forms of feudal and non-feudal split ownership in Roman law vocabulary, the jurists of the thirteenth and fourteenth century perfected the concept of divided *dominium* (*dominium divisum*) that Pillius had proposed in his commentary.[226]

While it may appear relatively straightforward, the concept of divided *dominium* required a good dose of juristic creativity and a fundamental

---

[223] Emanuele Conte, "Pillio da Medicina," in Italo Birocchi, Ennio Cortese, Antonello Mattone, and Marco Nicola Milletti (eds.), *Dizionario Biografico dei Giuristi Italiani (XII–XX secolo)* (Bologna: Il Mulino, 2013), 1587–1590.

[224] Stella, "Bringing the Feudal Law Back Home," 409.

[225] Antonio Rota (ed.), *L'apparato di Pillio alle* Consuetudines feudorum *e il Ms. 1004 dell'Archivo di Stato di Roma*. Studi e Memorie per la storia dell'Università di Bologna 14. (Mareggiani, 1938), 112–113.

[226] Paolo Grossi, *Il Dominio e le Cose: Percezioni Medievali e Moderne Dei Diritti Reali* (Milano: Giuffrè Editore, 1992); Robert Feenstra, "Les Origines du Dominium Utile Chez les Gloassateurs (avec un Appendice concernant l'opinion des ultramontane)," in Robert Feenstra (ed.), *Fata Iuris Romani, Études d'Histoire du Droit* (Paris: Presses Universitaires de Leyde, 1974), 21–259; Emanuele Conte, "Modena 1182, the Origins of a New Paradigm of Ownership: The Interface between Historical Contingency and Scholarly Invention of Legal Categories" (2018) *Glossae European Journal of Legal History* 5.

shift in methodological perspective. It is to the sheer creativity and sophisticated "naturalistic" methodology of Bartolus of Saxoferrato (1313–1357) that we owe the most comprehensive formulation of the theory. The most significant obstacle facing Bartolus was that, while Pillius had been able to find a Roman law peg for the idea of divided *dominium* in the *rei vindicatio utilis* granted to long-term tenants, Roman law explicitly denied that there could be double ownership. A passage of the Digest made it clear that "*Dominium* over the same undivided thing cannot be held by two persons."[227] What this rule meant was that there can very well be two or more co-owners of one thing, each owning a "share," but no two persons can own the entirety of the same thing at the same time. In light of this rule, the question, Bartolus acknowledged, was whether the holder of a right of *emphyteusis* or of a right of *superficies* were actual owners or merely holders of "rights over a thing owned by another."[228] Bartolus confidently declared that *both* are owners because there are two types of ownership, *dominium directum* and *dominium utile*.

> I ask, how many forms of *dominium* are there? A Doctor from Orleans says, as that German Doctor who yesterday gave a lecture here recounted, that there is only one form of *dominium*. But there are two, and I prove this by reference to Code 11.62.12, where it is said that the *emphyteucarius* is the *dominus*, but nevertheless another remains the *dominus* (see Code 4.66.1–2). And if there are two *domini*, then the forms of *dominum* are different, because the same *dominium* cannot be held by two persons as stated at the Digest 13.6.5.15.[229]

In Bartolus' reasoning, the rule of the Digest prohibiting full ownership of the same thing by two owners becomes an argument in favor of, rather than against, recognizing two types of *dominium*. Bartolus was certainly a skilled interpreter of Roman texts, but what allowed him to argue with confidence that there were two types of *dominium* was his method of legal analysis, which was fundamentally new. Bartolus could not be further from the formalistic classificatory zeal of the Roman legal

---

[227] Digest 13.6.5.15.
[228] F. Patetta (ed.), "*Excerpta Codicis Vaticani* Reg. 435," in A. Gaudenzi (ed.), *Bibliotheca iuridica medii aevi*, II (Bologna: Libreria Fratelli Treves di Pietro Virano, 1892), 134. See also Anna di Robilant and Talha Syed, "The Fundamental Building Blocks of Social Relations regarding Resources: Hohfeld in Europe and Beyond" (2019). Boston University School of Law, Law and Economics Paper No. 18-06, n. 64 (pp. 18–19).
[229] Bartolus ad Digest 41.2.17.1. See Bartolus de Saxoferrato, *In Primam Digesti Novi Partem* (Venice: Giunti, 1585), 84v. See p. 591.

scientists. Bartolus' main concern was the accurate description of the life of property law, where forms of split ownership in which the actual *uti* and *frui* and formal title belonged to two different "owners" had multiplied. Naturalism, that is, the careful observation of the actual facts of life, was the gist of Bartolus' methodology and the foundation for the concept of divided *dominium*. Bartolus' alert gaze saw that, in the lived experience of medieval society, having a broad right of enjoyment over the thing effectively makes you an owner. Andrea of Isernia, (1230–1316), an expert on feudal law who was a generation older than Bartolus, had already captured neatly this intuition when he wrote that: "He who has the effect of *dominium*, has *dominium*."[230] In other words, *dominium utile* was the effect, the fact, the substance of *dominium*, and it was this effect that mattered for the medieval jurists.

Bartolus' discussion of divided *dominium* is elegant and clever but not free from ambiguities. How are we to reconcile Bartolus' "naturalistic" acknowledgment that *dominium* is often split between two owners with the definition of *dominium* that made him a hero of the nineteenth-century architects of modern absolute *dominium*? Bartolus' definition is abstract and definitely "absolutist" and seems fundamentally at odds with his "naturalism": "What therefore is *dominium*? I respond, that it is the right of complete disposal over a corporeal thing, as long as it is not prohibited by law."[231] Medievalists have identified several possible keys to this puzzle. One key may be in the sentence that comes right before Bartolus' famous definition, where he explicitly mentions a number of the *iura in re aliena* before stating that "there is a different *dominium* for corporeal things than for incorporeal things." This sentence suggests that Bartolus was well aware that *dominium* was a broad concept, with many meanings, proper and improper, and that it comprised multiple species. Full *dominium*, giving the owner the right to completely dispose of a corporeal thing, was only one among these many species.[232] Others suggest that Bartolus focused in his definition on the owner's right of complete disposal in order to clarify the difference between the legal position of the owner, on the one hand, and, on the other, that of someone who is bound by a contract of *mandatus* – which obliges one

---

[230] Andrea of Isernia, *In usus feduroum commentaria* (Frankfurt: Andreas Wechelus [Heredes], 1598), 500.
[231] Bartolus ad Digest 41.2.17.1.
[232] Grossi, *Il Dominio e le Cose: Percezioni Medievali e Moderne Dei Diritti Reali*, 87.

to carry out another person's affairs with the utmost care – or of the possessor, who has a mere right to be on the land or to hold the thing.[233] No matter what one makes of the apparent tension between his definition of *dominium* and the theory of divided *dominium*, Bartolus' approach was fundamentally at odds with the methodology and the normative impulses of the jurists who invented modern *dominium*. While the latter were preoccupied with the conceptual architecture of property, Bartolus was interested first and foremost in accurately describing the living law of property. And while the nineteenth-century jurists placed normative emphasis on the owner's absolute sphere of control, Bartolus delved deep into the social relations that, in the fourteenth century, tied individuals to land and to one another.

The modern Romanists would eventually succeed in reconfiguring direct and useful dominium into full, "absolute" *dominium*. But the road from divided *dominium* to absolute *dominium* was long and tortuous and the concept of divided *dominium* would never completely disappear from property debates. Just as Roman *dominium* became the mythical archetype of the broadest and most robust idea of property, divided *dominium*, over time, came to signify a more pragmatic, realistic, and socially aware approach to property, an approach that attracted committed champions as well as vocal detractors. The former were a starkly diverse cohort that included strange bedfellows such as the utopian socialists of late nineteenth-century France and the conservative landed elites of the newly independent republics of Latin America. Utopian socialist reformers saw in divided *dominium* a blueprint for property institutions that would strengthen the position of the working-class vis-à-vis capitalist owners. By contrast, the landed elites of Chile or Mexico were eager to defend their economic power by presenting local forms of divided *dominium* as a means for improving the condition of the peasantry rather than as tools for economic and racial exploitation. The detractors of divided *dominium*, as we will see in the next chapters, far outnumbered its advocates. They were a large and outspoken crowd of liberal intellectuals, state bureaucrats, jurists, and political economists, who, in France, Germany, and Latin America, unabashedly denounced

---

[233] Thomas Rufner, "The Roman Concept of Ownership and the Medieval Doctrine of Dominium Utile," in John W. Cairns and Paul J. du Plessis (eds.), *The Creation of Ius Commune: From Casus to Regula* (Edinburgh: Edinburgh University Press, 2010), 141–142.

divided *dominium* as "feudal," oppressive, authoritarian, and inimical to economic productivity.

Divided *Dominium* in France on the Eve of the Revolution

In France, as in most of continental Europe, many forms of divided *dominium* had survived throughout the seventeenth century and well into the eighteenth century. On the eve of the revolution, French property law still appeared "feudal." There was almost no presage of the imminent reinvention of Roman absolute *dominium* for the modern world.

Prerevolutionary property differed from our contemporary notion of property in two fundamental ways.[234] Not only were ownership entitlements divided between different title holders and users, but, also, private ownership and public power were closely intertwined. Under the ancien régime, public administrative, judicial, and sovereign powers could be the object of private property. In the sixteenth and seventeenth century, one of the ways the absolutist state raised revenue and secured the allegiance of the aristocracy was the sale of venal offices.[235] Another example of private ownership of public power were the *seigneuries*, that is, the right to exercise civil and criminal justice over the inhabitants of a specific area, usually corresponding to the geographical boundaries of the fief with which the *seigneurie* was associated. Like venal offices, *seigneuries* could be transferred, by sale, gift, or inheritance, apart from its associated fief.[236]

The complexity of the law of feudal tenures was maddening. Even one of its most learned scholars, François Hervé, the author of a seven-volume *Théorie des Matières Féodales et Censuelles*, one of the last treatises on feudal law to appear before the revolution, could only warn that, "the study of our feudal law is extremely uninviting for the obscurity, the difficulty and the vastity of the matter."[237] And in the preface to his masterpiece, Hervé had to admit that:

> After long, hard work, I myself don't have an exact notion of the nature of the contracts of *fief* and *cens*, I ignore what constitutes the essence of each

---

[234] Rafe Blaufarb, *The Great Demarcation: The French Revolution and the Invention of Modern Property* (Oxford: Oxford University Press, 2016), 2.

[235] Id., 2–8.

[236] Id., 2–3, 24–26, 50–51.

[237] Francois Hervé, *Théorie des Matières Féodales et Censuelles*, vol. 1 (Paris: Knapen and Sons, 1785), i.

and all I can gather is that the definitions gave by my master author (Dumoulin) are wrong and faulty.[238]

Hervé's warning should not deter us from taking a quick glance at the different forms of landholding in France in the decades immediately prior to the revolution. Some forms of *dominium divisum* were feudal, involving a relation between a feudal lord and a subject, while others were not feudal and resembled a modern landlord-tenant relation. Among the feudal forms, the most well-known is the *fief*. One of the clearest definitions of the fief comes from Pothier, the forerunner of the advocates of modern absolute property, who also wrote a treatise on fiefs. Pothier explained that:

> The fief is a free, gratuitous and perpetual grant of a thing that is immovable or considered as such, in return for fidelity and homage and military service, and subject to the lord's direct *dominium (seigneurie directe)*.[239]

While initially, the relation between the seigneur and the vassal involved personal services such as military aid, judicial assistance, and advice (*de guerre, de cour et de conseil*), by the eighteenth century, the fief had largely lost its personal aspect and was simply one of the many forms of land-ownership. The actual nature of the feudal agreement varied significantly. Both the vassal's *dominium utile* and the lord's *dominium directum* could have different shape and content. As to the content of the seigneur's *directe*, the vast majority of fiefs were *fief de profit*, with the distinctive feature of the *droit de mutation*, by which the *seigneur* was entitled to receive a fee (*profit*) each time the fief was transferred.[240] Alongside fiefs *de profit*, there were fiefs *d'honneur*, for which the lord had perpetually renounced any monetary charge, retaining only the right of fidelity and homage, and fiefs carrying obligations in cash or kind, which, in the southern part of France where Roman law remained highly influential, were hardly distinguishable in substance from other forms of non-feudal long-term leases.[241]

Another form of feudal divided *dominium* was the *censive*, which was largely analogous to a fief, in substance and structure, with the only

---

[238] Id., iii.

[239] Robert Joseph Pothier, *Oeuvres posthumes de M. Pothier*, vol. 1 (Paris: Guillaume Debure, 1777) ; *Traité des Fiefs*, part 1, preliminary chapter, subsection 3, page 4.

[240] See Marcel Garaud, *Histoire Générale du Droit Privé Français: de 1789 à 1804, La Révolution et la Propriété Foncière*, vol. 2 (Paris: Recueil Sirey, 1958).

[241] Id., 22.

difference being that the grantee, the *censitaire*, was not a noble but a commoner.[242] The *censitaire* had rights and duties that were more limited than in the case of the fief. For instance, he could not transfer the land to another *censitaire* and had limited management powers; he could change the cultivation of the land or, potentially, leave it idle only to the extent that this did not compromise the payment of the *cens*. On the other hand, the *censive* was less onerous than the fief because it did not entitle the *seigneur* to the fruits of the land but only to a money payment, which, by the eighteenth century had become fairly modest. Also, over time, the powers of the inferior owner expanded and, by the eighteenth century, the *censive* could generally be passed to one's heir and transferred as a gift, free of any charge.[243]

Two other forms of divided *dominium* that were hardly distinguishable from the *censive* were the *bail à champart* and the *bail à rente seingeuriale*. Both were long-term leases and were significantly more lucrative for the seigneur than the *censive*. The *bail à champart* was characterized by a rent in kind (*champart*), which varied between one-twentieth and one-fifth of the total output of the land for the year, due at the time of harvest. The *bail à champart* was onerous for the "inferior owner" or lessee and, with time, came to be considered inimical to the development of agriculture because the lessee had very limited ability to manage the land. For instance, in most regional compilations of customary law, any change or innovation in the cultivation of the land that had the effect of reducing the value of the land, and, in turn, the *seigneur*'s portion of the fruits, would subject the lessee to the payment of an indemnity determined by experts.[244] The *bail à rente seigneuriale* was also a lease from a *seigneur* to a lessee, with a rent in money or kind, the amount of which was stipulated by agreement of the parties and was more onerous than the modest *cens*. To make things more complicated, the *rente* could be paired with a *cens* but it remained conceptually distinct from the *cens*.

Alongside these forms of feudal divided *dominium*, there were numerous non-feudal ones, which did not involve a relation with a feudal *seigneur* and were rather based on a perpetual or long-term lease contract. Of these long-term leases, which often had different names

---

[242] Id., 29.
[243] Id., 33–35.
[244] Id., 37.

depending on the region, the *bail à rente foncière* was common in both southern and northern France. It was a lease with rent in cash or kind and no further obligations. It often included a redemption clause that would allow the tenant to buy out the landlord's reversion.[245] Widespread, especially in southern France where Roman law dominated, was also the *emphyteusis*, the late-Roman long-term lease that we have already encountered in our chapter on Roman law (Chapter 1). For both these forms, the landlord retained a direct *dominium* that was purely a matter of private law and had no public or seigneurial dimension.[246]

Not all land was held as divided *dominium*. Allodial land, that is, land freely and fully owned, independently from any feudal lord and exempt from any charge, was particularly common in southern France. However, starting in the sixteenth century, the monarchy, pressed by fiscal concerns and the need to enhance its revenues, waged a powerful attack against free allodial owners through the creation of a new doctrine, the *directe universelle*. By this, the monarchy sought to place all lands that were not subject to the direct *dominium* of a lord under its ultimate proprietary sovereignty.

This brief glance at the many, complicated forms of divided *dominium* in France on the eve of the revolution gives us a good sense of the monumental scale of the property revolution that would happen between 1789 and 1848. The transition from divided *dominium* to a unitary and absolute concept of property would be a long and gradual process, characterized by jolts and ambiguities and fraught with practical hurdles as well as political and intellectual complexities. For modern property to take shape and assert itself, the spread of new ideological beliefs, the political and legislative action of the revolutionary elite, recurrent waves of peasant violence, and the jurists' legal-conceptual innovation would all be required. The development, starting in the eighteenth century, of new ideas of equality as well as of new economic theories would provide the impetus and the justification for modern property. The French Revolution, with its gradual and often insincere "abolition" of feudalism, would create the blank slate for the erection of the new modern property order. And the Napoleonic legislature, together with the "bourgeois" jurists, would give legal and conceptual form to the modern property system.

---

[245] Id., 122 ff.
[246] Id., 38–41.

Robert Joseph Pothier: The Last Jurist of the Old Regime or the Forerunner of Modern Property?

When the postrevolutionary jurists set out to develop modern property, they found themselves lacking conceptual tools. In the world of Old-Regime jurists, property had been the domain of the experts of feudal law as well as of the scholars of local customs. The "feudists" had made the intricate world of divided and dependent landholding their field of expertise, tirelessly investigating the historical basis and the legal and institutional details of feudal property. The experts of *droit coutumier*, the commentators on the various local customs compiled between the thirteenth and fourteenth century, had carefully described and patiently elucidated the details of the living laws of divided landholding. The former were the masters of feudal divided *dominium*, the latter the custodians of the intricacies of the living law of divided landholding; neither could foresee a new abstract concept of unitary and full property taking shape.

Enter Robert Joseph Pothier, a versatile and complex intellectual, whose place in the history of legal thought historians struggle to decipher. For some a radical innovator and the first of the modern jurists, for others the last and sharpest of the Old-Regime jurists, Pothier played a critical, if unintentional, role in paving the way for modern Romanist *dominium*.[247] While he did not invent anything new, Pothier reframed and foregrounded ideas developed by others and did so at the right time and in the right place. A native of a family of magisterial officers from the quiet, provincial town of Orleans, Pothier led a secluded scholarly life, rarely stepping into the public spotlight.[248] As his biographer reports:

> Although he was an enemy of noise and brilliancy, withdrawn into his studies and his room in the Rue de l'Ecrivinerie, Pothier escaped neither public honors nor the action and movement of his century. He was appointed alderman of Orleans, and took part, to a certain extent, in the quarrel of Jansenism. These are the only times in which our jurist touched public life.[249]

---

[247] Oberdan Tommaso Scozzafava, "La Soluzione Proprietaria di Robert-Joseph Pothier" (1980) *Rivista Diritto Commerciale* 327; Paolo Grossi, "Un Paradiso per Pothier, Robert-Joseph Pothier e la Proprietà Moderna" (1985) 14 *Quaderni Fiorentini per la Storia del Pensiero Giuridico Moderno* 401–456.

[248] See article on Pothier in Pierre Larousse, *Grand Dictionnaire Universel du XIXe Siècle* (Paris, 1877).

[249] A Frémont, *Recherches Historiques et Biographiques sur Pothier: Publiées à l'Occasion de l'Érection de sa Statue*, 4.

Despite his aversion to public life, in 1720, at the young age of twenty-one, Pothier was appointed to the Presidial Court of Orleans. Serving on the court made the young Pothier realize that, in order to fully understand French law, he had to study Roman law. For ten years, Pothier assiduously studied Justinian's Digest, making a name for himself as a talented Roman law scholar and, eventually, attracting the interest of the Chancellor of France, Henri François d'Aguesseau. As his many eulogies tirelessly repeat, Pothier brought to the study of Roman texts an analytical acumen and a clarity of sight that allowed him to discern the conceptual architecture of Roman law, which his contemporaries, all keen on minutia, could hardly grasp.[250] This talent for structural analysis and the flattering comparison with his fellow Romanists were emphasized in the *Éloge Historique de M. Pothier*, written by Guillaume-François Le Trosne (1728–1780), a disciple of Pothier:

> At the time, it wasn't the science of law properly that the law professors at the University of Orleans taught: of this beautiful and luminous science, they only presented the difficulties and the contradictions which were foreign to it and were introduced by the incompetence and bad faith of the Redactors of the Pandects. Instead of explaining the texts in a manner conducive to learning, they filled their lectures with small and subtle questions, invented and multiplied by the lovers of controversies . . . . Such a faulty and inadequate teaching could not satisfy a spirit as solid and just as M. Pothier: fortunately, he was able to reject this teaching; he saw the flaws and he made up for them through his own effort. In every science, it is the first steps that are the most difficult; he overcame the difficulties alone guided only by the hard study of the Institutes of Justinian in the pages of the Commentary of Vinnius and prepared himself to draw directly from the very source of Law through the deep study of the Pandects.[251]

For Pothier, clarity of thought was not only a matter of innate talent. An avid reader of the Jansenist writer Pierre Nicole, Pothier found the ethical inspiration for his legal analytical work in the Jansenist duty to think clearly, a duty that he saw as integral part of his civic commitment.[252] A particularly vivid allusion to Pothier's religious zeal colors one

---

[250] M. Dupin, *Dissertation sur la Vie et les Ouvrages de Pothier* (Paris: Béchet Aîné, 1825); J. E. de Montmorency, "Robert Jospeh Pothier and French Law" (1913) 13 *Journal of the Society of Comparative Legislation* 265–287.

[251] Guillaume-François Le Trosne, *Éloge Historique de M. Pothier* (Orleans: Vve Rouzeau-Montaut, 1773), lix–lx.

[252] De Montomorency, "Robert Jospeh Pothier and French Law"; Grossi, *Il Dominio e le Cose: Percezioni Medievali e Moderne Dei Diritti Reali*.

celebratory account of his life, which compares Pothier's work on the Digest to that of the Church Fathers on the Scripture:

> It may be said that, during these ten years, Pothier did what the Church Fathers did to learn Holy Scripture. This divine book became their continual occupation; St. Augustine, St. Chrysostom, St. Basil, St. Gregory, and St. Bernard studied immersed themselves in the study of the Scripture and their works abound in quotations from the Scripture. Pothier did the same for the study of the Pandects, the Corpus Iuris and the Commentary of Bartolus which he found in a state of complete decay.[253]

When, in the last years of his life, Pothier set out to study the law of property, he brought to it this exceptional talent for conceptual analysis and his Jansenist ethos. But Pothier was not simply a good analyst of conceptual structures. He also had a solid and pragmatic understanding of the living law of eighteenth-century France. Indeed, as has been suggested, the impetus that moved Pothier to turn his attention to property was not the excitement of a new intellectual adventure but the needs of daily legal practice.[254]

This pragmatic eye for the law on the ground predisposed Pothier to appreciate how, in many forms of divided *dominium* still in use in pre-revolutionary France, the seigneur's direct *dominium* had been gradually emptied of any meaningful content, while the "inferior" owner's *dominium utile* had become more robust.[255] With regard to fiefs, this transfer of ownership was still underway and "new" for the feudists at the time of the Revolution. But for other forms of divided *dominium*, such as the *cens*, the transformation was more significant and, largely, complete by the 1780s. In most regional compilations of customary law, the inferior owner, or *censitaire*, could now pass his tenure to his heirs free of any fee and had virtually unlimited freedom to transfer the tenure.[256] Further, the *censitaire* could now merge *dominium utile* and *dominium directum*, thereby acquiring full, free ownership, through a formal renunciation of the *seigneur* and payment of a sum.[257] This transformation in the very nature of divided *dominium* troubled the scholars of feudal law, the

---

[253] A. F. M. Fremont, *Recherches Historiques et Biographiques sur Pothier* (Orleans, Gatineau, 1859), 78.
[254] Grossi, *Il Dominio e le Cose*, 499.
[255] Garaud, *Histoire Générale du Droit Privé Français*, 2.
[256] Id., 33.
[257] Id., 34.

experts of the *Libri Feudroum*, who were hesitant to acknowledge it and disinclined to conceptualize it. To be true, Hervé, the last of the great "feudists," was not blind to the new significance of the inferior owner's *dominium utile* and yet could not bring himself to admit that the inferior owner had effectively become the sole owner. Instead, Hervé reluctantly concluded that "property can be diminished without ceasing to be property."[258]

The pragmatic and far-sighted Pothier intuited the implications of this transformation for the future of property and conceptualized this augmented *dominum utile* as full, sole ownership. In his treatise *Traité du droit de domaine de propriété*, Pothier downgraded *dominium directum* to a simple "right of superiority" and elevated *dominium utile* to the status of full ownership. Let's hear from Pothier:

> The *direct dominium* that owners of the fief or the *cens* have over the land they have inherited is the old, original *dominium* from which the *dominium utile* was carved out when the fief or *cens* was inherited; hence, this original *dominium* is not different from a mere *dominium* of superiority, which is the right of the owner/lord to be acknowledged as such by the owners and possessors and to demand certain retributions because of their original *dominium*. This type of *dominium* is not property (*domaine de propriété*) which is the subject of the present treatise. We should call it *dominium of superiority* and will discuss it later in a treatise on fiefs. The *dominium utile* over the land granted comprises what the land has to offer that is of use, such as the right to receive the fruits of the land and to freely dispose of them, with the duty, of course, to acknowledge as *seigneur* the person who has *dominium directum*. The *dominium utile* on the land is called *domaine de propriété* and the person who has it is called *propriétaire*, or *seigneur utile*. The person who has *dominium directum* is called simply *seigneur*. The latter is truly only the owner of his right of superiority while the owner of the land, is properly speaking, the *seigneur utile*.[259]

Pothier's conceptual trick, which distinguishing between a mere "right of superiority" and actual property, was not his own invention. Generations of sixteenth-century French jurists, influenced by the Humanists' quest for a philologically pure Roman law, had dismissed divided *dominium* as a medieval aberration and sought to find a better alternative. Specifically, Charles Dumoulin (1500–1566), in his massive commentary on the

---

[258] Id.
[259] Robert Joseph Pothier, *Traité du Droit de Domaine de Propriété*, vol. 1 (Paris: Guillaume Debure, 1772), part 1, chapter 1, paragraph 3, pages 4–5.

Coutume de Paris, the customary law of the Paris region, had already described the title owner's direct *dominium* as a merely nominal *dominium superioritatis* and the right of the vassal, the *censitaire* and the holder of an *emphyteusis* as *verum dominium*, that is, actual, property. Pothier simply reproposed Dumoulin's conceptualization at the right time, when around him, political economists and philosophers were already sowing the seeds of proprietary individualism.

What was the essence of Pothier's *domaine de propriété*? Interestingly, Pothier has the reader wait until paragraph four for a formal definition:

> This right of property, considered in its effects, must be defined as the right to dispose of a thing as one pleases, provided one does not infringe on the rights of another or violate the laws, *jus de re libere disponendi*, or *jus utendi et abutendi*.[260]

Pothier may still have been, in many ways, a man of the seventeenth century, but, in this passage, he reads as the first of the modern jurists who will make it a habit to define modern property by borrowing one of a number of supposedly Roman definitions. In this case, Pothier's choice falls on Bartolus' famous *ius de re corporali perfecte disponendi*. But Pothier modified Bartolus' definition in a subtle, yet critical, way, replacing *perfecte* with *libere* to emphasize what will become the critical feature of modern property, that is, the owner's exclusive and ample liberty.[261] Yet, again, the word *libere* was not Pothier's own pick. The Belgian Matthaeus Wesenbeck (1531–1586), in his commentary to the Pandects and Justinian's Code, had proposed a strikingly similar reading of the definition of *dominium* of the medieval "doctors" that also highlighted the owner's liberty:

> *Dominium* is the right, by which a thing is ours. The doctors thus insist upon the definition, that *dominium* is the right to dispose freely of a corporeal thing, unless and until it is prohibited by the law.[262]

Again, Pothier simply reproposed Matthaeus Wesenbeck's definition of property, but he did so at the right moment, thereby earning the reputation of a prescient innovator. As André-Jean Arnaud has noted, not only does Pothier's definition literally anticipate the famous definition of art. 544 of the "bourgeois" Code Napoléon, but indeed virtually every

---

[260] Id., part 1, chapter 1, paragraph 4, page 6.
[261] See Scozzafava, "La Soluzione Proprietaria di Robert-Joseph Pothier," 4.
[262] Matthaeus Wesenbeck ad Digest 41.1. See Matthaeus Wesenbeck, *Paratitla in Pandectas Iuris Civilis* (Basel: Eusebius Episcopius, 1566), 382.

section of the core part of Pothier's *Traité* would be literally reproduced in the Code. As Arnaud suggests, Pothier, in his *Traité*, seems to have carried out and completed the French Revolution a couple of decades in advance.[263]

Having defined property, Pothier moves to explain the content of the owner's right. And, again, he does so in strikingly modern terms, emphasizing two features: the owner's freedom of action and right to exclude:

> This right has a wide scope; it comprises: 1) the right to receive all the fruits and profits of the thing, regardless of whether they are actually received by the owner himself or by another who does not have a right to appropriate; 2) the right to dispose of the thing, not only for the uses the thing is naturally suited for but for any other use the owner wishes. For example, while the rooms of a house are naturally devoted to lodge humans, the owner has the right to shelter cattle, if he finds it convenient; 3) this right to dispose includes the owner's right to change the form of thing, for example the right to convert a parcel of arable land into lawn or a pond or vice versa. The owner has the right not only to improve the thing but also to diminish it, for example by turning a fertile parcel of arable land into non-cultivated land suitable only for pasture; 4) this right to dispose also includes the owner's right to lose the thing entirely, if he considers it convenient. For example, the owner of a beautiful painting has the right to paint over it and the owner of a book the right to burn it or tear it, if he thinks it is convenient; 5) the right to exclude anyone else from the use of the thing, unless those who have a right to use the thing by virtue of a servitude, or those who through an agreement have the right to engage in a specific use of the thing; 6) the right to dispose includes the owner's right to transfer the thing and the right to grant others specific uses over the thing, as he wishes.[264]

While Pothier, in this passage, does not explicitly use the term "absolute," the entitlements he lists speak volumes about the scope of the owner's power. The reference to the owner's right to waste and destroy the thing is not surprising and yet telling. The word *abuti* could have been plausibly read as meaning "consume" rather than "destroy." But the examples Pothier chooses – erasing a valuable painting or burning a book – suggest arbitrary license rather than a rational determination, driven by identity or privacy interests, and are fully consistent with Pothier's choice to rephrase Bartolus' famous definition, replacing

---

[263] André-Jean Arnaud, *Les Origines Doctrinales du Code Civil Français* (Paris: Librairie Générale de Droit et Jurisprudence, 1969).

[264] Pothier, *Traité du Droit de Domaine de la Propriété*, vol. 1, part 1, chapter 1, paragraph 5, pages 6–7.

perfecte with *libere*. The essence of ownership is liberty, the most extensive and unrestrained liberty, encompassing the full spectrum of individual volition from rational decision-making to capricious and erratic
desire. Again, Pothier reads as the forerunner of the modern mythology
of the right to abuse one's property, concerning which the nineteenth-
century proponents of absolute *dominium* would pour rivers of ink.

Exclusivity is the other critical element in Pothier's analysis and a
recurrent theme throughout the *Traité*. In section sixteen, which intro-
duces the topic of joint ownership, Pothier suggests that exclusivity is the
very essence of property:

> The right of property is, as we have seen above, the right by which a thing
> belongs to us to the exclusion of any other; it is in the very essence of this
> right that two people cannot each have complete *dominium* of property
> (*domaine de propriété*) over the same thing.[265]

While Pothier described property as absolute and exclusive, in real life,
the owner's rights were often limited and lessened by one of the several
"rights over a thing owned by another" (*iura in re aliena*) that Roman
law allowed owners to parcel out. To preserve the coherence of his
concept of *domaine de propriété* while still accounting for these limitations, Pothier introduced the distinction between "perfect," "imperfect,"
and "very imperfect" property:

> Property is flawless and perfect when it is full and perpetual and not
> burdened by real rights in favor of persons different than the owner. By
> contrast, property is imperfect when it expires at a given term or at the
> happening of a certain condition. It is also imperfect when it is burdened
> by real rights in favor of a person different than the owner, since these real
> rights were carved out of the rights attached to the property. Finally,
> property is very imperfect when it is burdened by a usufruct and, in this
> case, it is called "naked ownership."[266]

This conceptual distinction between perfect, imperfect, and very imperfect would figure prominently in the treatises of the nineteenth-century
jurists, offering the occasion for endless virtuoso performances of logical
classification.

Another instance in which Pothier reads as the first of the modern
property theorists is his discussion of the limits to property. Once again

---

[265] Id., part 1, chapter 1, paragraph 16, page 17.
[266] Id., part 1, chapter 1, paragraph 8, page 10.

literally anticipating the text of the Code Napoléon, Pothier admits of two limitations to the owner's right, namely the similar rights of others and the limits introduced by statutes and regulations.

> We have defined property as the owner's right to dispose of a thing as he wishes and we added *provided one does not infringe on the rights of another*. By this, we mean not only the actual rights that others have on the thing … but also the rights of the owners and possessors of a neighboring land whom the owner, no matter how perfect his right, cannot injure. And neither can the owner do in his parcel of land what the duties and obligations of neighborly relations proscribe. Finally, in our definition, after the language *"provided one does not infringe on the rights of another,"* we added *"nor the laws,"* meaning that, no matter how broad is the owner's right to dispose of the thing as he wishes, he cannot engage in uses that are prohibited by the laws. For example, while the owner of a field can plant what he wishes, he cannot plant tobacco since there are laws that prohibit tobacco plantations in the kingdom because they are contrary to the interests of *la Ferme du tabac*. Similarly, while property includes the right to sell and transport whatever thing one wishes, the owner is not allowed to take his fodders out of the kingdom if there is a law that prohibits the export of fodder.[267]

Pothier's discussion of the limits to property is minimalist and terse. Pothier does not feel the need to elaborate at length on the orderly coexistence of neighboring owners' spheres of absolute power, as the nineteenth-century jurists would do profusely. Nor does he dwell on the conflict between the owner's interest and the public interest. The notion that property necessarily implicates the public interest is mentioned only in passing, when Pothier clarifies that hurting the public interest by spoiling a first necessity is an injustice as a matter of natural law:

> Similarly, while ownership of a thing includes the right to misuse it and to lose it, a merchant who has waited a long time to sell a large amount of wheat, hoping that prices will rise, and then lets the wheat spoil in times of famine, would be guilty of a grave injustice towards the public because natural law does not allow him to spoil a commodity that is a first necessity, such as grain, in prejudice of the public interest.[268]

Pothier sees the grain merchant's egregious violation of the public interest as a breach of natural law, but this discussion of the relation between private property and the public interest is also fully consistent with ideas

---

[267] Id., part 1, chapter 1, paragraphs 13 and 14, pages 14–15.
[268] Id., part 1, chapter 1, paragraph 14, pages 15–16.

about the role of virtue that were gaining support in French political economy circles of the time. Pothier's example engages a question that was hotly debated by political economists: how to reconcile wealth and virtue by curbing the excessive pursuit of private self-interest to protect the nation's well-being.

The new, "perfect," absolute, and exclusive *droit de domaine de propriété* that Pothier's outlined in his treatise was entirely built with Roman law materials and heavily indebted to the work of sixteenth-century scholars like Dumoulin and Wesenbeck; and yet because of it, he can be seen as the first modern jurist, a forerunner with a lucid grasp of a seismic shift in the world of property that escaped his contemporaries. However, Pothier the man of the seventeenth century, fully immersed in the living law of the world that surrounded him, reappears in other treatises. The pluralism and relativism of Old-Regime property forms fills the pages of the *Traité de la Possession*, and the Roman "law of things" is examined in the *Traité des personnes et choses*. Pothier also devoted a separate treatise to the topic of possession. As he explained:

> While possession has nothing in common with *domaine de propriété*, *Nihil commune habet proprietas cum possessione* (Digest 41.2.12.1) since it is possible to have possession of something without having *domaine* of it and vice versa, someone can have *domaine* without having possession; nonetheless, because possession makes us presume that the possessor also has *domaine* and because possession is one of the modes of acquiring *domaine*, we thought we would add to the *Traité du Domaine de Propriété* a *Traité de la Possession*.[269]

The Pothier who authors the *Traité de la Possession* is not a visionary but, rather, the solid Roman law scholar with a rare talent for analytical clarity portrayed in Le Trosne's *Éloge*. In Pothier's treatise on possession, we find what we will vainly search for in the nineteenth-century property literature: a neat and clear account of the confusing topic of possession, free of ideological overtones. It is a dry account, tightly organized around a number of firm analytical fault lines. The first fault line is that between possession and property. Possession and property have nothing in common because possession is the mere *fact* of controlling the thing, while property is a *right* over the thing. The difference is a qualitative, fundamental one. Pothier's explanation is terse:

---

[269] Robert Joseph Pothier, *Traités de la Possession et de la Prescription: Traité de la Possession* (Paris: Guillaume Debure, 1772), preliminary chapter, pages 1–2.

We can define possession as the detention of a corporeal thing that we have under our control, either directly or through another person who detains the thing in our name and for us. Possession is a fact rather than a right over the thing that one possesses. No doubt a usurper has possession of the thing he misappropriated; but it is evident that he has no right over the thing.[270]

However, while possession is not, in itself, a right, it is the source of rights. Pothier's description of the legal consequences that spring from the fact of possession, that is, a presumption of ownership, namely the right to bring legal actions for the protection of possession and prescription, is succinct and clear. Another clear fault line in Pothier's discussion of possession is that between *civil* possession, that is, possession based on a title or in good faith, and *natural* possession, that is, possession that lacks title or is in bad faith. Again, Pothier explains the distinction in two terse, if somewhat arid, pages of purely analytical labor, free of ideological overtones. Having established these two firm distinctions – that between the right of property and the fact possession, and that between civil possession and purely natural possession – Pothier then moves to explain the two constitutive elements of possession: control and intent. In the voluminous nineteenth-century literature on possession, control and intent would be the object of long and elaborate digressions permeated by a robustly individualistic ideology. But, in Pothier, there is no paean to the individual's will to possess. Pothier's voice is that of a gifted analyst of Roman law, not an ideologue:

It is evident that one cannot acquire possession of a thing if he does not have the intent to possess it. For example, if I go to the study of a friend whom I am visiting and, while waiting for my friend, I take a book that I find on the table in order to look at it, it is clear that, even though I hold it in my hands, I do not acquire possession of it, because I do not intend to possess it. The same is true for land. If while travelling, I stop to spend the night in the château of a friend who is not there, even though I am alone in this château, I do not acquire possession because I do not intend to possess it.[271]

The Structural Foundations of Modern, Unitary, and Absolute Property: A New Constitutional Theory

The journey from divided *dominium* to Romanist-bourgeois property would have been more arduous without Pothier. But Pothier's new

---

[270] Id., chapter 1, article 1, paragraphs 1–2, page 3.
[271] Id., chapter 4, section 1, subsection 1, paragraph 40, page 35.

conceptual scheme would have remained a dead letter, a brilliant but abstract analytical exercise, without the work of a group of seventeenth-century constitutional theorists and eighteenth-century political economists who explained why a new concept of property was needed.

Pothier's *droit du domaine de propriété* required, as a fundamental theoretical premise, the development of a new constitutional theory of the relation between private property and public power. Pothier developed a new concept of unitary and full private property but did not explain the relation between this new concept and public sovereignty. As we have seen earlier, in the Old-Regime system of landholding, based on divided *dominium*, property, and sovereignty were closely intertwined. Not only did lords "own" venal offices and jurisdictional rights, so too the superior owners, that is, the owners of *dominium directum*, had a variety of entitlements that were partly "public" in nature. To become meaningful, Pothier's property had to be situated in a larger constitutional scheme that clarified the relation between these two forms of "sovereignty" over things and persons, private and public. This new constitutional vision had been developed by seventeenth-century jurists who argued for purging private property of any sovereign and public prerogative. In a recent book, Rafe Blaufarb describes the work of these jurists as establishing a "great demarcation" between property and sovereignty.[272] The idea that property and sovereignty ought to be distinguished and their respective domains neatly separated took shape gradually. The jurist Charles Dumoulin (1500–1566) was the first to suggest that royal power was purely sovereign, rather than comprising both a proprietary element and a sovereign one, and to try to mark off a purely proprietary realm distinct from state sovereignty.[273] And the great political philosopher Jean Bodin (1530–1596) further developed the notion that royal sovereignty is unique to the Crown and incapable of being alienated as private property.[274] In turn, the *Abbé* Claude de Fleury (1640–1723), a scholar and tutor of princes, was adamant that liberty

---

[272] Blaufarb, *The Great Demarcation: The French Revolution and the Invention of Modern Property.*

[273] Daniel Lee, *Popular Sovereignty in Early Modern Constitutional Thought* (Oxford: Oxford University Press, 2016), 79–120.

[274] See Richard Tuck, *The Sleeping Sovereign: The Invention of Modern Democracy* (Cambridge: Cambridge University Press, 2015), 1–62; Daniel Lee, "'Office Is a Thing Borrowed': Jean Bodin on Offices and Seigneurial Government" (2013) 41(3) *Political Theory*, 409–440; Martin Wolfe, "Jean Bodin on Taxes: The Sovereignty-Taxes Paradox" (June 1968) 83(2) *Political Science Quarterly* 268–284.

depended on separating property from power. He argued that "there is liberty where the individual enjoys the entire disposition of private law; and the Sovereign and his Officers the entire exercise of public law."[275] While Dumoulin and Bodin were the first to have an intuition of the "great demarcation," we owe the most coherent and detailed theorization of the new constitutional vision to Charles Loyseau (1564–1627), a judge in local and seigneurial court and, eventually, a lawyer in the parliament of Paris. It is worth taking a look at Loyseau's *Traité des Seigneuries* because it encapsulates the distinction between property and sovereignty in strikingly modern terms. The gist of Loyseau's analysis is immediately clear in the very first paragraph of the *Traité*. Feudal government was illegitimate, because it was based on the lords' usurpation of royal lands and royal justice, and *seigneurie* is a confusing term that blurs two distinct forms of authority over persons and things: private ownership and sovereignty. Let's hear from Loyseau:

> It is thus (as the divine Plato wrote) that these words, *yours and mine*, which concern only the private lordship, whose possession is real and quite apparent, are nonetheless cause of wars, troubles and lawsuits. How much more conflict must cause the public seigniory, which is only an intellectual right and an authority that one has on free persons and on things possessed by others? [It is thus] that, if the possession of this authority is uncomfortable to delimit, it is even more difficult to ground its title and its right in reason; because the Lordships were originally established by force and usurpation, it has since been impossible to bring order to this confusion, to legitimize this force and to settle by reason this usurpation.[276]

Aptly couched in stirring language are two distinct arguments, one historical and one conceptual. Historically, feudal lordships originated in an act of usurpation. Taking advantage of the weakness of the early Frankish kings, the lords had gradually converted their seigneuries, which initially were only offices, into patrimonial property, linking them to their feudal landholdings. Conceptually, Loyseau proposes a new vocabulary, capable of dispelling the fog that muddles the term *seigneurie*. Conceptual clarity calls for distinguishing between *private seigneurie* and *public seigneurie*. In a subsequent passage, Loyseau neatly encapsulates the distinction between these two forms of *seigneurie*:

[275] Quoted in Blaufarb, *The Great Demarcation*, 18.
[276] Charles Loyseau, *Traité des Seigneuries* (Paris: Abel L'Angelier, 1608), 1.

As to its division, the *seigneurie* has two species: private and public. The public *seigneurie* consists in the superiority and authority over persons or things, which however are peculiar to the lord, whereas the superiority of the simple officer is more limited, as I proved at the beginning of the second book of the "*Treatise on Offices.*" And this kind of public *seigneurie*, which concerns command or public authority, can only be exercised by public persons. As for the private *seigneurie*, it is the actual ownership and its enjoyment of something and it is called private because it concerns the right that each individual has over his thing. Hence, the lord who has the public *seigneurie* exercises it over his subject, while the one who has private *seigneurie* exercises it over his slave. The public *seigneurie* is called κυριότης, ἐξουσία, or ἀρχή in Greek, *imperium, potestas* or *dominatio* in Latin and, for us, domination or *seigneurie* properly. The private *seigneurie* is called δεσποτεία in Greek, *dominium* in Latin and, in French, *sieurie* properly.[277]

This paragraph is strikingly modern but also fully consistent with the traditional classical vocabulary. Retrieving Greek and Latin terms, Loyseau anticipates by over a century the "great demarcation" between ownership and sovereignty that only the revolution would, slowly and gradually, accomplish. Having introduced the "great demarcation," Loyseau then delves deeper into the nature of these two types of authority. Once again, Loyseau strikes the reader as fully projected into the future, anticipating two themes that would be dear to the Romanist-bourgeois jurists: eminent domain and private sacrifices in the public interest, and the absolute and despotic nature of private ownership.

Someone, who wishes to gain a fuller understanding, will find that this public *seigneurie* has effects on both persons and goods. As for persons, it is by virtue of [the public *seigneurie*], that we are forced sometimes to go to war, that we are imprisoned, that we are corporally punished, that we are put to death, when the case requires it. As for goods, it is by virtue of this [public] *seigneurie* that subsidies are raised for the necessities of the State, that goods are sold by the authority of justice, and that goods are taken from one and given to another. In short: that goods are confiscated in case of a delict, thereby reuniting private and public seigniory … and we must highlight that there is a very important difference in the use of these two forms of *seigneuries*. The ones who have private *seigneurie* may exercise it according to their discretion and free will, *quilibet enim est arbiter et moderator rei suae*,[278] because it is not wrong to use as we wish that which consists in what is ours. But because the public *seigneurie*

[277] Id., 6–7.
[278] See p. 9.

concerns the things which belong to others, or persons who are free, it must be used with reason and justice. And the one who uses it with discretion usurps an authority which does not belong to him: in the case of persons, holding them as slaves; in the case of goods, usurping the things of another. This is a thing that princes might well consider. And remember the response that Antigone gave to the king who said that kings could do anything they wish: not kings, she said, but tyrants.[279]

Loyseau's explanation is meant to dispel any further confusion caused by the fact that, actually, both private and public *seigneurie* may be exercised either over a person or over a thing. The distinction is practical as much as it is one of ethos. The ruler's public *seigneurie* involves command over his free subjects as well as the power to take private property through eminent domain when necessary; this authority must be exercised according to the principles of justice and reason and not usurped. By contrast, the owner may exercise his power over the things he owns as he wishes. To a seventeenth-century reader, still fully immersed in a world of divided *dominium* and private lordships, Loyseau's words must have sounded all the more powerful.

Property and the New Political Economy

Along with the new constitutional ideas about neatly demarcating private property and public sovereignty, political-economic ideas also played a critical role in preparing the ground for Romanist-bourgeois absolute property. The idea that a modern, productive agricultural economy requires a robust concept of property began to crystallize in the new cultural space of eighteenth-century political economy. By the 1760s, the term "political economy" was coming into fashion to describe a new, voluminous body of literature that discussed the organization of agriculture, trade, and manufacturing and their impact on the public welfare. Between the 1750s and the outbreak of the French Revolution, an educated reading public composed of the middling elites of the Old Regime became anxious about the effects of economic policy on their own social position, as well as on the nation's capacity to compete internationally, and started taking an active interest in economic policy and in agricultural improvement. The ensuing public conversation took place in the pages of books, treatises, and pamphlets penned by

---

[279] Loyseau, *Traité des Seigneuries*, 7–8.

economists and administrative experts but also by ordinary members of the educated elite.

Historians of economic thought call this conversation the "political economy of virtue," because participants viewed the promotion of economic development as a patriotic endeavor, aimed at regenerating the country by fostering both wealth and virtue.[280] The Seven Years War exposed France's weaknesses and triggered a wave of patriotism. Eradicating luxury and promoting agricultural improvement were the central elements of this patriotic agenda. Patriots imagined an economic order free of luxury as the basis for a regenerated polity. Excessive luxury and its counterpart, extreme poverty – in other words, inequality – were at the root of French weakness. Luxury and inequality were associated with despotism. Societies plagued by luxury would sooner or later become despotic because neither the elite, content with the pleasures of a luxurious life, nor the poor, pinched by need, would fight to preserve liberty. Hence, the first imperative of the new political economy was the fight against luxury.[281]

Along with the attack on luxury, the new patriotic political economists launched a concerted effort to reinvigorate agricultural production. A real craze for "agricultural improvement" swept France and was largely based on the comparison between France and England. Agriculture was critical in two respects: it was the most stable foundation for the nation's wealth, and it stimulated virtues such as responsibility, generosity, and frugality. The text that most effectively popularized the idea that the fortunes and the virtue of the nation might be revived by stimulating agriculture was *L'ami des hommes, ou traité de la population*, published by the Victor Riquetti, Marquis of Mirabeau in 1756. A central figure in the new political economy circles, Mirabeau (1715–1789) anticipated what would become the core argument of the Physiocratic School: the primacy of agriculture over manufacturing and commerce as a source of revenue. In the pages of his popular treatise, Mirabeau profusely elaborated on both the economic and social benefits of agriculture:

> Agriculture is not only one of the most admirable arts, the most necessary in the primitive state of society; it is still in the most complicated form that this same society can receive, the most profitable: it is the kind of work which renders the most to human industry, with the effort and labor

---

[280] John Shovlin, *The Political Economy of Virtue: Luxury, Patriotism, and the Origins of the French Revolution* (Ithaca, NY: Cornell University Press, 2006).
[281] Id., 13–48.

it requires. The ocean expects everything from the land and from the one who works on it: it is useless to repeat it; but I maintain that the profits of agriculture are safer and more considerable than the profits of maritime trade, or the pursuit of gold . . . . Agriculture is of all the most sociable arts. What nobility, what generous hospitality in the *mores* of those who spent their lives at the head of their workers and their flocks. But, without going so far, when you go into the garden of a poor man, he offers you, free of charge and ostentation, what an artisan seeks to sell to you. When a farmer makes a discovery he hastens to communicate it to his neighbors. All these arts are secrets that had to be stolen or expensively bought.[282]

Mirabeau's passage is a hymn of praise to the hard labor, the entrepreneurial spirit, and the generosity of those who devote their lives to agriculture and a not-so-thinly-veiled critique of mercantilism. Between the lines, Mirabeau expresses all his skepticism that manufacture and commerce could be genuinely productive and that they could be separate and independent sources of capital accumulation. Even in the advanced society of eighteenth-century France, agriculture is still the main source of wealth, superior to maritime commerce because it generates a stream of revenue that is not only greater but also more stable. And, while commerce encouraged the competitive and self-interested pursuit of private economic profit and the cultivation of luxury, agriculture fosters generosity and an ethos of cooperation.

Property was central to the political economy of virtue. The new field of political economy was populated by a variety of schools of thought, each proposing differing policy prescriptions, but the question of how property law could promote economic improvement was a shared concern. The agronomists of the Royal Agricultural Societies had a technical approach to agricultural improvement, one that emphasized the importance of crop rotation, land reclamation, and improving livestock breeds. Yet, property rights were never far from the minds of the royal agronomists. Launching a concerted assault on the commons, the agronomists called for the enclosure of common lands and the restrictions of communal use rights over privately owned lands, which they saw as inimical to innovation and improvement.[283]

---

[282] Victor Riquetti Mirabeau, *L'Ami des Hommes ou Traité de la Population* (Avignon, 1756), part 1, 32–33.
[283] Andre J Bourde, *The Influence of England on the French Agronomists, 1750–1789* (Cambridge: Cambridge University Press, 1953); Andre J Bourde, *Agronomie et Agronomes en France au XVIIIe Siècle* (New York: Sevpen, 1967).

But it was the Physiocrats who most forcefully advocated for a new law of property.[284] The Physiocrats prescription was simple: France could succeed by implementing an economic policy that privileged agriculture over industry and commerce, and that reorganized agriculture on a proto-capitalist basis. Proto-capitalist agricultural production was what really distinguished Physiocracy from the other approaches to agricultural improvement that had emerged in the context of the new political economy of virtue. While the agronomists emphasized the importance of extensive agriculture, the Physiocrats maintained that it was critical to farm existing lands effectively and intensively. Property was central to the Physiocrats' vision because the reorganization of agriculture on a proto-capitalist basis required a class that owns the means of production and whose ownership is fully protected. The type of property law that the Physiocrats envisioned looked very much like Pothier's *droit du domaine de propriété*.

It is therefore not surprising that the Physiocrat who developed the most detailed legal agenda for the movement was Guillaume-François Le Trosne, a disciple of Pothier and author of the hagiographic *Éloge Historique de M. Pothier*, written at the time of his mentor's death.[285] Le Trosne perfectly exemplifies the new breed of political economist that had gained influence in late eighteenth-century France. A jurist and economist by training, Le Trosne had an unshakable faith in natural law, an expertise in feudal law and the living law of divided landholding, and a keen interest in questions of institutional design. Le Trosne was also an active participant in the political and cultural life of his time. He followed his mentor's steps, becoming *avocat du roi* and *conseiller honoraire* at the Presidial Court of Orleans, and was a founding member of the Royal Agricultural Society of Orleans and an associate member of the Royal Academy of Fine Arts in Caen. In this last capacity, Le Trosne wrote a series of lectures, collected in a volume entitled *De l'Ordre Social*.[286] The lectures are framed as recommendations on policy-making

---

[284] On the Physiocrats, see Henry Higgs, *The Physiocrats: Six Lectures of the French Economistes of the Eighteenth Century* (London: MacMillan and Co., 1897); Liana Vardi, *The Physiocrats and the World of the Enlightenment* (Cambridge: Cambridge University Press, 2012), 3, 21; Elizabeth Fox Genovese, *The Origins of Physiocracy* (Ithaca, NY: Cornell University Press, 1976), 13; Warren J. Samuels, 'The Physiocratic Theory of Property and the State" (1961) 75 *The Quarterly Journal of Economics* 96–111.

[285] Le Trosne, *Éloge Historique de M. Pothier*.

[286] Guillaume-François Le Trosne, *De l'Ordre Social: Ouvrage Suivi d'un Traité Élémentaire sur la Valeur, l'Argent, la Circulation, l'Industrie et le Commerce Intérieur et Extérieur* (Paris: Guillaume Debure, 1777).

and institutional innovation addressed to Prince Charles Frederic of Baden-Durlach. A philanthropist and patron of philosophers and economists, the Prince of Baden had developed a keen interest in agricultural improvement and Physiocracy and, therefore, was a sympathetic ear for the economists. Pothier's spirit and teachings permeate the advice Le Trosne offers to the Prince. Liberty and absolute property are the two fundamental laws, enshrined in both natural law and the "physical order," which an enlightened ruler should secure and protect. In a passage that encapsulates all of the new ideas dear to both the economists and the most advanced jurists, Le Trosne declares that:

> Justice does not have the purpose of making fortunes equal, but of ensuring to each one what belongs to him: it guarantees to all liberty and the absolute and indefinite *propriété* of their person, their work, their industry, their personal wealth and the faculty of acquiring. It also guarantees land-ownership to the person who owns it; it makes him the recipient of the fruits and the arbiter of their distribution. But this liberty, which derives from his right, in no way hurts the liberty which other men have to share. Because they are the owners, in the same way, and sellers of their work, their industry, the use of their personal wealth. It is just what they offer them in exchange. While they have an indispensable need of substances, he who wants to increase his production has an equal need of their help, and has no right to force their work or to fix the price, just as they have no right to attribute to themselves the productions, or to restrict their value. It is only through this free exchange of labor and substances that we can ensure that the production and distribution of goods are of the greatest advantage to all.[287]

The new social order Le Trosne is describing here is nothing less than agrarian capitalism, the agrarian capitalism that France would have to wait decades to see fully realized. In the social order Le Trosne outlines, capitalist owners, endowed with robust property rights over the land, and free laborers, who are absolute owners of their labor and industry, bargain over the terms of their exchange. Feudal coercion is replaced by purely economic coercion. But in Le Trosne's preview of agrarian capitalism, there is no mention of economic coercion, and wealth inequality is a fact of life and does not violate justice. The question of inequality is relegated to a lengthy footnote in which Le Trosne takes great pains to rebut the philosophers' concerns about distributive fairness. The philosophers are caught in hopelessly abstract speculations and lack a full, realistic understanding of how society naturally works. Wealth inequality is the

[287] Id., 36–38.

inevitable consequence of the natural inequality of talents, effort, luck, character, and number of children. So what ought an enlightened sovereign do to establish a just social order? Le Trosne is adamant: acknowledge that the laws of liberty and of personal and real property are the essential and fundamental laws of human society, perfectly true to human nature, human needs, and the laws of reproduction.[288] And once liberty and property are secured, is there anything else the sovereign ought to do?

> Nothing more than to let the citizens enjoy it without intervening and to persuade them that pursuing their own interest is the most valuable thing they can do for society. As to other rights, the sovereign authority must regulate the exercise by positive laws which are simple, advantageous to the subjects, and which have their reason in the first laws.[289]

Le Trosne's recommendations neatly encapsulate the basic principle of the new political economy of virtue: reconciling individuals' private interest and the public good. Secure in their full and robust property rights, landowners will freely go after their private gain and, in turn, will expand the wealth of the nation.

Le Trosne was neither the most prominent nor the most sophisticated of the Physiocrats but he was the one who, because of his legal training and familiarity with Pothier's oeuvre, could most effectively relate his mentor's legal conceptualization of property to the prescriptions of the economists. The ideas we have seen formulated in Le Trosne's lectures are restated, with slight variations in emphasis, in virtually all the major Physiocratic works. Property figures prominently in the *Maximes générales* of François Quesnay, the most well-known and methodologically sophisticated on the Physiocrats. The fourth maxim declares that:

> That the ownership of the landed properties and the mobile wealth be assured to those who are their legitimate possessors; for the security of property is the essential fundamental of the economic order of society.[290]

In the same vein, Pierre-Paul Mercier de La Rivière, who through his *Journal d' agriculture, de commerce et des finances*, successfully popularized Quesnay's teachings, emphasized the happiness and freedom of action that absolute property would produce:

---

[288] Id., 29.
[289] Id., 40–41.
[290] François Quesnay (Auguste Ocken [ed.]), *Oeuvres Économique et Philosophiques de F. Quesnay* (Paris: Peelman, 1888); *Maximes générales du gouvernement économique d'un royaume agricole*, 331.

The greatest possible happiness of the community as a whole consists in the greatest possible abundance of useful goods and in the greatest possible liberty to make use of these goods. I have made clear that this maximum of enjoyment is the necessary consequence of the establishment of the right of property and that it is only by establishing this right that we are able to attain happiness.[291]

The Physiocrats were not only a school of economic thought, they were also a school of political action, aimed at influencing kings and princes.[292] Despite their ambitions, their teachings suffered reverses in the eighteenth century and, for the most part, fell on deaf ears. Yet, their role in the development of Romanist-bourgeois property was critical. In the writings of the Physiocrats, the nineteenth-century jurists, enamored with science, found a full-blown theory of the economic benefits of absolute property, a theory deserving all the deference owed to the founders of a new science, political economy.

Conclusion

The road from divided *dominium* to modern, absolute *dominium* would turn out to be long and tortuous, but it would have been even harder without the foundational work done by these seventeenth- and eighteenth-century forerunners. Pothier spared the architects of Romanist-bourgeois property the effort of developing from scratch a conceptual framework for modern property. Loyseau and the "political economists of virtue" saved the modern jurists the effort of conjuring up a scientific theory explaining the economic benefits of absolute property. Pothier may not have been a visionary animated by an interest in innovative conceptual design, as some suggest.[293] And he was definitely not an ideologue of bourgeois individualism. Yet, aided by his talent for conceptual clarity and his realistic grasp of the living law of his time, he provided the nineteenth-century jurists with a ready-made conceptual scheme that they could simply import into their treatises and codes. All that the architects of Romanist absolute *dominium* would have to do would be to couch Pothier's concepts in the language of modern bourgeois individualism.

The constitutional theorists of the seventeenth century, by demarcating the realm of private property from that of public sovereignty,

---

[291] Quoted in Philip Charles Newman, Arthur D. Gayer, Milton H Spencer (eds.), *Source Readings in Economic Thought* (New York: Norton, 1954), 103.

[292] Higgs, *The Physiocrats*, 7.

[293] See Scozzafava, "La Soluzione Proprietaria di Robert-Joseph Pothier."

established the foundations of the modern liberal constitutional order. But they also inspired one of the central, and most enduring, ideas of legal modernity: the notion that there exists a rigid separation between private law and public law, which are two coherent and distinct realms. The former comprises the rules that facilitate the horizontal interaction between individuals and is the domain of freedom. The latter consists of the rules regulating the vertical relation between the state and its citizens and is the territory of necessary coercion. This rigid dichotomy would allow generations of modern jurists to disguise and ignore the fact that property, always and necessarily, entails coercion and to denounce government regulation of property as coercive of private freedom. The task of disabusing the horde of lay as well legally trained champions of modern dominum of this deceitful separation between private and public will be taken up by the social jurists later in the century.

Finally, of enormous import was the work of the economists. By grounding Pothier's concept of full and secure property in the new science of political economy, Le Trosne, Mirabeau, and Quesnay conferred on absolute property legitimacy and credibility. The economists also provided the architects of Romanist-bourgeois property with a set of well-rehearsed arguments responding to two obvious concerns: the risk that absolute property would lead to wealth inequality and, eventually, to a political oligarchy, and the danger that absolute property would encourage owners to pursue their private gain at the expense of the public good. The *économistes* of the eighteenth century had an answer to both. As to the first, we have seen Le Trosne explain away wealth inequality as a natural fact of life, the effects of which would be periodically readjusted by the market and could be mitigated by promoting a culture of cooperation and sociability. As to the second, the need to reconcile private gain and public virtue was the core insight of the political economy of virtue. We read Le Trosne advising the Prince of Baden that allowing owners to exercise their absolute rights in pursuit of their private interest was the best way to expand society's wealth and to regenerate the economy. These arguments may have seemed simplistic and narrow to the philosophers and would certainly be dismissed as such by later generations of thinkers. But, for vast segments of the rising educated and entrepreneurial bourgeoisie of the eighteenth and early nineteenth centuries, who shared the skepticism of the abstract speculations of the philosophers that Le Trosne expressed in his lectures, they had the appeal of realism and pragmatism.

3

Crafting Romanist-Bourgeois Property

Roman Antiquity, Political Reaction, a Rising
Bourgeoisie, and Scientism

"Our New Modern Times"

By the late eighteenth century, in France, the foundations for modern
Romanist *dominium*, or la *propriété*, were solidly in place. Pothier had
conceptualized the *droit de domaine de propriété* as a unitary, robust, and
exclusive right. This new concept of property had a central place in the
new constitutional scheme developed by the most sophisticated
seventeenth-century jurists, where it stood alongside public sovereignty
but was neatly separated from it. Meanwhile, political economists and
policy-makers were actively disseminating the idea that broad and secure
property rights were critical for economic growth. However, this new
way of thinking about property had not gained widespread acceptance
and was confined to relatively small, elite policy circles. It had certainly
not spread to the insular and conservative world of academic jurists.

It was only in the early nineteenth century, with the onset of long-
term, structural transformations in the economy and society, that the
idea that France was entering new, "modern" times started appearing in
the pages of the jurists' treatises. A number of developments prompted
academic jurists to discuss legal modernization: the *reaction
napoléonienne*, that is, the conservative turn to a new political order;[294]
the beginning of the gradual and uneven transition toward a capitalist
economy; the slow ascendance of a new class, namely the bourgeoisie;

[294] Albert Soboul, *La France Napoléonienne* (Paris: Arthaud, 1983), 112; André Cabanis, "Le
Courant Néo-Monarchiste sous le Consulat," in J. Tulard (ed.), *La Contre-Révolution.
Origines, histoire, postérité* (Paris: Perrin, 1990), 313–324.; Jean-François Niort, "Le Code
civil ou la réaction à l'œuvre en Métropole et aux Colonies," in Niort (ed.), *Du Code noir
au Code Civil. Jalons pour l'Histoire du Droit à la Guadeloupe. Perspectives Comparées
avec La Martinique, La Guyane et la République d'Haïti* (Paris: L'Harmattan, 2007),
59–86.

and the proliferation of ambitious disciplinary reform agendas, such as political economy. Because property was critical to the social and economic transformations that had just begun, this reformist drive was particularly intense in the field of property law. As Hippolyte Taine (1828–1893) wrote in his monumental *Les Origines de la France Contemporaine*, the Revolution was, essentially, a radical transformation of property by a modern state.

> Whatever the great names, freedom, equality and fraternity, with which the Revolution is adorned, it is, in essence, a transformation of property; in this consists its intimate support, its permanent force, its primary engine and its historical meaning. In the past, in antiquity, we saw similar transformations being accomplished, with debt abolished or reduced, the land of the wealthy confiscated and public lands divided. But it was always contained in a city and confined to a small territory. For the first time [in the Revolution] it is accomplished on a grand scale and in a modern state.[295]

In this initial, post-revolutionary and early nineteenth-century phase, the project of modernizing property was by no means a coherent one shared by a supranational, cosmopolitan class of elite legal academics across Europe. Rather, reforming property law was a vague and ill-defined ambition, felt with varying intensity and different sensibilities throughout the European continent. A number of factors contributed to this diversity. The transition toward liberalism and capitalism happened along different paths and at different speeds across the emergent European nation-states and in the imperial periphery: in France, it was dramatically accelerated by a "bourgeois revolution" from below, while in Germany it would take a much later "revolution from above."[296] The rise of the bourgeoisie as a self-conscious and unified class was also a slow and highly uneven process: in France, a coterie of prominent liberal politicians sought to make the bourgeoisie central to political life, while the supine and backward bourgeoisie of the German states proved incapable of capturing state power for itself.[297] The cohesion and the

---

[295] Hippolyte Taine, *Les Origines de la France Contemporaine: La Révolution* (Paris: Hachette and Co., 1882), volume 1, book, 3, chapter 2, section 4, page 386.

[296] Ellen Meiksins Wood, *The Pristine Culture of Capitalism: A Historical Essay on Old Regimes and Modern States* (London: Verso, 2015), 2–8; Robert Brenner, "The Agrarian Roots of European Capitalism," in T. H. Aston and C. H. E. Philpin (eds.), *The Brenner Debate: Agrarian Class Structure and Economic Development in Pre-Industrial Europe* (Cambridge: Cambridge University Press, 1985), 282–283.

[297] Colin Mooers, *The Making of Bourgeois Europe: Absolutism, Revolution, and the Rise of Capitalism in England, France and Germany* (London: Verso, 1991), 137–143.

power of the jurists as a professional class also varied nationally, as did the jurists' level of insularity, provincialism, and interdisciplinary dialogue. Yet, despite these differences, European jurists started engaging explicitly with a discourse of "modernity" in the prefaces to their property law treatises and monographs. Allusions to a new era or a new state of affairs became ubiquitous in the jurists' writing.

Sympathetic to this discussion of modernity, but retaining many of its own intellectual commitments, was another powerful conversation that continued to gain momentum throughout Europe, namely the critique of feudalism. In France, *féodal* and *féodalité* ceased to be technical legal terms and became the bête noire of the modernizers, symbolizing oppressive hierarchies, an illiberal political order, and a property system inimical to growth and productivity. However, not all jurists saw the new times as uniformly bright. Many embraced its transformations, viewing them as a step toward a more liberal and prosperous society; others believed that modern property harbored new forms of inequity and servitude and were determined to resist them; and still others viewed this growing contestation of the ostensibly ageless institution of private property as a sign of the moral corruption and political instability of the new times.

Jurists who embraced the new times had strikingly consistent ideas about property. The new *droit de propriété* ought to be a robust and secure right, shaped in the image of Roman *dominium*. However, crafting and operationalizing this modern concept of *dominium* was a complicated and multifaceted project. The jurists had to select the relevant Roman legal texts and to engage in contentious disquisitions about their meaning and import. They also had to deploy all their intellectual creativity to organize their Roman-inspired property concepts coherently. Along with deep learning in Roman law and conceptual creativity, crafting modern property also required methodological sophistication, as the analysis of the modern law of *dominium* had to appear consistent with the latest trends in scientific thought. Finally, ideological appeal was just as crucial as legal analysis: modern *dominium* had to adhere to the prescriptions of neighboring disciplines, such as political economy, and to bear an ostensibly direct relationship to the ideas of liberty and equality that were the ideological currency of the day.

Needless to say, this complex project was also highly local in nature: throughout continental Europe and its periphery, jurists had to respond to different social and economic problems, were inspired by different scientific methodologies, proposed different conceptual solutions, and appealed to different philosophical concepts. In other words, modern *dominium* was both "universal" and intensely "local." The supranational dimension of the changes associated with modernity did not escape the jurists' notice, and references to the "universal" march toward modern property abounded. Similarly, the prefaces to property treatises and monographs were often explicitly addressed to a supranational, cosmopolitan audience, familiar with the larger ideas that the Enlightenment(s) and the modern revolutions had helped spread. But, as the reader delved into the chapters where the jurists struggled to retrofit modern, Romanist *dominium* into the preexisting national social and economic structure, the tone changed, often becoming eminently practical, and the analysis zeroed in on the concerns and debates of the local juristic community.

The complex legal and ideological project of crafting the law of modern *dominium* started in France and Germany, the intellectual leaders of continental Europe, capable of exerting a profound influence not only within closely related legal systems but also more broadly. It is to France and Germany that we will turn in this and the next chapter.

The Attack on Feudalism and the Property Revolution

By the late eighteenth century, in France, divided *dominium* had morphed significantly and in seemingly contradictory directions. On the one hand, as Dumoulin and Pothier had foreseen, many holders of *dominium utile* had come to resemble actual owners. On the other hand, a growing number of business-savvy landlords with precapitalist impulses had perfected strategies to augment their profits by shrewdly exercising their entitlements as "direct" owners. Yet, despite these concretizations, in the years that led to the Revolution, divided *dominium* was the target of virulent criticism. Studies of the *cahiers de doléances*, that is, the list of grievances compiled by local assemblies to instruct the deputies in the *États-Généraux*, offer a unique perspective on the range of views on seigneurial rights expressed by various social groups. For the peasants, the most detested aspect of seigneurial divided landholding regime were the periodic dues they had to pay and the seigneur's recreational privileges, such as the rights to hunt or to raise pigeons or rabbits, which exposed fields and crops to the threat of incursions and destruction.[298] By contrast, the notables of the Third Estate were primarily concerned with barriers to the development of the market, such as seigneurial monopolies, seigneurial

---

[298] John Markoff, *The Abolition of Feudalism: Peasants, Lords and the Legislators in the French Revolution* (University Park: Pennsylvania State University Press, 1996), 42–45.

compulsory labor services (*corvées*), and seigneurial tolls.[299] Further, evidence that the new ideas about "agricultural improvement" had spread well beyond elite circles is that almost every Third Estate *cahier* had something to say about agricultural progress.[300]

These broadly shared complaints about the burdens and inefficiencies of divided *dominium* coalesced in a mounting and virulent anti-feudal discourse. *Féodal* and *féodalité* had, until then, been trade terms of the *feudistes*, the jurists who specialized in the body of law that had developed over the centuries around the *Libri Feudorum*, the twelfth-century collection of feudal customs compiled in Lombardy.[301] However, in the decades preceding the Revolution, among jurists and pamphleteers steeped in Enlightenment and liberal thought, the word *féodal* started taking on a different, intensely derogatory connotation. So widespread were the negative feelings about *féodalité*, that the jurist Joseph Renauldon (1709–c. 1790), an expert in feudal law, opened his *Traité historique et pratique des droits seigneuriaux* by noting that "every day, I hear people say that seigneurial rights are odious."[302] Renauldon devoted a full section of his treatise to "the seigneurial rights that have resulted in servitude," in which he bluntly stated that "at every step, nature and humanity shudder, one finds everywhere the sad vestiges of our father's slavery."[303] By the early nineteenth century, *féodalité* had become a powerful intellectual and political construct and a denunciatory call for change. Not only did the French jurists of the revolutionary and Napoleonic era reinvent Roman *dominium*, they also reinvented *féodalité*. Their individual accounts differed in their relations to reality, but collectively these jurists both created and sought to subdue a threatening vision of feudalism; they would have agreed whole-heartedly with J. Q. C. Mackrell that "when the sleep of reason brought forth monsters, one of the first to appear was 'feudalism,'" and they were determined to slay it.[304]

---

[299] Id., 50–53.

[300] Id., 50–52.

[301] For a fascinating discussion of issues implicating the *Libri Feudorum* in a different context, see J. G. A. Pocock, *The Ancient Constitution and the Feudal Law: A Study of English Historical Thought in the Seventeenth Century* (Cambridge: Cambridge University Press, 1987).

[302] Joseph Renauldon, *Traité Historique et Pratique des Droits Seigneuriaux* (Paris: Despilly, 1765), iii.

[303] Id., book 3, chapter 1, page 197.

[304] John Q. C. Mackrell, *The Attack on "Feudalism" in Eighteenth Century France* (London: Routledge, 2013), 1.

The critique of *féodalité* was one of the central themes of the influential pamphlet that the *Abbé* Emmanuel-Joseph Sieyès (1748–1836), a prominent constitutional theorist and public intellectual, published shortly before the outbreak of the Revolution in 1789. Noting that "the innumerable vexations of the agents of *féodalité*" still afflicted the French countryside in the eighteenth century, the *Abbé* Sieyès challenged the jurists and legislatures that enabled these feudal vexations:

> If you don't want to proscribe the crowd of the inequitable and anti-social privileges, then recognize and legalize them; oh, blood boils at the mere idea of legalizing the abominable fruits of the abominable *féodalité* at the end of the eighteenth century.[305]

This powerful anti-feudal cry also pervaded the writings of Joseph Barnave. A leading figure in the Constitutional Assembly of 1789–1791, Barnave was not an academic jurist but a lawyer with a passion for a readable and generalist "philosophical history." His *Introduction à la Révolution Française* is a window onto the views and concerns of the revolutionary elites and is punctuated with invectives against all things "feudal":

> Then, Europe found itself divided into large monarchies, where the prince had almost no power and the people had no industry. There were two classes of men, one with the power of arms, which is everything in a country where the public power has no strength; the other with the force of superstition, so common among a people of extreme ignorance. Together they possessed the land, which then was the only wealth and, by the nature of things, carried with it all the power. They soon succeeded in subjugating the people, in freeing themselves from the control of the prince and by their progress, by the hierarchy that developed among them, and by the laws that they created to regulate this strange regime, founded what we call feudal government . . .. But the gradual influence of nature always prevails in the long run over that of accidental causes. Men, changed by great events, return slowly to what the soil, the climate and all general causes demand that they must be. Nature destined the Europeans to surpass all inhabitants of the globe in their active industry, or at least all those of the ancient world.[306]

In Barnave's account, feudal government is a "strange" regime, where hierarchy, the brute force of arms, ignorance, and superstition reign.

---

[305] Emmanuel-Joseph Sieyes, *Qu'est-ce que le tiers état?* (Paris: Correard, 1822), 186–187.
[306] Joseph Barnave, *Oeuvres Posthumes. Introduction à la Révolution Française*, vol. 1 (Paris: Bérenger, 1842), 27.

However, there is optimism and a sense of urgency in Barnave's pages: feudalism was the product of a specific turn of historical events, and the industrious peoples of Europe, whom nature had destined to great things, seemed ready the shake off the feudal yoke.

The actual dismantling of *féodalité* and of divided *dominium* started on the night of August 4, 1789, when, in a sudden, unexpected, and highly emotional turn of events, the National Constituent Assembly "destroyed the feudal regime in its entirety," as dramatically stated in the Assembly's own report.[307] That famous night, following the news of an escalation of peasant violence in the countryside, the National Assembly was considering a statement that would declare the sanctity of property rights and reaffirm existing laws. As the discussion was about to start, the Viscount de Noailles seized the floor and proposed that some seigneurial rights be abolished without compensation and others be subject to indemnification.[308] Suddenly, in an atmosphere of growing exaltation if not delirium, many deputies started renouncing a variety of rights and privileges.

Yet, the end of divided *dominium* was neither swift nor uncontroversial. For one thing, the motivations behind "the abolition of feudalism" were complex and mixed. The events of that night were probably driven by a combination of exaltation, fear, impulses of generosity, and careful calculation aimed at preserving entitlements that benefited many of the deputies who themselves held seigneurial rights.[309] Further, not everyone believed that expanding access to property required abolishing all forms of divided *dominium*. The *censive* was a case in point. In the prerevolutionary decades, the *censive* was the most common form of landholding in France and the chief means through which peasants acquired access to land. Unsurprisingly, the abolition of the *censive* caused some uproar. In 1790, in his address to the National Convention, the Archbishop of Paris, De Juigne, could hardly conceal his distress when he asked:

> To make people happy, you need to make them owners. How will the peasants become owners if we do not allow the *bail à cens*?[310]

---

[307] For a translation of the report, see John Hall Stewart (ed.), *A Documentary Survey of the French Revolution* (New York: Macmillan, 1951), 107.
[308] Raffe Blaufarb, *The Great Demarcation: The French Revolution and the Invention of Modern Property* (Oxford: Oxford University Press, 2016), 48–57.
[309] Markoff, *The Abolition of Feudalism*, 430 and 456.
[310] Marcel Garaud, *Histoire Générale du Droit Privé Français: de 1789 à 1804, La Révolution et la Propriété Foncière*, vol. 2 (Recueil Sirey, 1958), 30.

Was the mounting antipathy toward feudal divided *dominium* a sign that a "bourgeois" consciousness was taking shape and that a new class, the capitalist bourgeoisie, was emerging? The answer to this question is far from straightforward. To be sure, prior to the Revolution, a class of capitalist farmers who relied on wage labor and sought to maximize profits by improving labor productivity had started to emerge. Yet, well into the nineteenth century, the "bourgeoisie" was a *congérie* of socially and economically disparate middle classes with diverging interests.[311] Further, the most active leaders of the Revolution were not capitalist entrepreneurs in agriculture, manufacturing, or banking but lawyers and officeholders. This professional middle class shared in the anti-feudal discourse but was less interested in a new economic order than in the impact of status restrictions on their social and professional mobility.[312] They continued to invest in land and to aspire to join the aristocracy. However, it is also the case that, in the twenty-six years of revolutionary government, this diverse bourgeoisie, pressured by the dual threat of revolt from below and counterrevolution, steadily acquired self-confidence as a class, consolidated its hold on political power, and forged an agenda focused on modernizing property, rolling back labor protections, and liberalizing the market that proved vital to the long-term development of capitalism.[313]

Certainly, divided *dominium* was not abolished once and for all on the night of August 4th. The *député* Michel-René Maupetit's proclamation that, on the night of August 4, 1789, "the famous tree of feudalism was knocked down and, that night, all its roots were eradicated"[314] was wishful thinking. Outright abolition would have hurt many of the deputies, who were themselves owners of seigneurial rights, and would have jeopardized plans to restructure state finances. Rather, divided *dominium* was dismantled gradually over the course of the Revolution, as the succeeding revolutionary legislative bodies reacted to recurring waves of peasant unrest in the countryside.[315] The main architect of the plan for a gradual abolition was Philippe-Antoine Merlin de Douai

---

[311] Sarah Maza, *The Myth of the French Bourgeoisie: An Essay on the Social Imaginary 1750–1850* (Cambridge, MA: Harvard University Press, 2005), 5–13.

[312] Mooers, *The Making of Bourgeois Europe*, 95.

[313] Id.

[314] Michel-René Maupetit, *Lettres de Michel-René Maupetit: Député à l'Assemblée Nationale Constituante* (Charleston, SC: Nabu Press, 2010), 149.

[315] Markoff, *The Abolition of Feudalism*, 11. Peter M. Jones, *The Peasantry in the French Revolution* (Cambridge: Cambridge University Press, 1988), xi–xv and 248ff.

(1754–1838), a jurist who, before the Revolution, had earned a reputation for his ingenious defense of lords' claims against their peasants. Merlin chaired the committee in charge of operationalizing abolition and, in his report, he drew a clear line between different types of seigneurial rights:

> From the fact that the feudal regime is destroyed it follows that we must regard as eliminated without indemnity all the rights that do not derive from a contract of infeudation or a contract of access and have no basis other than a usurpation emboldened, sanctioned and legitimated by feudalism. You know, *Monsieurs*, how numerous is the list of these rights, for the most part bizarre and capricious.[316]

In this short passage, Merlin is both a masterful rhetorician and a consummate lawyer. Merlin indulges in all the tropes of the anti-feudal rhetoric: the "feudal regime" that has sanctioned acts of "usurpation," its effective "elimination," and the "capricious" nature of seigneurial rights. Yet, camouflaged by this popular anti-feudal rhetoric is a lawyerly distinction that, in effect, saves from destruction a significant part of the "feudal regime." Merlin differentiated between seigneurial personal rights obtained through force, which would be abolished without compensation, and seigneurial rights in land arising from freely entered contracts, which would be extinguished gradually and with indemnification. Merlin put to work two fundamental legal distinctions that were modern in flavor but Roman in origin. The first was the distinction between rights obtained through *coercion* and rights arising from a *freely entered contract*. The second distinction was that between *personal rights*, rights that a person has against another person, and *real rights*, rights in a thing, in this case land.[317] Merlin's strategy of using the concept of real rights arising from free contracts to justify seigneurial claims was not new. By the eighteenth century, the modern language of property and contract was gaining traction among the legal elites and was used both to attack the "feudal" and to defend it.[318] In their treatises, the most sophisticated *feudistes* of the prerevolutionary decades tried to present seigneurial rights as property rights originating in contracts, rather than as coercively imposed.

Merlin appropriated the move of the *feudistes*, hoping to placate the peasantry and undercut the possibility of more radical measures, while at

---

[316] Philippe-Antoine Merlin, *Rapport fait au comité des droits féodaux, le 4 septembre 1789, sur l'objet et l'ordre du travail dont il est chargé* (Versailles: Baudouin, 1789), 6.

[317] Markoff, *The Abolition of Feudalism*, 461, 467–468; Blaufarb, *The Great Demarcation*, 83–89.

[318] Markoff, *The Abolition of Feudalism*, 467.

the same time preserving many aspects of the seigneurial system.[319] However, working out the details of the system of gradual abolition and indemnification was no easy task. In 1792, under the pressure of a second wave of peasant insurrection, all seigneurial dues were declared presumptively coercive and thereby abolished without compensation. The final blow to seigneurial, divided landholding came on July 17, 1793, when the National Convention simply declared all seigneurial rights abolished without compensation. Finally, the *député* Maupetit's wish that the tree of feudalism be uprooted came true.

What Was Novel in the Code of Property: An Experimental Physics of Legislation and the Values of Modernity

By finally uprooting the tree of feudalism, the National Convention cleared the terrain on which the Napoleonic legislature would plant the seeds of modern Romanist *dominium*. The thousands of pages of grand-iloquent declarations that introduced the draft Code Civil des Français to the courts, the Conseil d'État, and the nation leave no doubt that the Code was, essentially, the code of property. André-Jean Arnaud and others have argued forcefully that it was a code written by property owners for property owners.[320] The *Exposé des motifs* that accompanied the Code warned the reader that:

> You should not be surprised that this draft [of the book on property] is limited to a few definitions and general rules because the entire body of the Code is devoted to defining everything that relates to the exercise of the right to property, the fundamental right on which all social institutions are based and that, to each individual, is as precious as life, to provide him with the means to preserve it .... Citizens-legislators, the law recognizes that property is the right to use one's things in the most absolute manner and that this right is sacred even for the humblest person. What principle is more fertile of useful consequences! ... It is to this respect for property that modern nations owe their spirit of justice and liberty.[321]

---

[319] Id., 456.

[320] See, e.g., André-Jean Arnaud, *Les origines doctrinales du Code civil française*. Bibliothèque de philosophie du droit, vol. 9 (Paris: Librairie Générale de droit et de jurisprudence, 1969).

[321] Jean-Étienne-Marie Portalis, "Exposé des motifs du projet de loi sur la propriété, titre II, livre II du *Code Civil*, présenté le 26 Nivôse an XII," reproduced in *Ecrits et discours juridiques et politiques* (Marseille: Presses Universitaires d'Aix, 1988), 126–127.

That property was the cornerstone of the new legal order set forth in the Code Civil was also clear to Jean Guillaume Locré de Roissy (1758–1840), the *secrétaire général* of the Conseil d'État, who played a prominent role as observer in the drafting process:

> But a sentiment more moving than that of Glory, your love for this people that you have just saved, Your Majesty, induced you to devote your work to reestablishing the shaken social edifice on the most solid base, the laws that regulate and protect property.[322]

Literally reproducing Pothier's words, article 544 of the Code Civil of 1804 defined modern property as "the right of enjoying and disposing of things in the most absolute manner, provided they are not used in a way prohibited by the laws or statutes."[323] Hardly any legal definition has proven more influential than this one. Generations of sympathetic readers around the world have praised it as the clearest expression of the commitment to a robust concept of private property, while hordes of critics have seen it as the embodiment of a simplistic individualism, permeated by a materialistic ideology that reduced individuals to a mere "mechanics of appetites."[324] However, the new *droit de propriété* sketched in the Code Civil was more complicated than its sympathizers, as well as its opponents, would have us believe. It was both old and new, deeply rooted in history and yet ambitiously innovative, ideologically more diverse and strikingly incoherent.

The *Discours de Présentation du Code Civil* and the *Exposé des Motifs* penned by Jean-Étienne-Marie Portalis (1746–1807), one of the four jurists charged by Napoleon with preparing a draft Code Civil, are the best guide to the old and the new in the Code's book on property. Portalis was a prominent lawyer, who had gained a reputation in his years as *avocat* in the *Parlement* of Aix en Provence, and an influential public figure active in conservative political circles. The *Discours* and the *Exposé* are rich and multifaceted texts, serving as methodological declarations, ideological manifestos, and exhibitions of conceptual *bravura*. The tone of these writings emphasized novelty, with Portalis making ubiquitous

---

[322] Jean Guillaume Locré de Roissy, *Esprit du Code Napoléon*, vol. 1 (Paris: de l'imprimerie impériale, 1805), ix.

[323] English translation from Anon (A Barrister of the Inner Temple), *The Code Napoleon; or, the French Civil Code* (London: William Benning, 1827), 150.

[324] Xavier Martin, "Nature humaine et Code Napoléon" (1985), 2 *Droits. Revue francaise de theorie juridique*, 2, 117–128, at 118.

allusions to "our modern times"[325] and to progress. The remarks about science also signaled novelty. Portalis was adamant that recent decades had brought not only great political and societal transformations but also significant intellectual turmoil:

> Since the middle of the eighteenth century, there is a great agitation in the minds. Our discoveries and our progress in the exact sciences and in the natural sciences have exaggerated in us the consciousness of our own strengths and have produced this live fermentation which has gradually extended to all that have fallen under our hands. Having discovered the functioning of the physical world, we now have the ambition to rebuild the moral and political world . . . . Has a nation ever given itself a brand-new code that totally disregards past practices? Let us interrogate history, which is the experimental physics of legislation, and teaches us to respect the old maxims, which are the product of a long series of observations.[326]

Portalis was a writing at a time in which scientism proliferated. The rising elites had invested the natural sciences, positive and descriptive, with substantial authority and the transfer of ideas and practices from the study of nature into that of humans and their institutions proliferated.[327] Illustrative of this trend were that Voltaire and other eighteenth-century writers had created the genre of popular science and that the physician Pierre Cabanis (1757–1808) had revived Hippocratic practices of non-speculative physiological description and had sought to apply them to humans and their society. Over the course of the century that was just starting, a variety of scientific positivisms, from Henri de Saint Simon (1760–1825) to Auguste Comte (1798–1857), would burgeon. Immersed in this cultural milieu, Portalis used the language of science, presenting history as "the experimental physics of legislation" and old maxims as the product of the repeated, factual observations performed by generations of Roman and French "legal scientists." At the dawn of the nineteenth century, a reader enamored of Roman antiquity and enthralled by the new scientism must have found Portalis' words all the more powerful.

---

[325] See, e.g., Jean-Étienne-Marie Portalis, "Code Civil. Théorie du Code Civil: II. Exposé general du système du Code Civil," in Jean Guillaume Locré de Roissy, *La législation civile, commerciale et criminelle de la France, ou Commentaire et complément des Code Français. Vol. 1. Code Civil*, vol. 1 (Paris: Treuttel and Würtz,1827), section 6, page 324.

[326] Id., sections 5–6, pages 322–324.

[327] Richard Olson, *Science and Scientism in Nineteenth-Century Europe* (Champaign: University of Illinois Press, 2007), 19–62; Robert Fox, *The Culture of Science in France, 1700–1900* (London: Routledge, 1992), 30–56.

Also in tune with "our new modern times" was Portalis' discussion of the relationship between property, social interdependence, and equality. To the reader who expects a magniloquent statement about *dominium*'s absolute character, similar to the many that would punctuate property law literature later in the century, Portalis' discussion may come as a surprise. Portalis did indeed state that property is the right to dispose of a thing in the most absolute manner, but he also introduced a notion of reciprocity and interdependence.

> And you, citizens legislators, will consequently endeavor to consecrate by your vote the great principle of property, presented in the bill as the right of enjoying and disposing of things in the most absolute manner. But as men live in society and under the laws, they cannot have the right to violate the laws that govern society. In a well-ordered legal system, the exercise of the right of property is regulated as is the exercise of all other rights. One thing is independence, another thing is freedom. True freedom is acquired only through the sacrifice of independence. True liberty consists in a wise composition of individual rights and powers with the common good .... Hence, we need laws to regulate how individuals can use their things just as we need laws to regulate how individuals can use their personal faculties. One must be free within the laws and not against the laws. Hence, in recognizing that one has the right to dispose of his things in the most absolute manner, we have added "provided that he does not use them in a way prohibited by the laws or regulations."[328]

Portalis' notion of interdependence was neither particularly elaborate nor sophisticated and, ultimately, fully consistent with the examples of the limits of the owner's rights that we read in Pothier's treatise. Yet, the acknowledgment that "real freedom" has to account for social interdependence is a sign that the drafter's vision of property was richer and more sophisticated than the simplistic property individualism that would come to pervade property law treatises only a few decades later. Portalis' discussion of interdependence was rooted in the cluster of ideas that would allow for what Pierre Rosanvallon has called "the society of equals," the aspiration to a society of free and equal citizens who are also autonomous, although interdependent, owners.[329] In this discourse, equality was a form of social relation, in which no person is subject to the will of another, all are equal before the law, each is necessarily engaged in a larger web of social connections, and people are responsible for their

---

[328] Portalis, "Exposé des motifs du projet de loi sur la propriété," 114–115.
[329] Pierre Rosanvallon, Arthur Goldhammer (trans.), *The Society of Equals* (Cambridge, MA: Harvard University Press, 2013), 20ff.

own material subsistence.[330] Property was central to all three dimensions: it was a right, equally recognized to each individual, that enabled autonomy and promoted interdependence.

No writer expressed this vision of property and society with greater clarity than Paul-Henri Thiry, Baron d'Holbach (1723–1789), a critical figure of what Jonathan Israel has called the "Radical Enlightenment."[331] Between the 1770s and the 1780s, d'Holbach published, anonymously, a series of books that greatly influenced the top vanguard of the democratic republican leadership of the Revolution. In his *Politique naturelle* (1773), d'Holbach elaborated at length on the relation between property, sociability, and equality:

> Individuals join together in society to put themselves in the position of being able to receive the assistance they want, not only the security of their person but also the possessions necessary to their conservation and welfare . . . .. Hence, Natural laws have given to each individual a right called property, which is the faculty to enjoy exclusively the things they have earned through their talent, labor and inventiveness . . ..[332] The inequality that natural laws have laid among individuals, far from being the source of their ills is the real basis of their happiness. Because of it, individuals are invited and forced to rely on each other and to provide reciprocal help . . ..[333] The natural inequality of men renders the equality of possessions impossible . . ..[334] An equitable government is one that makes sure that each individual enjoys with the greatest equality possible the rewards that come from social association . . ..[335] Under the democratic form of government, each individual remains, so to say, independent: his liberty is not limited by anything other than the laws that he sets for himself. We believe with no doubt that laws established to bind all citizens equally are the most appropriate means of remedying the inequality that natural laws have laid among individuals.[336]

To be sure, the notion of equality articulated by d'Holbach was ultimately thin, downplaying wealth inequalities as natural and relying on virtue,

---

[330] Id., 21–22.

[331] Jonathan I. Israel, *Radical Enlightenment: Philosophy and the Making of Modernity 1650–1750* (Oxford: Oxford University Press, 2002); Jonathan I. Israel, *The Enlightenment That Failed: Ideas, Revolution, and Democratic Defeat* (Oxford: Oxford University Press, 2019), 178–214.

[332] Paul-Henri Thiry D'Holbach, *La Politique Naturelle, ou Discours sur les Vrais Principes du Gouvernement* (London, 1773), vol. 1, discours 1, section 25, page 38.

[333] Id., discours 1, section 11, page 21.

[334] Id., discours 1, section 27, page 40.

[335] Id., discours 2, section 21, page 74.

[336] Id., discours 2, section 14, page 63.

formally equal rights and the quality of the social bond to correct them. D'Holbach's ideas were formative for leaders like the *Abbé* Sieyès and Mirabeau, both vocal critics of *féodalité* and passionate advocates of modern property. Portalis was, in many ways, a reactionary and an unlikely devotee of the "Radical Enlightenment"; yet his discussion of property, sociability, and equality still echoed themes of this earlier optimistic vision.

> Nor is the right of property the cause of inequality among men. Men are not born equal, neither in size, nor in strength, nor in skills, nor in talents. Chances and events still differ from one another. These inequalities, which are the very work of nature, necessarily comprise those which are found in society. It would be a mistake to fear the abuses of wealth and of the social differences which may exist between men. Humanity, beneficence, pity, all the virtues the seed of which has been thrown into the human heart, supersede these differences, and have the purpose of softening and compensating for the inequalities which form the picture of life.[337]

These ideas about the relation between property, formal equality, and sociability that had circulated among the liberal elites of eighteenth-century Europe, and of which we see a pale reflection in Portalis' writings, proved critical to the success of modern *dominium* over the course of the nineteenth century. They made the concept of *la propriété* introduced by the Code Civil appealing not only to the conservatives who supported the *réaction napoléonienne* but also to segments of the republican and liberal elites, who saw *la propriété* as one of the cardinal formally equal rights granted to all in a democratic republic.

What Was Old in the Code of Property: Roman *Dominium* and Natural Law

The references to social progress and the epistemological turmoil of modernity, the appeal to scientism and to an experimental physics of legislation, and the vision of a "society of equals" are what was novel in Portalis' approach to property. All else was not new. The concept of *la propriété* enshrined in the Code Civil was nothing other than Pothier's *droit du domaine de propriété*; the constitutional theory behind it was largely based on the work of the seventeenth-century theorists of the "great demarcation" between property and sovereignty; and many of the

---

[337] Portalis, "Exposé des motifs du projet de loi sur la propriété," 114.

arguments justifying modern *dominium* were drawn from a centuries-old natural law tradition. That not much was novel in the Code Civil's book on property Portalis himself was happy to admit:

> Some people seem to regret not seeing any new grand vision in the draft of the *Code Civil* which has been submitted for discussion. They complain of seeing in it only a recasting of Roman law, of our old customs, and of our ancient maxims. It would be desirable to add some precise ideas to what is meant by grand vision. Does grand vision mean some new bold institution in the manner of Solon and Lycurgus? But let us not deceive ourselves, fellow citizens-legislators: bold innovation is often a brilliant error, the sudden burst of which resembles that of lightning striking the very spot it illuminates.[338]

Skeptical about grand visions of a wholly new law of property, Portalis and his fellow drafters turned instead to the reliable guidance of Roman law. Theirs was, in many ways, an obvious choice. The myth of Rome enthralled the revolutionary generation in France. As students in the *colleges* of the ancien régime, the revolutionaries-to-be had been taught Livy and Cicero, in which they found compelling discussions of republican principles and republican heroes.[339] Jacques-Pierre Brissot (1754–1793), a lawyer and leader of the moderate faction of the Girondins, turned to Cicero when describing the ideal of learning and action:

> The model of the orator was so well realized by Cicero .... A lawyer, according to Cicero, must be universal. If he wants to open the doors of immortality, he must not limit himself to browsing the arid fables of jurisprudence. He must sprinkle them with the flowers of literature. He must combine the depth of reasoning with delicacy of thought, with the art of numbering the prestige of declamation. National and foreign poetries, fine arts, dialectic, history, morality, physics, philosophy above all, he must know everything, and read, reread, and discuss the best authors in each genre.[340]

Further, parallels between the struggle for republican freedom in Rome and in France were ubiquitous in the pamphlets of the firebrands of the Revolution. Throughout his widely read *La France Libre*, Camille

---

[338] Portalis, "Code Civil. Théorie du Code Civil: II. Exposé general du système du Code Civil," section 6, page 323.

[339] Harold Talbot Parker, *The Cult of Antiquity and the French Revolutionaries: A Study in the Development of the Revolutionary Spirit* (London: Octagon Books, 1965), 8ff.

[340] Jacques-Pierre Brissot, *Un indépendant à l'Ordre des Avocats: sur la décadence du barreau en France* (Berlin, 1781), 11–12.

Desmoulins (1760–1794), a lawyer and influential crowd orator, elaborated at length on this theme:

> The restoration of this liberty in France is reserved for our days. Yes, it is already back among us. It has not yet had a temple for the Estates General as the Greeks had in Delphi for the meetings of the Amphictyonic League, or the Temple of Concord for the meetings of the Senate in Rome; but it is no longer the case that we adore it quietly. It is everywhere a public cult. After forty years, philosophy has undermined the foundations of despotism and, as Rome before Ceasar was already shackled by its vices, France before Necker was already freed by *les lumières*.[341]

A decade later, in Napoleonic France, the cult of antiquity became particularly germane to law, where the parallels seemed striking.[342] In the preparatory works for the Code Napoléon, these parallels were tirelessly rehearsed: the jurist Domat was the French Gaius, the Code Civil the modern counterpart to Justinian's codification, and Napoleon the new Justinian. The *Essai sur l'utilité de la codification* recited an even longer and more elaborate series of analogies:

> There is no doubt that this work could be done by jurists who are not vested with any official authority, Gaius for the Romans, Bisson, Lamoignon and Domat for the French. But the dogmatic authority of scholars is insufficient. For the advantages of a good classification, of a clear reform and of a reasoned reorganization to benefit society, they ought to be consecrated by the irrefutable authority of the law .... This was the glorious task achieved by Lycurgus for the Lacedaemonians; Draco and Solon for the Athenians; for the Romans, after Numa, by the *decemviri*, Theodosius and Justinian; and for us by Charlemagne, Saint Louis and Napoleon.[343]

Yet, despite this pervasive cult of Roman antiquity, the early nineteenth century was a time of uncertainty for the scholars of Roman law in France. Over the course of the sixteenth and seventeenth centuries, the Romanists had played a central role, putting into practical use their conceptual schemes and analytical techniques. In this period, France had been home to a vibrant community of "Legal Humanists" and scholars, from Dumoulin to Pothier, who, inspired by Roman law, had

---

[341] Camille Desmoulins, *La France Libre*, 3rd ed. (1789), 1–2.
[342] Donald R. Kelley, *Historians and the Law in Postrevolutionary France* (Princeton, NJ: Princeton University Press, 1984).
[343] Jean-Étienne-Marie Portalis, "Essai sur l'utlité de la codification," in *Discours, Rapport et Travaux inédits sur le Code Civil* (Paris: Joubert, 1844), v–vi.

systematically reorganized and rationalized French customary law. However, the general enthusiasm for the novelty of the Code Napoléon risked obfuscating the role of Roman law. Many believed that Roman law had lost its vitality, becoming "dead legislation."[344] This idea lingered in juristic circles well into the 1820s. Joseph Louis Elzéar Ortolan (1802–1873), the author of a highly popular *Explication historique des Institutes de Justinien* (1827) that went through several editions, felt the need to note that:

> It is this body of law [Roman law] that, more than any other, calls for the use of the historical method, in France more than elsewhere, because, in France, Roman legislation is dead legislation; and, for the dead, what is left other than history?[345]

The mounting antipathy toward Roman law was also announced in the work of publicists and opinion writers. In 1785, the Basque writer and politician Dominique-Joseph Garat (1749–1833) had published in the *Mercure de France* a vitriolic attack to Roman law. Garat urged readers to find out for themselves what Roman law really was about, instead of accepting the long-dominant, optimistic image of a law of freedom and reason. Personally, Garat confessed, what he had found in his exploration of the Roman sources was a haphazard collection of abstract and impenetrable rules adopted by tyrannical emperors. Of the Roman jurists and the Digest, Garat scornfully wrote:

> These self-important men who found the laws to be too clear, too easy for their superb acumen transformed the simple and positive knowledge of law into complicated and controversial science[346] . . .. These Pandects or Digest which organize under the same title the vague and general maxims of the ancient jurists that often bear no relationship to each other or to the title under which they are assembled; that repeat innumerable times the same principles in twenty different ways without adding any clarity or depth; that decide the same question in absolutely opposite ways without any hint that helps decide whether one should prefer the opinion of Ulpian to that of Paul or of Paul to that of Ulpian.[347]

---

[344] Jean Gaudemet, "Tendances et Méthodes en Droit Romain," *Revue Philosophique* (1955) 145 *de la France et de l'Étranger* 145.

[345] Joseph-Louis-Elzéar Ortolan, *Explication Historique des Instituts de l'Empereur Justinien*, 6th ed., vol. 1 (Paris: H. Plon, 1857), v.

[346] Dominique-Joseph Garat, *Mercure de France*, n. 8, 19 février 1785, 112, https://gallica .bnf.fr/ark:/12148/bpt6k3745571q/f7.item.

[347] Id., 116.

In this climate of rousing provocations, Portalis' tribute to Roman law must have sounded very much like a call to arms for the jurists, and for the Roman law scholars in particular, an invitation to reclaim their role as the expert craftsmen of legal doctrine. Interpreting and operationalizing the new, Romanist law of property for modern France was undoubtedly an opportunity for academic jurists to expand their professional power and, in turn, to strengthen their place in the social and political order.[348] The law faculties, which had been suppressed in 1793 due to a spate of revolutionary distrust of lawyers, had just been reestablished. A law of 22 Ventôse of the Year XII (March 13, 1804) restored the *écoles de droit* and clarified the role of Roman law, prescribing that Roman law could be studied only in relation to French law.[349] Portalis was an obvious advocate for Roman law. A native of Provence, a *pays de droit écrit* where Roman law had been in effect until the Revolution, Portalis had received the rigorous university legal training prescribed by a 1679 edict, largely focused on Roman law. Therefore, it is no surprise that Portalis was eager to give credit to the jurists, modern and ancient, for the great bulk of the conceptual work for the new Code Civil.[350] Addressing the Académie de Législation, Portalis admonished that:

> You will never have real knowledge of the new Code if you only study the Code. The Roman philosophers and jurists are still the educators of humanity. It is in part because of the rich materials they have passed down to us that we have built the edifice of our national legislation.[351]

In the rich archive of concepts that the Roman "educators of humanity" had handed down to modern jurists, the fabled and largely imaginary concept of *dominium* seemed the ideal blueprint for *la propriété*, and Portalis and his fellow codifiers made it the centerpiece of the new law of property.

---

[348] On the renaissance of legal studies in France during the Napoleonic period, see Henri Hayem, "La Renaissance des Études Juridiques en France sous le Consulat" (1905) *Nouvelle Revue Historique de Droit Français et Étranger* 96–122; Frédéric Audren and Jean Louis Halpérin, *La Culture Juridique Française: Entre Mythes et Realités, XIX–XX Siècles* (Paris: CNRS Éditions, 2013); Philippe Jestaz and Christophe Jamin, *La Doctrine* (Paris: Dalloz, 2004).

[349] Loi relative aux Écoles de droit (N° 3678), Paris, le 22 Ventôse, an XII de la République.

[350] Portalis, "Code Civil. Théorie du Code Civil: II. Exposé général du système du Code Civil," section 6, pages 323–326.

[351] Jean-Étienne-Marie Portalis, "Discours de rentrée à l'Académie de législation. Paris – 26 novembre 1803" (2014) 1(1) *Les Cahiers Portalis* 33.

Inaugurating a very un-Roman habit of virtually all the nineteenth-century jurists, Portalis started his *Exposé des motifs du project de loi sur la propriété* by discussing the definition of modern *dominium*. And yet, once again, the reader who expects a magniloquent statement about the absoluteness of modern *dominium* will be surprised. The preparatory works reveal a much more nuanced understanding of the scope of the owner's entitlements. The remarks on the *ius abutendi* presented by the *Tribun* Jean Grenier (1753–1841) when the draft Code was submitted to the Tribunat are a good example. Grenier proudly noted that the defin-ition of property in the Code Civil was superior to the Roman definition because it refused to elevate the owner's abuse into a right:

> Property is defined as follows: "the right to enjoy and dispose of things in the most absolute manner, provided they are not used in a way prohibited by statutes or regulations." We see at first sight the correctness of this definition; it recalls that which is found in Roman law, which also seems to have been conceived with care, *jus utendi et abutendi re sua, quatenus ratio patitur*. But, dare we say it, the definition contained in the bill is more accurate; the mind refuses to see the misuse of property transformed into a right; it is well tolerated by civil law so long as it does not harm another; but, in the laws of natural law and morality, misuse is not allowed. Hence it was suggested that by these expressions, *jus abutendi*, the Romans really meant only the right to dispose of one's property in the most absolute manner and that this formula *jus abutendi* was only used to mark the contrast with, *jus utendi and fruendi*, which are the definition of the usufruct. The condition of not making of one's property a use prohibited by the laws and by the regulations is of evident justice.[352]

The *Tribun* Grenier was not alone in believing that *la propriété* does not encompass the right to abuse of the thing. In his *Analyse Raisonnée de la Discussion du Code Civil au Conseil d'État*, Jacques de Maleville (1741–1824), another of the Code's drafters, made the same point, briefly but forcefully. Article 544, Maleville noted, is the literal translation of the Roman definition of *dominium* as *jus utendi et abutendi re sua, quatenus ratio patitur*; however, the Latin word *abuti*, far from meaning "abuse," refers to the owner's right to fully enjoy and dispose of the thing to the point of consuming it. *Abuti*, Maleville continues, stands in opposition to

---

[352] "Discours prononce par le tribun Grenier, Discussion devant le corps legislatif," in Pierre-Antoine Fenet (ed.), *Recueil complet des travaux preparatoires du Code Civil*, vol. 11 (Paris: Videcoq Libraire, 1836), 158–159.

uti, which is to use the thing while preserving its substance.[353] Only a couple of decades later, the idea that owners have the right to misuse and, possibly, destroy their property became a mantra of the advocates of Romanist-bourgeois property.

Similarly, in the preparatory works, the idea that property is "absolute" only appears in the final stages of the drafting process. The earlier drafts of Article 544 omit any reference to property's absolute nature. Jean-Jacques Régis de Cambacérès (1753–1824) presented an early draft of the code that defined property as "the right of the person who possesses the thing to enjoy and dispose of it."[354] A subsequent version of Cambacérès' draft not only made no reference to property rights' "absolute" nature but in fact emphasized the need for legislative and regulatory limits to property. The owner, the second draft read, "has the right to enjoy and dispose of his property in conformity with the law."[355]

The question of whether the owner's right was "absolute" was also closely related to a critical constitutional question, the question of *domaine éminent*, that is, of the nature and scope of the sovereign's power over private property. Did *domaine éminent* refer to the sovereign's power to regulate, or take, private property in the public interest, or to the fact that the sovereign was the ultimate, superior owner of all property in the kingdom? This question, Portalis noted, had long "prompted the most solemn discussions in all the universities of Europe."[356] Portalis' answer came straight from Loyseau and the theorists of "the great demarcation." Feudalism, Portalis argued, had obfuscated all long-held, fundamental principles governing property, but the truth was that:

> Property belongs to the citizen, *imperium* to the sovereign. Such is the maxim of all countries and all time . . . . *Imperium*, which belongs to the sovereign, contains no aspect of property in its proper sense. It consists of the power to govern. It is the right to prescribe and order what is required for the common good and to direct accordingly things and persons . . . . When it comes to citizens' property, sovereignty gives the state the right

---

[353] Jacques de Maleville, *Analyse Raisonnée de la Discussion du Code Civil au Conseil d'État*, vol. 2 (Paris, 1805), 25.

[354] "Premier Projet de Cambacérès, Livre II, Titre II, Des Différentes Manières de Jouir des Biens, Par I, De la Propriété," in Fenet (ed.), *Recueil complet des travaux preparatoires du Code Civil*, vol. 1, 39.

[355] "Deuxième Projet de Cambacérès, Livre II, titre I, note 71," in Fenet (ed.), *Recueil complet des travaux preparatoires du Code Civil*, vol. 1, 116.

[356] Portalis, "Exposé des motifs du projet de loi sur la propriété," 116.

to regulate the use of their property through the civil laws, the power to dispose of their property for a public purpose and the power to levy taxes on citizens' property[357]

Portalis concluded his analysis with a resolute statement, meant to dispel any lingering confusion: when the sovereign regulates, takes or taxes private property, "the sovereign is not acting as the superior and universal owner of all land but rather in his capacity of supreme administrator of the public interest."[358]

Portalis' discussion of the moral, social, and economic benefits of a robust *droit de propriété* was also not novel. Portalis marshalled ideas from a long-standing natural law tradition and from the teachings of the Physiocrats and political economists. Portalis began by faithfully reiterating natural law arguments that had been articulated by Grotius and Pufendorf, who in turn had taken them from the sixteenth-century Spanish Late Scholastics, who, in turn, had relied on Aquinas. Property, Portalis argued, is a natural right, not an institution created by men, a right justified by human needs, and the duty of self-preservation:

> Man, when born, has only needs; he is charged with the duty of his preservation; he cannot exist or live without consuming: he has a natural right to the things necessary for his subsistence and maintenance. He exercises this right by occupation, by labor, by the reasonable and just application of his faculties and his forces. Therefore, necessity and industry are the two principles that create property.[359]

This argument about need and self-preservation raised a difficulty: justifying the transition from common ownership to private property. Did the passage from an original moment, in which God had made things available to all, to the later stage in which things are appropriated by individuals, accord with or contradict the law of nature? Again, Portalis' answer echoes well-established natural law doctrine, dating back to Cicero and the Stoics. Original common property was common only in the sense that it was available for anyone to take, Portalis argued, but its beneficial use required security of possession.

> Providence, no doubt, offers its gifts to universality, but to the utility and needs of individuals. The land is common, said the philosophers and jurists of antiquity, as is a public theater, in which everyone is expected to

[357] Id., 115.
[358] Id., 117.
[359] Id., 111.

take a seat. Common property before occupancy is in fact vacant property waiting for someone to take it. After occupation, they become proper to the person or persons who occupy them. Necessity constitutes a real right; but it is necessity itself, that is to say, the most imperious of all laws, which commands us the use of things without which it would be impossible for us to subsist. But the right of acquiring these things, and of using them, would be entirely useless without the appropriation, which alone can render it useful by linking it to the certainty of preserving what one acquires.[360]

As we know, the example of the seat in a public theater was not Portalis' own; it came straight from Cicero's *De Finibus*.[361] It is a counterintuitive and puzzling example, as it does not seem to justify permanent appropriation but mere temporary use, and yet it had become standard in the natural law property story line.

Portalis was also eager to have the ear of the educated public that had taken an interest in questions of political economy. It was not a long stretch to give these natural law arguments about property and security a spin that would lure the followers of the *économistes*:

> What would agriculture and the arts become without property in land, which is nothing other than the right to possess the portion of soil to which one has applied his hard work and justified expectations …. Hence, industry, encouraged by the security of enjoying one's conquered properties, transforms deserts into fertile lands, digs canals, dries swamps, and covers plains, where there was nothing but contagion and death, with abundant crops.[362]

Portalis' passage echoes the writings of the "political economists of virtue." The broad freedom granted to the cultivator and the owner, Portalis concluded, brings great benefits and negligible disadvantages; the public interest is safe when it has an ally, and not an enemy, in the private interest.[363]

This quick peek into Portalis' writings suggests that the normative underpinnings of the drafter's property discourse were richer and more diverse than often assumed. Also, their ideas about the scope of property entitlements was more nuanced than the "absolutist" view that would come to prevail only a couple of decades later. The task of developing and

---

[360] Id., 111–112.
[361] See Cicero, *De Finibus* 3.20.67–68.
[362] Portalis, "Exposé des motifs du projet de loi sur la propriété," 113.
[363] Id., 112.

popularizing a full-blown Romanist-bourgeois property individualism would fall on the next generation of jurists.

Absolute *Dominium* and Proprietary Individualism

By the mid nineteenth century, the jurists' property discourse noticeably changed: the tone became vehement and the normative arguments more simplistic, and the myth of absolute *dominium* put down deep roots. It is at this moment that modern Romanist *dominium* became a coherent ideological and professional project informed by a grandiloquent liberal individualism. A professional juristic class, drawn from an increasingly self-conscious bourgeoisie and openly supportive of its political and economic interests, took up the task of honing and expanding the property concepts outlined by the Napoleonic legislators. The names of these interpreters of the Code, collectively known as the *École de l'Exégèse*, are well known to generations of students in Europe but are hardly ever heard in contemporary property theory debates: Jean Baptiste Victor Proudhon (1758–1838), Charles Bonaventure Marie Toullier (1752–1835), Raymond Troplong (1795–1869), and Charles Demolombe (1804–1887). The name "Exegetists" is meant to convey these scholars' methodological commitment to a narrow and literal exegesis of the Code Civil.[364] But not all Exegetists were pedestrian interpreters of the Code and arid textualists. Their treatises and monographs on the law of property reveal methodological diversity and varying levels of sophistication. Some Exegetists were sophisticated historians and theoreticians; others were skilled conceptual architects who, in their massive treatises, sought to clarify the larger conceptual structure beyond the outline of the Code.[365] Certainly many shared ambitious agendas for

---

[364] On L'École de l'Exégèse, see Julien Bonnecase, *L'École de l'Exégèse en Droit Civil: Les Traits Distinctifs de sa Doctrine et de ses Méthodes d'Après la Profession de Foi de ses Plus Illustres Représentants* (Paris: E. de Boccard, 1924); Mikhail Xifaras, "L'École de l'Exégèse: Est Elle Historique? Le Cas de Raymond-Théodore Troplong (1795–1869), Lecteur de Friedrich Carl von Savigny," in Mohnhaupt Heinz, Kervégan Jean-François (eds.) *Influences et Réceptions Mutuelles du Droit et de la Philosophie en France et en Allemagne* (Frankfurt: Klostermann, 2001), 177–209; Michel Vidal, "La Propriété dans L'École de l'Exégèse en France" (1976) 5(1) *Quaderni Fiorentini per la Storia del Pensiero Giuridico Moderno* 7–40; Audren and Halpérin, *La Culture Juridique Française*, 47–56; Philippe Rémy, "Le Rôle de l'Exégèse dans l'Enseignement du Droit aux XIXe Siècle" (1985) *Revue d'Histoire des Facultés de Droit et de la Culture Juridique, du Monde des Juristes et du Livre Juridique* 91.

[365] Nader Hakim, "La Contribution de l'Université à l'Élaboration de la Doctrine Civiliste au XIXe siècle," in Maryvonne Hecquard-Théron (ed.), *Les Facultés de Droit inspiratrices du droit?* (Toulouse: Presses de l'Université des Sciences Sociales, 2005), 15–33.

the new science of law and were eager to underscore the intellectual gulf that separated them from practicing lawyers. As Charles Bonaventure Marie Toullier put it:

> What is the science whose temples are reopened with great solemnity? . . . We need to look for it, to discover the science of law and where else if not in the study of man? . . . Let's be careful not to confuse this vast and wonderful science with one of its branches and to confuse the jurist with the practitioner.[366]

The world in which these jurists operated was one in which a liberal bourgeoisie was finally emerging and a capitalist economy finally taking off. Under Napoleon, a new social class came on the scene, comprising provincial merchants, bankers, upstart landowners, imperial administrators, and lawyers as well as members of the old nobility. This new class drew income, social prestige, and qualifications for public office from ownership of land, and land was the primary means of credit for commercial or manufacturing ventures. In short, land had become capital. The top layer of this class took control of the state bureaucracy and the heights of the economy and became a powerful political force, dominating the July monarchy established in 1830.[367] Largely drawn from this political bourgeoisie, the jurists put their expertise to work in service of the interests of their own class.[368]

The stakes were high. As the inequalities of the new bourgeois order became deeper and more obvious, the believers in "absolute property" were confronted by a diverse cohort of social reformers and utopian socialists. These critics questioned private property and brought to the fore the issues of wealth inequality and the conditions of the propertyless working class. That the debate about property was a heated one transpires with clarity even in the otherwise measured and unemotional pages of juristic treatises. In his treatise on property, part of a monumental *Cours de Code Napoléon* in thirty-one volumes, Charles Demolombe[369] described the new contestations around private property as a telling sign of the level of moral corruption that France had reached:

---

[366] Charles Bonaventure Marie Toullier, *Le droit civil français*, Vol. 1 (Paris: F. Cotillon, 1846)m Titre préliminaire des lois en general, paragraph 149, page 114.

[367] Maza, *The Myth of the French Bourgeoisie*.

[368] Vidal, "La Propriété dans L'École de l'Exégèse en France"; Arnaud, *Les origines doctrinales du Code civil française*; André-Jean Arnaud, *Les Juristes Face à la Société du XIXe Siècle à nos Jours* (Paris: Presses Universitaires de France, 1975).

[369] On whom, see Olivier J. Motte, "Demolombe, Jean Charles Florent," in Michael Stolleis (ed.), *Juristen: ein biographisches Lexikon; von der Antike bis zum 20. Jahrhundert*, 2nd ed. (Munich: Beck, 2001), 173.

And it is God himself who established the right to property, of all rights the one that most vividly manifest itself in the instincts of conscience, the one which the universal agreement and free respect of the people proclaim to be inviolable regardless of positive laws; the one where the disastrous doctrines and detestable agitations of the parties have not clouded good faith and common sense . . . . Nothing better attests in front of history the state of moral perturbation in which French society has fallen in recent times than the monstrous controversies that we have to witness.[370]

Even more dramatic was Adolphe Thiers (1797–1877), the conservative liberal historian and prominent politician, who in his widely read essay *De la propriété* (1848) described the critics of property as "born like insects from the decomposition of all governments."[371]

In this climate of heated controversy over private property, the jurists of the *École de l'Exégèse* energetically took up the task of defending *la propriété*.[372] Naturally, economic interests and class politics were closely intertwined with professional power. Pierre-Louis Roederer (1754–1835), an economist and a highly influential political figure during the Napoleonic years, explicitly theorized the alliance between the emerging capitalist class and the jurists. Landowners and, most importantly, owners of industrial and financial capital, Roeder explained, were the backbone of a stable political and economic order, and the jurists were to be the experts who committed all their knowledge and skill to the defense of property. In Roeder's own words:

Without the capitalists of all types, the State cannot obtain any of the services necessary for its needs; it cannot even obtain the revenue necessary to pay for these services. Only capitalists immediately transfer revenue to the public treasury[373] . . . . A distinguished lawyer is a citizen who devoted to the maintenance of property and liberty all his talent for words, his deep knowledge, his high probity and his vigorous courage; and whose virtuous eloquence obtained triumphs that are recognized by justice and shared by all good people.[374]

---

[370] Charles Demolombe, "Cours de Code Napoléon," in *Traité de la Distinction des Biens, de la Propriété, de l'Usufruit, de l'Usage et de l'Habitation*, 2nd ed., vol. 1 (Paris: Durand, 1861), book 2, title 2, paragraph 534, page 479.

[371] Adolphe Thiers, *De la Propriété* (Paris: Paulin, l'Heureux et Cie, 1848), book 1, chapter 1, page 14.

[372] See the description of Henri Baudrillart in Kelley, *Historians and the Law in Postrevolutionary France*, 144.

[373] Pierre-Louis Roederer, *De la Propriété Considérée dans ses rapports avec les droits politiques*, 3rd ed. (Paris: Hector Bossange, 1830), chapter 4, page 32.

[374] Id., chapter 4, page 36.

By taking up the role of defenders of property, the liberal jurists were staking their claim to power, professional and temporal. Jurists were, obviously, not new to power. The Legal Humanists of the sixteenth and seventeenth century enjoyed high intellectual prestige, the Parisian barristers had achieved significant political clout already under the Old Regime, and lawyers were numerically well represented among the revolutionary elites. But, as we have seen, academic jurists, and the Romanists in particular, had suffered professional setbacks in the revolutionary decades. However, the Exegetists appreciated that the Code Civil, initially perceived as a threat, was a phenomenal opportunity to consolidate their academic and political capital, and they used it do to just that. Between 1804 and the 1890s, the academic study of law boomed, undergoing a radical transformation. Law faculties grew in number, the scope of the curriculum expanded and legal "science" achieved intellectual prominence and became methodologically more diverse. Perched on their academic chairs, clinging to the Code Civil, and secure in their interpretive science, the jurists posed as the "high priests of a new religion," of which, *la propriété* was a fundamental article of faith.[375] The "high priests" of property took up two critical tasks: operationalizing the bare outline of property law sketched in the Code Civil and disseminating the new culture of *la propriété* throughout French society.

While the exegetic property writers developed an almost superstitious cult of Pothier and closely followed his conceptual blueprint, their method and style could not be further from Pothier's.[376] Insomuch as Pothier's pages were plain, terse, and solidly grounded in the real life of property relations, the pages of the exegetic writers were grandiloquent, abstract, and often ideological. These writers viewed *la propriété* as the unique bond between the owner and a thing, tangible or intangible. Unmistakably, their property treatises opened with lengthy discussions of minute conceptual distinctions that were meant to elucidate the many facets of this unique bond but that, for the most part, read as abstract and purely academic exercises. Take the distinction between *propriété* and *domaine* outlined by both Proudhon and Toullier. As Toullier explained:

---

[375] Arnaud, *Les Juristes Face à la Société du XIXe Siècle à nos Jours*, 70; Philippe Rémy, "Le Rôle de l'Exégèse dans l'Enseignement du Droit au XIXe Siècle" (1985) *Revue d'Histoire des Facultés de Droit et de la Culture Juridique, du Monde des Juristes et du Livre Juridique* 91–105.

[376] Vidal, "La Propriété dans L'École de l'Exégèse en France," 29.

> *Propriété* is considered an inherent quality. Some authors establish a difference between *domaine* and *propriété*. They mean by *propriété* that quality in the thing itself, by which the thing is considered as belonging to this or that person exclusive of others. And by *domaine*, they mean the right to dispose of the thing, which they regard as the effect of property; So that according to them, *domaine* is attached to the person, whereas *propriété* is attached to the thing itself. Thus *domaine* and *propriété* are two correlative terms; one would be the active right of disposal, the other a passive quality which always follows a thing and submits it to the owner's disposal.[377]

At the end of this long paragraph, Toullier himself had to admit that this distinction between a passive *propriété*, by virtue of which the thing is submitted to the owner's will, and an active *domaine* was a subtle theoretical distinction, of little practical use. Another conceptual distinction was that between *chose* and *bien*. Warning the reader that he had "no intention of engaging in a philosophical controversy or in a vain dispute over words," Demolombe, explained:

> We designate as *biens*, in the technical language of jurists, the things that can procure an exclusive utility to men and that can become the object of property . . . . The word *chose*, in the indefinite flexibility of its meanings, includes everything that exists, not only the things that can become the property of men, but also everything that in nature escapes exclusive appropriation: the air, the sea, the sun. Hence, all *biens* are *choses*, but not all *choses* are *biens* . . . . *Chose* is the genre, *bien* the species . . . .[378] This character of utility is what effectively distinguishes *biens*. And it is from this that name *bien* seems to have derived, from the word *bonum* which conveys the idea of prosperity [*bonheur*] and well-being [*bien-être*]. Let's hear the jurist Ulpian: ". . . *bona ex eo dicuntur, quod beant, id est beatos faciunt; beare enim est prodesse.*"[379]

The gist of Demolombe's discussion of *chose* and *bien* was to highlight that the appropriation of value is what property is about. Yet, despite his

[377] Charles-Bonaventure-Marie Toullier, *Le Droit Civil Français Suivant l'Ordre du Code*, 6th ed., vol. 2 (Paris: Cotillon, 1846), book 2, title, 2, chapter 1, section 3, paragraph 82–83, pages 33–34. A discussion of this distinction also appears in Jean-Baptiste-Victor Proudhon, *Traité du Domaine de Propriété* (Brussels: Meline, Cans et compagnie, 1842), part 3, chapter 17, section 1, paragraphs 604–606, page 234.

[378] Demolombe, "Cours de Code Napoléon," book 2, title 1, chapter 1, section 1, paragraphs 8–9, page 6.

[379] Id., book 2, title 1, chapter 1, section 1, paragraph 16, page 11. The Latin text, found at Digest 50.16.49, translates as *"Bona* are so called from the fact that they make forturate, that is make someone *beatus*; for to make fortunate is to profit."

resolution to refrain from vain abstractions, Demolombe ended up enmeshed in long-winded, theoretical disquisitions that shed little light either on how specific doctrines helped secure or maximize the owner's value or on the normative trade-offs between the owner's *bonheur* and the *bonheur* of neighbors and the public.

Having clarified that property is about the utility that *biens* afford to the owner, Demolombe then embarked on a long analysis of the different types of *biens*, which is the most intriguing part of his treatise. Demolombe's pages on the distinctions between *biens* prove, once again, that it is when examining the "things," or resources, that the jurists trained in the Roman law tradition were most clearsighted and perspicuous. The echoes of the Roman "law of things," with its unique blend of formalism and sheer pragmatism, still reverberated in Demolombe's analysis. Demolombe relied on what may seem yet another arid distinction, that between the *physical* and the *juridical* substance of the thing – the *chose* – to convey the fundamental insight of the Roman "law of things." Ownership entitlements ought to be to be shaped with an eye not only to the physical characteristics of the thing but also to its social, cultural, and economic value and use.

> This first consideration, what we deduce from the constitutive elements of the *chose* and from its physical qualities, this consideration, I say, has, unquestionably, its importance when one seeks to assess and qualify juridically a *bien*. However, this consideration is not the only one; it is necessary to add that it is neither the primary nor the most decisive. What we assess above all in law is the external form of the *chose*, its distinctive and organizational form, that characteristic form that distinguishes the *chose* from other things, that renders it especially suited for a certain use or function, and makes it apt, to the exclusion of all other differently conformed things, to render a particular service or to procure a certain type of utility. *Voilà*, for us what matters is the substance of the *chose*, not as in physics or chemistry, the material, elemental substance of the thing, but the juridical substance that constitutes a certain entity, designated with a certain name and given a certain shape especially conceived to give it that destination.[380]

The "juridical substance" of the *chose* is, for Demolombe, the particular legal regime that reflects the specific social values and use practices that have developed around different resources. The Roman jurists had actually integrated insights drawn from external disciplines, be it philosophy

---

[380] Id., book 2, title 1, chapter 1, section 1, paragraphs 18–19, pages 12–13.

or religion, into the legal rules that applied to specific types of *res*. Demolombe, by contrast, stopped short of a self-consciously "externalist" approach.

In the section on *biens*, Demolombe also addressed the question of whether human beings could be the object of property. The maxim that *nul n'est esclave en France*, allegedly based on a fourteenth-century ordinance of Louis X, by virtue of which every enslaved individual who set foot on French soil would become free, had been a powerful element of the national political imagination since the sixteenth century.[381] Yet, the question of the ownership of enslaved individuals and their legal personality continued to haunt France until the *décret* of April 27, 1848, which entirely abolished slavery in all the French colonies and possessions.[382] Over the course of the seventeenth century, as France's colonial empire expanded and the country became more dependent on colonial commerce, the most powerful court, the Parliament de Paris, as well as the Amirauté de France (Admiralty Court) had started eroding the principle of freedom for enslaved individuals traveling to France with their masters. Even Enlightenment thinkers often celebrated for their abolitionist commitments, such as the *Marquis* de Condorcet (1743–1794) and the *Abbé* Gregoire (1750–1831), both actively involved in the Societé des Amis des Noirs, hardly called for immediate abolition, proposing instead a process of phased emancipation.[383] And the forebearer of modern property, Robert Jospeh Pothier, had no doubts that Black enslaved individuals in the French colonies were things, either moveable or "attached to immovables." Commenting on the Code Noir, the 1865 collection of laws that regulated French Caribbean slavery, Pothier noted that:

> however great the dignity of man in our colonies, the Blacks, who are our slaves, are regarded as movable property . . . . The Declaration of the King of March 1685 made an exception to this rule; it states that slaves are movables, *if they are not attached to land*; by these terms, *not attached to land* . . . the ordinance means these slaves who are principally and perpetually deployed for the cultivation of land on an estate; these slaves are

---

[381] Sue Peabody, *There Are No Slaves in France: The Political Culture of Race and Slavery in the Ancien Regime* (Oxford: Oxford University Press, 1996).

[382] See Hélène Servant, "Les registres d'état civil en Guadeloupe: le reflet d'une histoire mouvementée," in Jean-François Niort (ed.), *Du Code noir au Code Civil. Jalons pour l'histoire du Droit en Guadeloupe* (Paris: L'Harmattan, 2007), 152 n. 36.

[383] Louis Sala-Molins, *Les Miseres des Lumieres* (Paris: Editions Robert Laffont, 1992).

not movables, because they are considered to be part of the parcel of land, that is, of the estate the lands of which they are deployed to cultivate.[384]

By the time of Demolombe's treatise, the 1848 *décret* that abolished slavery in the colonies had rendered the question of the legal status of enslaved individuals in the French Caribbean islands moot, and Demolombe could hastily dismiss the topic of ownership of human begins:

> Is it even necessary to say that in no relationship, a man himself, the person of man, can be considered a *bien*? We do not need to occupy ourselves with slavery here, if not to say that our laws do not recognize it, at least on the continental territory of France . . . . No doubt, man can contract personal obligations, obligations to do or not to do, he can rent out his skills, and hire his service to another, and the different rights that result from these obligations are *biens* for those for whose benefit they contracted. But it is not the person of the debtor himself that is the object of this *bien*, even if this obligation can be enforced directly against him.[385]

And yet, only a couple of decades earlier, in 1826, well into the age of liberty and property ushered in by the Code Civil, one of the most prominent French jurists, Jean-Marie Pardessus (1772–1853), had expressed a very different view, squarely grounded in Pothier's understanding of the Code Noir. The context was the debate over the *projet de loi* on the compensation for the loss of property to be paid to the former French colonists in Saint Domingue after France recognized the independence of Haiti. The proposed law limited compensation to the loss of real property, excluding moveables. This limitation generated vocal opposition among French colonists, worried that, because Article 46 of the Code Noir defined enslaved individuals as *choses meubles*, they would not receive any compensation. The colonists argued that the value of their properties in Saint Domingue resided largely in the free labor of the enslaved African agricultural laborers and that the land in itself had limited value. Pardessus, in his report written on behalf of the legislative commission charged with examining the *projet de loi*, cited Pothier and reassured the colonists that enslaved Black laborers were to be considered "attached" to the real property on which they labored.

---

[384] Robert Jospeh Pothier, *Traite de la communaute*, vol. 1 (Paris: Debure, 1770), part 1, chapter 2, section 1, article 1, subsection 1, paragraph 30, pages 30–31.

[385] Demolombe, "Cours de Code Napoléon," book 2, title 1, chapter 1, section 1, paragraph 13, page 9.

But the same article [Article 46] admits exceptions. The slaves that work in a home are considered by Article 48 as part of it, and, except for debts contracted for their purchase, they cannot be seized by anyone else if not with the home and with execution of attachment of real property. Hence in the spirit, and, we would say, in the words of the ancient legislation, slaves were one and the same with the *bien-fonds* to which they were attached. Evidently, this is the meaning of Article 2 of the *projet de loi*. It is the consequence of the principle that the objects placed on the land for the enjoyment and use of the land are to be considered immovables by destination (*immeubles par destination*). This is incontestably recognized for the colonies and it was attested by Pothier, the most famous of the French jurists of the last century.[386]

Pardessus' paragraph reveals the racialized architecture of modern *dominium*, in which the Code Civil and its abstract idea of property as liberty existed side by side with the Code Noir and its monstruous denial of humanity and liberty. This dual structure enabled and protected the all-powerful white owner and citizen of the metropole and deprived Black enslaved individuals in the colonies of legal subjectivity, relegating them to the status of *non sujets de droit*, to be treated as objects of property.[387]

After a long rehearsal of the various types of *biens*, Demolombe moved to examine the scope of the power the owner has over his *biens*. In the lengthy section on *la propriété*, the minute conceptual distinctions of the law of *biens* gives way to grandiloquent ideological statements. Demolombe illustrates the gulf that separates the most perfect of the real rights, *dominium*, and personal rights with hyperbole and color:

> The difference between a real right and a personal right, with regards to their effects, is momentous. The real right produces *dominium*, the other a mere *obligation*. The real right creates the owner, the personal right only creates the creditor. The distance between one and the other is enormous. Place to the real right! And all the ranks open to make it pass, as it advances, powerful and absolute, by its own and sole force without the help of any intermediary, towards the thing on which it bears directly.[388]

---

[386] Jean-Marie Pardessus, "Rapport de la commission," in Charles Vanufel and Clément Felix Champion de Villeneuve, *Code des Colons de Saint-Domingue* (Paris: Vergne, 1826), 110–111.

[387] Jean Carbonnier, *Flexible droit. Pour une sociologie du droit sans rigueur*, 10th ed. (Paris: LGDJ, 2001), 247–254.

[388] Demolombe, "Cours de Code Napoléon," book 2, title 1, chapter 2, section 1 ("Qu'est-ce qu'un droit réel? Qu'est-ce qu'un droit personnel?"), paragraph 473, page 379.

Demolombe's call to open all the ranks and let absolute *dominium* advance is one of the most vivid images in the literature of the time, but similar verbiage appears in virtually every property treatise. "Sovereignty," "despotism," and "omnipotence" were the jurists' favorite terms to characterize *la propriété*. For example, in his *Explication théorique et pratique du Code Napoléon*, Victor-Napoléon Marcadé (1810–1854) explained that:

> We have already seen in Article 526 that *la propriété* is the broadest right one may have over a thing. This right renders the owner master and lord of the thing and gives him an absolute omnipotence and despotism over it.[389]

For quite a few jurists, the owner's "despotic" power also included the *ius abutendi*, the right to misuse and, possibly, destroy the thing. Resolutely departing from the cautious and moderate approach to the *ius abutendi* that we have seen in the preparatory works for the Code Civil, Frédéric Mourlon (1811–1866), wrote that:

> the owner can do anything he wants: he can use and dispose of his thing as he pleases; he is the absolute master of the thing. If he doesn't use it productively, if he keeps his fields fallow, if he lets his buildings perish, if he destroys, without any profit for himself, things that can be useful to others, he engages his conscience before God but not before the law. He is a bad owner, and consequently, a bad citizen. But while these acts are morally reprehensible, they are not offenses, they are not punishable under the civil laws. And, by the way, the right to misuse is not as dangerous as it may seem. The very self-interest of the owner acts as a counter-weight. The law cannot, without becoming tyrannical, concern itself with all the particular facts that constitute the exercise of property .... Regarding the acts that are less prejudicial for society, the law tolerates them for reasons that have to do with the respect of natural liberty which would succumb if the law regulated the exercise of property in its most specific details.[390]

In other words, for Mourlon, the owner's conscience and self-interest were sufficient to discourage the most obvious abuses and any effort to regulate the exercise of property rights ran the risk of being tyrannical. The same idea, the risk of tyranny, we also find in Demolombe:

> The word *abuti* of the Romans expressed only the idea of consumption and disposition, not of destruction; and, to the contrary, Roman law

---

[389] Victor-Napoléon Marcadé, *Élements du Droit Civil Français ou Explication Méthodique et Raisonée du Code Civil*, vol. 2(Paris: Cotillon,1842), 438.
[390] Frédéric Mourlon, *Répétitions Écrites sur le Code Civil*, 13th ed., vol. 1 (Paris: Garnier,1896), paragraph 1437, pages 767–768.

proclaimed this maxim: *Expedit rei publicae ne sua re quis male utatur* (Institutes 1.8.2). From this perspective, the French word *abuser*, which is synonymous with "misuse", does not represent fully the Roman idea of the word *abuti*. And, in our case, one can also take safely the maxim that it matters to the interest of society, if individuals govern their fortune well rather than misuse it. We also know that in the case of excesses of misuse, the owner may be, depending on the case, interdicted on account of insanity or provided with the assistance of a *conseil judiciaire* (a guardian). But, to conclude, it is important to recognize that property confers to the owner, if not as a matter of law, as a matter of fact, the right to misuse their property; because property would not be absolute without this right. And any preventive restrictions, infringing on the *droit de propriété* itself, bring more dangers than advantages. As a philosopher says, if the government become the judge of abuse, it will soon become the judge of use and the very idea of property and liberty would be lost (Thomas Raynal).[391]

In this passage, Demolombe is willing to acknowledge that the *ius abutendi* is one of the cases in which modern *dominium/propriété* departs from the supposed Roman "original" and to recognize that the owner's misuse may in fact harm society. Yet he still concluded that the *ius abutendi* is a logical and necessary consequence of property's absoluteness.

Another feature of modern *dominium/propriété* that took up innumerable pages in the jurists' treatises was its perpetual and inviolable character. Pothier and the Code Civil had hardly anything to say about the perpetual nature of property, but the Exegetists were eager to read this additional feature of perpetuity into the text of the Code. As Laurent candidly put it:

> Although the law does not say this, it is accepted by everyone that property is perpetual. Perpetuity results from the absolute right of the owner to dispose of the thing, a right that would not be conceivable if property was temporary.[392]

More firmly grounded in the text of the Code Civil and in the Chartes Constitutionnelles of 1814 and 1830 was the principle of the inviolability of property. Yet despite its solid, albeit recent, textual foundations, the idea of the inviolability of property had been questioned throughout the Revolution, with the more radical fringes openly advocating a modern *lex*

---

[391] Demolombe, "Cours de Code Napoléon," book 2, title 2, chapter 1, paragraph 545, page 495. The Latin in the quotation translates as "It is advantageous to the republic that no one use their things [lit. 'thing'] badly."

[392] François Laurent, *Principes de droit civil Français*, vol. 6 (Brussels: Bruylant, 1871), 139–140 n. 104.

agraria for France. In his pamphlet *De la Législation* (1776), *the Abbé* de Mably was the first to propose the confiscation and redistribution of property, and other similar proposals followed. These proposals generated real panic. In 1793, on the proposition of Bertrand Barère, the National Convention decreed the death penalty for anyone who would propose an agrarian law.[393] This recent wave of enthusiasm for land redistribution was obviously still very much in the minds of the jurists of the *réaction napoléonienne*, a fact that may explain the hyperbole in their reaffirmation of the inviolability of property.

Clarifying and operationalizing the Code's book on property was only part of the task of the Exegetists. Equally important was propagating and entrenching the new culture of property in French society. Unsurprisingly, the arguments of the Exegetists about the many benefits of property were far-reaching but simplistic. It is worth turning to Jean-Baptiste Proudhon because his ideas about property read as a vigorous rebuttal of the critique of property offered by his younger, and more famous, cousin. While the younger Proudhon penned a blunt critique of the proprietary ideology and raised the question of whether and how property may be a just institution, the older Proudhon viewed property as the basis of civic virtue and a safeguard against social and political turmoil.

> The right to property inspires in the owner a sentiment of security for the future; it makes the owner more docile and less turbulent; it encourages the owner to labor to create or acquire new properties by giving him the certainty that he will be able to fully enjoy of his property at his will; Now, laborious men are always the best citizens and the most useful to society. Property encourages the owner to conserve his property with the desire to pass it to his children, relatives or friends. And for those who receive it, this property is a cause of affection and gratitude. Property allows parents to give a good education to their children, making them better servants of their homeland . . . . It is through property that a good man can lift the unhappy and spark virtue in hearts that felt only desperation.[394]

Not all Exegetists were simplistic theoreticians. Raymond Troplong opened his treatise *De la Propriété d'Après le Code Civil* with a fascinating, and rare, discussion that grounds property in both democracy and natural law, going well beyond the simplistic natural law jargon of some

---

[393] R. B. Rose, "The 'Red Scare' of the 1790s: The French Revolution and the 'Agrarian Law'" (1984) 103 *Past & Present* 113.
[394] Proudhon, *Traité du Domaine de Propriété*, part 1, chapter 4, paragraphs 58–59, page 13.

of his colleagues. Troplong started with a brief reflection on the relation-ship between property and democracy.

> While many institutions fall or grow old, property remains standing, seated on justice and made strong by the law. It is property that, along with the family, keeps society powerfully anchored on the mobile surface of democ-racy. And how is it that democracy, which consumes so fast men and things, gives property more energy, youth and solidity than ever?[395] ... If liberty is the foundation of property, equality makes property sacred. All men are equal, meaning, equally free, and everyone must recognize in each other this independent sovereignty .... Thus conceived, property is the most democratic of all institutions because it is based on the two essential elements of democracy: liberty and equality.[396]

Once again, as in Portalis, in Troplong's passage we can hear faint echoes of some of the more sophisticated Enlightenment discussions about the "society of equals."

Conclusions

The development of Romanist-bourgeois property in France is a well-known story and historians have copiously examined the many facets of this juristic project. One aspect, however, has been largely overlooked. The arguments that the drafters and some of the more sophisticated nineteenth-century jurists deployed to justify modern *dominium* were more diverse and richer than often assumed. This diversity proved critical to the success of the project. The Exegetists' grandiloquent statements about an absolute *droit de propriété* could be easily dismissed as aberra-tions of a simplistic and extreme individualism and were soon forgotten. Demolombe, Marcadé, and Mouron would hardly have succeeded in making modern *dominium* such a pervasive and powerful legal and ideological construct. What made Romanist-bourgeois property so appealing and resilient were its diverse normative underpinnings. The more sophisticated among the jurists successfully marshalled an eclectic set of arguments – about natural law but also about sociability, interde-pendence, and political equality – in support of modern *dominium*. These arguments were rooted in earlier ideological traditions and proved immensely resilient, entrenching a simplistic and optimistic view of property.

---

[395] Raymond-Théodore Troplong, *De la Propriété d'Après le Code Civil* (Paris: Pagnerre, 1848), introduction, 1.
[396] Id., chapter 1, 12.

4

Reform, Not Revolution

Modernizing Property in Germany

While the foundations of modern Romanist *dominium* were outlined by Pothier and entrenched by the Napoleonic legislature, it was the German Roman law scholars who perfected the law of modern *dominium*, attempting to give it a coherent structure organized around one central idea: the owner's will. It is somehow paradoxical that what is arguably the most sophisticated conceptualization of modern, Romanist-bourgeois *dominium* was produced in Germany, known for its slow and difficult "separate path" to capitalism and bourgeois modernity.[397] The German professors' reconceptualization of property was obviously Romanist in its inspiration and sources. Whether it was also "bourgeois" is less obvious. If the notion of a self-conscious French capitalist bourgeoisie calling for a modern property law is simplistic and in need of qualifications, wholly inaccurate would be the idea of a liberal German bourgeoisie demanding a new set of property rules that would promote the development of capitalism. A small elite of reformers, inspired by English-style agricultural improvement, did exist in the German states in the late eighteenth and early nineteenth century.[398] However, their property reform ambitions were frustrated by a powerful feudal landowning aristocracy. When,

---

[397] Historians of Germany and Prussia emphasize the peculiarities of German development in regard to its separate path into modernity and capitalism, stressing that there was no bourgeois revolution leading to capitalism but rather a late revolution from above carried out by Bismarck in the 1860s. See Barrington Moore, *Social Origins of Dictatorship and Democracy: Lord and Peasant in the Making of the Modern World* (Boston: Beacon Press, 1966); Colin Mooers, *The Making of Bourgeois Europe: Absolutism, Revolution, and the Rise of Capitalism England, France and Germany* (London: Verso, 1991), 103–147; Ellen Meiksins Wood, *The Pristine Culture of Capitalism: A Historical Essay on Old Regimes and Modern States* (London: Verso, 1991), 26–27; Perry Anderson, *Lineages of the Absolutist State* (London: Verso, 1979), 236–237; Theda Skocpol, *States and Social Revolutions* (Cambridge: Cambridge University Press, 1979), 144–147.

[398] See above.

in the 1820s, this small cadre of agrarian reformers dispersed, the task of completing the abolition of feudalism and modernizing property law was taken up by the Roman law scholars. The Roman law professoriate had a number of comparative advantages over the reformist administrators and the divided and reluctant liberal intelligentsia. Professors had a strong and time-honored professional identity and the ability to disguise their political beliefs behind a sophisticated and ostensibly apolitical method of legal analysis. Secure in their position, Roman law scholars and historians of Rome joined forces to make emancipation and full ownership a reality for the German peasants. Animated by sincere scholarly devotion, and yet not shy to use Roman law and agrarian history to support their political agenda, historians of Rome built a powerful narrative equating the liberation of the German peasantry to the struggle of the dispossessed Roman free peasant described in the pages of Appian and Plutarch. Simultaneously, Roman law scholars outlined a new Romanist architecture for the law of property designed to enable and protect the full mastery of the owner's will over a physical thing. Over the course of this chapter, we will trace a progression from the overtly political and pragmatic attempts at reform by the Stein ministry, through the historical and conceptual legal work done by Barthold Georg Niebuhr and Friedrich Carl von Savigny to link the struggles of the Roman past to the pressing political and legal issues of their day to the abstract and often dogmatic fixations of the Pandectists; in this last stage, ideology and politics, although unacknowledged were no less present. We will also consider the interplay between, on the one hand, a supposed German uniqueness deriving in important ways from its mythologized past, and, on the other, contemporary cosmopolitan intellectual developments and international political and economic forces in influencing the course of this progression.

Optimism, Ambitions, and Enlightenment Ideas: The Stein-Hardenberg Reforms

Although not nearly as dramatic as the year 1789 in France, the reform year 1807–1808 in Prussia marked a similarly momentous turning point in the path toward modern property. The sensational events in France elicited strong emotions in Germany, running the gamut from the ecstatic joy of those who glimpsed the beginning of a new era of freedom and equality, to the utter terror of those who feared the violent destruction of a social and political order that had remained stable for centuries.[399] The revolution stirred passions, but it also made Germans realize that the conditions that led to the outbreak of the Revolution in France could be observed in Germany as well.

The feudal landholding system was the cornerstone of society virtually throughout Germany. The status and financial position of peasants were defined by two criteria: their personal legal status and the rights of tenure they had on their land.[400] These two criteria were related in regularized (or standard combinations? Regularized seems unclear to me after re-reading) combinations, specified by customary law, that differed regionally. Free peasants were few in number and had the same freedom status as free commoners; their obligations were limited to the fees, dues, and services owed to the landlord as ground rent. By contrast, servile peasants accounted for the vast majority of the peasant population. Servile status was inherited, and serfs had an inherent personal tie to the landlord, were bound to the land, and were subject to a variety of obligations and services. By the eighteenth century, the harshest type of servile condition – called "servitude in thralldom" (*leibeigen*), in which the serf had no legal personality and belonged to the lord, who could sell or alienate him or her at any time – had virtually disappeared. As to land tenure forms, very few free peasants were full, independent owners; those who were lived mostly in the northwest. The vast majority of peasants held more limited rights, coupled with obligations, that could be described as forms of divided *dominium*. Among these various forms, the critical distinction was that between forms that granted the "inferior owner" the right to transfer the land and those that did not. Peasants in the first category could pass the land to their descendants or could sell or mortgage their rights over the land, either freely or with the consent of the lord. By contrast, peasants in the second category had limited use rights granted either for life or for a specified period for time. In the least favorable

---

[399] John G. Gagliardo, *From Pariah to Patriot: The Changing Image of the German Peasant* (Lexington: The University Press of Kentucky, 1969), 151; Marion W. Gray, *Prussia in Transition: Society and Politics under the Stein Reform Ministry of 1808* (Philadelphia: The American Philosophical Society, 1958), 1.

[400] On this topic, see Wilhelm Abel, *Geschichte der deutschen Landwirtschaft vom frühen Mittelalter bis zum 19. Jahrhundert* (Stuttgart: Eugen Ulmer, 1962); Heinrich Bechtel, *Wirtschaftsgeschichte Deutschlands* (München: Callwey, 1951–1956); Theodor von der Goltz, *Geschichte der deutschen Landwirtschaft* (Stuttgart: Cotta, 1902–1903); Georg Friedrich Knapp, *Die Bauernbefreiung und der Ursprung der Landarbeiter in den älteren Teilen Preußens* (Leipzig: Duncker & Humblot, 1887); Hans Mottek, *Wirtschaftsgeschichte Deutschlands: ein Grundriss* (Berlin: Deutscher Verlag der Wissenschaften, 1957).

tenure form, peasants were mere tenants at will, whose rights could be terminated at any time by the owner.

As in France, this feudal landholding system was the object of intense controversy in the German states and in Prussia by the late eighteenth century. It was fiercely defended by the landed aristocracy, who argued that the preservation of traditional society was preferable to violent revolutionary change as in France.[401] And it was vocally challenged by a class of liberal reformers committed to English-style progress. A small and variegated group, comprising practitioners of *Kameralwissenschaft* – the German science of state administration and political economy – as well as Physiocrats and Antiphysiocrats, the reformers sought to accelerate what they saw as an impending and preordained Europe-wide transition: the gradual collapse of feudalism and the movement toward agricultural improvement and the productive use of land. The reformers' specific policy prescriptions varied dramatically. They involved practical measures, such as crop rotation, the optimal partitioning of fields, and improvement in livestock breeding, as well as a reform of property law that would abolish feudal bondage and compulsory labor and expand peasant ownership.[402]

For a brief time, growing frenzy about peasant uprisings made the reformers' ideas attractive to the landowning class. The tension between the radicalized peasant movement and the more moderate revolutionary legislatures that propelled the transformation of the property system in France did not materialize in the German states and Prussia. Yet, in the aftermath of the Revolution in France, agrarian unrest did escalate in some of the German states, and German peasants appeared to be fairly well informed about the events in France through peasant newspapers and pamphlets. Peasant uprisings were neither as numerous nor as severe as the landowners feared and, yet, were sufficient to convince those who opposed reform that some kind of change was necessary.[403] The

---

[401] Martin Kitchen, *The Political Economy of Germany 1815–1914* (Montreal: McGill-Queen's University Press, 1978), 9. See also G. P. Gooch, *Germany and the French Revolution* (London: Longmans, Green, and Co., 1920).

[402] On the various strands of agrarian reform proposals, see Jürgen Georg Backhaus, *Physiocracy, Antiphysiocracy and Pfeiffer* (New York: Springer-Verlag, 2011); Marten Seppel and Keith Tribe, *Cameralism in Practice: State Administration and Economy in Early Modern Europe* (Woodbridge: Boydell Press, 2017); David F. Lindenfeld, *The Practical Imagination: The German Sciences of State in the Nineteenth Century* (Chicago: University of Chicago Press, 1997).

[403] Gagliardo, *From Pariah to Patriot*, 152.

admonition of the Leipzig philosopher and translator Christian August Wichmann (1735–1807) resonated even with the skeptics:

> The French Revolution has awakened a love of freedom; it is getting stronger as the bloody combat of the French nation in asserting its independence from arbitrary rules by foreign powers continues. Once this nation, which has come to be well-respected, achieves this goal, it will encourage alienated and oppressed classes in other countries to rise against these unnatural, arbitrarily imposed laws.[404]

> The smallest spark … is sufficient to excite a rebellion and to kindle a fiery conflagration, which thereafter will not otherwise be extinguished than with the blood of thousands.[405]

> An important observation for the landlords that have hitherto had their goods produced through forced labor is that there is cause for concern if they continue to insist on these abhorrent services and refuse to react to the ongoing changes.[406]

Along with peasant unrest, a military and political catastrophe also contributed to accelerating and strengthening the spread of reformist ideas, infusing them with patriotic meaning. Prussia's shattering defeat in the war of 1806–1807 against the Napoleonic army helped reform-minded officials present their ambitious agenda as a patriotic effort to remake society anew.[407] Further, on the ground, social and economic change was already happening within the interstices of the feudal property system. While Prussia remained largely unaffected by the proto-industrialization that transformed other parts of Europe, it was not immune to the lager European trend toward the commercialization of agriculture. At end of the eighteenth century, with the increase in foreign demand for grain, the great farms of East Elbia became major export centers. Most landowners sought to expand their profit by using the levers offered by feudal property. For example, they converted the peasants' dues into money or services and they shortened tenure terms, thereby intensifying their exploitation of servile peasants. However, some landlords deviated from this pattern, realizing that a rigid social order based on hereditary servile status and long-term tenure was incompatible

---

[404] Christian August Wichmann, *Über die natürlichsten Mittel die Frohn-Dienste bey Kammer- und Ritter-Güthern ohne Nachtheil der Grundherren aufzuheben*, 1st ed. (Leipzig: J. G. I. Breitkopf, Sohn und Comp, 1795), 3–4.
[405] Id., 276.
[406] Id., 280–281.
[407] Gray, *Prussia in Transition*, 44.

with the imperatives of a market economy. In particular, the burden of having to support servile peasants, regardless of whether the yield was good or poor, convinced many landlords to free their peasants and to employ them as wage laborers instead.[408]

While these transformations had started weakening many aspects of the feudal property system, a concerted effort to anchor the foundations of a modern economy in private property and a free land market only came with the Stein-Hardenberg reform period of 1807–1821. While the Stein-Hardenberg reforms applied only to Prussia, most other German states followed suit during, or shortly after, this period. The hero of the reformist circle, Baron Karl vom Stein (1757–1831), was summoned by King Frederick William III to head a ministry established to make Prussia as strong as France.[409] Stein was a divisive figure. He will be long eulogized in German conservative-liberal historiography as a man of the Enlightenment, a cosmopolitan who embodied the values that we have seen were central to the vision of a "society of equals" in France: political equality, personal autonomy and self-government, economic individualism, and social mobility.[410] However, others painted a much less flattering portrait of Stein.[411] For instance, Colonel Henry Aimé Ouvry

---

[408] For an assessment of the practical consequences of the commercialization of agriculture for the peasants, see Hermann Mauer, *Das landschaftliche Kreditwesen Preußens agrargeschichtlich und volkwirtschaftlich betrachtet: Ein Beitrag zur Geschichte der Bodenkreditpolitik des Preußischen Staates* (Straßburg: Verlag von Karl F. Trübner, 1907).

[409] Gerhard Ritter, *Stein: Eine politische Biographie*, 3rd ed. (Stuttgart: Deutsche Verlagsanstalt, 1958).

[410] Günther Ipsen, "Staat aus dem Volk: Scheitern, Wollen, Vollbringen des Freiherrn vom Stein in der Preußischen Reform" (1973) 12(2) *Der Staat – Zeitschrift für Staatslehre* 157: "If there is one thing about Stein that accurately represents the inner nature of his era, it is his ingenious way of thinking …. His reforms laid the foundation for increased participation by ordinary citizens and peasants in public life."

[411] For negative views of Stein, see Eckart Kehr, "Zur Genesis der preußischen Bürokratie und des Rechtsstaats," in Hans Ulrich Wehler (ed.), *Der Primat der Innenpolitik: Gesammelte Aufsätze zur Preussisch-Deutschen Sozialgeschichte im 19. und 20. Jahrhundert (Veröffentlichungen der Historischen Kommission zu Berlin)*, vol. 19, no. 10 (Berlin: Walter de Gruyter & Co, 1965), 31–52; Karl Obermann, "Bemerkungen über die soziale und nationale Bedeutung der preußischen Reformbewegung unter dem Ministerium des Freiherrn vom Stein," in Hans Joachim Bartmuss et al. (eds.), *Die Volksmassen: Gestalter der Geschichte – Festgabe für Leo Stern* (Berlin: Rütten & Loening, 1962); Hans Rosenberg, *Bureacracy, Aristocracy and Autocracy: The Prussian Experience 1660-1815* (Boston: Beacon Press, 1968); Reinhart Koselleck, "Preußen zwischen Reform und Revolution: Allgemeines Landrecht, Verwaltung und soziale Bewegung von 1791 bis 1848," in *Industrielle Welt: Schriftenreihe des Arbeitskreises für moderne Sozialgeschichte,*

(1813–1899), who became a writer with an interest in agrarian policy and a member of the London-based Cobden Club of believers in free trade, viewed Stein as a conservative aristocrat "whose ideas of freedom did not square with the enthusiastic theories of Rousseau and still less with those of Voltaire" and whose political and private views clashed with any "philosophic and impracticable ideas of equality and fraternity as well as with the French scheme of the universal rights of man."[412] Stein, Ouvry concluded, was, first and foremost, interested in reestablishing German independence and, had 130-148the Prussians been victorious in their wars with the French, "most certainly we never should have heard of the Stein reforms."[413]

For a little over a decade, Stein's reformers enjoyed the support of the Prussian state. However, despite their aspiration to English-style agricultural progress, the Prussian state administrators did not seek to reshape the social relations of production along the lines of English agrarian capitalism. Frederick William and his administrators did not envision a wholly new socioeconomic system in which capitalist landowners competed to maximize profit by improving the productivity of property-less wage laborers. Rather, their interest in agrarian reform sprang from an essentially anti-capitalist interest: increasing peasant productivity, and in turn peasant taxation, to enhance the revenue of the Prussian absolutist state.[414]

Stein's reformers supported their proposals to abolish feudalism and establish full private property and a free market in land with a variety of arguments drawn from political economy and the agrarian sciences but also from moral and philosophical thought. Economic arguments about the critical importance of property reform for agricultural improvement had been circulating in Physiocratic and Cameralist circles since the mid-eighteenth century. As were their French counterparts, the relatively small group of German Physiocrats was philosophically committed to the idea that agriculture is the ultimate source of wealth, as well as to a

vol. 7 (Stuttgart: Ernst Klett Verlag, 1967), 56–70 and 206–210; Hanna Schissler, "Preußische Agrargesellschaft im Wandel – Wirtschaftliche, gesellschaftliche und politische Transformationsprozesse von 1763-1847," in *Kritische Studien zur Geschichtswissenschaft*, no. 33 (Göttingen: Vandenhoek und Ruprecht, 1978), 130–148.

[412] Henry Aimé Ouvry, *Stein and His Reformers in Prussia, with Reference to the Land Question in England: And an Appendix Containing the Views of Richard Cobden and J. S. Mill's Advice to Land Reformers* (London: Kerby and Endean, 1873), 11.

[413] Id., iv.

[414] Colin Mooers, *The Making of Bourgeois Europe*, 124.

robust notion of private property. While their ideas derived almost entirely from the works of the great French masters of Physiocracy, it was in Germany, and not in France, that the only attempt to fully implement Physiocratic orthodoxy was made. The Margrave Karl Friedrich of Baden engaged in a lengthy and detailed correspondence with Mirabeau and the French Physiocrats on how best to apply their policy prescriptions and actually implemented the *impot unique* and other measures in small sections of Baden.[415] The essential nexus between agriculture and property was also central to the agenda of the practitioners of Cameralism. Contrary to the Physiocrats, the strong focus on agriculture in the Cameralists' agenda was not based on any conviction that agriculture is the only source of real wealth – the Cameralists sought to increase productivity wherever possible, in agriculture, manufacturing, and commerce – but rather on a realistic assessment that, at the time, agriculture was the greatest source of wealth in the German states. For Johann Heinrich Gottlob von Justi (1717–1771), the most influential Cameralist of the eighteenth century, free and secure ownership and trade were key to the prosperity of the state:

> The freedom of a ruler's subjects is absolutely imperative for their happiness. Freedom, secure property and flourishing trades – so that each and every person is rewarded for their diligence with life's conveniences; these are the three primary reasons upon which the happiness of a nation and its subjects depends . . . . Where all three powers of state fall into the hands of one individual there is no real freedom; the subjects are dependent upon the stubbornness and arbitrariness of that very power. Freedom truly exists where a subject can do anything that the laws, in accordance with the overall welfare of the state, permit without worrying about displeasing someone or risking persecution and oppression.[416]

---

[415] David E. Lindenfeld, *The Practical Imagination: The German Sciences of the State in the Nineteenth Century* (Chicago: The University of Chicago Press, 1997), 26–28; Sophus A. Reinert, "Another Grand Tour: Cameralism and Antiphysiocracy in Baden, Tuscany and Denmark-Norway," in Jurgen Backhaus (ed.), *Physiocracy, Antiphysiocracy and Pfeiffer: The European Heritage in Economics and the Social Sciences* (New York: Springer, 2011), 39; Marten Seppel, "Cameralism in Practice," in Marten Seppel and Keith Tribe (eds.), *Cameralism in Practice. State Administration and Economy in Early Modern Europe* (Woodbridge: The Boydell Press, 2017), 4–8; Liana Vardi, *The Physiocrats and the World of the Enlightenment* (Cambridge: Cambridge University Press, 2012).

[416] Johann Heinrich Gottlob von Justi, *Staatswirtschaft*, 2nd ed., vol. 1 (Leipzig: B. C. Breitkopf, 1758), part 1, book, 1 section 32, page 66.

Along with these familiar economic arguments, the reformist discourse of vom Stein's circle also relied on a new vocabulary of freedom and equality that was being forged in cities like Königsberg, Kant's hometown, which was the main center of the German Enlightenment and a thriving harbor for the export of grain. In this new vocabulary, freedom took up a new meaning. In early modern Prussia, freedom was a term used to refer to a privileged status granted by an authority or purchased by its beneficiaries, for example, the right of a guild to engage in trade or the right of a village to elect its elders. By the late eighteenth century, philosophers and jurists reconceptualized freedom as a universal right independent from constraint by another's choice, a right granted to humanity as a matter of natural law.[417] This new notion of freedom was, obviously, typified by Kant's philosophy, but it was directly brought to bear on the question of property reform and integrated with economic arguments in the work of Christian Jacob Kraus, a lesser-known colleague of Kant, who taught cameralism at the university of Königsberg. An avid reader of Adam Smith, Kraus wrote a small pamphlet arguing for the abolition of serfdom that weaved together Kantian freedom, cameralism's commitment to enhancing agricultural productivity, and Smithian political economy.

> Laws against these sufferings cannot help the serf. To whom shall he appeal? To a patrimonial court presided by his lord? To a government court two or more days of journey away? Nothing can help him but the right to be master of his own affairs.[418]

The most significant expression of the reformers' aspiration to universal freedom and property was the Edict of October 9, 1807. Titled "Edict Regarding Facilitated Ownership and Free Use of Real Estate and

---

[417] Jürgen Schlumbohm, "Freiheit: Die Anfänge der bürgerlichen Emanzipationsbewegung in Deutschland im Spiegel ihres Leitwortes," in Géza Alföldy and Winfried Schulz (eds.), *Geschichte und Gesellschaft: Bochumer Historische Studien*, vol. 12 (Düsseldorf: Pädagogischer Verlag Schwann, 1975), 39; Werner Conze, "Nation und Gesellschaft: Zwei Grundbegriffe der revolutionären Epoche," in *Historische Zeitschrift*, vol. 198 (Oldenburg: Walter De Gruyter & Co, 1964), 1–43; Otto Dann, "Gleichheit und Gleichberechtigung," in Otto Brunner, Werner Conze, and Reinhart Koselleck, *Geschichtliche Grundbegriffe: Historisches Lexikon zur politisch-sozialen Sprache in Deutschland*, vol. 2 (Stuttgart: Klett-Cotta, 1972), 1006–1026.

[418] Christian Jacob Kraus, "Gutachten über die Aufhebung der Privatuntertänigkeit in Ost- und Westpreußen (1802)," in Werner Conze (ed.), *Quellen zur Geschichte der deutschen Bauernbefreiung* (Göttingen: Musterschmidt, 1957), 75.

Personal Conditions of the Rural Populace," it sought to dismantle feudal servitude and establish a free market in land through a number of core provisions.[419] The edict declared that all servitude was abolished and eliminated the existing class restrictions on land ownership, thereby fulfilling the promise of a free real-estate market in which land would be available for purchase to anyone who could make it profitable, regardless of class or status. The edict also abolished the entail, which prevented the alienation of aristocratic lands from family possessions and granted "free choice of profession" to all. The potential combined effect of these measures was far-reaching: the transformation of the rigidly hierarchical Prussian society into a mobile market society where only resources and talent established a person's place in society. Nobles would be allowed to enter a middle-class profession without detriment to their status and able to freely sell their family lands or purchase peasant farms or properties within urban municipal borders; similarly, middle-class urban citizens with capital to invest would gain the ability to purchase agricultural, noble, or peasant lands.

However, the path from formal servile emancipation to actual peasant ownership proved difficult. The balance of power between the landed nobility and the liberal reformist forces was quite different than in France. The German landed aristocracy exerted greater power than its French counterpart, and the revolutionary bourgeoisie of professionals and officeholders that proved critical to the property revolution in France hardly emerged in Germany. A liberal *Mittelstand* of university-trained bureaucrats and professionals committed to change did exist.[420] However, its strength, as well as its reform proposals and strategies varied significantly by region.[421] Overall, this liberal middle class was timid, uneasy about rebellion, and reluctant to pose a clear alternative to absolutist rule.[422] From the moment of his appointment, Stein had faced strong opposition from the landowning aristocracy who feared that the agrarian reforms would jeopardize their established prerogatives. In November 1808, following a vicious conspiracy that also involved some

---

[419] *Edict den erleichterten Besitz und den freien Gebrauch des Grundeigentums so wie die persönlichen Verhältnisse der Land-Bewohner betreffend* (Memel: Königreich Preußen, 1807).

[420] James Sheehan, *German Liberalism in the Nineteenth Century* (Chicago: University of Chicago Press, 1979), 19.

[421] Id., 25.

[422] Id., 43.

of his closest collaborators, Stein formally resigned.[423] In his *Politisches Testament*, drafted after his resignation, Stein played up his legacy, emphasizing the scope of reforms already completed:

> The last remains of slavery, hereditary serfdom is abolished, and the will of free people, that unshakable pillar of every throne, has been established. The unlimited right to acquire property is proclaimed. The privilege of determining one's own vocation has been returned to the people.[424]

Stein invited his successors to carry on with the interrupted reforms, but the following administrations lacked the enthusiasm and sense of urgency of the Stein ministry. The reformist discourse faded and would not be heard again in official circles until the revolutions of 1848. More generally, the reformist and cosmopolitan ideas of the Stein circle gradually fell into oblivion and soon seemed at odds with the changed ideological and political landscape that privileged Romantic, nationalist, and conservative-liberal ideas. Practically, the legislative effort to abolish feudalism and establish a new property system had slow and marginal impact in Prussia and in virtually all the German states. Historians' assessments of the Hardenberg-Stein reformers vary dramatically, with some seeing the reformers as manipulators of peasants in a larger struggle between aristocratic and bourgeois elites and others casting them as self-deluded optimists who believed they could remake society anew.[425] Regardless of whether one sees the reformers as motivated by a selfish class interest or by a naïve idealism, the great wave of Prussian

---

[423] Marion W. Gray, *Prussia in Transition: Society and Politics under the Stein Reform Ministry of 1808* (Philadelphia: The Society, 1986), 9; Richard C. Raack, *The Fall of Stein* (Cambridge, MA: Harvard University Press, 1965); Walter M. Simon, *The Failure of the Prussian Reform Movement 1807–1919* (Ithaca, NY: Cornell University Press, 1955).

[424] Quoted in Gray, *Prussia in Transition*, 150.

[425] Positive assessments present Stein as an alternative to Prussian traditions of militarism and authoritarianism who, with fewer obstacles, might have successfully transformed an authoritarian state into a modern republic. The reform era was characterized by noble enthusiasm. Gerhard Ritter, *Stein: Eine politische Biographie*, 3rd ed. (Stuttgart: Deutsche Verlagsanstalt, 1958); Golo Mann, *Deutsche Geschichte des 19. und 20. Jahrhunderts* (Frankfurt a.M.: Fischer, 1969). Historians who view Stein in the context of larger socioeconomic process and changing conditions of the rural masses in Prussia see him as a manipulator of masses rather than crusader for progress. Georg Friedrich Knapp, *Die Bauernbefreiung und der Ursprung der Landarbeiter in den älteren Teilen Preußens* (Leipzig: Duncker & Humblot, 1887); Walter Schmidt, "Marx und Engels über den historischen Platz der preußischen Reformen," in *Preußische Reformen – Wirkungen und Grenzen. Aus Anlass des 150. Todestages des Freiherrn vom und zum Stein* (Berlin: Akademie-Verlag, 1982), 54–74. Still others saw the Stein reforms as part of the oppressive bureaucratization and officialism of the early nineteenth century. They

land reforms failed to produce a prosperous peasantry, as Frederick's administrators had hoped.[426] Rather, it strengthened the aristocracy and generated a dislocated rural proletariat. Lack of credit, the limited size of parcels, the loss of the forms of support previously provided by the lord, and the unavailability of the resources offered by common lands in the wake of the enclosures forced many newly created peasant-owners to sell their land to the owners of large estates.

The Romanists Take up the Task of Modernizing Property Law

As the reformist spirit of Baron vom Stein's circle started waning, the task of sweeping away feudal *dominium divisum* and shaping a new law of property was taken up by the Roman law professors. A number of factors made the Romanists the actors best positioned to continue the work of Frederick's legislators. To begin with, some of the Romanists had important ideological and political affinities with the reformers. In the early stages of their careers, two of the scholars who would be most actively engaged in the effort to shape a modern Romanist law of property, Barthold Georg Niebuhr (1776–1831) and Friedrich Carl von Savigny (1779–1861), had been members of Stein's reform party. Savigny and Niebuhr were moderate conservatives and espoused the reformers' commitment to building a framework of property concepts that would transform semi-feudal Prussia into an ethical community of free citizens and full owners capable of resisting foreign powers, while avoiding the excesses of a radical, liberal property revolution as in France.[427] While they broadly shared a number of the reformers' beliefs, the Roman law professors had greater pull as agents of property modernization than the partisan politicians who made up the state legislature. The Romanists were perceived as a venerable and independent group of scientists who, over time, had perfected a set of ancient and apolitical legal tools capable

emphasized administrative reorganization at the expense of social change. Reinhart Koselleck, "Preußen zwischen Reform und Revolution: Allgemeines Landrecht, Verwaltung und soziale Bewegung von 1791 bis 1848," in *Industrielle Welt: Schriftenreihe des Arbeitskreises für moderne Sozialgeschichte*, vol. 7 (Stuttgart: Ernst Klett Verlag, 1967), 206–210; Hanna Schissler, "Preußische Agrargesellschaft im Wandel – Wirtschaftliche, gesellschaftliche und politische Transformationsprozesse von 1763–1847," in *Kritische Studien zur Geschichtswissenschaft*, number 33 (Göttingen: Vandenhoek und Ruprecht, 1978), 130–135.

[426] Gray, *Prussia in Transition*, 152.

[427] James Q. Whitman, *The Legacy of Roman Law in the German Romantic Era: Historical Vision and Legal Change* (Princeton, NJ: Princeton University Press, 1990), 165.

of effectively protecting individual freedoms against the state.[428] In the unique context of early nineteenth-century Germany, each of these elements mattered.

The jurists' ability to present themselves as neutral scientists has always proven key to the group's ambitions, from Rome to today. But, in the Germany of the early 1800s, the claim to disinterested scientific competence resonated with particular force for a number of reasons. To begin with, the anxiety about politics interfering with private law was growing. In the many states that made up Germany, as the old social order of competing estates started to crumble and the state asserted its authority, public law grew in scope and significance.[429] This massive expansion of public law prompted jurists to draw attention to the importance of private law as the bulwark to protect individual freedoms, in particular economic freedoms, against politics and the state. As the century progressed and the revolution of 1848 loomed large, political meddling in matters of private law, and property law more specifically, appeared increasingly suspicious.[430] In response, the Roman law professors promised to develop a private law untainted by politics. Constitutional and legislative protections of individual private rights appeared to be "political," in the sense that they were either the product of political bargaining or the monarch's concession, and, as such, vulnerable to being taken back by royal autocracy or undermined by revolutionary upheavals. By contrast, the professors' Roman law–based property concepts could be easily cast as a body of long-lived scientific concepts devoid of political content and hence immune from political attacks.

Not only did the Romanists offer a technical private law, ostensibly without politics, they also promised a unitary national body of private law without a state. At a time in which German nationalism was at its height but Germany was fragmented and the prospect of political unification seemed remote, this was an appealing promise. A cohesive and nation-wide professional group, the Romanists had the actual ability to shape a body of property law that would apply nationally and to do so without the support of the state.[431] Further, the Roman law scientists

---

[428] Id., ix, 92–120.
[429] Hans-Peter Haferkamp, "The Science of Private Law and the State in Nineteenth Century Germany" (2208) 6(3) *The American Journal of Comparative Law* 676–677.
[430] Id., 676.
[431] Id., 673, 676. For a window onto this question in an earlier period, see Charles Donahue, "Private Law Without the State and During its Formation" (2008) 56(3) *The American Journal of Comparative Law* 541–566.

promised to solve an epistemological problem: the need to develop a new type of legal science after the demise of the old legal science rooted in natural law ideas.[432] Kant's critical philosophy had exposed the weakness of the natural law approach dominant throughout the seventeenth and eighteenth centuries. The seminal idea of a timeless set of rationally organized natural law principles, Kant had shown, in fact uncritically mixed ethics and law, positive law and natural law, observation and speculation. Since each of these elements involved different thought processes, mixing them resulted in a fundamental confusion and lack of rigor. The Romanists of the early nineteenth century promised to replace this un-rigorous natural law approach with a rigorous science of positive law.[433] Finally, in a German society with a tradition of long-lived professional corporate institutions, the Romanists' venerable professional identity gave them a unique legitimacy. The Romanists had earned this professional aura because, at critical moments of political strife in German history – from the violent political and religious conflicts of the late Middle Ages to the conflict between Joseph II and the League of Princes in the late eighteenth century – they had come forward as the protectors of freedom and peace and the opponents of princely absolutism.[434]

Yet, despite their credentials and professional power, the Romanists' effort to reshape the law of property in the image of Roman property faced a nontrivial challenge. In a Germany now permeated with Romantic culture, Roman law seemed a foreign element, at odds with the Romantic emphasis on the German nation and its cultural traditions. Herder's philosophy of history, which rested on the idea of cultural nationalism, had set the tone for any discussion of social and cultural change. Herder argued that the development of a national culture on native foundations was not only desirable but necessary. For Herder, the most natural state was one nation with one national character, which is the product of the family features, the climate, the ways of life, and the education of a people.[435] In other words, romantic nationalism praised all things that were a manifestation of Germanic culture, either historical

---

[432] Mathias Reimann, "Nineteenth Century German Legal Science" (1990) 31(4) *Boston College Law Review* 843.
[433] Id., 844.
[434] Whitman, *The Legacy of Roman Law in the German Romantic Era*.
[435] Walter Schmidt, "Marx und Engels über den historischen Platz der preußischen Reformen," in *Preußische Reformen – Wirkungen und Grenzen. Aus Anlass des 150. Todestages des Freiherrn vom und zum Stein* (Berlin: Akademie-Verlag, 1982), 410.

or contemporary. This celebration of a uniquely Germanic tradition extended to law, with successive generations of "Germanist" scholars, from Karl Friedrich Eichorn (1781–1854) to Otto von Gierke (1841–1921) to Georg Beseler (1809–1888), praising an ancient customary Germanic law that was wholly particularistic, that is, developed within narrow legal spheres that were partly geographical, partly personal or social, and based on practical common sense.[436] If contrasted with this Germanic legal heritage, Roman law, despite the long tradition of the study of the classics in Germany, seemed an abstract legal framework produced by a distant and foreign civilization.[437] Also, to the extent that Romanticism favored a new love for classicism, it was a love of Greece rather than of Rome. Johan Joachim Winckelmann, one of the founders of modern scientific archaeology, was probably the most influential name in the neoclassical movement that sought to revive Greek antiquity. The longing for classical Greece was such a significant element of the cultural landscape of Romantic Germany that some scholars have provocatively alluded to "the tyranny of Greece over Germany."[438] Further, Roman law seemed particularly unsuitable in matters of property where the idea of a uniquely Germanic customary law fundamentally at odds with Roman law was deeply entrenched. For the "Germanists," the figment of a supposedly Roman absolute *dominium* that cosmopolitan liberals were promoting throughout Europe was fundamentally at odds with a Germanic law of ownership "that always recognized the superior claims of society and abstained from exaggerating the rights of individuals."[439]

It was Savigny, probably the most celebrated German jurist of the nineteenth century, who found the key to reconciling Roman law and the German nation. The dilemma that Savigny and the Romanists faced has been vividly described by the German historian Hermann Kantorowicz: could Savigny and his fellow Romanists be expected to sacrifice their beloved *Corpus Juris Civilis* to nationalist and patriotic doctrines? Obviously not. In his 1814 pamphlet *Vom Beruf unserer Zeit für Gesetzgebung und Rechtswissenschaft (On the Vocation of Our Age for*

---

[436] Paul Vinogradoff, "Introduction," in Rudolf Huebner, *A History of Germanic Private Law* (Francis S. Philbrick, trans.) (Boston: Little, Brown & Company, 1918), xxvii.

[437] Id., 412; Hermann Kantorowicz, *Was ist uns Savigny?* (Berlin: C. Heymanns Verlag, 1912), 338.

[438] Eliza Mariab Butler, *The Tyranny of Greece Over Germany: A Study of the Influence Exercised by Greek Art and Poetry over the Great Writers of the Eighteenth, Nineteenth and Twentieth Centuries* (Cambridge: Cambridge University Press, 1935).

[439] Vongradoff, "Introduction," xxxiv.

Legislation and Jurisprudence), Savigny concocted what Kantorowicz, with veiled criticism, dubbed a "fantastic doctrine."[440] In the early stages of the life of a people, Savigny argued, law develops organically from the consciousness of the people, as language and custom do. In this early stage, law does not consist of abstract rules but rather of intuitions of the principles governing human relations, expressed in symbolic acts and rituals. However, as civilization progresses and knowledge specializes, professional jurists, acting as the representatives of the people, organize this early organic customary national law into a scientific "system" of concepts and doctrines.[441] Savigny applied this theory to justify the use of Roman law in Germany. As the first great historian of medieval Roman law, Savigny argued that Roman law had never truly disappeared, even with the fall of the Roman Empire, but rather it had continued to be used and developed in the actual life of Germany throughout the Middle Ages.[442] Thereby, this Roman law, produced and reproduced in the life of medieval Germany, could be said to be the product of the consciousness of the German people and was now to be systematically ordered by the jurists to reveal its formal, abstract, and universal structure.

Savigny's "fantastic" theory of the life of Roman law in Germany, Kantorowicz suggested, was an act of love for Roman law and, Kantorowicz concluded (quoting Maitland), all is fair in love.[443] Yet not everyone was convinced and, decades later, in the preface to his monumental *System des heutigen Römischen Rechts*, Savigny felt the need to address his critics who feared that Roman law, a foreign law of the past, would overwhelm German law:

> It has often been asserted by opponents that the members of the historical school ... would subject the present to the government of the past and in particular would improperly extend the dominion of the Roman law in opposition partly to the German law, partly to the new legal culture which, by means of science and practice, has stepped into the place of

---

[440] Kantorowicz, *Was ist uns Savigny?*, 338.

[441] Friedrich Carl von Savigny, *Vom Beruf unsrer Zeit für Gesetzgebung und Rechtswissenschaft* (Heidelberg: Mohr und Zimmer, 1814); for an English translation, see Friedrich Carl von Savigny, *Of the Vocation of our Age for Legislation and Jurisprudence* (Abraham Hayward, trans.), 2nd ed. (London: Littlewood & Co, 1831).

[442] Friedrich Carl von Savigny, *Geschichte des römischen Rechts im Mittelalter*, vol. 1 (Heidelberg: Mohr und Zimmer, 1826); for an English translation, see Friedrich Carl von Savigny, *The History of the Roman Law During the Middle Ages* (Elias Cathcart, trans.), vol. 1 (London: Adam Black, 1829).

[443] Kantorowicz, *Was ist uns Savigny?*, 338.

the pure Roman law. This reproach ... ought not to be passed over in silence. The historical view of legal science is completely mistaken and disfigured when it is frequently so conceived.[444]

Savigny's rebuttal reads as firm. The Romanists' work of conceptual recreation and systematization will not assign Roman law "an improper mastery over us." Rather, the Romanists will produce a new, authentically German and yet methodologically Romanist law of property. In Savigny's words:

> We will not possess merely a weak imitation of Roman culture but our own completely individual and new culture. We will have gained something greater than a more rapid and effective judicial practice. The condition of clear, perceptual self-possession which is characteristic of the law of youthful peoples will be united with the heights of scientific culture.[445]

By salvaging Roman law from the attacks of its critics through his "fantastic" theory, Savigny paved the way for an ambitious retrieval and reinvention of Roman property. The new, uniquely German law of property was to be Romanist down to its very core. It relied on Roman concepts; it was conceptually organized through a systematic methodology inspired by the legal science of the Roman jurists; and it was fueled and justified by an ideological re-interpretation of Roman agrarian history. It is to this complex and creative legal and cultural operation that we will now turn.

The Free Roman Peasantry and the *freie Bauerngemeinde*

When the Roman law professors took up the task of completing the abolition of feudalism and liberating the German peasant, left unfinished by the Stein-Hardenberg ministries, the reformist enthusiasm of the years 1807–1808 had somehow vanished, as had the arguments and the rhetorical strategies that had supported the reform agenda. Along with the economic and moral arguments we have seen, a powerful rhetorical tool of the reformist effort of the beginning of the century had been the

---

[444] Friedrich Carl von Savigny, *System des heutigen römischen Rechts*, vol. 1 (Berlin: Veit, 1840), xi–xii. For the English translation, see Friedrich Carl von Savigny, *System of Modern Roman Law* (William Holloway, trans.), vol. 1 (Madras: J. Higginbotham, 1867), iv.

[445] Friedrich Carl von Savigny, *Vom Beruf unsrer Zeit für Gesetzgebung und Rechtswissenschaft* (Heidelberg: Mohr und Zimmer, 1814), 133–134.

gradual emergence of a new image of the German peasant.[446] In the decades of the reforms, in the public mind, the servile and dependent peasant of feudal Germany had been transformed into a free citizen and a patriotic, economically independent, and prosperous yeoman. To support their reinvention of Roman property, the Romanists appropriated the reformers' image of the German free peasant and gave it a new Romanist spin, connecting it to the similarly idealized persona of the Roman free and prosperous peasant.[447]

The scholar who brought his vast knowledge of Roman agrarian history to bear on the struggle for the liberation of the German feudal serfs was none other than Barthold Georg Niebuhr, whom we have already encountered as the youngest member of Stein's circle. Niebuhr, who would eventually become one of the most prominent modern historians of Rome, had started studying Roman agrarian history even before joining Baron vom Stein's party, when he was still a civil servant, the manager of the Danish State Bank. The liberation of the serfs was a central political question in both his native Denmark as well as in Germany, and Niebuhr developed his interest in Roman agrarian questions as he started reflecting, and preparing to act, on the contemporary Danish and German situations.[448] As did his fellow members of the Stein circle, Niebuhr believed that a free and moderately wealthy landowning peasantry was critical to the prosperity of the state and represented the best safeguard against foreign attacks.

Niebuhr approached Roman history with the devotion and rigor of a scholar but also the passion of a consummate politician. Like others in his generation, Niebuhr was not shy of using his immense knowledge of Roman history for the political causes that were dear to him.[449] As the historian and politician George Peabody Gooch put it, Niebuhr, like many historians of his time, was not interested in "just Roman history" but in the history of a "*freie Bauerngemeinde*."[450] More specifically, he was interested "in institutions, not in events, in social classes, not in

---

[446] Gagliardo, *From Pariah to Patriot*, x–xi.

[447] Zvi Yavetz, "Why Rome?: Zeitgeist and Ancient Historians in Early 19th Century Germany" (1976) 97 *American Journal of Philology* 289.

[448] Arnaldo Momigliano, "Niebuhr and the Agrarian Problems of Rome" (1982) 21(4) *History and Theory* 8.

[449] Yavetz, "Why Rome?," 284. Another towering figure in the study of Roman history who also devoted significant time to politics was Theodor Mommsen (1817–1903).

[450] George Peabody Gooch, *History and Historians in the Nineteenth Century* (London: Longman, Green and Co, 1913), 14. See also Yavetz, "Why Rome?," 285

individuals, in customs, not in lawgivers."[451] The early history of Rome fired Niebuhr's imagination because it offered a repertoire of usable tropes and institutions. That recent political events, from the scare of French Revolution, to the Prussian defeat against the Napoleonic army, to the agrarian question and the liberal movement that would lead to 1848, were very much present in Niebuhr's mind is clear from his private letters, in which he admits turning to Rome for hope and understanding:

> The evil time of Prussia's humiliation had some share in the production of my history. We could do little more than ardently hope for better days and prepare for them. I went back to a great nation to strengthen my mind and that of my hearers.[452]

The usable past that Niebuhr found in early Roman agrarian history was, first and foremost, the ethical model of the free and the virtuous plebeian. Niebuhr's sympathies were for the plebeians, the free peasants of early Rome.[453] The example of the mythical free Roman peasant could help reinforce the transformation of the German peasant from a pariah shut out of civilized society to a patriotic and productive citizen at the center of national life. Further, in Roman agrarian history, Niebuhr found a striking analogy between the social structure of early Rome, with its conflict between plebeians and patricians, and the social structure of contemporary Germany.[454] For Niebuhr, the struggle for freedom of the Roman peasant resembled that of the German feudal peasant. The situation of the German peasants in the east was one of gloomy servitude that, in the words of an observer of the time, made peasants "the hapless missing link between man and beast of burden."[455] In Niebuhr's mind, this servitude and the effort of the Junker landlords to put down the peasants echoed the narratives of Appian and Plutarch describing how the rich Roman patrician class accumulated vast estates, pushing the free, plebeian peasants off their lands and turning them into a landless proletarian. The history of the struggle between the plebeians and the patricians was appealing to Niebuhr also because it had a happy ending

---

[451] Yavetz, "Why Rome?," 285.
[452] Francis Lieber, *Reminiscences of an Intercourse with Mr. Niebuhr, the Historian During a Residence with Him in Rome, in the Years 1822 and 1823* (Philadelphia: Carey, Lea & Blanchard, 1835), 81.
[453] Momigliano, "Niebuhr and the Agrarian Problems of Rome," 8.
[454] Id., 14.
[455] Georg Friedrich Knapp, *Die Bauernbefreiung und der Ursprung der Landarbeiter in den älteren Teilen Preussens*, vol. I (Leipzig: Duncker & Humblot, 1887), 77.

that resonated with Niebuhr's own hopes. Niebuhr was no radical and was firmly committed to a landholding system based on full private ownership. What he hoped for, and worked for, was a peaceful reconciliation, whereby the aristocracy would recognize and coexist with a freed land-owning peasantry. In the Roman story of the plebeians and their final reconciliation with the patricians, Niebuhr saw a desirable example for contemporary Denmark and Prussia.[456]

However, when it came to developing a legal strategy to move Germany away from feudal serfdom and toward a land economy based on full private property, Roman agrarian history, at least in the dominant understanding of the time, was a double-edged sword. The problem was the infamous *lex agraria*. In the dominant historiographical narrative, the plight of the dispossessed Roman peasant finally ended with Tiberius Gracchus' *lex agraria*, which set a limit to individual landownership and assigned all the land in excess to the agrarian poor. In Niebuhr's time, the conventional understanding was that the Gracchan law applied not only to public lands but also to large privately owned estates and, hence, it was seen as a redistributive attack on private property. And, in fact, as we have seen, in late eighteenth and early nineteenth century, under the revolutionary impulse coming from France, there was much talk, among radical egalitarians all over Europe, of a modern *lex agraria* and of a modern Tiberius Gracchus. These calls, we saw, generated significant alarm and violent rebuttals even from moderate political voices. Hence Niebuhr was eager to keep the cause of peasant freedom and ownership neatly distinct from any proposal involving the redistribution of private property.

To successfully use Roman agrarian history in support of private property, Niebuhr set out to refute the "mad and detestable sense" given to the agrarian law by the French "gang of criminals" and to prove that the latter's idea that the *lex agraria* applied to private property was based on an erroneous reading of the historical sources.[457] Building on the work done by classical scholar Christian Gottlob Heyne (1729–1812), Niebuhr argued that the agrarian law applied exclusively to the occupants of public lands (*ager publicus*).[458] It was only the private assignees of parcels of public lands, not private proprietors, that saw their maximum

---

[456] Momigliano, "Niebuhr and the Agrarian Problems of Rome," 14.
[457] Id., 9.
[458] Heyne made this argument in a lecture given in Latin in 1793, under the title "*Leges agrariae pestiferae et execrabiles*," which was subsequently published in Christian

amount of land capped and the excess confiscated and redistributed. Proponents of the *lex agraria*, Niebuhr suggested, had failed to grasp the distinction between two modes of "owning" land that appeared similar, involving similar entitlements and powers but were in fact quite different: private *property* and private *possession* of public lands. The target of the Gracchan agrarian law were *possessors*, not *owners*. Niebuhr, who was primarily a historian even though he had a law degree, struggled throughout his career to understand the exact nature of private possession of public lands and recounted his struggle with vivid language:

> It is to Heyne's essay that I myself owe my conviction of this truth [that the *lex agraria* only applied to possessors of public lands] which I have firmly retained ever since I began my researches on Roman history: but at the same time this merely negative certainty threw my mind into as painful a state of perplexity as was ever experienced. This torment, of being utterly unable to conceive a proposition, the reverse of which I saw it absolutely necessary to reject – a feeling very nearly akin to the despair excited by vain efforts to fathom the mysteries of theology – grew as I advanced to manhood and engaged in public business; still, in intervals of leisure, turning my eyes toward my beloved field of antiquity, while with the ripening of experience I felt a more pressing desire to comprehend the ancient world no less distinctly than the present, more especially in those relations of civil life with which my professions rendered me conversant.[459]

The answer to Niebuhr's torment finally came from Savigny, whose *Das Recht des Besitzes* (*On the Law of Possession*) helped Niebuhr gain a firm grasp of the difference between possession and property. Title to public land was vested in the Roman state that informally transferred portions of it, not exceeding a certain size, to individual "possessors." The grant involved ample rights to use and transfer but the state could take the parcels back at any time. Further, the protection from interference or dispossession by others was limited to the relatively informal "possessory interdicts."[460] Because the use and transfer rights of possessors of public lands were broad and effectively resembled those of actual private

---

Gottlob Heyne, *Opuscula Academica Collecta*, vol. 4 (Göttingen: Dieterich, 1796), 350–373.

[459] Barthold Georg Niebuhr, *Römische Geschichte*, vol. 2, 2nd ed. (Berlin: 1836), 149–150. For the English translation, see Barthold Georg Niebuhr, *The History of Rome* (Julius Charles Hare and Connop Thirlwall, transs.), vol. 2 (Philadelphia: Thomas Wardle, 1835), 99.

[460] Id., 97–115.

owners, generations of lawyers, public intellectuals, and political agitators had been under the impression that the agrarian law applied to private property. With Niebuhr straightening the historical record, the Romanists could now shape the "system" of modern property law in the image of Roman property without having to worry about the *lex agraria*.

The Place of Property in the "System" of Private Law

The fundamental outline of the "system" of modern property law was laid out by Savigny. We have encountered Savigny in the small circle of active members of Baron vom Stein's reform party. However, Savigny's role in the history of modern property is much more consequential and complicated than that of a reformer. A member of the social, intellectual, and political elite of reactionary Prussia, Savigny quickly became the most prominent of the German jurists and was appointed by the king *rector magnificus* of the prestigious University of Berlin in 1812. Academic power soon translated in political power. In 1817, Savigny was nominated to the Staatsrat (State Council, an assembly that advised the Chancellor and his ministries on matters of legislation) and, in 1819, to the Obertribunals für die Rheinprovinzen (the court of appeals for the Rhine province). Savigny's career in public office reached its apex in 1842 when he was selected to head the Ministry for Legislation.[461] Savigny, whose personal interests aligned with the feudal nobility, had significant reservations about particular aspects of Stein's emancipatory edicts. Yet, he was convinced that emancipation was necessary and he believed in the need for a property law, which, in conformity with the post-Kantian idealist and Romantic traditions, would promote the essential freedom of the individual with regard to itself, the external world, and relations with other free individuals.[462]

Faithful to his two cardinal methodological commitments that we already saw neatly encapsulated in his 1814 pamphlet *Vom Beruf,* that is, historicism and systematic legal science, Savigny outlined a "system" of property concepts that was both empirically grounded – because its "materials" were drawn from the actual " living" reality of property relations in Germany – and logically organized to reveal an inner

---

[461] John Edward Toews, *Becoming Historical: Cultural Reformation and Public Memory in Early Nineteenth-Century Berlin* (Cambridge: Cambridge University Press, 2004), 139.
[462] Id., 152, 154.

conceptual and normative coherence. The idea that law is to be organized into a logical system and that legal analysis is a science was, as we know, a Roman one. Over the course of the sixteenth century, the idea that law is a science had gathered steam. The philosopher, polymath, and jurist Gottfried Wilhelm Leibniz (1646–1716) had emphasized the specific connection between law and geometry, presenting the natural law of reason as a body of law endowed with mathematical exactness, and the German jurist Christian von Wolff (1679–1754) had further popularized this ambition to scientific precision. Savigny combined these ideas with his commitment to empiricism. In the preface to his *System des heutigen römischen Rechts* (*System of the Modern Roman Law*), Savigny described the essence of his systematic method as the work of discovering the innate connections that give legal concepts their greater unity:

> I place the essence of the systematic method in the knowledge and exhibition of the innate connection or of the relationship, by which the single ideas and rules of law are attached to a greater unity. Such relationships are at first often hidden, and the discovery of them will then enrich our research. They are moreover very manifold and our view will become more complete in proportion as we succeed, as to an institution of law, in discovering and pursuing its relationships on various sides.[463]

For Savigny, the overarching principle that bound together, logically and normatively, the concepts and rules of property law was the commitment to enabling and protecting the will of the individual. Faithful to post-Kantian idealist and Romantic traditions, Savigny placed at the center of his property system the autonomous individual, capable of determination by self-imposed ethical commands.

To fully understand Savingy's reorganization of the law of property, we have to start from the place of property law in the larger private law "system." Property is one branch of the "system" of private law concepts and rules and, within this larger system, it belongs to what Savigny calls the law of "potentialities." Comprising both the law of property and the law of obligations, the law of "potentialities" derives its name from the fact that it forms "an extension of the individual power beyond its natural limits," enabling the individual's will to exert its mastery respectively over things (law of property) and over individual acts of extraneous persons (law of obligations). The function of the law of property (and of the law

---

[463] Friedrich Carl von Savigny, *System des heutigen römischen Rechts*, 8 vols. (Berlin: Veit, 1840–1849). For the translation, see Friedrich Carl von Savigny, *System of Modern Roman Law* (William Holloway, trans.), vol. 1 (Madras: J. Higginbotham, 1867), xix.

of obligations) Savigny repeatedly explains in his *System* is to govern and coordinate relations among individuals, which Savigny calls private "jural relations," by assigning to each individual will a "sphere" within which the will has absolute mastery.

> Man stands in the midst of the outer world, and the most important element, to him in this surrounding of him, is the contact with those who are like him by their nature and destination. If now in such contact free natures are to subsist beside one another mutually assisting, not hindering themselves, this is possible only through the recognition of an invisible boundary within which the existence and activity of each individual gains a secure, free space[464] .... From the stand-point now gained each single jural relation appears to us as a relation between person and person, determined by a rule of law. This determination by a rule of law consists in the assignment to the individual will of a province in which it is to rule independently of every foreign will.[465]

The image described in this passage, that of infinite, independent individual spheres of action that are marked by invisible boundaries and seamlessly coexist, would influence modern property discourse immensely.

Enabling the mastery of the individual was, for Savigny, the fundamental moral principle that informs the law of potentialities, but it was a minimalist principle, beyond which morality has no place in the law of potentialities. In Savigny's words:

> The law serves morality not by performing its bidding but by securing the free development of its power dwelling in each individual will[466] ....
> Property and obligations are only significant and valuable to us, as an artificial extension of our own personal faculties, as new organs artificially added to our nature in essence.[467]

For Savigny, the moral or immoral exercise of property entitlements was not a question for private law but rather for the individual's own conscience. Further, Savigny believed, the inequities resulting from individuals' absolute exercise of their wills are addressed through specific institutions of public law or taxation. To illustrate this point, Savigny contrasted the minimalist moral content of the law of potentialities with that of family law, the other branch of the private law "system," which, by contrast, has significant moral content.

---

[464] Id., 269.
[465] Id., 271.
[466] Id., 270.
[467] Id., 273.

To the assertion here made that potentiality's law does not, like family law, include in it a moral element, it might be objected that the moral law is to rule over every kind of human action and that therefore the relations of potentialities also must have a moral foundation. Of course they have such inasmuch as the rich man ought to regard his wealth as goods entrusted to his management; only this view remains completely foreign to the dispositions of law. The distinction therefore lies in the family-relation being only incompletely governed by the institutions of law so that a large part of it is abandoned exclusively to moral influences. On the contrary in the potentiality's relations the mastery of legal institutions is completely accomplished and that without reference to the moral or immoral exercise of a right. Hence the rich man can allow the poor one to perish either through the denial of assistance or the harsh exercise of the right of a creditor and the remedy admitted against this springs not from the ground of private, but from that of public law; it consists in the institutions for the relief of the poor to which of course the rich man can be compelled to contribute although perhaps his contribution is not immediately perceptible. It remains therefore true, in spite of this, that no moral constituent is ascribable to potentiality's law as an institution of private law, and through this assertion neither the absolute domination of the moral law is mistaken nor the nature of private law placed in a doubtful light.[468]

Having clarified that the law of property and the law of obligations serve the common function of enabling the will of the individual, Savigny then moved on to investigate the boundary between these two bodies of law. In Roman law, Savigny explained, the boundary between property and obligations appears to be neatly marked. In the law of property, the will exerts its mastery directly upon the thing itself while, in the law of obligations, the will exerts its power on the acts of another person. However, at closer inspection, Savigny recognized, the boundary between property and obligations is fuzzier than the Roman jurists made it seem and, rather than a clear break, we see a spectrum of forms. Absolute property, protected by the action of vindication, and the contract of hired service and mandate are the two opposite poles of the spectrum, the former falling squarely in the realm of property, the latter in the realm of obligations. Between these two poles lies a variety of hybrid forms that exhibit elements of property as well as of obligations.

At the first glance the relation to one another of the two divisions of potentiality's law stated, seems so immutably determined by their object

---

[468] Id., 301–302.

matter, that it must everywhere be found to be the same. On closer examination however a very free playroom for manifold determinations of the positive law of different nations is shown in this law .... So far as the settlement of boundaries is concerned, certain extreme points doubt-less present themselves in which the special nature of one or the other division is wholly unmistakable: thus rigid property with unlimited vin-dication on the one side, the contract of hired service and mandate on the other, but between these lies a natural approximation, indeed a gradual transition, in the fact that the most numerous and important obligations aim at acquiring by the acts of others a right over a thing or at least the use and enjoyment of such.[469]

While acknowledging that the line between property and obligations is fuzzy, Savigny was careful to avoid "aberrations" that would completely dissolve the distinction, such as the temptation to see all real rights simply as consequences of obligations or conversely to view obligations as modes of acquiring real rights. Rather, the most precise and safest way to characterize the distinction between property and obligations, Savigny maintained, is that, in property, the opponent is undetermined while, in the law of obligations, the opponent is determined. In other words, property rights are exercised against the world at large, while the rights arising from obligations are exercised only against a specific person.

To conclude, in his "system" of modern Roman private law, Savigny downplayed the fault line between the law of property and the law of obligations, emphasizing instead their common function of empowering the individual will. This system logically organized each of the many property forms and doctrines that constituted the actual fabric of prop-erty relations in Germany based on the role each played in empowering the individual to exercise their will over a resource.

The Internal Conceptual Organization of the Property System

The property forms that Savigny sought to logically organize under the overarching principle of enabling the owner's will were multifarious and incoherent. Some forms were Roman in origin, such as the usufruct and the different types of servitudes, but others were local, German forms of limited and divided *dominium* that did not fit easily into a property system system designed to glorify the will of *the* owner, as the . Faithful to his empirical and historicist approach, according to which law derives

---

[469] Id., 302–303.

from the entire lived past of a nation, Savigny did not gloss over this complexity but rather fully accounted for it. The key to Savigny's effort to organize all these disparate forms was the concept of *Besitz* (possession). Savingy defined possession capaciously, as "the mastery over things in point of fact" and organized all these different instances in which an individual actually controlled a thing under the category of either possession or quasi-possession.[470]

Possession occupied Savigny's mind since the very early days of his academic career. Written in less than seven months and published in 1803, *Das Recht des Besitzes* (*On the Law of Possession*) was Savigny's first publication and instantly made him a celebrity. It is in this first major work that Savigny's system of modern, Romanist property started taking shape.

Savigny defined possession as "the mastery over things in point of fact," based on the "state of consciousness of unlimited physical power" over the thing.[471] In other words, the possessor is someone who has full control of the thing with the intent of exercising such control. From this definition, he noted, it follows that property is the most perfect juridical instance of possession: "As law, it [possession] appears simply and completely in the shape of property or the unlimited and exclusive mastery of a person over a thing."[472]

More precisely, possession is the condition of *fact*, or the practical consequence, corresponding to the legal *right* to property (*das Recht auf Eingentum*). As Savigny explained:

> By the possession of a thing, we always conceive the condition in which not only one's own dealing with the thing is physically possible, but every other person's dealing with it is capable of being excluded …. For, as property consists in the legal power of dealing with a thing at will and of excluding everyone else from its enjoyment, the exercise of property takes place by means of possession which thus is the condition of fact, corresponding to property as the condition of law.[473]

However, possession, Savigny warned, was broader than the condition of fact, or the consequence that follows from property. Possession is a

---

[470] Id., 299.
[471] Friedrich Carl von Savigny, *Von Savigny's Treatise on Possession: Or, the Jus Possessionis of the Civil Law* (Erskine Perry, trans.), 6th ed. (London: S. Sweet, 1848), 170–171.
[472] Friedrich Carl von Savigny, *System of Modern Roman Law* (William Holloway, trans.), 299.
[473] Von Savigny, *Von Savigny's Treatise on Possession*, 2.

distinct category that only partially overlaps with property because Roman law protected possession independently of property. As Savigny explained:

> If this juridical relation of Possession [the fact corresponding to the right to property] were the only one, all that need be predicated of it in juridical terms might be comprehended in the following proposition: the owner has the right to possess; he also, whom the owner permits to possess, has the same right; no one else has this right. But the Roman Law defines the modes of acquiring and of losing Possession, as well as of property; it treats Possession, therefore, not merely as the consequence of a right but as the foundation of rights[474] . . . . Now the whole right of Possession consists in the protection against certain kinds of disturbance given to the mere exercise of the right, without any reference to the existence of the right itself.[475]

In other words, in Roman law, the very fact of possession gave the possessor rights, regardless of whether the possessor was also the owner by title. An individual who had full enjoyment of the thing, with both the intent to control the thing and the actual physical control, had the right to be protected against interferences or dispossession through the remedies called "possessory interdicts." But why would a system as rational and equitable as Roman law protect possession regardless of title? It could seem somehow unfair to protect the possessor who does not also have title. The reason why Roman law protected the mere *fact* of possession regardless of right, Savigny explained, was that dispossession or disturbances by means of force or violence were, in themselves, unlawful, a violation of the public order that the possessor should not have to suffer, regardless of whether the possessor has a right worthy of protection.[476]

> [The right to possessory interdicts] found themselves on *obligationes ex maleficio*[477] . . . . [In the case when the violence offered to the person disturbs or puts an end to possession a]n independent right is not . . . violated with the person, but some change is effected in the condition of the person to his prejudice; and if the injury, which consists in the violence against the person, is to be wholly effaced in all its consequences, this can only be effected by the restoration or protection of the status quo, to which the violence extended itself. This is the true ground of possessory suits.[478]

---

[474] Id., 3.
[475] Id., 391.
[476] James Gordley and Ugo Mattei, "Protecting Possession" (1996) 44(2) *The American Journal of Comparative Law*.
[477] Von Savigny, *Von Savigny's Treatise on Possession*, 21.
[478] Id., 28.

In sum, for Savigny, the possessor deserves protection, regardless of the right, because their situation is changed to their disadvantage through the use of force.

In his effort to systematically organize the law of property, Savigny stretched the concept of possession even further to include not only the actual exercise of property, with full control and intent, regardless of the right, but also the actual exercise of a more limited real right over a thing owned by another, such as in the case of *emphyteusis*. Usufruct, the right of *superficies*, or the servitudes were still have been in need of a place in the property system. The challenge of using possession to describe these smaller rights over a thing owned by another was that, with the possible exception of *emphyteusis*, they all involved neither of the two defining elements of possession, that is, the full physical control over the thing and the intent to exercise such control. *Emphyteusis*, which, as we know, was a long-term lease that effectively granted the right-holder a degree of control over land owned by another similar to that of an owner, was somehow an exception. Because of the robust entitlements it involved, it could comfortably fit it into the category of possession. But the other more limited real rights over a thing owned by another could hardly be organized under the label of possession.

Savigny's answer to this challenge was to retrieve another Roman, post-classical, concept: *quasi-possessio*. The actual exercise of these more limited real rights over a thing owned by another, Savigny noted, are cases of *quasi-possessio*. Possession is the condition of fact corresponding to the right to property; by contrast, *quasi-possessio* is the condition of fact corresponding to one of the more limited real rights over a thing owned by another. For Savigny, the reason to treat the more limited real rights over a thing owned by another as instances of *quasi-possessio* lies in the very purpose of the possessory interdicts. Let us hear from Savigny himself:

> The right to Interdicts founds itself on any unlawful interference with the exercise of property; by violence, for instance. If now, a forcible disturbance of the mere exercise of any other right could be conceived it would be strictly logical to protect such rights by similar Interdicts. But this is the case as to all the elements of property which are capable of existing as independent rights severed from property itself. *Usufructus* is a right of this sort, as to which it is clear, on the first glance, that a violent disturbance may be as easily conceived as with respect to property itself; so also with respect to all other servitudes; and also with *superficies* .... It has been shewn above, with respect to these separate rights, that no *animus domini* exists and, consequently, no true possession can be ascribed to him who enjoys them. But as the enjoyment of them may be

interfered in exactly the same way as the enjoyment of property, it follows
that Possession may have reference to other rights besides property . . . .
Thus, as true *possessio* consists in the exercise of property, so this *quasi-
possessio* consists in the exercise of a *ius in re.*[479]

What Savigny is trying to get at in this passage is that the possessor and
the quasi-possessor suffer the same injury when they are disturbed in the
actual exercise of their right. If it is true that the interdicts protected an
individual who was forcibly disturbed in the actual physical control of a
thing because such forcible interference is, in itself, an unlawful injury,
then it follows that the quasi-possessor, who is similarly disturbed in the
actual exercise of the more limited control over a thing granted by these
other real rights, deserves the same protection.

Having accommodated the more limited real rights under the category
of quasi-possession, the last challenge for Savigny were the Germanic,
semi-feudal forms of divided *dominium* that still existed throughout
Germany. Savigny acknowledged that these feudal forms were un-
Roman and yet he still found a place for them in his "system" because
they were part of the consciousness and custom of the German people.
The stumbling block was that these forms, extraneous to the "pure"
Romanist system, involved limited and divided control of the land, rather
than full control. Savigny's twin concepts of possession and *quasi-possessio* proved useful once again. Savigny fit forms of divided *dominium*
that granted the "inferior owner" ample control over the land into the
category of possession and forms in which the inferior owner had more
limited use rights into the category of *quasi-possessio.*

> Possession, in the Roman law, refers only to property and *iura in re* . . . .
> Now the whole right of possession consists in the protection against
> certain kinds of disturbance given to the mere exercise of the right,
> without any reference to the existence of the right itself. This protection,
> therefore, can only extend to such rights as allow of these kinds of
> disturbances being conceived, and except property and *ius in re*, no such
> rights existed. But by the constitution of the Christian Church and of the
> European states, rights were created and were bound up with the posses-
> sion and enjoyment of the soil such as the Roman either knew nothing of
> or never contemplated as the special rights of individuals. Thus the
> exercise of episcopal jurisdictions depends on the possession of the See
> and its temporalities, and a similar relation of state-jurisdiction, or of
> individual branches of it, occurs both in the palatinate authority of princes
> and the jurisdiction of certain owners of estates. The same relation exists

[479] Id., 130–131.

with the real charges established by the German law, such as tithes, ground-rents and services. For all these rights a similar protection to that afforded to property may be conceived and the possession of these rights which have been established in the above manner may be resolved in the most frequent and important cases into possession of land, i.e. into the exercise of property . . .. But even in the cases where the exercise of only one of these rights, jurisdiction for instance, is prevented by violence, although the above reference to the soil does not then exist, still something analogous to it is conceivable just as in the case of the Roman *juris-quasi-possessio*.[480]

Savigny's willingness to include forms of Germanic divided and limited ownership in his logical systematization of the law of possession was not only a matter of methodology. It also signaled an element of complexity in Savigny's ideological beliefs. While Savigny designed his property system to promote the full mastery of the individual's will, his attitude toward economic individualism was ambiguous and coexisted with a communitarian streak. Savigny was skeptical of what he saw as the tendency of the Stein-Hardenberg reforms to define freedom purely in terms of the individual pursuit of economic self-interest, unrestricted by communal bonds. In fact, in his work on the *Staatsrat*, Savigny tried to modify the procedures for rural emancipation in ways that would sustain communal restrictions on economic individualism.[481] In a way, Savigny's approach foreshadows what is, as we will see, a central feature of the Romanist-bourgeois property tradition: the constantly uneasy balance between the individual and society in the law of *dominium*. By clarifying the notions of possession and quasi-possession, Savigny was able to connect logically all instances in which the will of an individual actually exercised its mastery, either full or more limited, over a thing.

The Pandectists' Flight into Abstraction: A Property Architecture with a Life of Its Own

Savigny struggled to build a system of property law that was both rooted in history and organized logically. By contrast, the next generation of German jurists largely neglected the historical and empirical element and drove the systematic method to new extremes. These jurists were

---

[480] Id., 391–392.
[481] John Edward Toews, *Becoming Historical: Cultural Reformation and Public Memory in Early Nineteenth-Century Berlin* (Cambridge: Cambridge University Press, 2004), 154.

collectively known as *Pandectists* for their reliance on the *Pandects*, which is another name for the compilation of juristic writings more commonly known as Digest, published by Justinian in AD 533. In their hands, property took on a life of its own, organized in an abstract legal architecture of the individual will that aspired to be "real," "closed," and "gapless."[482] The claim that private law concepts, such as property, were "real" marked a qualitative leap in the jurists' methodology and is certainly difficult to fathom for the contemporary reader. The *Pandectists* argued that property is "real" in the sense that its concepts really exist, that is, they are not merely useful for purposes of explanation but, as Franz Wieacker put it, are "real entities subject to the laws of physical nature."[483] In other words, rights and legal effects are like bodies and their physical attributes; similarly, property rules are just like the rules of mechanics or physics in that they are permanently valid propositions relating to physical facts, the logical application of which leads to decisions that are "correct," "right," and hence also "just." Further, the *Pandectists* viewed the property system as closed and gapless because the correct answer to any specific real-world property question could be easily deduced from the system's own internal concepts, with no need to rely on any extralegal consideration of administration, morality, or politics.[484]

The *Pandectists'* property system owes its normative impulse and its fundamental internal organization to Savigny. As in Savigny's "law of potentialities," the property system is organized around the central idea of enabling the owner's will to exert its full mastery over a physical thing. Further, as for Savigny, property and possession – the right and the fact – are the two pillars of the architecture of the will. And yet, despite their debt to Savigny, the *Pandectists'* pages read very differently than do Savigny's. The real life of German property relations receives little attention, displaced by lengthy and abstract discussions of the essence and structure of property.

The opening paragraphs of the numerous *Lehrbücher der Pandekten* published in the mid-nineteenth century invariably start with lengthy examinations of the unique, immediate, and direct relationship between the will of the owner and the thing. For example, Karl Ludwig Arndts

---

[482] Franz Wieacker, *History of Private Law in Europe: With Particular Reference to Germany* (Tony Weir, trans.) (Oxford: Clarendon Press, 1995), 343–344.
[483] Id., 344.
[484] Id., 343.

(1803–1878), whose *Lehrbuch der Pandekten* went through fourteen editions, declares that:

> Property, its fundamental idea, is a right by which a person has absolute ownership of a thing, so that the thing belongs entirely to the owner and is subjected, exclusively and in all respects, to the owners' will.[485]

Even more bizarre and convoluted is the description of this unique relation offered by Burkard Wilhelm Leist (1819–1906) in his *Civilistische Studien* (1854):

> The thing is materially and forever interfused with the person, completely assimilated by the person. The subject almost absorbs the substance of the thing, depriving it of its objective independence and attracting it to himself.[486]

The *Pandectists, who were also steeped in historical study and therefore thoroughly familiar with the obviously relational and pluralistic nature of many of the property forms of the Germanic living law, could not have been oblivious to the fact that* ultimately, property involves relations among individuals with regard to the thing. Yet, in their rarefied and streamlined architecture of property, others were hardly ever mentioned. The essence of property was that the owner, having subjected a tangible, physical thing to their will, stands as its lone, exclusive gatekeeper facing a whole world of unspecified others who owe them deference. In Windscheid's words:

> Real rights are rights by virtue of which the will of the right-holder decides over a thing. Obviously, this does not mean that it is the thing itself to which the legal system, by granting a real right, imposes this subjection. This would not make sense as all rights exist between person and person not between a person and a thing. What we mean is that the will of the holder of a real right governs the behavior of all others, not this or that one, with respect to the thing.[487]

To preserve the linear clarity and coherence of the architecture of property, not only were others treated as an unspecified universe owing the owner a duty of noninterference, but the thing itself was also shorn of

---

[485] Ludwig Arndts, *Lehrbuch der Pandekten*, vol. 4 (Munich: J. G. Cotta'sche Buchhandlung, 1861), 191.
[486] Burkard Wilhelm Leist, *Civilistische Studien auf dem Gebiete dogmatischer Analyse*, vol. 3 (Jena: Fromman, 1859), 52–53.
[487] Bernhard Windscheid, *Lehrbuch des Pandektenrechts*, 6th ed., vol. 1 (Frankfurt: Rütten & Loening, 1887), 101.

any possible complexity. The thing that the owner subjects to their all-powerful will is a tangible, corporeal thing.

> In the definition of the concept of thing we have to start by noting that thing means every single object [*Stück*] that is part of inanimate nature, which is to say that the concept of thing refers to the real material existence.[488]

Intangibles that have no material reality and exist as things only in the imagination can be part of an individual's patrimony but cannot be the object of ownership.

> As to the object of property, we have stated that it is a material thing. The only deviation from this principle is that a plurality of material things (*universitas rerum*) may be the object of property. But there cannot be property over what Roman law technically calls *res incorporales*. *Res incorporales*, in this sense, are rights and if someone wants to attribute to himself the property of rights this can only mean that these rights compete to him. Hence, you need to say this right competes to him, not he has property over this right . . .. Similarly, one ought to be careful about the expression "intellectual property". The things produced by our intelligence are a species altogether different from material things and hence cannot be subject to the same rules.[489]

The *Pandectists* always described the tangible thing that is the object of property in abstract terms. The complexity of the Roman "law of things," its detailed distinctions that accounted for the physical, economic, or cultural significance of different things, in the treatises of the *Pandectists* is considered purely historical material that hardly affects the writer's understanding of the present and future law of Germany. Between the 1850s and the 1880s, Germany underwent dramatic transformations, with the reorganization of its agricultural production, the expansion of railroads, and the intensification of coal mining. And yet in the many *Lehrbücher des Pandektenrechts* (*Textbooks on the Law of the Pandects*) that were published in these years, the resources that were critical to this changing economy receive only scant attention.

Because of this virtual fusion between the owner and the thing, listing the owner's entitlements over the thing, which as we have seen was a regular drill for the writers of the French treatises, was not the *Pandectists*' main preoccupation. Rather, the *Pandectists* preferred to convey the idea that the owner's power manifests itself in infinite and

---

[488] Id., 449.
[489] Id., 521–522.

diverse ways. The reason why the *Pandectists* insisted that it is difficult and pointless to pin down the specific entitlements is that it would risk obscuring a critical structural feature of property: property is a monolithic totality, not the mere sum of the owner's distinct entitlements. As Windscheid puts it:

> One could also list the various entitlements that comprise the owner's property right, for example, the right to use, the right to exclude, the right to prevent interferences by third parties, the right to demand the thing from any third party who possesses it or the right to transfer the thing. But it cannot be said that property is the sum of all these rights. Property is the full totality of the power over the thing, and the individual entitlements are simply different manifestations of this totality.[490]

This point about the structural unity of property forced the *Pandectists* to confront another question.[491] If property is a monolithic totality, limitations to single entitlements present a problem. How can the owner transfer single entitlements by, for example, granting others a right of usufruct or a servitude without diminishing or emptying property? And how can the state curb or disallow single entitlements through statues and regulations without destroying property? Arndts' answer is one that we have already seen in the work of Pothier and of other French jurists.

> The concept of property is not destroyed because partial limited rights over the thing are granted to others or because general provisions of law take away from the owner faculties that would otherwise be comprised in his unlimited power, just as the concept of liberty is not destroyed when one has to carry out duties which correspond to the rights of others and to obey the laws. But when these rights of others cease, property becomes again unlimited and exclusive.[492]

In other words, property is not destroyed or diminished because property is an "elastic" totality, subject to contractions and re-expansions. Any grant of rights to others or legislative limitation only temporarily contracts property, which re-expands to its original shape whenever the grant or limitation ceases.

The problem of reconciling the owner's grant of entitlements to others with the idea that property is a unitary totality presented itself most glaringly in the case of divided *dominium*, in which the owner transferred

---

[490] Id., 560–561.
[491] Not all Pandectists share this view of property as a monolithic totality. Some, like Arndts, conceptualize property as the total sum of the entitlements it comprises.
[492] Arndts, *Lehrbuch der Pandekten*, 192.

to another such a robust set of entitlements as to justify calling both owners, albeit "superior" and "inferior," respectively. In this case, the superior owner's property seemed effectively emptied of most of its content, and over the long term, the answer that property is elastic appeared less convincing. But, interestingly, for the *Pandectists*, *dominium divisum* was no longer a question deserving extended scrutiny. The methodological difference with Savigny could not be starker. Committed to both historicism and system-building, Savigny could not ignore the many existing forms of *dominium divisum* and treated them as instances of either possession or quasi-possession. By contrast, in Arndts's *Lehrbuch der Pandekten*, divided *dominium* is confined to a footnote and explained away as a non-Roman aberration.

> The Glossators recognized a *dominium utile* 1) in cases in which according to Justinian's law there was full ownership but the owner had no *rei vindicatio*; and 2) in cases such as emphyteusis and *superficies* where, in fact, there is a simple *ius in re aliena*. In the latter cases, the Glossators juxtapose to *dominium utile* all the entitlements retained by the real owner and call them *dominium directum*. This juxtaposition was then extended to similar legal relations that emerged in the new law. However, after Thibaut, it is now generally admitted that *dominium divisum* has no place in Roman law. And also, in German law, this contrast between *dominium utile* (Nutzeigethum) and *dominium directum* (Obereigenthum) is very difficult to explain.[493]

Similarly evasive are the pages on the limits to property in the interest of neighbors and the public. The discussion is often historical and retrospective, focused on a distant and abstract world of Roman neighbors and there is no premonition of the complexities that the transition to capitalism and industrialization, which was just around the corner, would bring. Windscheid's treatment of the limits to the owner's rights is emblematic:

> The strictly logical, unqualified explication of the concept of property is not possible without significant difficulties. No system of positive law can avoid somehow deviating from this logical rigor[494] . . .. Not all of the legal system's limitations to property rights that existed in Roman law are today appropriate. We will list below the ones that are. Among these limitations, a particularly important set concerns relations among neighbours and it is from these that we will start.[495]

---

[493] Id., 197.
[494] Windscheid, *Lehrbuch des Pandektenrechts*, 564–565.
[495] Id., 565–566.

This brief introduction is followed by a list of twelve rules addressing issues such as boundary walls, trees and vegetation, watercourses, air and light, and excavations, and then by a cursory reference to limits on the right to transfer. This minimalist approach to the limits on property was clearly inadequate to govern property relations in a rapidly industrializing society. As we will see Chapter 5, it would not be long before the Romanists would have to struggle with neighborly relations, specifically with conflicts between static uses of property and industrial uses.

Conclusions

Because the power of the landowning aristocracy and the weakness of the liberal middleclass in the German states prior to unification prevented a "property revolution" as in France, the task of reforming the property system was taken up by a prestigious cohort of "scientists" of Roman law. These legal "scientists" were prominent academics enmeshed in the larger conversations about science and epistemology triggered by the Kantian critical project. They were also influential players in the world of politics, serving in courts, ministries, and legislative committees, and their moderately conservative political beliefs about agrarian class relations were never far from the frontline of property debates. Animated by scholarly zeal but also guided by a political agenda that aimed at freeing German peasants from feudal servitude and reconciling the interests of freed peasants with those of the landowning nobility, different generations of German Roman law experts reshaped Roman property concepts and produced a property "system." This architecture of property was highly sophisticated and was sober in tone, with none of the bombastic statements we saw in the pages of the French treatise-writers but was nonetheless pervaded by the same robust individualistic ideology. The German Roman law scholars aspired to a property system that would be coherent, both normatively and conceptually, with each property form or doctrine logically organized based on the role it played in enabling the will of an individual to freely govern a physical thing to the exclusion of all others. This idea of property as a coherent architecture of the will proved immensely influential, casting a long shadow over property debates throughout the twentieth century and is still with us today.

5

The Tensions of Absolute Property

The nineteenth-century theorists of modern Romanist *dominium*, the great French treatise-writers and the German Romanists, embarked on a quest for coherence, aspiring to develop a body of property law that was both normatively and conceptually coherent. These jurists sought to build an architecture of logically interrelated property doctrines informed by the unifying commitment to maximizing the owner's freedom of action. At first glance, they may appear to have succeeded in their aspiration to coherence. As we have seen in the previous chapters, writers tried hard to describe property as a doctrinal field coherently organized around the principle that the owner's will is "absolute." They touted *dominium* as a right unique in kind that gives the owner virtually unlimited control over a thing, to the exclusion of all others. Further, they argued the simple fact that an individual, exerting their will over a thing by exclusively possessing it, deserved protection against disturbances and dispossession by others, regardless of whether the possessor was the rightful owner. Writers also took great pains to clarify that, even when the owner granted others a limited and temporary right to use the thing, such as a servitude or a right of usufruct, the "fullness" of the owner's right was in no way diminished because property is "elastic" and therefore capable of contracting and re-expanding without losing its essence. Finally, our jurists presented the limits on owners' entitlements as a minimally invasive set of juristic doctrines and statutory provisions meant to secure the harmonious coexistence of neighboring owners and to protect a small number of fundamental public interests.

Yet, this coherence was illusory. Far from being coherent, modern *dominium* and the concepts it inspired – *la propriété, la proprietà, Eigentum* – were riven with tensions that could hardly be disguised. Some of these tensions were already present in Roman law itself. For instance, the tension between property and possession was a legacy of Roman law, which pledged full protection to the owner but also granted significant protections to the person who possessed the thing, regardless of whether they were the owner. Similarly, the tension between *dominium* and *emphyteusis*, the long-term lease that granted the tenant many of the entitlements typical of ownership, was also Roman. It had originated in the tension between *dominium ex iure Quiritium* and a more limited form of private tenure in land owned by the state (*ager vectigalis*). Other tensions, however, were the product of the dramatic acceleration in social and economic change over the course of the nineteenth century. As industrialization and the development of commercial agriculture picked up, property law faced new practical problems that could only be answered by significantly straining the simplistic framework of absolute *dominium*.

Despite all their talk about modernization and improvement, the first generation of jurists who, in the late eighteenth and early nineteenth century, set out to reinvent Roman *dominium* for modern Europe were hardly preoccupied with the needs of the capitalist economy. Their objective was to build the property infrastructure of the new liberal political order. Obviously, they were keen on accommodating the interests of the political and economic elites that backed the new order, but these goals still seemed well served by the simplistic, and apparently coherent, "system" of absolute *dominium*. However, as social and economic change accelerated, and, with it, class antagonism, the demands of capital and labor on property law multiplied. The most advanced sectors of the nascent entrepreneurial bourgeoise understood that development required a more flexible set of property doctrines that would empower owners to parcel out entitlements and thereby expand investment and access opportunities for both owners and productive users. Further, a growing chorus of "social" and "socialist" writers and pamphleteers of all stripes vocally denounced the role that "absolute" property played in the "social question." As legislatures started responding to these demands by expanding or reshaping property forms and doctrines, the jurists found it harder to accommodate these new legislative developments while also preserving the appearance of property's coherence. With impressive displays of conceptual *bravura*, conspicuous omissions, and evasive commentary, they struggled to smooth the conceptual inconsistencies of the modern Romanist property system without fully succeeding.

In the pages that follow, we will take a close look at the jurists' attempts to deal with four doctrines that threatened to strain the coherence of the property system: *emphyteusis*, possession, limits on ownership, and common ownership. While ultimately unsuccessful, these attempts are nonetheless worth exploring. For one thing, these failed attempts opened rifts in the apparently solid edifice of modern *dominium*, rifts that, a couple of decades later, the social critics would be quick to exploit. Most importantly, the jurists' efforts to smooth these tensions throw into sharp relief a diversity of ideological and methodological views that hardly surfaces in the nineteenth-century property treatises. Today, the grandiloquent introductions and the prolix theory chapters on *dominium* read as the uniform orthodoxy of delusionary formalists and simplistic liberals, invariably repeating similar platitudes about property being absolute and exclusive. However, in the more technical sections of their treatises, when faced with these hard questions, the jurists were forced to clarify their methodology and make plain their ideological commitments, revealing important rifts, varying degrees of analytical skill, and indeed surprising moments of doubt.

No less fascinating, and today largely forgotten, is the rivalry between emerging national property cultures competing to achieve global influence that pervades the jurists' writings on these difficult topics. The arguments and the rhetoric of modern *dominium* were largely supranational but its methodology, that is, property formalism, had distinctively national flavors. When testing their analytical skills on these hard puzzles, French, German, and Italian property scholars often indulged in bursts of cultural and methodological nationalism, claiming the superiority of their respective national brand of formalism. With colorful language, the Germans took pride in their conceptual rigor, while the Italians cautiously distanced themselves from the excesses of German conceptualism, and the French ridiculed German theories as useless, reveling in their more pragmatic attitude.

The jurists' effort to ease these points of stress within the property "system" also places into sharp relief the diversity of practical concerns and policy agendas that motivated the architects of modern *dominium*. These differences are largely obscured in the property literature addressed to a generalist audience, which seldom moves beyond bold but vague claims about the relation between modern *dominium* and "improvement" or "productivity," but they stand out neatly in the highly technical analyses of *emphyteusis*, common ownership, possession, and expropriation for a public purpose. Not only did these topics involve logical difficulties, they also implicated pressing local economic and social issues. The logical solutions jurists devised, as well as their varying degree of discomfort with these logical difficulties, speak volumes about the specific local or regional needs they faced and the authors' ideological beliefs and policy preferences. Writers who were familiar with the many forms of communal ownership that had existed for centuries, and still thrived, in the Alpine region and throughout Italy sought to make room for them within their national property systems. In a similar fashion, jurists in semi-peripheral Sicily or peripheral Latin America – who faced the ills of *latifundia*, agrarian turmoil, and lagging economic growth – were more comfortable with different strategies for reconciling *emphyteusis* with *dominium* because they saw *emphyteusis* as the tool to achieve the twin goals of development and a modicum of redistribution. In France, the combination of the enforced destruction of titles by a law of 1793, the social chaos of the Restoration, and the rise of large-scale manufacture made the tension between securing title owners and protecting useful possessors an eminently practical and quite controversial question. These local concerns were highly diverse and yet they all muddled the coherence of the property system.

Emphyteusis: A Form of Quasi-Property?

By the mid-nineteenth century, *emphyteusis*, a form of long-term lease that was incorporated into late Roman law and became widespread in medieval times, had turned into a highly controversial issue that made sparks fly in juristic circles. As the French jurist Jean Charles Florent Demolombe put it:

> The right of *emphyteusis*! There has never been a real right as important and renowned as the right of *emphyteusis*. Of all the real rights, it is the one that has generated the most difficulties and controversies and is discussed everywhere in legislation and in the writings of the jurists.[496]

The reason for such drama was that, since its very beginning and throughout its long life, the right of *emphyteusis* appeared as a maddeningly confusing hybrid form: part lease, part ownership, part limited real right over a thing owned by another. *Emphyteusis* had its origins in the granting of state or municipal land, in Rome called *ager privatus vectigalisque*, for long periods of time or even in perpetuity in exchange for the payment of an annual rent; it was one of the many, smaller "ownership" forms made available by Roman law. Following the Gracchan agrarian law, the public lands held by private possessors in excess of

---

[496] Charles Demolombe, "Cours de Code Napoléon," in *Traité de la Distinction des Biens, de la Propriété, de l'Usufruit, de l'Usage et de l'Habitation*, 2nd ed., vol. 1 (Paris: Durand, 1861), book 2, title 1, chapter 2, paragraph 491, page 408.

the prescribed limit were confiscated and redistributed in small parcels to private "tenants" who were granted broad entitlements in return for the payment to the Roman state of an annual rent (*vectigal*). The tenants' entitlements were robust and included the right to use the parcel, the right to transfer it to one's heirs and to grant limited rights to use to others. Besides these robust entitlements, another feature made this landholding form unique. In case of disturbances and interferences, the tenants of parcels of *ager vectigalis* – who, initially, could only avail themselves of the *actio conducti* resulting from the standard contract of lease – were soon given by the magistrate known as the *praetor* an action *in rem* (*actio utilis in rem*). By the time of the later Roman Empire, this "ownership" or tenancy form had become known by the Greek name *emphyteusis*. The term derived from the Greek verb "to plant" and referred to a new feature that, in time, had become essential to the relation between the title owner and the holder of the right of *emphyteusis* (*emphytecarius*). In addition to the duty to pay the annual rent, the latter now also had an affirmative duty to improve the land.

A ubiquitous form of structuring agrarian relations in France and in Italy between the fourteenth and the late eighteenth centuries, *emphyteusis* acquired distinct features in different regions and became further muddled by its resemblance to a host of other landholding forms introduced by feudal law. Despite these local variations, by the eighteenth century, *emphyteusis* was a standard form with a number of essential features: a perpetual or long-term transfer of land from a private or public landlord, who retained title, to the holder of the *emphyteusis*, who acquired a set of inheritable and transferable rights and duties. Along with the duty to pay the annual rent, the holder of a right of *emphyteusis* had an unrestricted right to use, the duty to make improvements, the right of first refusal if the landlord decided to transfer title, and the right to acquire the actual title by paying the capitalized rent.

As the enthusiasm for the project of a modern law of property centered around the idea of absolute *dominium* spread through law faculties and legislatures, *emphyteusis*, with its unique combination of robust entitlements but also important duties, presented jurists with two intractable questions, one conceptual and one about policy. The conceptual question interrogated the nature of *emphyteusis* and its place in modern property law. Is *emphyteusis* a simple contract of lease? Or an instance of divided *dominium*? Or the most robust of the real rights over things owned by another? Could *emphyteusis* be a form of quasi-

dominium or temporary *dominium*? Finally, what if *emphyteusis* is a hybrid creature deserving its own, separate place in the property system? Equally contentious was the policy question regarding the desirability of *emphyteusis* in modern society. Is *emphyteusis* a remnant of feudalism, an inherently hierarchical landholding form fundamentally at odds with the values of a modern society of free and equal owners? Or is *emphyteusis* a property form designed to expand access to land and to promote the productive use of land, entirely in accordance with modern egalitarian values and with the principles of modern political economy?

Jurists and legislatures throughout continental Europe and its peripheries offered widely divergent answers to these questions, but both diffidence and a hostility toward *emphyteusis* prevailed. At a time when the anti-feudal rhetoric was widespread and strident, jurists were diffident toward this property form that smacked of feudalism. But equally pervasive was the hostility to recognizing a new form of quasi-property that could overshadow the centrality of *dominium*. The section about *emphyteusis* in Demolombe's *Cours de Code Napoléon* is a remarkable instance of this widespread juristic hostility. *Emphyteusis* was a hot topic in France. The evasive and confusing treatment of *emphyteusis* in revolutionary legislation and in the Code Civil had generated a heated debate among French jurists over the status of *emphyteusis* in France. A *loi* of December 18–19, 1790 had explicitly abolished perpetual *emphyteusis* but seemed to allow temporary *emphyteusis* that did not exceed ninety-nine years. The Code Civil restated the prohibition on perpetual *emphyteusis* but was silent about temporary *emphyteusis*, failing to list it among the real rights over things owned by another enumerated in article 543. The Court de Cassation, on the other hand, had repeatedly stated that, under the new Code Civil, the grant of an *emphyteusis* operated as a transfer of ownership of a parcel of land for a specific term, effectively treating *emphyteusis* as a form of temporary ownership.[497] Demolombe decried the Court's idea of temporary ownership and argued instead that the Code Civil's silence was to be interpreted as implicitly abrogating temporary *emphyteusis*. Demolombe's tone was sarcastic:

> What! Is it the *Code Napoléon* that changed and modified the nature of *emphyteusis*? But it does not say a single word! *Emphyteusis* is a temporary transfer of property and the holder of an *emphyteusis* is a temporary

---

[497] Civ., April 1, 1840, S 40-I-433; Civ., July 24, 1843, S-43-I-830; Civ., March 6, 1850, S 50-I-210.

owner? But, in truth, can there be a temporary owner? Can the right of property, which consists in disposing of the thing in the most absolute manner (art. 544), be limited to a certain time?[498]

No less disparaging was Demolombe's rebuttal of the idea that *emphyteusis* could a form of quasi-*dominium*, surprisingly endorsed by his colleague Troplong, who, once again, proved to be one of the most open-minded and historically aware of the Exegetists.

> But what is this quasi-*dominium*? It is not enough to answer that Cujas called it so. We are now in the presence of a Code, under which this designation of quasi-*dominium* must refer to a right, one of the real rights recognized by this Code. Now, what is the right that quasi-*dominium* refers to? We do not say it. It is very difficult indeed to answer![499]

The truth, Demolombe concluded, is that *emphyteusis* is part lease, part usufruct, and part ownership without really being any of them. Rather, Demolombe suggested, *emphyteusis* is a sui generis form, an agreement between the parties that has the effect of "dismembering" property. It is no surprise that this effective dismemberment of ownership was favorably viewed by the jurists of the ancien regime, given its affinity with the values and needs of a hierarchical political and social order. However, Demolombe resolutely asserted, this dismemberment of ownership has no place in modern society. Rehearsing the standard arguments of what he called "wise" liberalism (as opposed to "revolutionary" liberalism), Demolombe explained why the Napoleonic legislature's decision to abrogate *emphyteusis* was the right decision:

> And all this explains why our new laws, our liberal and democratic laws (wisely democratic and liberal, not revolutionary!) that regulate the relationship between those who own land and those who do not, reject *emphyetusis*, admitting only the lease. It is because the new legislature not only aimed at freeing persons and things, securing their respective independence (Marcadé, t. II art 526). The legislature also sought to simplify the legal regime of landownership, suppressing all the divisions and subdivisions that complicated it and prevented its free alienability.[500]

---

[498] Charles Demolombe, "Cours de Code Napoléon," in *Traité de la Distinction des Biens, de la Propriété, de l'Usufruit, de l'Usage et de l'Habitation*, 2nd ed., vol. 1 (Paris: Durand, 1861), book 2, title 1, chapter 2, section 2, paragraph 491, page 410.
[499] Id., book 2, title 1, chapter 2, section 2, paragraph 491, page 411.
[500] Id., book 2, title 1, chapter 2, section 2, paragraph 491, pages 414–415.

Demolombe went beyond simply airing the platitudes of "wise" liberalism about freedom and alienability; he also directly engaged the most powerful argument of the few supporters of *emphyteusis*, who viewed *emphyteusis* as a means of expanding access to land for peasants who did not own land or for small owners who sought to enlarge the size of their farms. Turning on its head his opponents reasoning, Demolombe denounced *emphyteusis* as an instrument of inequality, one that fails to adequately serve the needs of small peasants with limited financial resources. To prove his point, Demolombe contrasted the position of the tenant in a standard lease with that of the holder of an *emphyteusis*. At first glance, *emphyteusis* may appear more advantageous than a simple lease because it does not expire upon the death of its holder and because it can be mortgaged. However, at closer inspection, the legal regime of *emphyteusis* is, in fact, harsher on direct producers with limited means. While the tenant is not responsible for the payment of taxes, is only held to simple rental repairs, and may be entitled to rent reduction if the crop is lost, the holder of an *emphyteusis* pays all taxes, is in charge of all repairs, including major ones, and bears the full risk of crop loss.[501]

Demolombe's rejection of *emphyteusis*, while thorough and full-throated, was by no means the only, or even the dominant, characterization of *emphyteusis*. Among the German Romanists, for example, many showed greater openness. Preoccupied first and foremost with logical systematization, the Pandectist scholars were less interested in taking sides in the debate about the desirability of *emphyteusis* in modern society. Rather, they viewed *emphyteusis* as an intellectual puzzle, as a concept in search of a place in the modern property "system," and they strove to find a satisfactory answer. While some were not afraid to describe *emphyteusis* as an instance of divided *dominium*, and a few were not shy to consider *emphyteusis* as a type of quasi-*dominium*, most viewed *emphyteusis* as one of the real rights over a thing owned by another. Arndts' treatment of *emphyteusis* in his *Lehrbuch der Pandekten* well exemplifies this growing consensus. To Arndts, it seemed relatively straightforward that *emphyteusis* is simply one of the limited real rights over a thing owned by another. As Arndts explained:

> *Emphyteusis* [and the right of *superficies*] are real rights of enjoyment over immovables that, because they are so broad as to allow the right holder to enjoy and dispose of the thing in a virtually unlimited way, and because

---

[501] Id., book 2, title 1, chapter 2, section 2, paragraph 491, page 414.

they are alienable and inheritable, so closely resemble property that they are, sometimes, considered forms of limited property. But, to be true to their conceptual nature, they are nothing other than real rights over a thing owned by another.[502]

The debate over *emphyteusis* was not all conceptual abstractions or "wise" liberal platitudes. At the semi-periphery of Europe, in the Kingdom of the Two Sicilies, the largest state of pre-unitary Italy, *emphyteusis* was a central political question that prompted creative juristic analyses and galvanized activists. In the new market in land opened up by the abolition of feudalism in 1812, *emphyteusis* was the centerpiece of a grand bargain between two different segments of the elite: the former feudal lords and an emerging entrepreneurial middle class. By entering into contracts of *emphyteusis*, the former feudal lords could retain ultimate title to the lands to which their titles of nobility were attached, while smaller landowners were able to expand their farms, turning previously uncultivated or underutilized land into a productive resource. Hence, contrary to the Napoleonic legislature, the drafters of the 1819 Leggi Civili per lo Regno delle Due Sicilie[503] (Civil Laws for the Kingdom of the Two Sicilies) explicitly regulated *emphyteusis*, and local jurists produced a flurry of treatises that portrayed *emphyteusis* as a tool for economic growth and moderate redistribution.

In the pages of the jurists of the Italian South, *emphyteusis* was, for all matters, a "type" of ownership because it granted the holder long-term use and transfer rights, similar in effect to those of an owner, as well as a privileged path to full ownership through the payment of the capitalized rent. Retaining this ancient ownership form was, the Southern jurists argued, a matter of good economics and common sense. The difference when compared with the French and German treatises could not have been greater. In the works of these Italian jurists, feudalism does not project its ghostly shadow over *emphyteusis*, references to divided *dominium* have no pejorative overtone, and the arcane conceptual dia-tribes of the mandarins of French and German legal academia receive scant attention. Instead, patriotic aspirations and more local anxieties

---

[502] Karl Ludwig Arndts, *Lehrbuch der Pandekten*, 5th ed., vol. 1 (Munich: Cotta, 1865), 304 ff. For a translation, see *Trattato delle Pandette del Cavalier Lodovico Arndts. Prima edizione italiana sulla settima tedesca* (Filippo Serafini, trans.), vol. 1 (Bologna: Tipi Fava & Gragnani, 1872), part 2, chapter 4, paragraph 195, page 362.

[503] *Codice per lo Regno delle Due Sicilie, Parte I, Leggi Civili*. Seconda edizione uffiziale (Naples: Real Tipografia del Ministero di Stato della Cancelleria Generale, 1819).

loom large in this regional literature on *emphyteusis*. For the Sicilian jurists, *emphyteusis* was the occasion to assert their intellectual autonomy from the small cohort of French and German writers that dominated property debates and to emphasize the unique challenges faced by the Italian South. The reader may be surprised to learn that one of the first treatises on *emphyteusis* to appear, Pasquale Liberatore's (1763–1842) *Trattato dell'Enfiteusi*, was published as an appendix to Liberatore's Italian translation of Delvincourt's *Cours de Code Civil*.[504] In France, Delvincourt was among those who argued that the Code Civil had effectively abolished *emphyteusis*, and Liberatore's decision to supplement his translation of Delvincourt's *Cours* with a vocal defense of *emphyteusis* reads as a defiant vindication of national and intellectual autonomy. A similar assertion of autonomy appears in the 1864 treatise of another Southern Italian jurist, Gaetano Arcieri (1794–1867), who was actively involved in the *Carbonari* movement that fought to liberate Italy from foreign oppressors. Arcieri briefly explained the argument that induced the Napoleonic legislature and many French jurists to expunge *emphyteusis* from the property system, that is, that *emphyteusis* effectively splits *dominium* in two, negatively affecting land values. In France, Arcieri concluded, "these arguments have triumphed, however this is not a reason to abide by the example of the French."[505] The question of whether to retain *emphyteusis* in a modern legal system is an eminently local and practical one, Arcieri explained.

> To solve the question of *emphyteusis* we need to move from the level of ideology to that of practical common sense. To decide this question [what to do with *emphyteusis*], we need to consider our customs and traditions, the needs of our agrarian economy and of our industrial development . . . . And even the most obstinate advocates of economic principles have to agree that *emphyteusis* is perfectly suited to the need for the division of latifundia and their improvement. Hence even if we consider the question from this perspective only, it would be good advice to preserve the contract of *emphyteusis* in our law books.[506]

---

[504] Pasquale Liberatore, "Trattato dell' Enfiteusi," in *Corso di diritto civile del Signor Delvincourt, novellamente tradotto dall'ultima edizione francese ed accompagnato dalla nuova giurisprudenza civile del Regno delle Due Sicilie*, vol. 10 (Naples: Nel Nuovo Gabinetto Letterario Largo Trinità Maggiore, 1841). See also Claude-Étienne Delvincourt, *Cours de Code Civil*, vol. 3 (Paris: Fournier, 1819).

[505] Gaetano Arcieri, *Trattato dell'enfiteusi* (Naples: Morelli, 1864), book 3, title 9, chapter 2, paragraph 33, page 17.

[506] Id., book 3, title 9, chapter 2, paragraph 32, page 17.

Along with agricultural improvement, access to land was the theme that pervaded the pages of the Sicilian jurists. Arcieri, who had participated in the revolutionary insurrections of 1848, dwelt at length on the perils of an unequal distribution of a critical productive resource such as land.

> The motor of prosperity is the equal distribution of wealth. When property is concentrated in the hands of a few, two negative consequences follow that gravely damage the economy of a nation. The first is that agricultural land is left vacant and desolate; the second is that it leads to misery because the worth and welfare of the individual is based on labor.[507]

Arcieri noted that because *emphyteusis* has the potential to effectively remedy inequities in the distribution of land, to promote productivity, and to restore the dignity of agricultural laborers, very few modern nations had entirely discarded this ancient form and many more still were weighing its benefits. For Arcieri, the case for *emphyteusis* was even stronger in Sicily where, until very recently, land had been concentrated in the hands of a small number of large owners and agricultural development had faltered.

In the treatises of the Sicilian jurists, *emphyteusis* also provided the impetus for a pragmatic focus on actual and specific economic resources that foreshadowed the call for a new resource-based property analytic that would come to dominate property debates toward the end of the century. For example, in his treatise on *emphyteusis* published in 1852 in Catania, jurist Francesco Duscio discussed *emphyteusis* as a property form with the potential to boost the improvement and productivity of resources that were critical to the economy of the region.[508] By the mid-nineteenth century, as the demand for sulfuric acid in the French and British chemical industries kept growing and Sicily was emerging as one of the most important sulfur-producing areas of Europe, Duscio's hope was that *emphyteutical* leases for sulfur mines would encourage investment. *Emphyteusis*, in Duscio's view, could also bring new capital to the Sicilian *tonnare*, the tuna-fishing enterprises that had also historically been concentrated in the hands of a few large entrepreneurs. And *emphyteusis*, Duscio suggested, could also encourage investment in water mills and steam-powered mills, thereby supporting the larger effort to spur industrialization in Sicily.

---

[507] Id., book 3, title 9, chapter 2, paragraph 33, page 17.
[508] Francesco Duscio and Vincenzo Vecchio, *Dell'enfiteusi, o commentario del tit. 9 nel libro 3 delle Leggi per lo Regno delle Due Sicilie*, vol. 1 (Catania: Pietro Giuntini, 1852), 156.

Demolombe may have been right: among the real rights, *emphyteusis* was the one that posed the greatest difficulties for the proponents of a coherent will-based modern property system. Yet it was also the one that generated the richest and most forward-looking juristic debate, pushing the boundaries of nineteenth-century property theory and anticipating a pragmatic, policy-oriented approach focused on resources that would fully bloom only decades later.

The Quandaries of Possession

The doctrine of "possession" was another point of stress in the "system" of modern Romanist property. Savigny's treatise *Das Recht des Besitzes* (*On the Law of Possession*) published in 1803 went through seven editions and made the young Savigny a star in juristic circles. Savigny's intention, as we know, was to bring clarity to the knotty questions surrounding the concept of possession in Roman law. However, Savigny's treatise, far from settling the controversy, further inflamed it, and the debate was still raging in the 1870s, when the Italian Ilario Alibrandi compared possession to a distant land still waiting to be discovered:

> The process of revealing the truth is similar to the discovery of distant lands. The first explorers capitulate and dying half way through while the last voyagers happily reach their destination.[509]

The obstacles on the road to possession were both conceptual and practical. To begin with, jurists could not agree on the very nature of possession. Is possession a right or a mere fact? The answer, for Savingy, was straightforward. The mere detention of a thing, which the Romans called *naturalis possessio*, Savigny noted, is a nonjuridical physical relation. However, he added, under certain conditions, possession acquires a legal character, becoming *possessio civilis*. Hence, Savigny concluded, it is self-evident that possession is *both* a right and a fact and that the complex and lengthy analyses of his fellow jurists were simply unhelpful.[510]

---

[509] Ilario Alibrandi, *Teoria del Possesso secondo il diritto romano* (Rome: G. Aurelj, 1871), part 1, chapter 2, paragraph 40, page 37.
[510] Friedrich Carl von Savigny, *Das Recht des Besitzes* (Giessen: Heyer, 1837), section 1, subsection 7, pages 58–101.

> It is clear that possession in itself, according to the original notion of it, is a simple fact; it is just as certain that legal consequences are bound up with it. Therefore, it is at the same time both a right and a fact, namely, a fact according to its nature, and equivalent to a right in respect of the consequences by which it is followed, and this double relation is a very important one to keep in mind throughout.[511]

The legal rights that the fact of possession confers, Savigny further explained, are two: prescription (*usucapio*), or the right of the possessor who has possessed a thing for certain period of time to become its owner, and the right to possessory interdicts, that is, the possessor's ability to obtain the remedies known as "possessory interdicts" in case of disturbance or dispossession.[512]

However, what appeared plain to Savigny seemed shrouded in fog to the many others who, for decades, continued to apply themselves to the question of the nature of possession, reaching widely divergent conclusions. Particularly sharp were the disagreements among those who concurred that possession was a "right" but parted ways when asked what kind of right. For some, possession was a *ius in re*, the fifth to be added to the traditional four identified by the medieval jurist Baldus (ownership, servitude, pledge-right, and the right of inheritance).[513] Others viewed possession as provisional ownership and the interdicts as temporary remedies introduced for the sake of convenience in the early stages of lawsuits in which ownership is disputed.[514] Still others described possession as "incipient ownership" protected in Roman law because it has the requisites necessary to, potentially, lead to full ownership through prescription (*usucapio*).[515]

These disputes over the nature of possession may seem the pedantic elucubrations of Roman law scholars obsessed with minute conceptual distinctions. But possession also posed important questions of fairness and efficiency. A fascinating discussion, rich in philosophical and political implications, probed the reasons why Roman law protected

---

[511] Id., section 1, subsection 4, page 23. For the translation, see Erskine Perry, *Von Savigny's Treatise* On Possession, 6th ed. (London: S. Sweet, 1848), 17.

[512] Id., 5.

[513] See Henricus Hahn, *Dissertatio inauguralis de iure rerum et iuris in re speciebus harumque divisionibus in genere* (Helmstedt: Heredes Lucii, 1639), conclusio 1, paragraph 14, section 2, for a treatment of Baldus' schema.

[514] Savigny, *Treatise* On Possession, 26.

[515] Eduard Gans, *System des Römischen Civilrechts im Grundrisse* (Berlin: Ferdinand Dümmler, 1827), 201–216.

possession regardless of whether it was accompanied by the right of ownership. Why should modern law follow Roman law in protecting a possessor who did not have a right?[516] Rudolf von Jhering (1818–1892) bluntly posed the question at the outset of his monograph on possession:

> Why do we protect possession? No one asks this question for property, so why raise it with regards to possession? Because the protection of possession stands out for all its contradictions. Protecting possession, by implication, means protecting robbers and thieves. How can the law, which condemns robbery and theft, recognize and protect the possession of the fruits of such acts? Isn't this equivalent to condoning and approving with one hand what is rejected and prosecuted with the other hand?[517]

Yet, if possession is an institution that has existed for centuries, Jhering continued, there must be a good reason. Participants in the debate had quite different ideas about what this good reason could be. The first to offer an answer had been the young Savigny who argued that possession is protected to preserve the public order.[518] In the successive editions of his treatise, Savigny perfected his explanation that dispossession or disturbances by means of force or violence are, in themselves, an unlawful personal injury that the possessor shall not have to suffer, regardless of whether he or she has a right worthy of protection. Savigny was concerned mostly with the private law dimension of this disturbance of the public order, that is, with the harm suffered by the individual possessor. By contrast, others shifted the focus toward the larger, "public" aspect of forceful interferences with possession. For instance, Adolf August Friedrich Rudorff (1803–1873), who had studied with Savigny in Berlin, insisted that the reason modern property law should protect possession is that any disturbance suffered by the individual possessor is also, fundamentally, an injury to the community and to the legal system itself.[519]

As Savigny's treatise went through successive editions, more German jurists started challenging his attempt to ground the protection afforded to possession in the need to preserve the public order. Ultimately, this

---

[516] See James Gordley and Ugo Mattei, "Protecting Possession" (1996) 44 *American Journal of Comparative Law* 293–334.

[517] Rudolf von Jhering, *Über den Grund des Besitzschutzes* (Jena: Maute's Verlag, 1869), 3. For a translation, see Rudolf von Jhering, *Sul fondamento della protezione del possesso* (Francesco Forlani, trans.) (Milan: Vallardi, 1872), 3.

[518] Savigny, *Treatise On Possession*, 32.

[519] Adolf August Friedrich Rudorff, "Rechtsgrund der possessorischen Interdicte" (1831) 7 *Zeitschrift für geschichtliche Rechtswissenschaften* 107.

controversy about the rationale for protecting possession independent of ownership implicated larger questions about the very values that inform private law. At a time in which jurists were intent on reorganizing the private law system as a mighty architecture of the individual will, some sought to find an alternative justification for the protection of possession, one more directly related to the dominant will-based theory of private law. The rationale for protecting possession independent of the right of ownership, these jurists argued, lies in the deference owed to any manifestation of the individual will, even before the lawfulness of its volition is established. Proponents of this will-based theory of possession charged one another with formulating the theory in the most persuasive terms. Eduard Gans (1797–1839), an independently minded jurist influenced by Hegelian thought, and who had long been in disagreement with Savigny, offered one variant of the argument. Gans explained that:

> If possession is accompanied solely by the individual's specific will to possess, it is but inchoate direct property. If, however, a right to possess can be asserted against anyone, it is real property. The reason why we recognize and protect the mere will is that it is, in itself, a substantial element that deserves protection, and it may only be set aside by a universal right of possession. Therefore, the legal basis of possession lies neither in the control exercised over a thing, nor in any presumption relating to it, but rather in the will of the individual relating to that thing; it is a right in itself and ought to be treated as such.[520]

Another champion of the will-theory of possession, Carl Georg Bruns (1816–1880), explicitly discussed the methodological concerns behind the effort to ground the protection of possession in the respect owed to individual will. In his *Das Recht des Besitzes im Mittelalter und in der Gegenwart*, published in 1848, Bruns noted that theories that justify the protection of possession by citing "external" policy factors, such as the protection of the public order, miss the point. The task of a positive legal science is to identify an "internal" justification for possession:

> It may be convenient to adduce empirical and practical reasons for the protection of possession, but there is little to gain from such efforts in a matter in which legal science resolutely demands an internal juridical necessity, deduced from the nature of possession.[521]

---

[520] Gans, *System des Römischen Civilrechts im Grundrisse*, 211–212.
[521] Carl Georg Bruns, *Das Recht des Besitzes im Mittelalter und in der Gegenwart*, vol. 1 (Tübingen: H. Laupp'schen Buchhandlung, 1848), section 8, subsection 58, page 487.

Unconvinced by theories that emphasized the public order and approaches that foregrounded the will, Rudolf von Jhering sought to move the debate beyond the impasse it had reached in a monograph published in 1869 and titled *Über den Grund des Besitzschutzes* (*On the Justification of Possession*). Jhering conceded that the will is the force that animates private law but firmly noted that the will finds its measure and limitation in the law and is given legal power only if it stays within the limits of the law. In Jhering's words:

> One has to keep separate its personality from the relationship arising by virtue of an unlawful act. The former, regardless of the wrongs committed, remains what it is and does not lose any of its legal protection. But it does not follow that the personality, like a saint capable of miracles, can elevate, cure and purify, by simply touching it, everything that is malignant, ill or unclean, and can cover with the ample mantle of its legal protection all the unlawful acts in which the will may manifest itself.[522]

After a lengthy and detailed critique of each of the many theories of possession that circulated among jurists, Jhering proposed yet another answer to the puzzle of possession: *ownership* is the key to understanding possession. Protecting possession, Jhering argued, is only a means that makes it easier to secure effective protection of ownership. In Roman law, possession was a needed supplement to ownership, introduced to spare the true owner the burden of proving title in case of disturbances. Because, in Roman law, proving ownership was often difficult – as it required evidence of an uninterrupted chain of transfers of title going back to the first owner – the magistrate known as the *praetor* made available to the owner who suffered disturbances the remedies known as interdicts, which did not require proof of title. Indulging in a military metaphor, Jhering describes possession as an outpost positioned to guard against intrusions and surprise attacks on property:

> According to this notion of possession, one may characterize possession as a "military outpost of property," a fortification of property that exists not for its own sake but because of property. Through possession, the owner fends off the first attacks on his ownership rights. On the battlefield of possession, what takes place is not a full, decisive battle over title, but rather a skirmish in which, if you allow me, heavy artillery is not

[522] Jhering, *Über den Grund des Besitzschutzes*, 32. See also Jhering, *Sul fondamento della protezione del possesso*, 26.

necessary and light artillery suffices. You do not use cannons to drive back thieves and burglars.[523]

But if effectively protecting ownership is the key, how to explain the protection given to the possessor who is not the true owner? Jhering seems to suggest that the protection given to possessors who were not the true owners was an unavoidable side-effect, the price to be paid for protecting owners.

> The protection of possession was introduced because of property. However, this protection cannot be granted to the owner without also giving it to the non-owner. In fact, if you limit the proof of ownership to the mere exterior condition that corresponds to ownership, this assistance to the owner ends up benefitting anyone who can show this factual condition of possession presupposing ownership. Hence, possession acquires an independence vis-à-vis property that allows it to turn against property, rather than exclusively to assist it.[524]

The lofty theoretical disquisitions that fill the pages of the German jurists obliterated the practical questions posed by possession. However, these factual questions were front and center in France, where the destructive impetus of the Revolution and the chaos of the Restoration period had muddled the question of who could occupy and use the land. In the first half of the nineteenth century, property, grandiosely invoked in the revolutionary and Napoleonic literature, was, on the ground, a largely irrelevant concept. The Revolution had led to the massive confiscations of the lands of the *emigres*, the aristocrats who fled France, and titles had largely been destroyed following a law of 1793. With the Restoration, the question of whether and how to compensate the *emigres* whose lands had been taken became incendiary and conflicts between "old" owners, that is, pre-revolutionary owners, and "new" owners who had subsequently acquired these lands multiplied.[525] Further, starting in the 1820s, with the expansion of the textile, pottery, and iron industries, conflicts between agricultural "inertial" users and manufacturing "productive" interests further complicated land disputes. Property was abstract and seemed of no avail; instead, what mattered was possession.

---

[523] Jhering, *Über den Grund des Besitzschutzes*, 54. See also Jhering, *Sul fondamento della protezione del possesso*, 43.

[524] Jhering, *Über den Grund des Besitzschutzes*, 54. See also Jhering, *Sul fondamento della protezione del possesso*, 43.

[525] Kelley and Smith, "What Was Property?," 212.

With both feet on the ground, French jurists dismissed Savigny's sophisticated abstractions as useless and turned instead to the real life of possession in France. This shift in focus came with declarations of methodological independence and assertions of the unique history of possession in France. In the preface of his *Traité de droit de possession*, published in 1842, William Belime (1811–1844), professor at the University of Dijon, took Savigny to task:

> The most well-known jurist of contemporary Germany, M. de Savigny, recently appointed minister of justice in Prussia, did not disdain to write a treatise on possession, which is his most popular title in the universities on the other side of the Rhine. One has to acknowledge that so divorced are the principles of Roman law from ours, particularly when it comes to possession, that this work, so remarkable in many ways, for the sagacity of its exegesis and for its skilled analysis of the sources, this work in which Savigny, one could say, became Roman to interpret the Roman laws, this work that could have been written by a jurist of the second century, by Gaius or Ulpian, is of little or no avail in practice. Hence, despite my admiration for the learned professor of Berlin, I will rarely have the occasion to cite his work.[526]

Belime doubled down on the practical irrelevance of the Germans' theoretical investigations in the first chapter of his treatise when he attributed the endless controversy over whether possession is a fact or a right to the *philosophisme* of the *savants* on the other side of the Rhine and to their lack of interest in real-life problems. Belime was not alone: virtually all the works on possession published in France in the mid-nineteenth century dwelt upon the unique practical, legislative, and historical dimensions of possession in France.

Not only were French jurists less inclined to lofty philosophizing, possession was an altogether different matter in France. The legal sources that governed the law of possession were different, with customary law playing a major role. To truly understand the history of the law of possession in France, Belime warned, one had to look away from Roman law and turn instead to the great experts of the *coutume*, from Beaumanoir to Boutillier, and to the royal ordinance on procedure of 1667.[527] Similarly, to fully grasp the complexities of the modern *droit de possession*, one had to shove aside academic literature and examine

---

[526] William Belime, *Traité du droit de possession et des actions possessoires* (Paris: Joubert, 1842), preface, viii.
[527] Id., x.

instead the work of the *juges de paix* (justices of the peace), who had competence over possessory actions. Created by a law of 1790 and reorganized by a law of 1838, the justice of the peace was an eminently practical role, in Belime's words, "a paternal court in which the subtleties of positive law count less than common sense and the rectitude of intentions."[528] To be helpful to the *juges de paix*, who often did not have legal training, the very vocabulary of possession needed to be simplified. In the lengthy chapter on possession that opens his treatise on prescription, Raymond Troplong laid out the basic types of possession in France. The Roman law language of the German theorists who distinguished between "natural" and "civil" possession is obscure, Troplong noted, and French courts prefer a more mundane classification, intelligible to practitioners:

> I no longer hear [courts] speak of natural and civil possession because the obscurity of this distinction does not even begin to do justice to it. Rather, what I hear every day is precarious possession; possession grounded in a property title or *animo domini*; possession sufficient to give rise to acquisitive prescription, to designate the possession described by article 2229 of the Civil Code, which leads to prescription; and "*possession annale*" (year-long possession) or *saisine* to designate the possession which is the foundation of our possessory actions and that gives rise to a presumption of ownership. With this simple and unpretentious vocabulary we always understand each other. With the words *naturalis possessio* and *civilis possessio*, we would always have to explain and argue.[529]

This "simple and unpretentious" four-fold classification recurs in virtually all the French treatises on possession. While the first three types of possession are intuitive for a lawyer trained in Roman law, the fourth, the *saisine*, is distinctively French, and treatise writers took great pains to explain its uniqueness. As Troplong explained:

> Here we find a great innovation. For Roman law, it was sufficient to have possession at the time of the lawsuit to be able to use the interdicts. In France, simple possession is not sufficient. A *saisine* is necessary, which is to say, one needs to have possessed for a year and day. This point is important and quite consequential.[530]

---

[528] Id., xi.

[529] Raymond Troplong, *Commentaire sur la prescription* (Brussels: Meline, Cans et Compagnie, 1843), chapter 2, section 2, paragraph 239, page 156.

[530] Id., chapter 2, section 7, paragraph 295, page 178.

Another authority in matters of possession, Pierre-Paul-Nicolas Henrion de Pansey (1742–1829), whom Napoleon had appointed Premier President of the Court de Cassation in 1809, had earlier described simplicity as the virtue of the *saisine*. Instead of a confusing variety of interdicts with different requirements, Henrion de Pansey noted, French law makes available to the possessor who has possessed for one year and one day a straightforward, but limited, action, the *action en complainte*. In this action, Henrion de Pansey continued, all the plaintiff needs to prove is the *saisine*, that is, possession for one year with *animo domini*; and all that the plaintiff can obtain is to be maintained in possession.[531]

While the *saisine* had the virtue of being simple, possessory matters were never simple. The practical conflicts that arose between competing possessors take up a large portion of the French literature on possession. In real life, treatise writers agreed, it is entirely possible to see three individuals, each claiming one of these types of possession. In Toulier's illustration:

> Mere detention (*possession*), possession grounded in ownership title (*droit de possession*), and saisine (*droit de posséder*) are three entirely distinct things and may belong to three different individuals. For example, if a negligent owner allows another to dispossess him, he still retains the right of ownership to which the right to possess is attached. At the same time, the usurper, after a year of possession, has the right to maintain possession of the land for the time being, to prevent anyone from disturbing him and to engage, like the owner, in the acts permitted by the right of ownership. Finally, a second usurper who has dispossessed the first by violence or otherwise, has the mere detention.[532]

Conflicts between different possessors arose in a variety of circumstances and treatise writers agreed that possession was largely a practical, empirical question in which the *juge de paix* was called to weigh facts and intentions, with little guidance from the black-letter law of possession or the academic literature. To illustrate that the meaning of possession, the scope of the acts that show possession, and the question of intent and *animus domini* are ultimately empirical questions, Troplong recounted an 1830 case that had attracted significant attention. Nicolas Foray, the

---

[531] Pierre-Paul-Nicolas Henrion de Pansey, "Justices de paix," in *Ouvres Judiciaires du President Henrion de Pansey* (Paris: Dussillon, 1843), 1–183; chapter 43, section 7, page 129.

[532] Charles-Bonaventure-Marie Toullier, *Le droit civil français suivant l'ordre du Code*, vol. 3 (Paris: Warée, 1824), book 2, title 2, chapter 1, section 2, paragraph 79, page 52.

owner of a mill and a canal had effectively abandoned the property, failing to operate the mill for sixty years. Taking advantage of the state of disrepair of the dams that formerly carried the water into the canal, occupants had cultivated the banks of the canal and part of the canal itself, which had become a little stream for the irrigation of the crops. When Foray sued, the occupants claimed ownership through acquisitive prescription. The occupants' possession was indisputable and one would have imagined they would have prevailed. But the court of Lyon held, and the Court de Cassation confirmed, that, because, over the sixty-year period, the canal had never become completely dry, the heirs of Foray had maintained possession.[533] While the court did not provide an explanation for this bizarre outcome, Troplong noted that the ultimate question was how to solve the conflict between passive possession and active, productive possession:

> It is likely that what remained of the canal appeared to the court a continuation of intentional possession sufficient to make the right of the owner prevail. But the court did not consider that the occupants of the banks, through their cultivation and labor, had also possessed what remained of the canal, and hence it was no longer possible to privilege an intentional but inactive possession over the possession of third parties who used the land, applied their labor to it, and harvested its fruits in broad daylight, finally claiming ownership.[534]

The case of Nicolas Foray was by no means exceptional: conflicts between active possessors and passive owners were a significant part of the daily work of the courts and the justices of the peace. The nature and scope of the activity possessors and owners engaged in, as well their relative economic power, varied significantly. "Active" possessors were often occupants who used the lands for grazing, timbering, and harvesting, and title owners could be idle landowners or large productive enterprises. The law in the books and the scholarly treatises were largely irrelevant to these daily conflicts and the outcomes of the cases were hardly predictable.

As this brief journey through the academic treatises on possession shows, in the 1840s, possession seemed a maddeningly complicated matter. Despite their different methodological approaches, neither the German theoreticians nor the French pragmatists could fully clarify the many conceptual and practical questions raised by possession.

---

[533] Troplong, *Commentaire sur la prescription*, chapter 2, section 2, paragraph 245, page 158.
[534] Id., chapter 2, section 2, paragraph 245, page 158.

Is Man the King of All Things? The Limits and Duties of Ownership

Perhaps less intellectually stimulating than topics such as *emphyteusis* or possession, but equally consequential, was another challenge facing our property writers. In the second half of the nineteenth century, in an effort to support economic and technological change and to address the negative externalities it created, legislatures started tightening the limits and duties of owners of specific types of property such as mines, water courses, woodlands, and wetlands. The tension between the jurists' ubiquitous grandiloquent statements about modern *dominium* being absolute and these statutes and regulations, which kept growing in number and significance, could hardly be concealed.

The jurists relied on a number of strategies to minimize this tension but they could not fully dispel it. One strategy was to carefully manage topic boundaries. Jurists would omit any mention of the limits to ownership in their chapters about *dominium*, instead confining their brief references to the new regulatory regimes to lengthy but inconsequential and largely antiquarian sections on the "law of things." This was the path followed by Jean Baptiste Victor Proudhon in his *Traité du Domaine de Propriété*. The high-sounding prelude sets the tone for the rest of the discussion: things exist to serve the needs of man, who is the king of nature.

> By *biens* we generally mean all the things that contribute to the welfare of man: *Naturaliter bona ex eo dicuntur, quod beant, hoc est beatos faciunt; beare est prodesse . . . .* Man is the king of nature, all other beings are meant to serve his needs, as declared by the Creator.[535]

Having declared man the king of nature, Proudhon then proceeds to describe the fundamental distinctions of the Roman law of things. The reader who expects Proudhon to then delve into a detailed description of the growing number of legislative limits to owners' entitlements over specific things will be disappointed. Proudhon's list of limits is relatively short and the duties imposed on owners are largely meant to secure public safety, the basic needs related to the transport infrastructure, or the peaceful coexistence of neighboring owners. For instance, owners of

---

[535] Jean-Baptiste-Victor Proudhon, *Traité du Domaine de Propriété* (Brussels: Meline, Cans et compagnie, 1842), part 1, chapter 1, section 1, paragraph 1, page 1. The Latin text, which deviates minimally from Digest 50.16.49, translates as "Naturally *bona* are so called from the fact that they make forturate, that is make someone *beatus*; for to make fortunate is to profit." See pp. 379.

buildings that pose safety risks have a duty to demolish them; owners of wooded land may not clear their land without the authorization of the competent authority; owners of forests situated in the proximity of the Rhine River may be requested to sell to the government fascines to strengthen the embankments in case of flood; and owners of wetlands may be forced to drain and fill their marshes.[536]

Downplaying the legislative limits to property was also the strategy followed in most of the many textbooks on the law of the Pandects published in Germany in the central decades of the nineteenth century. In the pages of the Pandectist writers, the Roman "law of things" became an abstract conceptual taxonomy, accurately reproduced but emptied of all its pragmatic, real-life flavor. Arndts' treatise, for example, explained the limits to ownership in general terms, relegating the list of specific limits to a lengthy footnote.[537] The nine limits listed in this footnote largely reproduce Roman law restrictions and are relatively trivial, ranging from the duty to grant rights of ways in specific instances, to the cutting of branches, to the encroachment of structures, to the respective rights and duties with regard to nuisances such as smoke.[538]

To get a detailed picture of the growing body of special legislation that was starting to transform property, one has to turn to Toullier's *Le droit civil français suivant l'ordre du Code*, the aim of which, as the subtitle recites, was to "reunify theory and practice." Rather than glossing over the tension between the dogma of "absolute" property and the innumerable new limits to owners' entitlements in the public interest, Toullier made this tension plain. In the opening paragraphs of the chapter entitled "Des Modifications de la propriété," Toullier acknowledged the general principle that the new limits effectively "modified" property itself:

> Modifications to property limit the exercise of property rights with regards to the things they apply to . . . . Modifications touch the right of property itself.[539]

The rest of Toullier's chapter featured a lengthy list of legislative limits that spanned over a century, including the *loi* of September 16, 1807,

---

[536] Id., part 1, chapter 2, paragraphs 14–22; pages 3–4.
[537] Arndts, *Lehrbuch der Pandekten*, 195; Serafini (trans.), *Trattato delle Pandette del Cavalier Lodovico Arndts*, vol. 1, part 2, paragraph 131, page 227.
[538] Arndts, *Lehrbuch der Pandekten*, 196 n. 1; Serafini (trans.), *Trattato delle Pandette del Cavalier Lodovico Arndts*, vol. 1, part 2, paragraph 131, page 228 n. 1.
[539] Toullier, *Le droit civil français suivant l'ordre du Code*, vol. 3, book 2, title 2, chapter 4, preliminary section, paragraph 242, pages 161–162.

which imposed a duty on owners to drain marshes and wetlands in conformity with government plans; the *loi* of April 21, 1810, which established a comprehensive legal regime for mineral resources, imposing limits on the rights of surface owners and regulating the requirements and procedures for mineral permits and leases; and, finally, a series of *lois*, *ordonnances*, and *decrets*, dating back to the eighteenth century, which reshaped the rights of owners of wooded lands, limiting their ability to cut down trees and clear their lands, in order to secure stores of wood for the French Navy.

The challenge posed by the growing legislative limits on ownership appeared even more stark when these limits were effectively confiscatory, depriving owners of core entitlements and significantly diminishing the value of the property. In his *Traité de l'expropriation pour cause d'utilité publique*, Charles Delalleau (1791–1850), who served as *avocat* in the royal court of Paris, compiled a long list of regulatory limits that may have been regarded as having an impact on owners similar to that of expropriation.[540] The list included, most notably, the physical invasion of privately owned land for an indefinite period of time, the temporary occupation or impairment of the use and value of property, the imposition on private owners of an easement or servitude for the benefit of the public or the expansion of an existing easement or servitude, the taking of a servitude enjoyed by a private owner on public property, the taking of a lessee's interest in a lease, as well as instances in which an owner was to lease their property to the government. While this list may not come as a surprise for today's reader, it was certainly at odds with the grandiose assertions – that property is absolute and inviolable and that expropriation is an exceptional sacrifice – that punctuated the jurists' treatises. The emphasis on the exceptional nature of expropriation translated into a very narrow formal definition of expropriation. Delalleau explained that *expropriation pour cause d'utilité publique*, properly defined, only referred to cases in which there was an actual *transfer* of title from a private individual to the state.[541] This narrow doctrine of expropriation failed to account for the many other instances in which the state demanded "sacrifices" from private owners, including "regulatory takings." Most cases did result in some amount of compensation but were not subject to the strict procedural and substantive requirements for expropriation.

---

[540] Charles Delalleau, *Traité de l'expropriation pour cause d'utilité publique*, vol. 1 (Paris: Cosse, Marchal et Compagnie, 1866), 81 ff.
[541] Id., 78–103.

Common Ownership: A Hieroglyphic that Cannot Be Deciphered

Few topics triggered emotions and reciprocal verbal attacks as intense as those generated by common ownership. In the scholarly debate over common ownership, Italian Romanist Sergio Perozzi lamented, "ideas usually considered axiomatically absurd are taken as valid and writers habitually clear and precise seem content with the strangest, most imprecise and empty ideas one could imagine."[542] The crux of the matter was how to reconcile two apparently contradictory ideas within the Roman legal tradition. The first was the principle, attributed to the Roman jurist Celsus the Younger, that two owners cannot own the same thing at the same time.[543] The second was the concept of *communio* or *condominium*, a form of common ownership, established by contract or by law, in which two or more persons owned an undivided fractional interest in the same thing.[544] How to conceptualize the relationship between the various co-owners in a *communio* without coming into conflict with Celsus' maxim? More generally, if property is the individual's exclusive and absolute control of a material thing, how could multiple owners have a right of the same nature and scope over the same thing at the same time? And the difficulties did not end here. For jurists who aspired to build a coherent property system, the fact that the rules about *communio* were scattered throughout the Roman law sources and that *communio* seemed to have no obvious logical place in the system was a source of angst. Should *communio* be discussed along with ownership? Or does it pertain to the "law of things," more precisely to the question of whether things are divisible? Finally, could *communio* be an altogether different concept that deserves its own separate place in the system? As a German jurist (and Dante reader) noted, if anyone managed to get out of this labyrinth of questions and opinions, they could happily declare themselves to have found their way out of Dante's *"selva oscura."*[545]

---

[542] Silvio Perozzi, *Sulla struttura tipica delle servitù prediali in diritto romano* (Rome: Forzani, 1888), 364.

[543] Digest 13.6.5.15. In another instance of a tendency by now familiar, the maxim illustrating this principle – *duo non possunt habere dominium eiusdem rei in solidum* – is not found in the ancient source but is in fact a later formulation.

[544] On the date of the emergence of the term *condominium*, see P. van Warmelo, "Aspects of Joint Ownership in Roman Law" (1957) 25(2) *Tijdschrift voor Rechtsgeschiedenis* 125 n. 1.

[545] Paul Steinlechner, *Das Wesen der iuris communio und iuris quasi communio*, part 1 (Innsbruck: Wagner, 1876), 148.

German and Italian jurists were the fiercest contenders in the debate over common ownership, and intra-European intellectual rivalry played a nontrivial role in the dispute. Theories of common ownership were one of the few areas in which the Italians, who were newcomers in the high echelons of European legal thought, explicitly questioned the "excesses" of German conceptualism. On the very first page of his essay, Perozzi explains that he felt the urge to bring clarity and real-world sensibility to a topic that "had too easily offered the German jurists the occasion to display their taste for abstraction which is their main weakness."[546] With lively prose and sharp wit, Perozzi walks the reader through the twists and turns of this seemingly unending juristic controversy and finds none of the many theories of *communio* offered by his fellow jurists fully convincing.

All these theories, Perozzi argues, are based on the same mistaken assumption that there is only one idea of property, that is, individual property, and that there must be a way to square the puzzle and to demonstrate that multiple co-owners can have a right over the same thing that is identical to the right of a sole owner. Take, for example, the oldest theory of common ownership, embraced by the German Pandectist Georg Puchta among many others, who sought to solve the dilemma by arguing that each co-owner had an identical right over an *ideal portion* of the thing. Puchta explained in very plain terms that:

> Given the nature of ownership, there cannot be multiple owners of the same thing. If a thing does in fact have multiple owners (aside from the case in which each owns a distinct corporeal, material portion of the thing, *pro diviso*) this is fathomable only so long as each owns only an ideal portion of the thing, but, because this portion exists only in the mind (*iuris intellectu*), it is impossible to mark its boundaries externally, on the thing. This state of affairs is called *condominium*. None of the co-owners can control the thing in its entirety or even a physical portion of it, but each can withdraw and ask for partition, thereby transforming their right of ownership *pro indiviso* into ownership *pro diviso*.[547]

Champions of this theory believed they had solved the puzzle by dividing up the thing in "ideal" portions that are then "incorporated" in the

---

[546] Perozzi, *Sulla struttura tipica delle servitù prediali in diritto romano*, 1.

[547] Georg Friedrich Puchta, *Cursus der Institutionen*, 3 vols. (Leipzig: Breitkopf und Härtel, 1841–1847). For the source of the quotation, see A. Turchiarulo (trans.), *Corso delle Istituzioni di G. F. Puchta*, vol. 2 (Naples: Tipografia all'insegna del Diogene, 1854), book 4, chapter 4, section 230, pages 111–112.

common thing so that the latter consists of the sum of these ideal parts and belongs jointly to the co-owners. For Perozzi, the fault of this theory is obvious: property is a right over a physical thing but, according to this theory, each co-owner has a right over a creation of the mind, a pure abstraction, and the actual physical thing is left with no owner. To say that these imaginary portions are "incorporated" in the physical thing is not an answer; how these imagined parts can be "incorporated" in the thing without losing their nature as mere ideas, Perozzi jokes, is a mystery.[548]

Equally faulty, Perozzi argues, is the theory according to which it is the right of ownership itself that is divided, not the thing. For Perozzi, this theory only generates further confusion because its advocates had widely different ideas on how exactly the right of ownership would be divided. For some, the right is one but mentally divided in *ideal* parts, which, together, form the whole, full right.[549] The idea of a unitary right divided into ideal parts is simply absurd for Perozzi because it leads to the inevitable conclusion that each co-owner has a right over the thing that *is* and *is not* property at the same time. If the thing is one, then, given the Roman maxim that two owners cannot own the same thing at the same time, it follows that each co-owner's right *is not* property but must rather be another type of real right, short of property. At the same time, each co-owner's right *is*, in a way, property because it is an ideal part of the common property right.[550] Others suggested that these portions of the right of ownership are *real* rather than ideal: the unitary right of ownership is actually and effectively divided up into multiple rights of identical nature.[551] Again, Perozzi is unconvinced. To avoid openly contradicting the maxim that two owners cannot own the same thing at the same time, its advocates are left with no choice but to argue that, while the thing is one and undivided, because the right is divided it *appears* that the thing itself is divided. Anyone can see, Perozzi notes with a hint of mockery, that the notion that the co-owners' distinct property rights have as an object not the actual physical thing but "fractions of the thing that seem to exist but in fact do not exist" is ridiculous and faces the exact same

---

[548] Perozzi, *Sulla struttura tipica delle servitù prediali in diritto romano*, 66.
[549] Eduard Böcking, *Institutionen*, vol. 2 (Bonn: Adolf Marcus/Georgi, 1843), 9.
[550] Perozzi, *Sulla struttura tipica delle servitù prediali in diritto romano*, 69–70.
[551] Carl Georg von Wächter, *Handbuch des im Königreiche Württemberg geltenden Privatrechts* (Stuttgart: Metzler, 1842), part 2, chapter 8, section 6, paragraph 43, pages 272–280; and Part 2, chapter 12, section 2, paragraph 75, pages 579–587; Id., *Archiv für die civilistische Praxis*, vol. 27, 155.

difficulties encountered by the theory of the division of the thing in "ideal" parts.[552]

While Perozzi was not kind to the supporters of these theories, he reserved his most vehement scorn for Windscheid's theory of *communio*, which was rapidly becoming the leading theory in Europe and was widely applauded as innovative. Rather than dividing up the thing or the right, Windscheid conceptualized common ownership as a unitary property right over an undivided thing residing in a collectivity of owners. In Windscheid's words:

> From the concept of property it follows that there cannot be multiple property rights over the same thing. On the other hand, it is possible that the one, unitary, property right over the thing belongs to multiple subjects. We call this *communio*. In this case, the relationship between the multiple owners is such that none of them can take any action with regards to the thing without the will of the others. The size of each owner's share does not matter and the majority does not decide. But this principle is not applied with abstract rigor and each co-owner has to allow the others to use the thing so long as this use does not damage the thing or diminish its use. If one's use precludes the others form using the thing, then the co-owners will parcel the use according to their respective shares. Similarly, the revenue or any other utility produced by the thing is to be divided among co-owners according to their shares and the same is true for the expenses. Each co-owner can represent the group vis-à-vis third parties but they will only receive what is due to them based on their share. In a similar way, the obligations contracted with regards to the thing bind each co-owner only to the extent of their respective shares.[553]

In this paragraph, Windscheid makes an argument that seemed anathema to most writers who approached the topic blinded by the idea that ownership always and only pertains to an individual. Property may pertain to a group of owners collectively, "so that it can only be set in motion by the collective will of the owners." While the right is exercised collectively, some of the *effects* of the right, most importantly the revenue *value* generated by the thing, is divided among them in proportion to each one's share. Having outlined his theory, Windscheid makes another argument likely to leave many fellow Romanists bewildered: Roman *communio* may not be the only form of common ownership.

---

[552] Perozzi, *Sulla struttura tipica delle servitù prediali in diritto romano*, 73.
[553] Bernhard Windscheid, *Lehrbuch des Pandektenrechts*, 6th ed., vol. 1 (Frankfurt: Rütten & Loening, 1887), 603–605.

In German law, Roman *communio* is often contrasted with so-called collective ownership (*Gesamteigentum*); while there is disagreement as to the details of this form, it generally describes a situation in which multiple owners collectively own the thing without an ideal, mental partition in arithmetic fractions. Many have expressed concerns about introducing a concept of common ownership different from the Roman one. The essential point in this controversy is to acknowledge that a plurality of property rights over the same thing is a possibility ruled out by the very nature of property and that the same logic precludes the possibility of conceiving of property as the sum of the single entitlements of the various co-owners. Beyond this, one has to confess that common property may be modified in ways not contemplated by Roman law and, in particular, that nothing precludes the possibility that the portion of value due to each may be determined according to principles different from that of fractional shares.[554]

The Germanic form of common ownership (*Gesamteigentum*) Winscheid alludes to in this paragraph was a hot topic in European juristic circles. Advocates described it as an altogether different property form rooted in an ancient German communitarian agrarian tradition. Whether *Gesamteigentum* was actually a thriving property form in the living law of Germany and the pre-unification German states was hotly contested and, yet, allusions to a radically "other" Germanic property tradition were ubiquitous in the Romanists' writings on common ownership. Germanic collective ownership may have been less an actual living institution than an ideological provocation on the part of scholars known as "Germanists," who rejected the idea of a modern German law based on Roman law and called instead for an authentically Germanic private law inspired by social and communitarian values. Most famously outlined by the great Germanist Georg Beseler, *Gesamteigentum* was heralded as the antithesis of the Roman *communio*, a diametrically opposed, non-individualistic way of thinking about ownership, of conceiving of the relation between the individual, the group and the thing.[555] Windscheid's overture to this fundamentally other property tradition is surprising for a member of the Pandectist School and a tribute to his methodological openness. Interestingly, Windescheid did not persuade Perozzi, who was himself known among the Italian Romanists for his

---

[554] Id., 606–607.

[555] Georg Beseler, *Volksrecht und Juristenrecht* (Leipzig: Weidmann, 1843), part 1, chapter 6, section 5, paragraph 4, pages 193–194. See also Georg Beseler, *System des gemeinen deutschen Privatrechts*, 4th ed., 2 vols. (Berlin: Weidmann, 1885); and Otto Friedrich von Gierke, *Deutsches Privatrechts*, vol. 2 (Leipzig: Duncker und Humblot, 1905).

intellectual and methodological autonomy. Windscheid's idea of a unitary property right held collectively by multiple subjects, Perozzi argued, is an "undecipherable hieroglyphic," an impossible attempt to reconcile two opposite assumptions: the idea that each member is an actual full owner and the notion that there can be only one property right over a thing.[556]

The reader who, after this series of firm and colorful rebuttals, cannot wait to hear Perozzi's own theory of common ownership will be disappointed. A sensible legal analysist with a distaste for extravagant conceptual schemata, Perozzi was less interested in proposing yet another theory of common ownership than in convincing the reader that, so long as we hold on to the traditional definition of property as one individual's right to exclusively control a physical thing, the puzzle of common ownership is simply impossible to solve. In other words, to allow for a form of property with multiple owners, we need a new definition of property. Perozzi concludes his essay with an admonition:

> To develop a theory of common ownership one needs to start with a revision of the concept of property. For too long legal science has been caught in a vicious circle; if we do not break this vicious circle, we will continue to do and undo, to play with ideas of property, things, subjects, parts, division, value and effects without ever finding an intelligible solution. This at least is my conviction, and I hope that, one day, it will become everyone's conviction.[557]

Perozzi's invitation to set aside property monism, that is, the belief that there exists only one concept of property, to discard formalistic and hyper-individualistic assumptions about Roman property, and to turn with fresh eyes to the pluralism of Roman property forms was largely ignored, and the question of how to conceptualize *communio* remained a highly contested one for many more decades.

Conclusion

The controversies over *emphyteusis*, possession, common ownership, and regulatory takings opened rifts, both methodological and normative, in the apparently cohesive cohort of theorists of modern *dominium*. These rifts made easier the job of the social jurists who, toward the end of the

---

[556] Perozzi, *Sulla struttura tipica delle servitù prediali in diritto romano*, 81.
[557] Id., 368.

nineteenth century, would challenge the idea that modern property ought to be shaped along the lines of a fictitiously Roman, hyper-individualistic "system" of property law. As we saw, the jurists' strategy to ease these tensions in the property system was either to engage in far-fetched conceptual virtuosity or to depart from the constraints of conceptual formalism and to loosen the very structure of the system's logical archi-tecture. In the long term, the former strategy backfired, further under-mining property formalism. The proliferation of bizarre theories about *emphyteusis*, possession, or common ownership made formalism look bankrupt. As Perozzi put it, ideas once considered absurd were now presented as valid, and the logical precision that was touted as the virtue of property formalism gave way to empty and unclear analysis. On the other hand, the theorists of modern *dominium* who responded to these difficulties by loosening the "rigor" of their conceptual formalism, by making overtures to empiricism and pragmatism, further reinforced the sense, increasingly shared by many in elite juristic circles, that a change in methodology was needed.

The controversies over these difficult doctrines, by throwing into sharp relief the sheer diversity of ideological beliefs and policy agendas embraced by the advocates of modern *dominium*, also weakened the broad consensus that the normative theory of modern *dominium* had attracted. In the last decades of the eighteenth century and well into the nineteenth century, when property seemed functionally related to auton-omy and political equality – themselves the grand ideas of liberal mod-ernity emanating from revolutionary France – modern absolute *dominium* seemed appealing to different sectors of the European elite. But the enthusiasts of the new science of political economy, the natural law believers, and the democratic egalitarians were strange bedfellows who had only temporarily found common ground. While the controver-sies over *emphyteusis*, common ownership, and possession were highly technical and hardly accessible for the larger public, the ideological divisions they created in juristic circles had echoes in broader public conversations.

6

Roman Dominium in the Republics of Latin America

Property, Nationhood, Race, and Economic Development

Introduction

In the waning days of the Spanish Empire and, later, in the newly independent republics of Latin America, the attack on feudal property was just as vocal as in the European metropole. As the liberal *creole* elites sought to integrate their countries into the world-market as primary producers, they understood themselves as partaking in a larger, foreordained, trans-Atlantic transition from feudalism to economic modernization and from mercantilism to commercial liberty. The before and after of this transition were described in a bourgeoning literature of broadsheets, *pasquinos*, and economic treatises, which portrayed Latin American societies and their economies as divided in two, largely independent, segments: a stagnant and retrograde feudal sector and an expanding and increasingly more dynamic modern sector.[558]

While the tones and the arguments of this anti-feudal discourse echoed the assault on feudal property in the metropole, the intellectual sources and the material interests of the detractors of feudalism in Latin America were far more complex. The liberal *creole* elites drew upon a vast and diverse political-economy literature that went beyond the obvious canonical authors of the French Enlightenment and included semi-peripheral regional traditions, such as the Neapolitan Enlightenment, that more closely resonated with their specific concerns about underdevelopment and metropolitan-satellite relations.

---

[558] D. F. Sarmiento, *Facundo* (Buenos Aires: Librería la Facultad, 1921); E. Laclau, "Feudalism and Capitalism in Latin America" (1971) *New Left Review* 19–38; A. G. Frank, *Capitalism and Underdevelopment in Latin America: Historical Studies of Chile and Brazil* (New York: Monthly Review Press, 1967).

Chile was a country that took pride in having advanced the furthest in the path toward modernization, while also securing political "order" and "stability."[559] Here, an elite of liberal *creole* statesmen with juristic training championed a concept of absolute *dominium* that was, initially, only a simple constitutional framework rather than a full-fledged regime of property doctrines. Its two pillars – the inviolability of property and the free alienability of property – were to facilitate the creation of a robust market in agricultural land, without disturbing the social and economic position of the land oligarchy. The incoherence and extreme malleability of these two principles were immediately obvious in some of the most important political and legislative debates of the 1820s–1860s: the question of the *mayorazgos*, the treatment of the property of the ecclesiastical orders, the abolition of African slavery, and the problem of *la propiedad en Araucania* (indigenous property). In each of these debates, the inviolability and the free alienability of property were in tension. The juristic elite struggled to mediate these tensions and to impress on their desired outcomes the appearance of a relative coherence. Despite the liberal flavor of these two principles of constitutional property, the outcomes that the liberal *creole* political elite sought to achieve were blatantly illiberal. By mediating these tensions, the jurists sought to justify the racial subordination and economic exploitation of the indigenous and *mestizo* population and to narrow the racial boundaries of the new nation's supposedly universal republican citizenship.

When Andrés Bello, the most legendary jurist of Chile and the author of the 1855 Código Civil, and a younger generation of sophisticated writers of *Comentarios* to the Código Civil finally constructed a more detailed doctrinal architecture from the simple constitutional framework of property, the tensions within the property system only became more evident. So too did the originality of the new country's law of property, which the Chilean juristic elite emphasized, taking great pains to explain the several critical problems on which they had chosen to depart from the French Code or the writings of the German jurists. Committed to agricultural improvement but also reluctant to undo the semi-feudal relations of production that allowed the landed elite to extract profit

---

[559] S. Collier, *Chile: The Making of a Republic 1830–1865* (Cambridge: Cambridge University Press, 2003), 124; I. Jaksić, *Andrés Bello: Scholarship and Nation-Building in Nineteenth-Century Latin America* (Cambridge: Cambridge University Press, 2001), xx–xxi.

from the peasantry, Bello crafted a system that combined feudal property and modern *dominium*.

The Liberal Creole Elites and the Attack on Feudalism

The feudal landownership structure that the liberal elites of the newly independent nations sought to dismantle rested on an intricate variety of forms of ownership, of varying scope and with features unique to colonial, export-driven societies. These forms are described in detail in a rich seventeenth-century scholarly literature penned by treatise writers such as Juan de Solórzano (1575–1675) and Antonio de León Pinelo (1589–1660),[560] who specialized in *derecho indiano*, the Spanish public and private law that applied to the Indies. While the specific forms varied regionally, the general landownership pattern was consistent throughout Spanish, and to some extent Portuguese, America. Owners with full *dominium* derived their titles either from the early land grants (*capitulaciones*) or from the later land sales made by the Castillian Crown to the private individuals who engaged in the "discovery and pacification" of the territories of the New World that the Spanish-born Pope Alexander VI assigned to Spain in 1493–1494 when he brokered the Treaty of Tordesillas. To summarize in broad strokes, these grants and sale agreements provided for a variety of conditions and privileges, which, typically, included a residency requirement, a duty to establish a *pueblo* with a required minimum number of inhabitants, the right to receive the work of groups of indigenous laborers in exchange for Christianizing them, and a variety of resource-specific obligations that applied to grazing, farming land, or to mineral resources.[561] These documents also featured a provision about the fair treatment of the indigenous population.[562] Aside from these conditions, owners had the full set of ownership entitlements that nineteenth-century jurists associated with Roman, and modern, *dominium*.

However, in Spanish America, *dominium* worked in combination with legal institutions designed to coerce and exact labor services from the

---

[560] See especially J. de Solorzano y Pereira, *Politica Indiana* (1647) and A. L. Pinelo, *Tratado de Confirmaciones Reales, Encomiendas, Oficios y Casos en que se Requieren para las Indias* (1630).

[561] J. M. Ots Capdequi, *España en América*, 2nd ed. (Bogota: Universidad Nacional de Colombia, 1952); M. C. Mirow, *Latin American Law: A History of Private Law and Institutions in Spanish America* (Austin: University of Texas Press, 2004).

[562] Ots Capdequi, *España en América*, 36ff.

indigenous, *mestizo*, and poor *creole* population. Hence, it operated very much like feudal property in Europe, mimicking, and exacerbating, the latter's hierarchical and exploitative effects. The *encomienda*, but also the *ripartimientos* and the *mita*, were legal structures by which Spaniards effectively tied large number of workers of *Indio* status to aristocratic lands and exacted from them labor or personal services. The rights granted by the *encomienda*, which were effectively equated to property rights, could not be alienated or mortgaged but were inheritable and passed by primogeniture. A revenue-neutral way to compensate *conquistadores* and a mode of exploiting indigenous labor critical to the colonial economy, the *encomienda* was abolished by royal legislation throughout Spanish America over the course of the eighteenth century, but its vestiges carried on well into the nineteenth century. Poor white or *mestizo* laborers were also incorporated into this feudal ownership structure through forms of landholding that were a hybrid of lease and labor contract. Variously described throughout Spanish America as *inquilinos*, *arrendatarios*, or *agregados*, these laborers received from their employer a small parcel of land adjacent to the estate (*hacienda*) with the obligation to provide labor, to assist with specific seasonal operations, and to pay a yearly rent in cash or kind. The *inquilinos* or *arrendatarios* also received a small salary for labor in excess of the services agreed upon and could be evicted at any time with short notice.[563]

Alongside full *dominium*, there also existed more limited forms of divided *dominium*. Private lands, but also vacant public lands (*tierras baldias o realengas*), were often granted to users by means of emphyteutic leases or a similar form known as *censo al quitar*. In both forms, ownership entitlements were split between a landlord – or "direct" owner – who had title, and a tenant – or "useful" owner – with perpetual or long-term use rights as well as a duty to pay an annual rent or pension to the former. This intricate pluralism of private landholding forms coexisted with communal ownership and Indigenous property (*la propiedad indiana*). Starting in early colonial times, the Spanish Crown endowed newly established towns and *pueblos* with communal lands to be used for pasturing, timber, and other activities. These lands, which were administered by the local municipal authorities (*cabildos*), could be used for a variety of purposes and were often leased to private tenants to generate revenue. *La propiedad indiana* was an altogether separate legal category permeated with

---

[563] Id., 37–45.

assumptions about racial inferiority and driven by the needs of the racia-lized, export-oriented satellite economy. Individuals of *Indio* status had the legal capacity to hold land as private property but restraints on alienation, designed to protect a racial group portrayed as inferior and immature, significantly burdened their right to transfer.[564]

While, at the time of independence, each of these various forms of land tenure had been slowly changing, the fundamental structure of this landholding system was still largely intact. The elites of the new inde-pendent republics, which had largely embraced different strands of liberalism, ranging from conservative to radical, turned against this landholding system with a vocal "anti-feudal" discourse. They character-ized the new republics as facing a critical choice between feudalism and liberal modernity. In essays and newspaper articles, liberals of all stripes argued that the challenge was to reform the old colonial landholding regime, with its servile labor forms and subsistence economy, and to promote free labor, agrarian improvement, and security of tenure. In Chile, the *inquilinaje*, a widely diffused tenure form, epitomized the "feudal," the "barbaric," and the "colonial," and a prolific literature addressed its many pitfalls. In a lengthy essay titled "Nuestro Sistema de Inquilinaje,"[565] Ramón Dominguez set up the analogy with European feudalism in stark terms:

> The most precise analogy is with the vassal of a feudal lord. The *inquilino* effectively bounds himself to the owner of a *hacienda* to have a place to live, a parcel to cultivate, and the material and moral protection of the landlord, which is so important for the *inquilino*'s relationship to the government and his ability to seek justice in court. In exchange for these trivial concessions, the *inquilino* commits to provide specific labor ser-vices on the *hacienda*, to help whenever needed, to perform whatever task he is given, regardless of how far away or difficult; in a word, to do whatever the owner of the *hacienda* asks him to do, no matter what.[566]

Addressing the land oligarchs who defended the *inquilinaje* system by downplaying its feudal nature and characterizing the *inquilinos* as modern employees, Dominguez described in detail the daily forms of oppression that the *inquilinos* had to suffer. While *inquilinos* were paid a salary for the extra labor they performed in addition to the customary tasks and obligations specified in the agreement, this salary was well

---

[564] Id., 40, 113.
[565] R. Dominguez, *Nuestro Sistema de Inquilinaje* (Santiago: Imprenta del Correo, 1867).
[566] Id., 40.

below market rate and, for the most part, in kind rather than in cash. Payments in kind were administered through the *hacienda*'s own *tienda-despacho*, a hybrid of bank and emporium, and yet another instrument for the landlord to gain profit at the expense of the workers. Because the *inquilinos* were only allowed to purchase necessary goods from the *tienda-despacho*, any cash salary they would receive from the landlord would ultimately end back in the latter's pockets; further, the lending practices of the emporium were actual debt-traps for many *inquilinos* and their families.[567] Other forms of oppression included "contracts" by which the *inquilino* would sell to the landowner the crop cultivated on the parcel in advance of the harvest well below market price. Unfair contractual terms placed all the risks on the *inquilino* and gave all the benefits to the landlord. The latter purchased the crop at half its market price and with no harvesting costs; any risk of crop loss was on the *inquilino*, whose obligation to deliver the crop would be simply postponed to the next harvest.[568]

The racial nature of the exploitation perpetuated through the *inquilinaje* system was not lost on critics such as Dominguez. The *inquilinaje* developed and expanded over the course of the eighteenth century in connection with transformations in the Chilean colonial economy and racial structure; specifically, the growth of the *mestizo* population and the surge of wheat export to neighboring Peru. As the separate racial status of *indio* subject to the payment of a yearly tribute to the Castilian crown loosened, under the impetus of both reformist legislation as well as successful resistance strategies on the part of the *indio* population, crossing the line between *indio* and *mestizo* became easier. Consequently, the *encomienda* proved less effective as a system for exacting indigenous labor. In late colonial times and after independence, the *inquilinaje* allowed the Chilean landowning class to effectively perpetuate the system of racialized labor exploitation by subjugating the increasing number of free *mestizos* seeking agricultural wage labor as *inquilinos*. Dominguez traced this progression in racial exploitation in very clear terms:

---

[567] T. M. Klubock, "Ránquil: Violence and Peasant Politics on Chile's Southern Frontier," in G. Grandin and G. M. Joseph (eds.), *A Century of Revolution: Insurgent and Counterinsurgent Violence during Latin America's Long Cold War* (Durham, NC: Duke University Press, 2010), 127–128.

[568] M. Gongora, *Origen de los Inquilinos de Chile Central* (Santiago: Editorial Universitaria, 1960).

The land cultivated by the *indio* at the time of the conquest, was tolled by the *mestizo* in colonial times and now by the *inquilino* who is his descendant. The same happened for the landlords, with the lands and the power associated with the *encomienda* passing from fathers to sons and, in part because of this transfer, which in regards to persons should have ended with independence, in part because of ignorance, bad faith or other reasons, the landlords rule and the workers obey. The constitutional precepts have no value.[569]

As this passage shows, the contrast between the *inquilinos'* feudal serfdom and the promises of freedom and citizenship contained in the many successive constitutions of the new republic could not have been starker. Accordingly, in the copious political economy literature published in the post-independence decades, the *inquilinaje* was presented as the one feudal remnant that emptied the new nation's promise of freedom of all its meaning. Dominguez himself conveyed this notion of a feudal anomaly in Chile's otherwise progressive and grandiose march toward freedom with flamboyant language:

> Then came the time of independence. The enslaved and oppressed peoples [of the colonial time] were succeeded by free people full of virility and energy. The ports of America opened up to all nations and thousands of foreigners were quick to show up with their industry and commerce. New towns emerged as if from nowhere and liberty established itself in them and a bright future opened up for Columbus' continent .... The liberty enshrined in all the constitutions of the American nations and granted to all who set foot on their soil is a powerful guarantee for its social classes or at least this is what their inhabitants believe. However, this freedom, recognized and put into writing, is dead letter with no meaning for the workers who with their hard labor procure the riches of their soil. In Chile, this anomaly is tacitly tolerated as we will demonstrate in this essay.[570]

For Dominguez, the *inquilinaje* system not only severely limited laborers' freedom; it also betrayed the promise of equality enshrined in Article 12 of the Chilean Constitution of 1833, which proclaimed that all citizens are equal before the law and that no one social class is privileged in Chile. The *inquilinos*, Dominguez noted, are a disfavored social class that endures in conditions of inequality, oppressed by the power of an old feudal social custom that is stronger than the law on the books.

---

[569] Dominguez, *Nuestro Sistema de Inquilinaje*, 32.
[570] Id., 30.

While liberal thinkers generally agreed that the *inquilinaje* was a property form that thwarted the liberal ambitions of republican Chile, few called for its abolition. For most, the *inquilinaje* was a landholding form in need of reform, with the scope and the nature of the proposed reforms varying dramatically. Dominguez, a progressive liberal, envisioned a multifaceted reform, comprising a new regulatory regime mandating security of tenure and clear and fair employment terms. Dominguez also suggested establishing special courts for agrarian matters in order to overcome the obvious disadvantage faced by the *inquilinos* in the regular courts, which were staffed with representatives of the landowning class. Dominguez was well aware that his proposals to regulate the terms and conditions landowners could impose on their *inquilinos* clashed with the unrestrained freedom that characterized "absolute" *dominum*, a concept that, as we will see in the next section, was starting to pervade the conversation about property in the newly independent nation. And yet, Dominguez insisted that the deference owed to liberal property should not condone landowners' oppressive behavior.

> The first difficulty one encounters is to reconcile the respect owed to property with the rights of the *inquilinos*. To be sure a landowner has the right to use freely his property and to employ the workers he wishes; nonetheless the relations with these persons and his proprietary rights need to be regulated and brought within the limits of what is just and beneficial. It is not equitable that the *inquilino* is deprived of what belongs to him with no reason; and, similarly, that his ignorance is exploited for the benefit of the employer; it is critical that he be guaranteed what is due to him so that he can devote himself to his work and provide for his children free of worries.[571]

Not all were of the same mind. A conservative liberal like Lauro Rafael Barros had very different ideas about the role of the *inquilinaje* in modern Chile and the wisdom of regulating the relationship between landlords and their *inquilinos*. In 1875, Barros, a landowner who, in the 1890s, would be appointed Ministro de Hacienda and would serve as president of the Sociedad Nacional de Agricultura, wrote a piece entitled *Ensayo sobre la condición de las clases rurales en Chile*.[572] Barros, dramatically recast the dominant narrative about the *inquilinaje* being a

---

[571] Id., 59.

[572] L. Barros, *Ensayo sobre la condición de las clases rurales en Chile. Memoria presentada al Concurso de la Exposición Internacional de 1875* (Santiago: Imprenta Agricola de Enrique Ahrens, 1875).

feudal anomaly. To be sure, in colonial times, the *inquilinaje* had been a tool of feudal oppression but, in modern Chile, the *inquilinaje* had effectively transformed into a type of freely entered contract between landlord and laborer, critical to expanding the productivity of the country's agriculture. Barros did admit that, in a country like Chile in which virtually all the land is controlled by a small number of large owners, the *inquilinos*, in order to have a parcel of land to cultivate, would have no choice but to accept the landlords' conditions. Yet Barros seemed oblivious to the overwhelming likelihood of coercion in such circumstances. A conservative animated by a blend of benevolent paternalism and die-hard laissez-faire ideas, Barros elaborated on the economic and moral benefits of the *inquilinaje*:

> The *inquilinaje*, in the form it takes in today's Chile, is a source of prosperity for productive and of welfare for the rural classes. The *inquilino* is today a provider of necessary extra labor without whom the expansion of our agricultural production would be almost impossible, and, in turn, the landlords, partly out of interest (interest is often an element of progress), partly due to the now more widespread education, know how to reward and give security to the laborers who, with them, take in the noble struggle of agricultural work.[573]

Barros was not the lone voice asserting the merits of the *inquilinaje*, and indeed the vocal critique of feudal property was in fact rather without substance. The *inquilinaje* survived well into the twentieth century.

A New Synthesis of Ideas for the Chilean Republic

In 1844, an incendiary essay entitled "Sociabilidad Chilena" appeared in the pages of the literary periodical *El Crepuscolo*. Its author, Francisco Bilbao, vocally incited fellow Chileans to exit once and for all the Middle Ages, which he identified with the Spanish colonial legacy of feudalism and Catholicism, and to develop a "new synthesis" of ideals for modern republican Chile.[574] Bilbao was a radical liberal whose essay earned him accusations of blasphemy and a conspicuous fine. But the idea that a new synthesis of ideas was needed to guide the new republic was widely shared among the politically active upper classes. What the specific elements of this new synthesis would be was the question that had

---

[573] Id., 18.
[574] F. Bilbao, "Sociabilidad Chilena," in *Obras Completas de Francisco Bilbao*, vol. I (Buenos Aires: Imprenta de Buenos Aires, 1865), 3–16.

dominated public debate since the 1820s. It was a contentious question, involving deep disagreements on issues such as how to balance the principles of liberal constitutionalism and the calls for a strong executive capable of securing political stability and how to reconcile the new ideas about secularism that came from France and the enduring power of the Catholic Church in the new republic. However, one notion seemed to elicit broad agreement, regardless of ideological inclination: that the path toward modernity ran through robust and inviolable property rights modeled after Roman *dominium*. Both *pelucones* and *pipiolos*, as conservatives and liberals were colloquially known, saw property as fundamental to the making of the nation and envisioned the fundamentals of property law in terms that, at first glance, appeared strikingly similar. Even Bilbao celebrated the virtues of property with words that scream individualism and hardly befit a rumored subversive:

> The Individual, the human I, body and soul, needs property to achieve his mission on Earth. He needs property to develop his intellectual life as well as his physical life and that of his children.[575]

In the cohort of politicians and statesmen that shaped the political structure of the Chilean republic, many had juristic training and could claim expertise in matters of property. The Spanish Crown's establishment of the Real Universidad de San Felipe in 1747, with three chairs, out of eleven, devoted to legal subjects (law, canon law, and Roman law), had given impetus to juristic studies. Manuel Montt, Mariano Egaña, José Victorino Lastarria, and Antonio Gracia Reyes had all studied law, either at San Felipe or at the Instituto Nacional, which was established later. They could cast themselves as simultaneously theorists and technicians of property. They were public intellectuals steeped in the property discourse of Spanish, French, and Atlantic liberalism, as well as experts in the technicalities of Roman property law and well-acquainted with the property treatises of the great masters of France and Germany. Despite their ideological differences, these jurists-statesmen shared a pragmatic and reformist attitude toward nation-building. They favored workable rather than ideal solutions and they focused on immediate goals such as stability, gradual liberalization, and economic development.

Because a Código Civil for the new republic was a monumental and controversial task that would not be accomplished until 1857, the general

---

[575] F. Bilbao, "Revolución," in *Obras Completas de Francisco Bilbao*, vol. I (Buenos Aires: Imprenta de Buenos Aires, 1865), 23.

contours of the new regime of property were first sketched in the several Chilean constitutions enacted between 1818 and 1833. Acclaimed by the newspaper *El Mercurio de Valparaiso* as the document that sanctioned the reawakening of Chile, the constitution of 1828 enshrined the two linchpins of liberal property: the inviolability and free alienability of property. Article 17 declared that "no citizen can be deprived of what he owns or has a legal right to, not even of a part of his property, no matter how small" without a judicial decision and the payment of just compensation. Article 126 declared that the *mayorazgos* and all other restrictions preventing the free transfer of land were "forever abolished."[576] The *mayorazgo*, a key albeit recent institution in Chile, was a property form originating in Castilian law and consisting of an individual's right to the enjoyment of certain aggregate property, with the condition that it be passed in its integrity, perpetually and successively to the eldest son. Virtually unknown in Chile until the mid-eighteenth century, *mayorazgos* became common when the growing colonial *creole* elite, which was amassing fortunes through the export of wheat and in mining, started seeking to consolidate its social and economic power. After independence, this *creole* aristocracy took the reins of the new country.

These two provisions sanctioning the inviolability and free alienability of property were hardly remarkable; they echoed the liberal property discourse that was sweeping through much of Europe and the Americas and hardly differed from analogous provisions in other constitutions of the time. And yet, both provisions, despite their universalist flavor and liberal appeal, and notwithstanding the broad political consensus around absolute property, stirred conflict, as they affected in complicated ways the economic and political interests of different segments of the Chilean elite.

Gaining a sense of the specific concerns that preoccupied Chilean jurists and politicians requires immersion in the juristic commentaries, political pamphlets, and political economy treatises produced from the 1820s on. In this copious literature, evidence of a burgeoning Chilean "Republic of Letters,"[577] one finds, below the surface of global liberal

---

[576] E. Cordero Quinzacara, "La Dogmática Constitucional de la Propiedad en el Derecho Chileno" (2006) 19 *Revista Chilena de Derecho* 125–148; D. Hugh Caldera, "La Garantía Constitucional del Derecho de Propiedad y la Expropiación" (1979) 6 *Revista Chilena De Derecho* 312–335.

[577] Collier, *Chile*, xix–xx.

property rhetoric, a vibrant regional property debate that implicated highly controversial questions about social hierarchy, racial oppression, slavery, and the role of the Church in the new republic. While all apparently subscribing to the agenda of modern absolute property, writers viewed the relation between property, liberty, and equality in starkly different terms. Who were the winners and the losers in the effort to make land freely alienable? What was the meaning of *igualdad*, and whose property was inviolable? *Pelucones* and *pipiolos* fought vehemently over these questions.

The Struggle over the *Mayorazgos* and the Tension between the Free Alienability and the Inviolability of Property

Despite the bold declaration that *mayorazgos* were "forever abolished," enshrined in the Constitution of 1828, the struggle to make land freely alienable proved intensely divisive in Chile and made slow progress between the days of independence and 1852, when the *mayorazgo* was finally repealed. As the tide of anti-feudal rhetoric kept mounting throughout Europe and the Atlantic world and political economists extolled the economic and social benefits of a free market in land, the continued existence of property forms designed to keep land in the hands of a small landowning class, such as the *mayorazgo*, became hard to defend. Further, the *mayorazgos* threatened the very liberal and egalitarian values that had animated the independence movement. In the words of Pedro José Prado Jaraquemada (1754–1827), one of the most influential political figures of the late colonial era and the early days of independence, the tension was obvious: how could Chile be called democratic if it still allowed *mayorazgos*?[578] No plausible arguments can be made in favor of the *mayorazgos*, Prado Jaraquemada noted, and "those who support retaining this barbarian institution do so only because of selfish personal interest, or fanaticism, or acritical respect for tradition, or capricious partiality and class solidarity."[579] While the champions of the *mayorazgo* may have been few, they were definitely illustrious and vocal. Prominent among them was Juan Egaña (1768–1836), one of the most influential figures in the cohort of jurists-statesmen that shaped the

---

[578] P. J. Prado Jaraquemada, *Los Actuales Poseedores de Mayorazgos de Chile Apoyan la Justicia con que la Representacion Nacional ha Derectado su Reduccion al Valor Primitivo en que se Fundaron* (Santiago: Imprenta de la Independencia, 1827), 3.
[579] Id., 4.

early republic. The debate between Egaña and the liberal critics of the *mayorazgo* laid bare the internal tensions of the idea of "absolute" property. Both sides rested their arguments on the platitude that modern property is "absolute," and yet they could hardly agree on the implications of this proposition for the institution of the *mayorazgo*. In the case of the *mayorazgo*, the two main features of "absolute" property, its free alienability and the inviolability of owners' rights, seemed to work at cross-purposes. Abolishing the *mayorazgo* would certainly facilitate the free circulation of property in the market, but it would also deprive the owners of future interests inherent in their rights.

The campaign to abolish the *mayorazgo* played up the argument that the "essence" of modern property is the owner's ability to freely dispose of his property and that the *mayorazgo* severely impinged on this ability. As Prado Jaraquemada noted:

> To deprive property of its alienability and transmissibility, which are its most precious qualities; to have the preservation of families rest on the endowment of one individual only in each generation, at the cost of condemning all others to misery; and to base this endowment on the random fact of the order of birth, rather than on merit or virtue, is not only repugnant to the dictates of reason and to the natural sentiment, but also contrary to the principles of the social contract and to the maxims of legislation and politics.[580]

However, the pamphlet also noted, this absolute right to freely dispose ends with death and to extend its reach beyond the owner's lifetime is to destroy property, not to consolidate it. Allowing owners to control their wealth after their death means depriving their successors of this same right. Owners of *mayorazgos*, the authors concluded, far from being true owners are in fact condemned to be mere usufructuaries, with no right to dispose of their property as they wish.

Juan Egaña and his fellow defenders of the *mayroazgo* were, by Egaña's own admission, in a difficult position. Well aware of the broad popularity that the idea of free alienability enjoyed among the liberal elites and mindful of the risk of being labeled retrograde supporters of feudalism, they were under no illusion about the likely final outcome of the contest. "Our pen," Egaña wrote at the outset of his *Memoria Sobre Los Mayorazgos de Chile* (1828),[581] "far from becoming excited in the hope

---

[580] Id., 13.
[581] J. Egaña, *Memoria Sobre Los Mayorazgos de Chile* (Santiago: Imprenta de R. Rengifo, 1828).

of a favorable outcome, moves slowly, with the fatigue and the discouragement that come from a long fight that started in 1818."[582] To avoid appearing the mouth of naked class interest or the backward-looking champion of the feudal, Juan Egaña cast his objections to the abolition of the *mayorazgo* in the same liberal language used by his opponents. Egaña crafted a narrative in which present owners of *mayorazgos*, impatient to sell their lands and blinded by "the damn greed of profit," sought to shatter a fundamental principle of natural law – the inviolability of property rights, present and future. Hoping to enlist more supporters among the juristic elite enamored with Roman law, Egaña skillfully folded into the narrative two of the dearest treasures of the nineteenth-century Romanists: absolute *dominium* and the *ius abutendi*. Regardless of its relatively recent appearance in Chile, Egaña argued, the *mayorazgo* is an age-old property form, a corollary of the principle that the owner has absolute *dominium*. Just as owners have every right to destroy their property at their whim, all the more so they have the right to bequeath their property to whomever they wish and to impose any restriction or condition they deem appropriate. However, for this absolute right to dispose to be meaningful, Egaña added, the owner ought to have security that his acts of disposition are fully protected and beneficiaries ought to be confident that their future interests are inviolable. As Egaña put it:

> To deprive successors of their expected legal rights is to impose on them the harsh punishment of deluding hope, as Bentham put it ... it is to sacrifice on the altar of self-interest the principle of security that provides the protection of all these expectations and prescribes that their fulfillment, to the extent that it depends on the laws, be commensurate to the hopes generated.[583]

Egaña also needed to confront his opponents' accusation that the *mayorazgo* was a feudal institution fundamentally at odds with the democratic commitments of the Chilean republic. Declaring himself unwilling "to be intimidated by the ghost of feudalism" too easily evoked by the liberals,[584] Egaña stressed the difference between the *mayorazgo* – which rested exclusively on private ownership rights – and actual feudal property – which impermissibly merged private property and public sovereignty. Similarly misplaced, Egaña argued, was the concern that

[582] Id., 1.
[583] Id., 8.
[584] Id., 18.

the *mayorazgo* threatened republican equality by perpetuating political and economic oligarchies. All that republican government demands, Egaña noted, is individuals' equality before the law, not actual equality of fortunes. Oligarchies rest on political inequality, Egaña continued, not on wealth inequalities, which are the result of natural differences in talent and effort.[585]

Hoping to stoke fears of expropriation and redistribution among the landowning class, Egaña, who had just denounced the liberals for shrewdly evoking the ghost of feudalism, was himself quick to reanimate another powerful ghost in the history of property, the Roman *lex agraria*. Not only is wealth inequality natural, Egaña argued, it is also hard to tackle effectively. When Rome passed the agrarian law to address the inequitable concentration of land, any resulting improvement was short-lived and its benefits were far outweighed by the long-lasting social turmoil the law caused.[586]

By the 1850s, the time was finally ripe for the abolition of the *mayorazgos*. The task of reconciling the free alienability of property with the inviolability of property was taken up by Andrés Bello, a poet, humanist, and the most prominent Chilean jurist. Bello devised an ingenious solution, making the land freely alienable but protecting vested property interests by converting the *mayorazgos* into an entailed stream of income at 4 percent of the value of the land.

The public discourse around property was also changing and, by the 1850s, Juan Egaña's denial that concentration of wealth perpetuated through the *mayorazgos* bred political oligarchies seemed disingenuous to many. Liberal writers started openly voicing fears that modern absolute property had generated a "new feudalism of wealth." In 1844, Bilbao had been the first to question whether the republican government was in fact intent in resurrecting the past, instead of continuing the revolutionary process set in motion by the independence movement. Now, new voices echoed Bilbao's concerns. Chief among them, was Pedro Félix Vicuña (1805–1874), the founder and publisher of the newspaper *El Mercurio de Valparaiso*. His treatise *El Porvenir del Hombre*, published in 1858,[587] proved influential and captured the concerns of a new generation of liberals. Dedicated to *La Juventud Chilena*, Vicuna's

---

[585] Id., 17.
[586] Id.
[587] P. F. Vicuna, *El Porvenir del Hombre* (Valparaiso: Imprenta del Comercio, 1858).

treatise urged young Chileans to rethink the relation between property and democracy:

> Let us shape democracy so that property be its primary foundation but also so that property not become a political power that can halt the triumph of freedom.[588]

Property remained a central element of liberals' vision for the future of Chile but their understanding of the relationship between property and equality was growing in complexity and sophistication. The security of property, Vicuna explained, is the fundamental condition of our sociability and the motor of progress and civilization. Yet, he warned, property is power, economic and political. Concentrated ownership of land and capital allows a new aristocracy to subjugate the working masses and to reshape for its own advantage the laws that govern society. To remedy the new feudalism, Vicuna called for the redistribution of property and the establishment of a national bank and of a robust public credit system.[589] Vicuna and Bilbao's ideas about property and power remained confined to a small group of progressives but they presaged themes that would become prominent in mainstream juristic circles when the 1925 constitution introduced the idea of the "social function" of property.

Feudal Reaction or Liberal Progress: The Inviolability of the Church's Property

Talk of a new feudalism also shaped another vexed debate in newly independent Chile, that over how to treat the property of the Catholic Church. The inviolability of property was one of the cardinal principles of the new republic, but did it apply to the immense wealth of the Church? After all, for the secular liberals who had fought for independence, the Church exemplified the feudal oppression that Chile had endured in colonial times. Would the extension of the principle of inviolability to the property of the ecclesiastical orders halt the progress toward liberalism and reinstate a new feudalism?

In colonial Spanish America, the Crown and the Church had an almost symbiotic relationship by virtue of the *Real Patronato de las Indias*. Established through three papal bulls starting in the fifteenth century, this system of patronage entrusted the Spanish Crown with

---

[588] Id., 3.
[589] Id., 12–16.

significant control over the Church, with regard to both ecclesiastical appointments and property matters. In return, the Crown pledged to assist in the Christianization of its colonial empire through the erection of churches and convents, the establishment of religious educational institutions, and the support of missionaries. Under this royal patronage, the Church became the single most influential institution in Latin America as well as the single largest landowner and credit institution.

At the time of independence, the place of the Church in the republic became a charged question and one of the points of greatest disagreement between *pelucones* and *pipiolos*. It was a question that involved ideology, property, and sovereignty. The political and ideological profile of the ecclesiastical elite, by and large royalist and conservative, hardly fit with the republican and liberal values of the political elite of the 1820s. Further, the vast property of the Church was held through ownership forms, such as tithes, *censos*, and *capellanias*, that resembled feudal dues, combining aspects of ownership and profit with sovereignty and social control as well as religious piety.

Inspired by French Enlightenment thought and its criticism of the role that the Church as an institution had played during the Old Regime, the Chilean liberals of the 1820s viewed the Church as one of the pillars of the oppressive feudal order that they sought to dismantle and its immense landed wealth as critical to expanding the economy. The most obvious effort to disestablish the Church in the new independent republic was a decree of September 6, 1824, that seized property belonging to the regular religious orders and abolished tithes. Title to the properties of the regular orders was transferred to the state and their management entrusted to the Ministerio de la Hacienda, and the state began to pay clerics a cash pension and to provide other forms of material support and supplies. Article 10 of the decree explained that the rationale for the transfer of the Church's property to the state was the need to relieve the regular clergy from the burden of property management, so that clerics could devote themselves exclusively to their spiritual ministry, free of any "prophane distraction."

Interestingly, the Church responded with arguments drawn from the liberal property discourse so influential among the liberal elites of Europe and the Americas: economic productivity and citizenship. In March 1825, the order of the Recoletos Dominicos pleaded to be exempted from the 1824 decree. The clerics noted that they had instantly complied when, in the middle of the night of the previous September, the government commissioner showed up at the door of their convent to enforce the decree. Yet, they believed that their rural and urban properties should be returned to them. Because of their long-standing involvement in the local agrarian economy, the friars, the petition argued, were best positioned to productively manage the lands and to employ the revenue to help the local population. More surprising was the Recoletos' reasoning on the relationship between property and citizenship:

> The more thoughtful politicians have vocally advocated that there be no clergymen who is not an owner, so that there be no individual who is not a good citizen.[590]

The Recoletos did not have to wait long to see their property returned. When the liberals were defeated in the Civil War of 1829–1830, the new conservative regime, which relied on the Church to secure political and social stability, embarked on an effort to re-entrench the Catholic Church. A law of September 1830 provided that properties confiscated from the Church were to be returned or compensation to be paid. But the most effective guarantee for the Church came with the constitution of 1833. Largely drafted by two prominent conservative San Felipe alumni, Mariano Egaña and Manuel José Gandarillas (1789–1846), the constitution of 1833 incorporated ostensibly liberal language, but the limits of its commitment to liberalism did not escape the more radical fringe of the liberal party. One of the most significant innovations in the constitution of 1833 was that the guarantee of the inviolability of property applied to all property, whether owned by individuals or by "communities." The term "communities," absent in the previous liberal constitution of 1828, referred primarily to the property of the ecclesiastical orders. The reaction to the new provision was mixed. Manuel Carrasco Albano (1834–1873), a liberal jurist and politician who, in the 1850s, penned a highly influential volume of *Comentarios sobre la Constitucion Politica de 1833*, saw the extension of the inviolability of property to ecclesiastical property as a laudable departure from the furious overreaction against the power of the Church in the Old Regime that swept through many European nations.

> This clarification seeks to prevent the confiscation of ecclesiastical properties or property belonging to religious orders that, since the eighteenth

---

[590] "Sesión del Congreso Nacional 66, en 21 de marzo de 1825, número 151, por Frai Matías Fuenzalida," in Valentín Letelier (ed.), *Sesiones de los Cuerpos Lejislativos de la República de Chile (1810–1845)*, vol. 11 (Valparaíso: Biblioteca del Congreso Nacional de Chile 1886–1908), 96.

century, have been the victims of the reaction against their wealth and ostentation. England, France, Germany, Spain and Piedmont, and later some of the American republics, have adopted this measure at different times, either as revenge, or as wrath, or as a response to the problems of the Treasury or as an economic measure to foster the circulation of the immense properties accumulated by the Church and augment the wealth of the nation.[591]

The interpretation of radical liberals was quite different. Francisco Bilbao denounced the restitution of ecclesiastical properties as a reactionary effort to undo the liberal revolution and resurrect the legacy of feudalism and Catholicism:

> The reaction is supported by the old unity of ideas. This unity was Catholicism. Accordingly, all its institutions are supported and its preoccupations satisfied. This is the reason for the restitution of all properties to the communities[592] .... The current government is committed to resurrecting the past, and, hence, is retrograde![593]

As in the case of the *mayorazgos*, in the political struggle over State-Church relations in the aftermath of independence, the constitutional framework of liberal absolute *dominium* proved rhetorically powerful but also fundamentally under-determined and malleable.

Property, Race, and Citizenship

Property and equality before the law were both central to the "new synthesis of ideas" that guided the Chilean republic. The constitution of 1833 promised a nation of equal individuals with inviolable property rights. Article 12 stated not only that all Chileans were equal in the eyes of the law but also that "there are no privileged classes in Chile."[594] In his 1854 *Comentario*, Manuel Carrasco Albano declared this principle to be "one of the most precious conquests of human reason against the unjust exceptions introduced because of social concerns and reinforced by the passage of time and by ignorance."[595] The narrative propounded by the

---

[591] M. Carrasco Albano, *Comentarios sobre la Constitucion Politica de 1833*, 2nd ed. (Santiago: Imprenta de la Libraria del Mercurio, 1874), 50.

[592] Bilbao, *Sociabilidad*, 31.

[593] Id., 33.

[594] Albano, *Comentarios sobre la Constitucion Politica de 1833*, article 12, paragraph 5, page 41.

[595] Id., 42.

liberal political elite described a linear progression from the inequalities of the colonial era to a present of equality. Slavery and the detailed racial hierarchy of the *Código de las Indias* were confined to a distant past and the Chilean republic now stood alongside France and the United States in affirming the equality of all. And yet, Carrasco Albano himself recognized that the promise of equality before the law could hardly be deemed fulfilled. Striking a sour note in the chorus of liberal public intellectuals, the prominent constitutionalist lamented that "even today, under our republican government, what deviations, what mitigations and infractions does this great principle of equality have to suffer!"[596] The relationship between modern property and equality before the law was more complicated than the dominant liberal discourse of the time made it seem and it was saturated with racial assumptions. Whose *dominium* was inviolable and whose freely transferable were divisive questions that consistently influenced two important debates of the time, namely those over the abolition of African slavery and over the question of indigenous property in the southern province of *Araucania*. Once again, absolute *dominium* proved a malleable and meaningless concept, a technical tool for policing racial boundaries rather than an instrument of equality and freedom.

In the early 1820s, as radicals and many liberals fought for the complete abolition of African slavery, the inviolability of property became the legal peg used to ward off the call for total and unconditional abolition. In Chile, enslaved individuals of African descent were a relatively small part of the workforce compared to other parts of Hispano-America. Comprising approximately twenty to twenty-five thousand individuals in the eighteenth century, the population of African descent had declined to ten to twelve thousand individuals by 1810. Their status and material conditions varied significantly: about half of the individuals of African descent were legally enslaved; others were free either because their owners had manumitted them in their wills or because they had purchased their own freedom. As France abolished slavery in 1794 and Saint Domingue did the unthinkable by overthrowing colonialism and slavery and becoming the first Black republic, Chilean liberals came to see African slavery in Chile as fundamentally at odds with the values that had inspired the independence movement and the establishment of the republic. In 1811, after a vocal campaign led by the patriot and social

---

[596] Id., 43.

reformer Manuel de Salas (1754–1841), Chile became the first republic in Latin America to enact a *ley de la libertad de vientres* (law on the freedom of wombs). While the law did not apply retroactively to existing enslaved individuals, it granted freedom to all individuals born in Chile after its enactment as well as to any traveling enslaved person who stayed in Chile longer than six months. The law was largely ignored by slave-owners and, a decade later, little had changed, leading liberals to intensify their call for total abolition.

On June 23, 1823, senator José Miguel Infante (1778–1844) presented the Senate with a proposal to "declare free all slaves still existing in Chile and all who set foot on the national territory."[597] Infante's proposal found a fierce opponent in Mariano Egaña, son of Juan Egaña and a prominent conservative jurist trained at the Universidad de San Felipe. Property was at the heart of the dramatic conflict between Infante and Egaña. Infante, like Egaña, was a lawyer and San Felipe alumnus and was an avid reader of the French encyclopedists and a passionate reformer whose moderate liberalism of the days of independence had turned into radicalism by the 1820s. Historians recount that, on the evening of June 23, in a senate hall lit by the feeble light of candles that accentuated the gravitas of the moment, Infante delivered a jarring denunciation of the inconsistency between slavery and republican values:

> It is four thousand citizens who are suffering from this barbaric law, four thousand consciences who lament their disgrace, four thousand victims who ask for protection from us who, in the name of Law and the dignity of the individual, made the Revolution. We cannot deny the freedom they are demanding from us because we would be disavowing the holy cause that led us to transform a political and social situation that mocked our redemptive ideal.[598]

A deep silence fell on the Senate hall and a visibly emotional Infante concluded that all he desired was to be remembered by posterity as the author of the motion to free the enslaved African population. The Senate approved the proposed law unanimously but objections that property is absolute and inviolable were immediate. In the same hours in which Infante was addressing the Senate, José Santiago Muñoz Besanilla, a veteran of the revolution and a liberal, penned an article for the

---

[597] G. Feliu Cruz, *La Abolicion de la Esclavitud en Chile*, 2nd ed. (Santiago: Editorial Universitaria, 1973).
[598] Quoted in id., 66.

periodical *El Tizón Republicano* demanding clarifications of the effects of the abolition of slavery on property rights:

> The Senate has sanctioned the freedom of slaves. We would like to learn the reasons the Senate invokes to dispose of the property of particular individuals; or whether the peoples who have entrusted the Senate with the protection of their security, have granted the Senate any right to do so.[599]

When the law was transmitted to the executive, the property argument found a receptive ear in Mariano Egaña, then serving as Ministro de Gobierno, who, in private conversations with members of the Senate, was adamant that the principle of the inviolability of property trumped any justified and laudable concern about the fate of Chile's enslaved population. Therefore, the note received by the Senate on July 1st, bearing the signature of the Supreme Director Ramon Freire and of Egaña himself, did not come as a surprise.

> While the Supreme Director is of the same opinion as the Senate with regards to the freedom of the slaves declared this past July 25th, nonetheless he would be remiss not to make clear that this provision is a direct attack on the sacrosanct right to property that is to be considered the first and foremost element of the social order, upon which neither the Senate, nor the Government, nor any other authority can infringe. Slaves belong exclusively to citizens whose property cannot be taken without paying compensation and for this reason the Director will never grant his approval until a fund sufficient to compensate owners for their loss of property has been set aside.[600]

In a matter of days, the debate over the abolition of African slavery had dramatically changed tone. Philosophical and moral arguments about freedom and human nature had slipped into the background and the battle over slavery was now fought on the terrain of modern property, absolute and inviolable. In his response to the executive, the president of the Senate, Augustin Eyzaguirre, went straight to the weakness of the property argument: the assumption that human beings can be owned. The fundamental right all humans have to freedom, Eyzaguirre wrote, makes slaveowners' property rights in human beings iniquitous and undeserving of compensation. But Egaña would not budge. Again, speaking through the office of the Supreme Director, he vigorously reasserted his conviction that property is absolute and inviolable, no matter what its

---

[599] Id., 67.
[600] Id., 76.

origin and how iniquitous. The inherent freedom of all individuals and the full eradication of slavery are laudable principles, Egaña wrote, but they are abstract theories. Wise policy is an altogether different matter, requiring appreciation of a people's actual customs and concerns and, in Spanish America, enslaved persons had always been deemed to be property.

> In politics what matters is not what is intrinsically just but rather what is attuned to people's usages and preoccupations. Slaves have always been deemed to be the exclusive property of their owners with only minimal limitations introduced in the last centuries as social practices softened. Slaves were bought and sold and subject to all the rules of property; this was authorized by the law of nations and by national laws; and when the nation of Chile, through its Congress, issued the memorable decree of October 15, 1811, it declared that from then on no slaves would be born in Chile but that the decree would not affect living slaves, explaining the reasons for this exception. It is good that philosophers, drawing closer to first principles, now agree that slavery is unjust. These sentiments are just and laudable and so are those of the Senate whose members seek to eradicate slavery. But is this enough of a reason to attack property, even if iniquitous in its origins? ... We should take the approach that best reconciles all rights and interests, securing the acquisition of freedom to slaves while also indemnifying those who have indisputably been deemed to be owners. This would be the best evidence of the determination with which the Nation and the authorities pursue this philanthropic providence.[601]

This dramatic confrontation between the Senate and the executive lasted a full month, until Diego José Benavente, a liberal who served as Ministro de la Hacienda in Freire's cabinet, persuaded Egaña to desist. The Senate's bill finally became law on July 23, 1823, with no provision about compensation.

Vocally asserted in the case of slaveowners, the inviolability of property was easily brushed aside when the republic sought to expropriate indigenous lands in the project of wealth appropriation and racial subjugation euphemistically known as *pacificacion de la Araucania*. In the early decades of the new republic, plans to develop the southern region of Araucania, inhabited by the Mapuche population, were hardly a priority in the government's agenda as the economic interests of the elite were largely concentrated in the Northern mining region and in the agricultural *Valle Central*. In the narrative of the creole liberal elite that had

---

[601] Id., 78.

fought for Chile's independence, the *Araucanos* were "el lustre de la America," valiant warriors who had successfully resisted the Spaniards and, hence, deserved to be included in the new nation. In a decree of March 4, 1819, Bernardo O'Higgins, Director Supremo del Estado de Chile, denounced the inhumane policy of the Spanish Crown with regard to the native inhabitants of Chile, which the *Leyes de Indias* relegated to the degrading status of *Naturales*, subject to the payment of a yearly personal tribute and deprived of political representation. The decree announced that this "precious portion of our species" was now "to be called Chilean citizens, free as the other inhabitants of the state, with the same voice and representation, the same capacity to enter any type of contract, to appear in court, to marry, to engage in commerce."[602] As equal citizens, the native inhabitants of Araucania were also to enjoy all the moral and economic benefits of modern *dominium*.

Despite O'Higgins' benevolent call to inclusive citizenship, the ultimate goal of racial domination and land annexation quickly became manifest. Only a couple of years after O'Higgins had welcomed the Mapuche as full citizens, a law of 1823 specified that citizens of indigenous origin were only granted full *dominium* over the land they individually "possessed and used," while all excess indigenous land, cultivated communally, belonged to the state and was to be sold at public auctions.[603] While individual Mapuche owners were free to exercise the other core entitlement of modern *dominium*, the right to freely alienate proved detrimental for indigenous owners, many of whom lost their land to creole and foreign speculators, often through fraudulent transactions.

In the 1850s, as the demand for agricultural products grew, fueled by the Californian and Australian gold rushes, the government turned to the southern region with new interest. In the public opinion, the *Araucanos* were no longer precious and equal members of the nation, but rather, in the words of a reader of the newspaper *El Mercurio*, published in 1859 "a barbarian and unyielding tribe, deaf to the Gospels and incapable of harboring any noble sentiment."[604] Wondering how the government could have allowed such a ferocious population "to be at the doorstep

---

[602] The decree is available at www.archivonacional.gob.cl/616/w3-article- 85377.html?_nor edirect=1.

[603] A. Jara, "Ley de 10 de junio de 1823," in *Legislación indigenista de Chile: Recopilación e introducción de Alvaro Jara* (Mexico: Instituto Indigenista Interamericano, 1956), 25.

[604] "Editorial de 'El Mercurio' sobre la ocupación de la Araucanía," *El Mercurio de Valparaíso* (May 24, 1859), 2.

of our homes, posing a perennial threat to property, liberty and order,"[605] the reader called for the valiant Chilean army to occupy the region and for the government to complete the appropriation of its lands. Some of the most prominent political figures in Chile had already started drawing up competing plans to conquer, "pacify," or develop the south in 1820s, and the merits and flaws of these plans were now before the Camara de Diputados.[606] Property was at the core of the *Diputados'* discussion with two related questions needing a resolution. The first was whether the Mapuches had full *dominium* or instead a smaller form of divided *dominium*. The answer to his first question determined the solution to the second dilemma, namely, whether the most appropriate legal means to acquire the Mapuches' land was expropriation or purchase.

In September 1863, Cornelio Saavedra (1821–1891) who, in 1857 had been appointed Comandante de armas de Arauco, presented a "pacification plan" involving expropriation. In this proposal, all the lands that the President of the Republic deemed necessary to establish settlements (*poblaciónes*) in the lands occupied by the Mapuches were to be declared of public utility and expropriated. Saavedra's plan caused concern. The Comision de Gobierno de la Camara de Diputados, worried that the indigenous populations of the South would experience expropriation as an act of outright plunder calling for revenge, moved to purchase rather than expropriate the Mapuches' land. Saavedra's expropriation plan also engendered unease among liberal *diputados* with juristic training, such as José Victorino Lastarria (1817–1888), a San Felipe alumnus who by the 1860s had become one of the most prominent constitutional law scholars. The question that preoccupied Lastarria was, as one *diputado* put it, "how to embark on the gradual conquest and civilization of *Araucania* with the constitution in our hands."[607] In the legislative session of August 30, 1864, Lastarria addressed directly the question of the nature of indigenous property. To make the case for the purchase plan of the *Comision*, Lastarria explained the difference between colonial divided *dominium* and modern property. A government taking of the Mapuches' lands, along the lines suggested by Saavedra, would have posed no legal problem under the old colonial law, Lastarria argued, because the indigenous populations had mere *dominium utile* (i.e., use

---

[605] Id., 2.
[606] Camara de Diputados, "Sesión 43 Ordinaria, 9/1/1864," in *Sesiones de Congreso Nacional* (1864), 562.
[607] Diputado Echaurren Huidobro, Sesión 43 Ordinaria, 9/1/1864, 563.

rights), over their lands, while *dominium directum* (i.e., actual title) belonged to the sovereign. However, the new independent Republic of Chile had rejected once and for all the medieval idea of divided *dominium*, granting all its citizens, no matter whether creole or indigenous, full *dominium*. Since the Mapuches were full owners, Lastarria forcefully argued, Saavedra's plan ran afoul of the constitutional guarantee of the inviolability of property.

> It is unconstitutional because, as I said in the last session, the practice and the laws established after our independence recognize that the indigenous have a real property right. Under the *Leyes de Indias*, the direct *dominium* over indigenous land belonged to the sovereign, the king of Spain, and hence could be transferred only by the king. After Chile abandoned these principles of the old law and recognized to indigenous individuals not only the possession but also direct *dominium* of the lands they occupy, no matter how they occupy them, and after laws were passed that regulated the transfer of these lands in order to secure individuals their rights, their *dominium*, isn't it unjust, unconstitutional and, effectively, an aggression to expropriate their lands?[608]

Lastarria believed in the rule of law and sought to uphold the constitutional principle of property that was hailed as the greatest sign of progress in modern Chile. However, that most liberal jurists viewed the principles of citizenship, equality before the law, and the inviolability of property with sheer cynicism became obvious when Benjamin Vicuña Mackenna responded to Lastarria. An alumnus of the law faculty at the Universidad de Chile and the founder of *La Asamblea Constituyente*, a political periodical that advocated for a reform of the 1833 conservative constitution, Vicuna Mackenna ridiculed the constitutional concerns raised by Lastarria. Expropriation, Vicuna Mackenna noted, was in the best interest of the *indios* themselves and, in any case, did the Constitution even apply in the remote southern lands of Arauco?

> I believe the project presented by Señor Saavedra to be much more sensible and larger in scope. It involves the gradual expropriation of the entire *Araucania* region, in the best interest of civilization and the *indio* himself. On the other hand, the counter-project backs off from expropriating the barbarians based on a constitutional concern . . . . But, I ask, does the Constitution apply in *Araucania*? Who can argue this? And if it does not apply, if it is not known and accepted, then where is the constitutional violation? We are reluctant to explore this question in a frank and honest

---

[608] Diputado José Victorino Lastarria, Sesión 43 Ordinaria 9/1/1864, 561.

way. A childish reluctance! Because our constitutional charter is not in force among the savages of *Arauco*, is *Arauco* not part of our national territory? Of course not![609]

A law governing indigenous property was finally passed in 1866 and it was largely consistent with the spirit of Vicuna Mackenna's remarks, making a mockery of the inviolability and free alienability of property. All land over which Mapuche owners could not prove actual and continued possession for at least one year was declared "vacant" (*tierras baldias*) and, hence, property of the Republic. State lands were to be transferred gratuitously but with conditions to settlers who would establish *poblaciones*, or who sold land through public auction in parcels not exceeding fifty hectares. The law also limited indigenous owners' ability to sell their land, requiring sellers to produce a registered title and to comply with special procedures under the supervision of a public official, the Intendente de Arauco. The constitutional principles of property – inviolability and free alienability – remained a dead letter, impotent in the face of the greed for land that moved the government and private land investors to colonize and "pacify" the Mapuche lands of the south.

A Law of Property for the New Republic: Roman Law, the Lessons of History, and the Neapolitan Enlightenment

By the 1850s, the liberal discourse of modern property pervaded public debates in Chile and the fundamental constitutional tenets of modern property were in place. However, Chile still lacked a new private law framework for *dominium*, that is, a set of property concepts and doctrines responsive to the unique needs of the new republic. For the first decades after independence, property law was a multilayered and disorganized body of law resting on the Castilian, Roman Law-based *Siete Partidas* of the thirteenth century as well as on a number of *Recopilaciones* of Spanish private law that applied solely to the Indies. The new national law of property was finally crafted by Andrés Bello, the Venezuelan-born poet and humanist who became Chile's most legendary jurist.

In the cohort of statesmen-jurists who shaped the new nation, Bello was, in many ways, a quirky character. He shared neither the thoroughly liberal political ideas of Infante or Lastarria nor their vocal calls for

---

[609] Diputado Vicuna Mackenna, Sesión 43 Ordinaria 9/1/1864, 559–560.

change, but he was also not a staunch defender of the old order like Mariano Egaña. Like many others in that cohort, Bello identified "order," in the sense of political and economic stability, as the fundamental challenge for the republics of Spanish America. The fear of disorder colored his views about the goals of a modernized law of property. For Bello, modern Chilean property law was to be a framework for order. Neither revolutionary as in France, nor feudal as in colonial Spanish America, the property law of the new Código Civil would be reformist and gradualist, facilitating the steady diffusion of landownership necessary for a stable society and promoting the establishment of a robust market for land that is the prerequisite of a productive economy without undermining the interests of the existing landowning elite.[610]

Despite the vehemence of the anti-feudal discourse of the *pipiolos*, the many pamphlets denouncing the *inquilinaje* as a feudal remnant and the 1852 law that converted the *mayorazgos* into income streams, the property forms that allowed the landowning class to perpetuate and expand its landed wealth were still semi-feudal. The great landowners controlled the transmission of their wealth through the *fideicommissum*, a property form of Roman origin that allowed an individual to transfer property to a fiduciary subject with the obligation of bequeathing it to another when a certain condition occurred. Further, the *inquilinaje* was still alive and well. Not only did the legislature take no action with regard to the *inquilinaje* until well into the twentieth century, but also, as Chile's participation in the world market increased, the *inquilinaje* became even more coercive. As the demand for wheat exports kept growing, landlords responded by increasing the servile exactions imposed on their *inquilinos* rather than by enhancing labor productivity. As he set out to codify the law of property, Bello's challenge was to strike a difficult balance between modernizing the economy and protecting the immediate interests of the powerful semi-feudal elite.

Bello's approach to property reform was inspired less by the work of the French Physiocrats and political economists than by the economic thought of Gaetano Filangieri (1752–1788), one of the central figures of the Neapolitan Enlightenment. Bello was not alone in his admiration of this regional Enlightenment tradition; contemporaries reported that the Spanish translation of Filangieri's *Scienza della legislazione* was also in prominent display in the library of Juan Egaña. In Filangieri's work,

---

[610] Jaksić, *Andrés Bello*, 156 ff.; Collier, *Chili*, 122–123.

Bello, Egaña, and the other members of the modernizing creole elite found insights that shed light on the unique challenges faced by post-colonial Latin America. In the Kingdom of Naples, at the very periphery of Europe, Filangieri had encountered some of the same problems: a weak agricultural economy, the concentration of land in the hands of few great owners supported by property devices such as primogeniture, the *maggiorasco* and the *fideicommissum*, the existence of large unproductive and inalienable ecclesiastical landholdings, and a lack of patriotic love and a tenuous connection to the state. For Filangieri, property was the answer to these problems.

> Property is what generates the citizen, and land what binds him to the *patria* .... Look at the state of all nations and you will see them divided in two opposite factions, owners and non-owners or mercenaries .... The common disgrace of Europe is that, because of defective property laws, the class of owners is infinitely small in comparison to the class of mercenaries.[611]

To increase the number of owners and nurture citizens' virtue, Filangieri proposed sweeping reforms in the Kingdom of Naples: abolishing the *fideicommissum* and the *maggiorasco*; reducing the burden of taxation over land; and actively promoting agriculture, the arts, and commerce which, Filangieri explained, are the three sources of wealth. The former generates actual products and is therefore "the matter"; the second increases the value and use of the products and thereby is "the form"; the third transports and distributes the products and, hence, is "movement."[612] The *Ciencia de la Legislacion* also spoke directly to a question that was vital for the reformers of the new republics: the metropolis' exploitation of the agricultural economies of the former colonies. Filangieri argued that the public interest of both the metropolis and the colonies demanded more equitable relations based on the respect of property and the abolition of commercial monopolies. For the elites of the new republics of Latin America, Filangieri foreshadowed a global market in which robust peripheral economies produced and freely exchanged high-quality agricultural products.[613]

---

[611] G. Filangieri, *Scienza della Legislazione*, vol. 2 (Milan: Società Tipografica de' Classici Italiani, 1822), 27.

[612] Id.

[613] Id., 170 ff.

Filangieri's lessons made a profound impression on Bello . Agriculture had been a central theme of Bello's work since his early days as a poet and humanist. In his poem, "La agricultura de la zona torrida" (1826), a young Bello had outlined the *estado agrario* he envisioned for the newly independent state of Gran Colombia, celebrating the fertility of its soil, its lush vegetation, the hard labor of its population, its peaceful polity, and its commitment to the rule of law.[614] Bello's vision for the *estado agrario* was imbued with references to ancient Rome. Bello's poem echoed Virgil's attitude toward nature and his expectations of a coming Golden Age and alluded to the example of the Roman republic in which hard laboring and virtuous citizens-farmers upheld the rule of law and avoided tyranny.

> Oh youthful nations crowned with laurel who rise before the West's astonished gaze! Honor the fields, honor the simple life, and the farmer's frugal simplicity. Thus freedom will dwell on you forever, ambition be restrained, law have its temple.[615]

By the 1850s, Bello's poetic celebration of agriculture had evolved into an agenda for property reform. Piecing together doctrines from Roman, Spanish, and French law, Bello shaped a body of property rules for the republic.

That Roman law would be such an essential building block of the new Chilean property law was unsurprising (after all, the *Siete Partidas* and French law were themselves based on Roman law) and yet not uncontroversial among the liberal juristic elite. For committed liberals like Infante and Lastarria who were committed to broad legal change, Roman law was the instrument of a despotic empire, further tarnished by its association with Spanish colonial oppression. Interestingly, during the 1830s, the place of Roman law in the new republic's legal system was not just a matter for specialists but rather a topic of interest for the larger educated public, and articles on the teaching of Roman law and the Latin language appeared frequently in the most important newspapers. In the pages of *El Valdiviano Federal* and *El Araucano*, Infante and Bello engaged in a heated polemic over the role of Roman law in the newly revised curriculum of the Instituto Nacional, one of the most prestigious institutions of

---

[614] A. Bello, *La Agricultura de la Zona Tórrida (1826), Poesías*, in *Obras Completas de Don Andrés Bello*, vol. 3 (Santiago: Imprenta Ramírez, 1883), 66; M. D. Ramírez Rondo, "Concepión del Estado Agrario en Andrés Bello" (2015) 41 *Revista de Derecho y Reforma Agraria* 91–96.
[615] Bello, *La Agricultura de la Zona Tórrida*, 75.

higher education. For Infante, teaching of Roman law was the "greatest disservice one could do to the education of our youth." Imbued with despotism, replete with minute and abstract distinctions and largely focused on obsolete problems, Roman law would be not only largely inaccessible to the people of the Chilean Republic but also of very limited use to lawyers. In Infante's own words:

> Bello's plan for the Republic! Once again, as in the time of servitude, we hear in our law schools that the *responsa* of the learned men, the edicts of the Pretors and the will of the Prince, *sed et quod Principi placuit*, have force of law and so have the multitude of other dispositions abundant on each page of this noxious code that today, as in the past, we force our students to memorize. Are we intending to bring them back? If not, why feed our students with lessons in despotism? ... And by reestablishing Roman law and its obscure expositions aren't we making law totally inaccessible to public knowledge?[616]

In his forceful reply, published in the pages of *El Araucano*, Bello dismissed the accusation that Roman law was infused with despotism by distinguishing between Roman constitutional law, possibly tainted with tyranny, and Roman private law, an atemporal law of equity and reason. In Bello's own words:

> It is said [in *El Valdiviano*] that Justinian was a tyrannical ruler and that, as good republicans, we should reduce to ashes anything that comes from such impure origin .... But the constitutional order of a state could be detestable and yet its civil laws excellent. The Roman civil laws have stood the test of time, have been probed in the crucible of philosophy and they conform to the principles of equity and reason.[617]

Bello also had an answer for critics who denounced Roman law as a foreign import of little use in answering present problems. Bello's answer closely echoed the scientific-historical method of Friedrich Karl von Savigny, the greatest German Roman law scholar of the time, of whom Bello was an avid reader. For Bello, modernizing the Republic's property law meant organizing with scientific rigor the existing and multifarious layers of legal rules regulating property that had developed over time in response to the unique circumstances of this corner of Spanish America. Echoing the fascination with science and geometry that enthralled so many of his fellow jurists in Germany, Bello believed that only a law of

---

[616] *El Valdiviano Federal*, no. 75, 1/20/1834.
[617] A. Bello, "Latín y Derecho Romano, Opusculos Literarios," in *Obras Completas de Don Andrés Bello*, vol. 8 (Santiago: Imprenta Ramirez, 1885), 211.

property organized around Roman law concepts would achieve scientific precision:

> Science impresses in the law its seal, its logic grounds, legal principles, formulates axioms, deduces consequences, and distills from the idea of the just inexhaustible developments. From this perspective, Roman law has no rivals. One may question some of its principles, but its method, its logic, its scientific system made it, and still make it, infinitely superior to any other law. Its texts are supreme examples of juridical style, its method is that of geometry applied, with all its rigor, to moral questions.[618]

To be sure, Roman law was heavy in distinctions and subtleties, but this, Bello argued, is the case for all sciences. This taste for minutia is no less useful in the case of law than in the case of zoology, when the scientist counts the colors that tint the wing of a butterfly, or in the case of botany, when the botanist describes the most minute details of a plant.

However, for Bello, in addition to the conceptual clarity of the Roman legal scientists, Chilean property reformers also ought to have a full grasp of the unique needs of their nation. Such understanding, Bello argued, had to come first and foremost from history. For Bello, the work of the liberal historians of Restoration France and of the German Romantic historians was a source of information to be adapted to the specific context of Chile.

> Let us read, let us study European histories; let us observe very closely the particular scenario that each of them develops and summarizes; let us accept the examples and lessons they contain . . .. Can we find Chile with all its accidents, its characteristic features in such books? The Chilean nation is not mankind in abstract, it is mankind under special forms as special as the mountains, rivers and valleys of Chile, its plants and animals, the races to which its inhabitants belong, the moral and political circumstances in which our society was born and is now developing.[619]

Using Roman law building blocks and with the guidance of the lessons of history and political economy,[620] Bello crafted a body of property law that, far from mimicking French and German modern Romanist property, was in many ways original.

---

[618] A. Bello, "Proemio del Derecho Romano, Opuscolos Jurídicos," in *Obras Completas de Don Andrés Bello*, vol. 9 (Santiago: Imprenta Ramirez, 1885), xviii.
[619] A. Bello, "Temas de Historia y Geografia," in *Obras Completas de Andrés Bello*, vol. 23 (Caracas: Fundación La Casa de Bello, 1981), 249.
[620] A. Bello, "Proyecto de Código Civil," in *Obras Completas de Don Andrés Bello*, vol. 12 (Santiago: Imprenta Ramirez, 1888), ix.

Between Feudal Property and Modern Property: An Original Conceptual Architecture

A compromise between the much-decried feudal property and the law of modern absolute *dominium* crafted by French and German jurists and favored by the modernizing elites of the periphery, the law of property for the Chilean republic was the collective work of Bello and of a small cohort of highly sophisticated legal scholars like Jacinto Chacón (1820–1893), Robustiano Vera (1844–1916), and, later, Luis Claro Solar (1857–1945). Similar to Bello, these jurists were also politicians, public intellectuals, and polymaths with interests ranging from poetry to theology to history. They refined and explained Bello's solutions and their *Comentarios*, which proved influential throughout Latin America and, in the case of Luis Claro Solar, even reached European juristic circles. The commentaries and hornbooks penned by Vera, Chacon, and Claro Solar are at times derivative but, in other instances, original and creative.

The treatment of the foundational concepts of property (*dominium*, possession, the law of things) largely redoubles the analysis found in the writings of the great masters of France and Germany. For example, Bello's definition of *dominium* tracked the language of the Code Napoleon and its commentators, emphasizing the owner's right to dispose of the thing *arbitrariamente*. Similarly, Jacinto Chacón reiterated a favorite theme of much European Romanist scholarship of the time when he connected the "abstract" notion of *dominium* to the "concrete" law of things; it is only when the idea of property is applied to actual things (*bienes*), Chacón argued, that the scope of the owner's *dominium* and the distinct entitlements it carries become clear.[621]

However, while the basic concepts were not new, the overall structure outlined by Bello and his colleagues was original. Pluralism and hybridity were its earmarks. To pursue his gradualist agenda of paving the way for diffuse ownership and a free market in land while also protecting the interests of the landowning oligarchy, Bello made some original choices. For José Clemente Fabres (1826–1908), another alumnus of the Instituto Nacional who went on to build a successful professional career as *profesor del Código Civil* and dean at the Universidad de Chile, the most original feature of Bello's *Código* was its treatment of the question of possession, which had fueled heated controversies between

---

[621] J. Chacón, *Exposición Razonada y Estudio Comparativo del Código Civil Chileno*, vol. 2 (Valaparaiso: Imprenta de Mercurio 1878), 19.

the leading German and French jurists. The theory of *la posesión inscrita*, Fabres wrote:

> is the greatest and most significant novelty introduced by our *Código* in the Spanish and Roman law, the deep roots of which [the Code] has preserved with religious and cautious respect.[622]

Fabres was not a lone voice. Luis Claro Solar went even further and called *la posesión inscrita* "a radical innovation."[623] What made *la posesión inscrita* such an important novelty was that it promised to mitigate the fundamental weakness of the theory that possession is a means to afford greater protection to owners, famously articulated by Rudolf von Jhering. Dispossessed owners, Jhering reasoned, would receive protection for the simple fact of their possession with no need to prove title, which was notoriously difficult, a *probatio diabolica*. The weakness of Jhering's theory was obvious. Jhering assumed that ownership and possession aligned and that, in the vast majority of cases, the possessor is also the owner by title. This assumption, however, was questionable, and Jhering himself had to admit that the risk of protecting possessors who were not in fact owners was real but inevitable. Unfairly protecting a relatively small number of possessors who did not have title was a risk worth running in order to afford more effective protection to the vast majority who were both possessors and owners. Bello's *posesión inscrita* sought to minimize this risk by protecting only possessors who have registered their possession in the *Registro Conservadorio*. According to article 728 of Bello's *Código*, the two traditional requirements for possession, that is the physical control of the thing and the intent to possess as an owner, "are not sufficient to establish possession unless the thing is also registered." In the *Mensaje del ejecutivo al Congreso proponiendo la aprobación del Código Civil*, Bello foreshadowed a modern Chile in which registration in the *Registro Conservatorio*, possession, and ownership would be perfectly aligned, and information about landownership in the Republic would be public and easily accessible to all. In Bello's own words:

---

[622] José Clemente Fabres, *Instituciones de derecho civil chileno*, vol. 1 (Valparaíso: Imprenta del Universo, 1863), 352. On the theory of *posesión inscrita*, see also Fernando Atria, "Derechos Reales" (2005) 2 *Revista de Derecho de la Universidad Adolfo Ibáñez* 29–105; Id., "El sistema de acciones reales, parte especial: la acción de precario" (2017) 30(2) *Revista derecho Valdivia* 57–86.

[623] Luis Claro Solar, "Nota a sentencia" (1905) 3(1) *Revista de derecho y jurisprudencia* section 1, page 130.

Registration is what confers real effective possession. And, as long as the registration has not been cancelled, he who has not registered his title does not possess; he is a mere holder. Since the *Registro Conservatorio* is open to all, there cannot be possession that is more public, solemn and indisputable than registration. The benefits that flow from this order of things are obvious. Possession of real property is manifest and indisputable, rapidly approaching an era in which registration, possession and ownership will be identical terms; land ownership in all the Republic visible to all in a full picture that represents, so to say, instantaneously its changes, burdens and successive divisions.[624]

And yet, as one commentator put it, the perfect alignment of registration, possession, and ownership remained a "glorious illusion."[625] Critics were quick to point out the many absurd and unfair instances in which *la posesión inscrita* pitted real owners against registered possessors. If someone sold to another a parcel of land they did not own and that the actual owner had never registered, the buyer, by simply registering the land in their name, would acquire ownership, through the doctrine of prescription, after thirty years of possession/registration.[626] While such cases of patent usurpation may have been relatively rare, so called *inscripciones de papel*[627] (paper registrations) were far from uncommon and an effective way for large absentee landowners to prevent direct producers from ever becoming owners of the land they cultivated. In his essay "Vulgarización sobre la posesión ante el Código Civil chileno," Leopoldo Urrutia Anguita (1849–1936), professor of civil law and twice president of the Corte Suprema de Chile, recounted in detail one of the many cases he had come across in his practice in which the owner of a large hacienda had sought to dispossess a peasant family, who had lived and worked on part of the estate's land from time immemorial, through an *inscripción de papel*.

> It was a large *hacienda* registered with these natural limits: to the north a lagoon; to the south, a river; to the east, the Cordillera de la Costa; to the west the Pacific Ocean. Within this large estate there were six or eight

---

[624] Mensaje del Ejecutivo al Congreso proponiendo la aprobación del Código Civil, 22 de noviembre de 1855, available at Biblioteca del Congreso Nacional de Chile, http://bcn.cl/2gzwx.

[625] Victorio Pescio Vargas, *Manual de derecho civil*, vol. 9 (Santiago: Jurídica de Chile, 1978), 148.

[626] Humberto Trucco, "Teoría de la posesión inscrita dentro del Código Civil chileno" (August 1910) 7(6) *Revista de derecho y jurisprudencia* 134.

[627] Leopoldo Urrutia Anguita, "Vulgarización sobre la posesión ante el Código Civil chileno" (March and April 1934) 31(1–2) *Revista de derecho y jurisprudencia* 11.

parcels that from time immemorial were possessed by a family of fishermen with fenced boundaries visible and notorious. Title had been transferred from father to son even if the title was not registered without any
difficulty arising. The registered owner sought to dispossess these occupants with registered title. The action was rejected despite the fact that the
possessors did not have registered title, based on the fact that the registration of the natural boundaries could not include these parcels the of the
fishermen family because neither at the time of the registration nor
afterwards had been occupied by the owners of the larger hacienda in
which they were located; de facto possession had always been with this
family.[628]

While in the case described by Leopoldo Urrutia, the possessors prevailed, in many other instances, the doctrine of *posesión inscrita* and the
common practice of *inscripciones de papel* proved effective tools to bar
access to landownership to direct producers. The property regime that
Bello envisioned, in which registration, possession, and ownership would
be synonymous and information about land easily accessible was
designed to benefit the landed elites who had access to lawyers and a
shrewd practical knowledge. As Fernando Atria noted, the Código Civil
of 1855 was not written for peasant communities and urban workers who
were, de facto, excluded from the newly reinforced system of *propiedad/
dominium*.

Bello's modernized property system also included two other innovations that were heralded as original products of Bello's genius: la
propiedad fiduciaria and the *censos*, a hybrid form found in the
Spanish law for the Indies that displayed features of both property and
contract. In the words of another great jurist of modern Chile, Miguel
Luis Amunategui Reyes (1862–1949), these well-crafted property forms
were further evidence that the Código Civil of 1855 was "not a servile
copy of any other" and that Bello had proven to be "a world-class jurist,
not an *amanuensis* or a scribe."[629]

Undoubtedly, Bello's reconfiguration of the *fideicommissum* as a type
of ownership – *propiedad fiduciaria* (fiduciary property), featuring a
more limited set of entitlements than *dominium* – was a radical departure from the Code Napoleon, then hailed as the leading example of
liberal modernization throughout Latin America. The *fideicommissum*

---

[628] Id., 11.
[629] M. L. Amunategui, "Introducción: Proyecto Inedito del Código Civil, Opuscolos
Científicos," in *Obras Completas de Don Andrés Bello*, vol. 13 (Santiago: Imprenta
Ramirez, 1890), xxi and xxxviii.

was a form of Roman origin that involved three subjects: an owner who, usually in his will, transfers property to a fiduciary owner subject to the obligation to transfer it to another, the *fideicommissarium*, or beneficiary, if a certain condition occurs. In revolutionary France, the *fideicommissum* was deemed to be incompatible with modern liberal and egalitarian principles and was abolished altogether. Bello and his fellow jurists were not oblivious to the arguments that had induced the French legislature to eliminate the *fideicommissum*, and they even avowed sympathy with these arguments. As Luis Claro Solar noted:

> The founders of our national independence were well aware of the serious problems the *fideicommissum* causes for the economic development of the country and they considered it as a monarchical institution contrary to the principles of equality that need to animate the Republic.[630]

Even more blunt was Jacinto Chacón who, in his *Esposición Razonada y Estudio Comparativo de Código Civil Chileno*, asserted that the *fideicommissum* enabled the formation of a despotic political and economic oligarchy, noting that:

> [the *fideicommissum*] perpetuates the transmission of significant wealth within certain families, which end up forming a sort of caste that, believing itself superior to the other social classes, seeks to exempt itself from the rule of law and to take control of the government.[631]

Yet, despite these candid analyses, for Bello and his fellow jurists, eliminating the *fideicommissum* altogether, as the French had done, would have meant losing the support of the economic and social elites, who had historically relied on the *fideicommissum* to build and transmit their family wealth. For Bello, the solution was to allow the *fideicommissum*, albeit in a limited form, and to reconceptualize it as a form of "fiduciary property." Bello's treatment of "fiduciary property" was clever: ideologically, politically, and conceptually. At a time when the liberal ideology of modern property had great traction and the rejection of the "feudal" was as vocal as ever, Bello astutely presented the *fideicommissum*, an institution that smacked of feudalism, as a logical consequence of the notion of modern property, not its negation. By establishing a *fideicommissum*, Bello reasoned, the owner was simply exercising his "absolute" right to dispose of the thing as he wishes, which, obviously,

---

[630] L. Claro Solar, "De los Bienes," in *Explicaciones de Derecho Civil y Comparado*, vol. 4 (Santiago: Jurídica de Chile, 1992), tomo 8, paragraph 910, page 18.
[631] Chacón, *Exposición Razonada y Estudio Comparativo del Código Civil Chilen*, xii.

includes the right to gift or bequeath the thing subject to any condition he may see fit.

While this argument was clever, it also exposed a conceptual contradiction. While the testator, by imposing on the fiduciary the obligation to transfer the property to the beneficiary if a certain condition occurred, was undoubtedly exercising his absolute *dominium*, he was also significantly impairing the fiduciary' s right to freely transfer the property, another core attribute of modern absolute property. In the *Mensaje* that explained the reasons why the Chilean Congreso should approve the new Código Civil, Bello addressed this tension head on:

> This draft code maintains the *fideicommissum*, despite the fact that many modern codes have abolished it. We recognized it [the *fideicommissum*] as an emanation of property because every owner has the right to impose any condition or limitation he wishes on his acts of liberality. However, taken to its full extension, this principle clashes with the social interest, both by hampering the circulation of wealth and weakening that natural solicitude in conserving and improving one's wealth that has its most powerful driver in the prospect of enjoying one's wealth perpetually, with no limits or responsibilities and with the ability to transfer it to whomever one wishes.[632]

In a similar vein, Jacinto Chacón described this puzzle as an intractable one: allowing the *fideicommissum* encourages one owner, the testator, to abuse his right to dispose by limiting the right of another owner, the fiduciary, to freely transfer; on the other hand, prohibiting the *fideicommissum* violates the testator's right to freely dispose of his property.[633] While both entitlements, the right to make plans for one's property and right to freely transfer the thing were described as critical attributes of modern property, the latter enjoyed an elevated status because it was deemed to serve both a private and a public interest. The right to transfer enabled the individual owner to invest and engage in profitable exchanges while also facilitating the establishment of a robust market and the social wealth it creates.

To ease this tension, Bello introduced an important limit, prohibiting the establishment of two consecutive *fideicommissa*. Owners were free to establish one *fideicommissum* only and any arrangement whereby the property would be effectively rendered inalienable in the long term, whether through consecutive *fideicommissa* or consecutive rights of

---

[632] Bello's message is available at www.derecho-chile.cl/mensaje-del-código-civil/.
[633] Chacón, *Exposición Razonada y Estudio Comparativo del Código Civil Chilen*, 215.

usufruct, was prohibited. The goal, Bello explained, was to reduce restrictions to the alienability of property that are prejudicial for the economy "to the minimum possible," short of eliminating altogether a tool that well served the estate-planning needs of the economic elite.[634]

Ideologically clever and a savvy political compromise, Bello's discussion of the *fideicommissum* was also conceptually sophisticated. Bello's choice as to the proper place of the *fideicommissum* in the conceptual architecture of property was intriguing. It suggested that Bello, contrary to many of his fellow Romanists in Europe who centered their property architectures around the one concept of *dominium*, had a pluralistic understanding of property as a graduated spectrum of forms of "owning." Bello's first innovation was to characterize the *fideicommissum* squarely as a matter of property. By and large, jurists, in Latin America and in Europe, viewed the *fideicommissum* as belonging to the law of succession. Jacinto Chacón himself was among the proponents of this traditional approach, explaining that the *fideicommissum* was, in essence, an entrustment (*encargo de confianza*) of property from the owner to a fiduciary to be fulfilled after the former's death.[635] By contrast, Bello placed the *fideicommissum* in the title on property under the heading "limitaciones del dominio."[636] Effectively, Bello, by reconceptualizing the *fideicommissum* as property, designed a spectrum of forms of "owning" of different scope, from full *dominium* to a more limited form of "fiduciary property" to the even more limited and temporary use and enjoyment of a thing by virtue of a usufruct.

It is in the detailed explanations of this graduated spectrum of property forms that the novelty and sophistication of the nascent modern Chilean property "science" becomes apparent. *Dominium*, our jurists explained, is the only full and unitary mode of owning, its essence consisting in the absolute and exclusive disposition of the thing. By contrast, the fiduciary owner is, until the moment of the transfer to the beneficiary, "the actual and only owner, but not an absolute owner."[637] Conceptualizing with precision what being an owner "but not an absolute owner" meant was no easy task, as the scope of the fiduciary owner's entitlements could vary significantly.

---

[634] Bello, *Proyecto de Código Civil*, title VIII, article 876, page 196 (epigraph).
[635] Claro Solar, "De los Bienes," paragraph 912, page 23; Chacón, *Exposición Razonada y Estudio Comparativo del Código Civil Chilen*, 225 ff.
[636] Bello, *Proyecto de Código Civil*, title VIII, article 876, page 196.
[637] Chacón, *Exposición Razonada y Estudio Comparativo del Código Civil Chilen*, 232.

Effectively, there were not one but three forms of fiduciary ownership. The broadest type of fiduciary ownership, the *fideicommisso de residuo*, was virtually indistinguishable from *dominium*. In this broader form, Claro Solar explained, the testator expressly granted the fiduciary both the right to "enjoy of the property according to his own *arbitrium*" and the right to "freely dispose of the property," effectively according the fiduciary rights similar to those of an absolute owner.[638] Why "effectively" similar and yet not absolute? Part of the answer was easy: the fiduciary owner still had the duty to transfer to the holder of the future interest what was left at the time the condition occurred. The more difficult part of the answer was the exact meaning of *arbitrary* enjoyment and *free* disposition. How to quantify the difference between absolute, arbitrary, and free? Claro Solar suggested that the fiduciary's right to arbitrarily enjoy of the thing does not go as far as to allow him to deliberately and maliciously ruin or destroy the thing.[639] Similarly, the right of free disposition does not allow the fiduciary to capriciously transfer the thing to others in fraud of the rights of the holder of the future interest (*fideicommissarium*). These limits – malice and fraud – were, Chacón noted, a matter of "public interest."[640] Since the legal system recognizes fiduciary property as a distinctive form consisting of two rights, the fiduciary's property right and the future interest of the *fideicommissarium*, the public interest in the certainty of the law requires limiting the ability of the fiduciary to maliciously destroy the expectations of the designated future owner. Effectively, these writers suggest, the fiduciary owner differs from the absolute owner in that the former may not "abuse" his right. Whether the *dominus* himself could actually commit abuse of right was a question that only a few decades later would become incendiary in property circles around the globe.

Fiduciary ownership could also be narrower in scope and further differentiated from absolute *dominium*. In a second variant, for example, the testator may have granted the fiduciary the right to enjoy the thing at his own *arbitrium* but not the right to freely dispose of the thing. Finally, in the standard *fideicommissum*, the fiduciary had an even more limited set of entitlements, comprising the right to use and enjoy and a significantly limited right to transfer or, possibly, no right to transfer at all. Despite these limitations to the right to transfer, fiduciary ownership is

---

[638] Claro Solar, "De los Bienes," 69–70.
[639] Id., 71–72.
[640] Chacón, *Exposición Razonada y Estudio Comparativo del Código Civil Chilen*, 225, 232.

still ownership. The fiduciary is the only owner until the condition occurs: he has broad rights to use and manage the property, including the ability to change its use or purpose, provided he does not diminish its value or quantity; and, he may eventually become the absolute owner if the condition never occurs.

The final form on the spectrum of forms of "owning" designed by Bello and his fellow jurists was the usufruct, which was not actually ownership but a temporary, limited, and yet robust mode of holding a thing. As we have seen, the question of the nature of the usufruct and its relationship to ownership had long been a vexed one. By the time Bello set out to reorganize Chile's law of property, there was wide agreement that the usufruct, despite its holder's robust right to enjoy the thing, was not a "lower" form of time-limited ownership but a qualitatively different right over a thing owned by another (*ius in re aliena*). However, the question of the differences with fiduciary ownership appeared more complicated and was the object of lengthy analyses in the treatises of the Chilean jurists. Practically, the fiduciary owner and the holder of a usufruct appeared to be in a similar situation: both held the thing only temporarily, subject, respectively, to the duty to transfer it to the holder of the future interest at the occurrence of the condition and to the duty to transfer to the title owner at the end of the usufruct period. The fiduciary and the holder of an usufruct also had a similar set of entitlements that comprised a robust right to use and enjoy but no right to transfer or a limited right to transfer. So what made it so obvious that the fiduciary was an owner while the holder of the usufruct was not? For Claro Solar, the difference was structural. Fiduciary ownership consisted of one right only, the property right of the fiduciary, and the *fideicommissarium* had a mere expectation to become owner if and when the condition occurred. By contrast, in the case of the usufruct, there existed two rights, that of the title owner and that of the holder of the usufruct.[641]

Another form that, in the mind of Chilean nineteenth-century liberal reformers, was associated with the feudal and colonial past was the *censo*. A Spanish institution, regulated in the *Leyes de Toro* and the *Siete Partidas* and included in the *derecho indiano* of the *Nueva Recopilación*, the *censo* was a form that lay in between contract and property law. Formally, it was a contract of sale by which one party purchased from another the right to receive an annual rent or pension.

---

[641] Claro Solar, "De los Bienes," 69 ff.

While framed as a sale, the *censo* practically operated similarly to a loan. In the *censo consignativo*, the most common form in colonial Spanish America, the lender (*censualista*) transferred a capital sum to the debtor (*censuario*) in return for the payment of an annuity equivalent to the original principal plus an interest secured by a parcel of real estate. For modern property reformers, the *censo* presented a challenge. Conceptually, because of its hybrid nature – partly contract, partly real right – the *censo* fit uneasily in the modern jurists' property architecture of neatly defined concepts. As for other hybrid forms, the legal essence of the *censo* was the object of a heated controversy among jurists in Roman law countries. For some, it was a right *in personam* against the *censuario*; for others, the *censualista* and the *censuario* were both owners with divided *dominium* over the parcel; still others, conceptualized the *censo* as a real right over land owned by another. The *censo* presented a challenge also because it contradicted the two central tenets of modern property science: enabling absolute *dominium* and facilitating the free alienability of property. Legal scientists and legislatures could only be skeptical of a burden that ran with the land, limiting the debtor's full *dominium* and making the parcel less attractive to prospective buyers. In addition to these flaws, over the centuries, the *censo* had gained the reputation of being an instrument of oppression and a "feudal" remnant of the colonial past. It was used by the greatest lender of colonial Spanish America, the Church, to cover up its unfair lending practices. Formally a sale, the *censo* allowed the Church and other lenders to circumvent the prohibition on usury. Another reason for the *censo*'s reputation was that it had been effectively repurposed by *encomenderos* and Spanish and creole speculators to appropriate the mining profits of the indigenous people of central Chile.

Between the sixteenth century and the days of independence, scores of reformist political and religious leaders had publicly decried the injustices perpetrated through the *censo* and sought to reign in such abuses. In 1580, the Bishop of Santiago wrote to the Spanish King informing him of the grave injustices that continued to be inflicted on the indigenous population (*naturales*) with regards to the *sesmo*, the 6 percent portion of the profits from the gold they mined, which, by law, belonged to the indigenous communities. He shared, by way of example, that he was aware of individuals who had mined gold for thirty years without ever seeing a cent because their *sesmo* had been invested in *censos* and the promised annuities had not been paid. In 1822, a decree bearing the signature of Bernardo O' Higgins, Director Supremo of the newly independent nation, declared that the use of the *censo* by the religious communities was, effectively, a form of usury prohibited by the law and capped the annuities on the Church's property at 4 percent. Faced with the question of how to treat the *censo* in the new Código Civil, Bello, once again, as for the *mayorazgo* and the *fideicommisso*, opted for a compromise.

The *Mensaje* that accompanied the Código suggests that Bello's preferred solution would have been to do away with the *censo*, following the example of the French legislature. Describing the new and more restrictive legal regime of the *censo*, Bello added that if this regime ended up discouraging the investment of capital in *censos*, "we would have accomplished, indirectly, a great good."[642] However, despite his own views, Bello was reluctant to alienate the economic elites by abolishing an institution that functioned as a critical source of credit in the country's semi-feudal economy. Bello retained the *censo*, placed it in the book on contracts but openly acknowledged its dual nature. "The right of *censo*," the Código recited, "is personal in that it is directed against the *censuario*, even if he is not in possession of the parcel, real in that it follows the latter."[643]

Bello was a conservative liberal, not a radical intent on questioning his contemporaries' idea that *dominium* is absolute; nor was he a methodological innovator who consciously sought to reveal the fuzzy nature of legal categories and replace the monistic architecture of property centered on *dominium* with a pluralistic constellation of properties. A deliberately pluralistic theory of property open to hybrid forms was not what Bello had in mind, and would only emerge decades later when the social critics would push the boundaries of the discourse and methods of modern property. Paradoxically, it was his reluctance to fully break with aspects of feudal property vital to the interests of the landed elite that led Bello to experiment with the pluralism and hybridity that would become critical to the understanding of property over the course of the twentieth century.

Conclusions

At the periphery of the Roman law world, in the newly independent republics of Latin America, modern absolute *dominium* proved a

---

[642] Bello's message is available at www.derecho-chile.cl/mensaje-del-código-civil/.
[643] Bello, *Proyecto de Código Civil*, article 683, page 156.

powerful nation-building tool. As the intellectual and economic elites of Latin America propounded a narrative that portrayed the societies and economies of the new nations as split between a "feudal" and a "modern" sector, absolute property signified the definite shift toward modernity. As in Europe, where Romanist *dominium* appealed to diverse audiences – from conservative liberals with a natural law perspective, to the reformist bureaucratic elites, and, in France, even to fringes of the post-revolutionary egalitarian republicans – modern *dominium* elicited broad consensus. In the republic of Chile, celebrated as the state that had advanced the most on the path toward a liberal and stable polity and a productive economy, virtually all segments of the large and varied spectrum of liberalism embraced the discourse of modern property and endorsed property reform.

Yet in Latin America as in Europe, nineteenth-century Romanist property was complex and riven with contradictions. While in Europe, where modern *dominium* was the distinctive domain of Romanists and private law scientists, in Chile, from independence until the 1850s, property was a matter of constitutional political economy that preoccupied an elite of statesmen with juristic training. The two pillars of the republic's new constitutional political economy, the principles of free alienability and inviolability of property, were malleable and could be easily appropriated for widely diverging, if not opposite, agendas. These two principles served well the liberal entrepreneurial class that advocated for the creation of a robust national market, as well as the small colonial creole elite seeking to secure its social and economic position; they also came in useful to the radicals, such as Bilbao and Vicuna, who called for the full material and moral emancipation of the individual. Finally, these two principles proved useful in the efforts of the secular republicans who hoped to undo the economic and cultural effects of the *real patronato de las Indias* yet were also mobilized by the conservative-ecclesiastical power block that resisted the separation of State and Church.

Not only were the politics of modern Romanist property in Chile complicated and contradictory, so too was its conceptual architecture. With the debates over the new Código Civil of the 1850s, *dominium* became a matter of legal conceptual analysis within the purview of an emerging class of jurists who saw themselves as part a global network of scientists of modern Roman law and on par with their French and German colleagues. In the new Chilean law of property, the conceptual tensions and contradictions of the "system" of modern property, which the great masters of private law in France and Germany had relentlessly sought to disguise, were acknowledged and creatively managed. Completely expunging from the property system forms that nineteenth-century jurists viewed as "feudal" but that were critical to the interests of the landed oligarchy, such as the *fideicommissum*, the *inquilinaje*, or the *censo*, was a political risk that the conservative liberal Bello would not take. The result was a conceptual architecture of property that, while replicating many of the solutions of the European property scientists, was more hospitable to hybrid concepts and plural ownership forms.

7

The Social Critics

The Critique of Absolute *Dominium* and the Retrieval of the Roman Social Doctrines

The Social Question and the End of Optimistic Liberalism

The nineteenth-century Roman law scholars of Europe and Latin America crafted the law of modern *dominium* in a world that was still pre-capitalist and in which liberal political institutions were in their infancy. Absolute *dominium* gained wide appeal because it promised a way out of the existing political and economic order, which growing segments of the elite believed to be in need of reform. Conservative liberals, who cherished the Kantian natural law tradition, valued absolute *dominium* because it afforded individual autonomy and agency; the various schools of political economists and the bureaucratic administrators of the absolutist states because it facilitated "agricultural improvement" and the development of a productive commercial agriculture; the liberal modernizing elites of Latin America because they saw absolute *dominium* as a central attribute of the exclusionary and racialized citizenship of the new republics and as the pillar of the "modern" sector of their national economies; finally, republicans and egalitarian liberals because *dominium* allowed them to envisage a future in which all individuals would have equal access to the benefits of full ownership. These diverse constituencies shared an "optimistic liberalism" that led them to believe in the transformative potential of the Roman law of property that the jurists were reinventing.

By the second half of the nineteenth century, the hopes of economic transformation harbored by these elites were actually coming to pass. Relations between the owners of capital and direct producers were changing to reflect the imperatives of competition, profit maximization, and increasing wage-labor productivity. The external competitive pressure of British capitalism and the availability of new productive technologies encouraged states to support economic growth through public investment. In France, during the Second Empire and the Third Republic, competition with Britain and the threat posed by the prospect of a unified and rapidly industrializing Germany prompted a major economic restructuring. Led by a class of high-ranking state adminis-trators, economists, and bankers, this transformation involved the liber-alization and unification of the internal market, the construction of modern transport infrastructures, and large investments aimed at mech-anizing the facilities of industrial firms. The property framework of *dominium* codified in 1804 and solidified by the jurists of the July Monarchy lent aid to this process as did other changes in legal doctrine, most notably, the Cour de Cassation's effort to grant employers arbitrary powers, by rolling back long-standing customary labor protections. Similarly, in the German states and principalities, despite the overwhelm-ing predominance of agrarian and semi-feudal relations of production, the momentum of capitalist development on a world scale was also starting to be felt. In Prussia, the property reforms of Baron von Stein accelerated the transition to agrarian capitalism. Rather than emancipat-ing feudal peasants, the reform efforts provided to *Junker* landlords more land, money, and an enlarged landless agrarian proletariat. Further, artisanal production began to contract and industrial development picked up, both in the Rhineland, where new markets for industrial products were developing, and in East Prussia, where the state was deeply involved in heavy industry for fiscal and military purposes.

The economic growth that economists and state administrators expected would result from this policy of public investment and property law modernization did materialize, albeit gradually and unevenly. However, the aspirations to autonomy, independence, and equality that had undergirded the discourse of modern *dominium* were never realized. The rationalization and expansion of the economy generated enormous wealth inequalities between the propertied classes and the large class of property-less wage laborers. The latter experienced oppression rather than autonomy, material dependence rather than the independence, and exclusion instead of equality. The "optimistic liberalism" that had propelled the reinvention of the Roman law of absolute *dominium* did not vanish all together, but talk of a looming "social question" came to dominate policy debates. The "social question" prompted social reform-ers of all stripes to interrogate the role of property law in the emergent industrial world. Social reformers questioned the economic power that the robust entitlements of modern *dominium* afforded owners of land

and industry; they also weighed how the corresponding disentitlements of neighbors, communities, and workers affected the weakest.

The new political and intellectual climate created by the "social question" transformed the ideological discourse about property, the concerns of the jurists, and, to an extent, the doctrines of property law. Alternative conceptualizations of property focused on social relations, redistribution, and cooperation started appearing in the writings of philosophers, economists, and pamphleteers. And a new generation of jurists, interested in functionalist and consequence-based approaches to property, gained power in law faculties in Europe, Latin America, and beyond.

While the conversation about the justification for private property and the goals of property law changed dramatically, one aspect of property debates remained the same: the place of Roman antiquity and Roman law in the imagination of the jurists. The architects of modern *dominium* had looked to Rome for inspiration, and so did the new critical vanguard. Rome continued to provide the analytical lens to understand the present. The inventors of modern *dominium* had sought insight in the virtuous Roman Republic; by contrast, the social critics drew cautionary tales from Rome's later turbulent political history. Roman law also continued to function as a repository of concepts and doctrines that could be reinvented and repurposed to tackle new problems. This time around, it was the relational and pluralistic features of Roman property law, which the architects of modern *dominium* had overlooked, that came in useful.

The New Discourse about Property and Inequality in Industrial Society

The writers and theorists who hoped that modern Romanist *dominium* would contribute to establishing a "society of equals" believed, optimistically, that they had a good answer to the criticism that this absolutist notion of property would likely exacerbate economic and political inequality. An ethos of moderation and rejection of luxury, the equalizing effects of the free market, and the strength of the social bond in the new liberal society, they argued, would mitigate any inequalities resulting from a property law designed to maximize the freedom of owners. However, as the development of agrarian and industrial capitalism accelerated throughout Europe and the resulting subordination and exploitation of wage laborers became manifest, these optimistic answers started to appear simplistic. Beginning in the 1830s, a growing and rich literature discussed the social ills of industrial society. Conservative liberals perse-vered in their attempt to naturalize and justify the new inequalities, presenting them as the result of differences in natural talent and virtue. By contrast, a diverse cohort of reformers – from utopian socialists, to radical republicans to, proponents of solidarism – sought to eradicate or mitigate wealth inequality by targeting the laws and institutions that were at its root. Chief among these was the law of property.

One of the first treatises to diagnose the causes of the new economic and social inequality that plagued industrializing society was *Nouveaux principes d'economie politique*, published by the Swiss political economist Jean de Sismondi (1773–1842) in 1819.[644] In the introduction to the *Nouveaux principes*, Sismondi, until then known as a sympathetic inter-preter of Adam Smith, announced a change of heart. Sismondi declared that he had been profoundly affected by the "commercial crisis that Europe has experienced in the last years and the cruel suffering of the workers of the manufacturing industry that I witnessed in Italy, Switzerland and France and that all public reports suggest is at least equal to that experienced in England, Germany and France."[645] This realization led Sismondi to refocus his interests from encouraging the creation of wealth to addressing its unequal distribution. Providing moving descriptions of the suffering of industrial workers, Sismondi presented a forceful indictment of how the owners of capital exploited labor. Owners of manufactures, Sismondi charged, lured workers with miserable salaries, exposed them to the mephitic air of cotton mills and the vapor of mercury, and pocketed the profits of their industy, passing on to society the cost of remedying worker's poverty and poor health.[646]

Like many before him, Sismondi sustained his diagnosis of the social question by drawing parallels with Roman history. The immiseration of the industrial working class, he suggested, was reminiscent of that of the Roman agrarian landless proletariat, whom Sismondi, following the historian of the second century AD Appian, described as having no attachment to any established political order and the single vocation to produce children. Further, in Sismondi's narrative, the incessant violence and political strife experienced by Rome in the transition from Republic

---

[644] J.-C.-L. Simonde de Sismondi, *Nouveaux principes d'économie politique ou De la richesse dans ses rapports avec la population*, vol. 1 (Paris: Delaunay Libraire, 1819).

[645] Id., vol. I, iv.

[646] Id., vol. I, 2–3, 92.

to Empire foreshadowed the future of industrial Europe.[647] The analogy between the misery of the industrial proletariat and the oppression of the Roman enslaved population quickly became an important theme in the literature on the evils of industrial society. De l'esclavage moderne, published in 1840 by Félicité Robert de Lamennais (1782–1854), was a must-read among reformers. Lamennais denounced the hypocrisy of those who had predicted an optimistic liberal egalitarianism that had helped usher in dominium and described the present as no different from the slave societies of antiquity.

> A new right, based on the principle of natural equality has become commonly accepted ... but this right, elevated to a religious dogma that can appeal to the consciences of Christian peoples ... has remained a simple idea, a pure sentiment, with no impact on exterior facts and no general practical application. In actual reality, we are still at the pagan solution of the social problem, at the slavery of ancient nations, only disguised in different name and forms.[648]

The glorification of the individual was another idea that had provided the normative impulse for modern dominium, and it was now being questioned also. Among the educated public with reformist leanings, individualisme took on a negative connotation, coming to be seen as the root cause of inequality rather than as an emancipatory aspiration. Denunciations of the ills of individualism punctuated the pages of Le Producteur, the short-lived journal founded by the disciples of Claude-Henri de Rouvroy, comte de Saint-Simon (1760–1825). In a letter published in the 1826 issue, an admirer of the English reformer Robert Owen (1771–1858) launched into a full-blown attack on individualism, private property, and the competitive market. It seems out of question, the author of the letter wrote, that the principle that generates wealth inequality, with all its ills, "is the spirit of exclusive individuality that leads us to pursue our own interest independently from and, too often, at the expense of the other members of society."[649] Instead of the unequal and atomized industrial society, the author of the letter imagined a new

[647] Id., vol. I, 182, 232–235.
[648] Félicité Robert de Lamennais De l'esclavage moderne (Paris: Pagnerre Editeur, 1840), 41–42.
[649] "Lettres au Redacteur du Producteur sur le systeme de la cooperation mutuelle, et de la communaute de biens, d'apres le pla de M Owen" (July 1826) 4 Le Producteur: journal de l'industrie, des sciences et des beaux-arts 539.

productive order, organized around the twin principles of cooperation and common ownership:

> It is to this principle [of competition] that [Owen] opposes the principle of cooperation . . . . But one would solve only a small part of the problem if this cooperation in labor were not accompanied by the communal enjoyment of the fruits of labor based on a principle of equality.[650]

The letter writer was not alone in advocating for cooperation and common ownership, as these ideas were rapidly gaining acceptance among the different strands of utopian socialists, who saw common ownership as critical to a new equitable and rationally organized economy and society.

In this climate of growing denunciation of proprietary individualism, a most powerful blow to modern *dominium* came with the publication of Pierre-Joseph Proudhon's incendiary essay "Qu'est-ce que la propriété?" (What is Property?) in 1840. Departing from the reassuring language of scientific planning *en vogue* among the utopian socialists, Proudhon launched a scathing assault on the discourse of modern absolute property. His first move was to ridicule the dearest treasure of the jurists, absolute *dominium*:

> The Roman law defined property as the right to use and abuse one's own as long as it accords with the reason of the law . . .. Some have tried to justify the word abuse on the grounds that it signifies not senseless and immoral abuse, but only absolute dominion. Vain distinction! Invented to sanctify property, and powerless against the delirium of possession, which it neither prevents nor represses. The proprietor may, if he chooses, allow his crops to rot; sow his fields with salt; milk his cows on the sand, change his vineyards into a desert and use his vegetable-garden as a park? Do these things constitute abuse or not? When it comes to property, use and abuse are necessarily indistinguishable.[651]

Having exposed the absurdity of any distinction between lawful absolute *dominium* and immoral abuse, Proudhon turned on their head, one by one, the justifications for private property dominant in the liberal property discourse.[652] Is property a natural right of all individuals? Modern legislators, Proudhon scornfully insinuated, pick and choose which rights

---

[650] Id., 540.
[651] P.-J. Proudhon, "Qu'est-ce que la propriété?," in *Oeuvres completes de P.-J. Proudhon*, Tome I (Paris: Lacroix Editeurs,1873), premier mémoire, chapter II, page 37.
[652] Mikhaïl Xifaras, "Ya-t-il une théorie de la propriété chez Pierre-Joseph Proudhon" (2004) 47 *Corpus, Revue de philosophie* 229–282.

are "natural" according to their own taste.[653] By way of illustration, Proudhon noted that the *Déclaration des droits de l'homme et du citoyen* of 1793 stated that property is a natural right, along with liberty, equality, and security, while the jurist Toullier, one of the great masters of modern *dominium*, dropped equality from the list.[654] May it be because property negates equality? Equally ridiculous was, for Proudhon, the attempt to justify property based on first occupancy. Here, Proudhon targeted another dearest treasure of the Romanists, Cicero's famous analogy between occupying a seat in a theater and the first occupation of property, which, as we have seen, was endlessly cited in the nineteenth-century property treatises. Cicero's analogy, Proudhon noted, far from justifying private property, invalidates it.

> Cicero compared the earth to a large theatre. *Quemadmodum theatrum cum commune sit recte tamen dici potest ejus esse eum locum quem quisque occuparit.* This passage is the most philosophical treatment of the origin of property that antiquity has left us. The theatre, says Cicero, is common to all; yet, the place that each occupies is called his own. This obviously means that it is a place possessed not appropriated. This comparison annihilates property; even more, it implies equality. Can I, in a theatre, simultaneously occupy a seat in the parquet circle, one in the balcony and a third one in the galleries? No, unless I have three bodies, like Geryon, or I have the power to be in different places at the same time, like in the story of the magician Apollonius.[655]

If the theories of natural right and first occupation seemed laughable, no less risible was, for Proudhon, the idea that property is based on the very idea of personality. If property is a fundamental expression of the self, then *all* free individuals should be owners, not some only. Could property ever be just for Proudhon? Only to the extent that it remunerates the individual's actual labor contribution to the collective effort of production and is proportional to that contribution's duration and intensity.[656]

The public conversation about property shifted gears when the writings of Karl Marx started gaining attention. Marx brought new urgency to the question of property. The utopian socialists believed that the ideal society could be achieved thought gradual change; even the incendiary Proudhon admitted, in an 1846 letter to Marx, that he

---

[653] Proudhon, "Qu'est-ce que la propriété?," 39.
[654] Id., 39–41.
[655] Id., 46.
[656] Xifaras, "Ya-t-il une théorie de la propriété chez Pierre-Joseph Proudhon," 248ff.

preferred "to burn property slowly, rather than to give it new strength by making a St. Bartholomew's Day of the owners."[657] Instead, Marx's goal was to "shorten and lessen the birth pangs of the new society."[658] Marx is most well known for foreshadowing a future in which the proletariat's struggle for self-emancipation would eventually lead to a society with no private property. This common perception of Marx as the atemporal revolutionary has overshadowed a more nuanced account of Marx's role in the debate on property. Marx was a man of his epoch, whose understanding of property was shaped by the French Revolution and the political and cultural conflicts that inflamed the German states between the 1820s and the 1880s but also, in fundamental ways, by the juristic debates of his time.[659] Marx clarified a fundamental analytical point: property is not an affirmation of the individual will but is, in essence, a social relation. This realization did not escape the most sophisticated scholars of Roman and medieval law, who were deeply familiar with the intricate relational nature of divided *dominium*, but it had fallen into oblivion because it hardly fit the ideological view of the liberal jurists. In a passage in the third volume of *Das Kapital*, Marx openly derided the will-based conception of property as ridiculously simplistic:

> Nothing can be more ridiculous that Hegel's development of private landed property .... Free private property in land – a very modern product – is not, according to Hegel, a specific social relation, but a relation of the human being as a person to "Nature," "an absolute right of appropriation with respect to all things of human beings." This much is immediately clear, that the individual person cannot affirm himself as a property owner through his "will" in opposition to an alien will that similarly seeks to embody itself in the same bit of earth. A great many other things are required for this besides good will.[660]

---

[657] "Lettre à Karl Marx, Lyon, 17 mai 1846," in *Correspondance de P.-J. Proudhon*, par A.-J. Langlois, vol. 2 (Geneva: Slatkine Reprints, 1971 [1875]), 200.

[658] Karl Marx, *Das Kapital*, vol. 1 in Karl Marx and Friedrich Engels, *Marx Engels Werke*, Band 23 (Berlin: Dietz, 1972), 16.

[659] On Marx's relationship with juristic thought of the time, see Jean Axelrad Cahan, "The Concept of Property in Marx's Theory of History: A Defense of the Autonomy of the Socio-economic Base" (1994–1995) 58(4) *Science & Society* 392–414; Donald R. Kelley, "The Metaphysics of Law: An Essay on the Very Young Marx" (1978) 83(2) *American Historical Review* 350–367.

[660] Karl Marx, *Das Kapital*, vol. 3, in Karl Marx and Friedrich Engels, *Marx Engels Werke*, Band 25 (Berlin: Dietz, 1981), 628–629, as quoted in Cahan, "The Concept of Property in Marx's Theory of History."

Rejecting the will theory, Marx recast property as a pattern of relations of production and extraction of surplus value that is consolidated and legitimated in a system of legal rights. This understanding that property is both a social relation and a legal institution Marx owed in part to Savigny's work on possession, which he probably encountered while attending Savigny's lectures at the University of Berlin.[661] Savigny had argued that law has its origin in a people's practices and customs and is then formalized into logically interrelated concepts by jurists. Echoes of Savigny's theory of possession are evident in a passage from *Zur Kritik der Hegelschen Rechtsphilosophie* (1843):

> The actual ground of private property, occupation, is a fact, an inexplicable fact, not a right. It is only through the juridical determinations which society attaches to factual possession that it acquires the character of legal possession, of private property.[662]

Marx's understanding that property originates as an economic fact, a pattern of social relations of production, and then evolves into a complex legal institution was no doubt a critical intuition, but one that was certainly facilitated by Marx's familiarity with the work of the German jurists. The debates around possession and property, fact and right, and the disquisitions about divided *dominium* – a concept that made explicit that property is a social relation with regards to a productive resource – equipped Marx to develop his theory that property is both structure and superstructure.

Yet another strand of thought that proved highly influential in reorienting the conversation around property was the now often forgotten "radical republicanism" that flourished in France toward the end of the nineteenth century. The optimistic liberalism of postrevolutionary republicans led them to see private property as a defense against domination and dependence. By contrast, the radical republicans of the end of the century thought of individual property as the source of domination and envisioned instead a form of social property. Wealth and property – Léon Bourgeois (1851–1925), the leader of the movement, wrote in his essay *Solidarité* – are created through the collective effort of past and present generations.[663] Accordingly, Bourgeois argued, each individual is

---

[661] See Kelley, "The Metaphysics of Law," 352.

[662] Karl Marx, "Zur Kritik der Hegelschen Rechtsphilosophie," in Karl Marx and Friedrich Engels, *Marx Engels Werke*, Band 1 (Berlin: Dietz, 1981), 315, as quoted in Cahan, "The Concept of Property in Marx's Theory of History."

[663] Léon Bourgeois, *Solidarité* (Paris: Armand Colin, 1896), 73.

born with a quasi-contractual debt toward the other members of society.[664] To realize the fulfillment of this obligation, the radical republicans proposed to establish institutions that would promote solidarity, a fair distribution of wealth, and the "free development of the human personality."

As these ideas about the role of property in industrial society started gaining more attention, the terms of the juristic debates also changed. The formalistic and individualistic approach to property did not disappear from one day to the next. Many jurists carried on with their "scientific" work of solidifying and tweaking the conceptual "system" of modern *dominium*. However, a new generation of critical jurists sought to translate the new ideas about property into actual legal doctrines.

A New Global Vanguard Redefines the Law of Property

The critics who sought to reform the law of property shared two commitments: making the law of property more equitable and approaching property as a social institution with specific purposes, rather than as a "system" of abstract concepts. The critics' actual political beliefs varied: some were liberals, others were social democrats, and still others were socialists. Their specific methodological views were also diverse, with some advocating a decidedly empirical and policy-oriented approach and others seeking an uneasy mediation between conceptualism and purposivism. Regardless of their political beliefs or their particular brand of sociological method, these critics saw themselves as innovators who challenged the formalism and individualism of the masters of modern *dominium*, the institutionally powerful academic "old-guard." As this new juristic vanguard gained intellectual prestige, many of its members also became institution-builders who shaped new international academic programs, published highly successfully property treatises, and founded new law reviews that came to rival the most established and prestigious work of earlier generations.

This rising generation of social critics differed from their older colleagues who had reinvented Roman *dominium* also in that they were able to establish a global scholarly network. While, for most of the nineteenth century, contacts among jurists in different countries of the Roman law world had been limited and the new theories about modern *dominium*

---

[664] Id., 115.

had spread mainly through the circulation of treatises and textbooks, this new generation of critics was more tightly connected. Young scholars from Latin America, the Middle East, and the more peripheral legal cultures of Europe obtained their doctoral degrees abroad and established long-term relationships with their mentors. Further, prominent academics traveled for international conferences and visiting professorships, which, in turn, prompted enduring correspondences and closer professional relations and thus more frequent intellectual exchange. In a word, the scholarly debate about property was becoming global.

This global network of social jurists retrieved and reinvented the concepts of Roman property law that spoke to the pluralism of property forms and to the relational nature of property rights. Their innovations included the doctrine of "abuse of rights," a new emphasis on the Roman law of things and the plurality of resource-based property regimes, the idea that property comes with a "social obligation" and the *lex agraria*. Each of these property doctrines reflected both the yearning for a new, purpose-oriented methodology as well as the substantive aspiration to greater equity and social cohesion. Unsurprisingly, each of these doctrines sparked intense controversy, had unintended consequences, and was repurposed in service of a variety of political agendas, some of which perverted the aspiration to equity that supposedly moved the social jurists or served the needs of authoritarian regimes.

Abuse of Rights: A Continental Drug with Disagreeable Effects or a Mild Corrective?

The doctrine of "abuse of rights," which prevents owners from "abusing" their proprietary entitlements, is probably the best-known of the proposals of the social jurists.[665] In late-nineteenth- and early-twentieth-century France and Italy, abuse of rights sparked a heated scholarly debate, characterized by harsh condemnation as well as hyperbolic encomium. Its critics envisaged it as "a barren logomachy,"[666] a "medieval

---

[665] Larissa Katz, "Spite and Extortion: A Jurisdictional Principle of Abuse of Property Right" (2012–2013) 122 *Yale Law Journal* 1444; Michael Byers, "Abuse of Rights: An Old Principle, A New Age" (2001–2002) 47 *McGill Law Journal* 389; Annekatrien Lenaerts, "The General Principle of the Prohibition of Abuse of Rights: A Critical Position on Its Role in a Codified European Contract Law" (2010) 18 *European Review of Private Law* 1121.

[666] Marcel Planiol, *Traité élémentaire de droit civil*, 4th ed. (Paris: Librairie générale de droit et de jurisprudence, 1907), tome II, sections 870–871.

relic thoughtlessly carried over,"[667] or, at best, "a pure piece of sentimen-tality."[668] By contrast, its champions acclaimed it as the triumph of a more perfect and broader vision of justice. The wave of emotionality stirred by abuse of rights continued well into the twentieth century. Writing in 1965, Italian jurist Pietro Rescigno noted that the changing fortunes of abuse of rights were evidence of "the jurist's agony in redeeming law's ancient misery."[669] More recently, an experts' report published by the Council of Europe concluded that abuse of rights makes it possible "to establish the connection between the justice ostensibly guaranteed by positive law and genuine justice."[670]

Such emotion may be surprising given that most scholars viewed abuse of rights as a relatively narrow "subjective" doctrine that focused on the owner's motive. While they varied in scope, these subjective articulations of abuse of rights introduced only modest limitations to proprietary entitlements. For example, in the variant known with the medieval name *aemulatio vicini*, the owner was said to abuse their right when driven solely by the malicious intent to harm another. In a second formulation, an abuse of a right was found any time malice was the dominant, though not the exclusive, motive animating the actions of the owner. According to a third, slightly broader, formulation, owners were deemed to abuse their right when they acted with a lack of "legitimate interest," though not necessarily spitefully.

These prevailing narrow and subjective formulations of the doctrine were for the most part inconsequential; objective formulations, however, could lead to a more significant compression of the owners' entitlements. In one variant, an owner acted abusively if she exercised her right contrary to the "normal function" of the right. In another variant, property rights were abused when exercised contrary to their "socio-economic purpose," which required weighing the owner's activity against larger social needs and interests. For example, a landowner who, in an arid region, drained ground water and diminished the community's supply in order to sell it for profit may be deemed to have used her right

---

[667] Vittorio Scialoja, "Aemulatio," in *Enciclopedia Giuridica Italiana*m, vol. 1, par 2 (Milan: Società Editrice Libraria, 1910), 426–452.

[668] H. C. Gutteridge, "Abuse of Rights" (1933) 5 *Cambridge Law Journal* 43.

[669] Pietro Rescigno, L'Abuso del Diritto, Riv. Dir. Civ. 1, 205 (1965); Id., *L'Abuso del Diritto* (Bologna: Il Mulino, 1998).

[670] "Abuse of Rights and Equivalent Concepts: The Principle and Its Present Day Application," in *Proceedings of the Nineteenth Colloquy on European Law, Luxembourg, 6–9 November 1989* (Strasbourg: Council of Europe, 1990), 10.

contrary to its "socioeconomic purpose." Two of the most prominent
social jurists of the time, Raymond Saleilles (1855–1912) and François
Gény (1861–1959), were vocal advocates of this broad objective notion of
abuse of rights. As Saleilles explained:

> Nothing is more dangerous, and more useless, than to leave the criterion
> of what constitutes abuse of right simply to individual psychology. There
> is no person who, in this case, does not have the ingenuity to argue that
> their intention was not to harm another; it would be very easy to point to
> an individual interest. The true formula is the one that identifies the abuse
> of a right in the abnormal exercise of the right, the exercise that is
> contrary to the economic or social purpose of the subjective right.[671]

The fact that abuse of rights could be formulated in such different
ways, with effects that varied dramatically, was certainly part of the
reason it generated such anxiety among commentators. In a 1933 article,
the English jurist H. C. Gutteridge described the indeterminacy of the
doctrine as a threat to individual liberty and noted, with great relief, that
abuse of rights was a purely "continental" doctrine, extraneous to the
common law.

> The conversations I have had with continental lawyers left me with the
> impression that *abus de droit* is regarded as a dangerous expedient which
> should only be utilized to prevent manifest injustice . . . .. It [abuse of
> rights] resembles a drug which at first appears to be innocuous, but
> may be followed by very disagreeable after effects. Like all indefinite
> expressions of an ethical principle it is capable of being put to an infinite
> variety of uses, and it may be employed to invade almost any sphere of
> human activity for the purpose of subordinating the individual to the
> demands of the State . . . .. But it is clear that the theories of abuse and of
> relativity of rights, in general, have no place in our law as it now stands.[672]

Abuse of rights quickly became a matter of legal-cultural identity. The
fact that there seemed to exist no doctrine of abuse of rights in the
common law was a source of relief for Gutteridge, but for many jurists
in France and Italy, it signified the ethical flaws of the Anglo-Saxon
tradition. These jurists were eager to demonstrate that altruism and
equity were the defining features of the "Latin race," as opposed to the
individualist and absolutist nature of the Anglo-Saxon tradition.

---

[671] Raymond Saleilles, *Étude sur la théorie générale de l'obligation d'après le premier projet de code civil pour l'Empire allemand*, 2nd ed. (Paris: F. Pichon, 1901), 370 n. 1.
[672] Gutteridge, "Abuse of Rights," 43.

The legal world is crossed by a twofold current: the individualist current and the social current. The individualist current, which deserves the epithet of absolutist, is the one which characterizes the Anglo-Saxon race. Profoundly individualist the Anglo-Saxons are in their institutions, in their philosophy, in their behavior. If their most outstanding philosophers praise with pleasure the inexorable laws governing the struggle for life and natural selection, their jurists, in nice symmetry, hold a rigorous and merciless conception of law; most of all they want legal weapons, means of action.[673]

The author of this passage is the French jurist Louis Josserand (1868–1941) who, in 1905, published a highly influential essay entitled *De l'Abus des droits*. Josserand was a sophisticated and often polemic methodological innovator, who relentlessly pushed the idea that law is a social science rather than a form of abstract geometry, as propounded by the formalist juristic old guard, which was largely concentrated in the prestigious *Faculté de Droit* of Paris.[674] One of the most prominent figures in the emerging global network of social critics, Josserand well exemplified the interests, commitments, and also the professional trajectory, of the rising global vanguard. After a slow start in legal academia, appreciation of his controversial and innovative work earned him an appointment as Professeur de Droit Civil in the Faculté de Droit of Lyon, then seen as marginal and provincial. Subsequently, as his reputation grew, Josserand climbed the ladder of professional and institutional power, becoming dean at Lyon in 1913 and, ultimately, conseiller à la Cour de cassation in 1935. Josserand's ambitions as an intellectual and a

---

[673] Louis Josserand, *De l'abus des droits* (Paris: Arthur Rosseau Editeur, 1905), 7 and 8. Josserand's rage seems irrepressible and does not spare Frederick Pollock: "The applications of this point of view are innumerable; English and American jurists apply it unpityingly and even with pride, and especially Frederick Pollock, justly among the most well-known jurists. In his outstanding work on tort law, *The Law of Torts*, this author shows, with a wealth of examples taken from everyday life, this principle cherished by his compatriots, i.e., immunity in the exercise of common rights."

[674] On Josserand, see *Un ordre juridique nouveau? Dialogues avec Louis Josserand, sous la direction de M. William Dross et Thierry Favario* (Paris: Mare & Martin, 2014); David Deroussin, "Josserand, Le Code Civil et le Code Libanais des obligations et contrats," in *Le Code civil français et le dialogue des cultures juridiques* (Paris: Bruylant, 2007), 49–94; F. Audren and C. Fillon, "Louis Josserand ou la construction d'une autorité doctrinale" (2009) 1 *Revue trimestrielle de droit civil* 39–76; D. Fenouillet, "Étienne Louis Josserand (1868–1941)" (1996) 17 *Revue d'histoire des Facultés de droit et de la science juridique* 27–46; C. Baillon-Passe, "Relire Josserand" (2003) *Dalloz* 1571; J.-P. Chazal, "'Relire Josserand', oui mais ... sans le trahir!" (2003) 27 *Recueil Dalloz Sirey de doctrine de jurisprudence et de législation* 1777–1781; S. Dumas-Lavenac, "Le Droit selon Louis Josserand" (2015) 2 *Revue juridique de l'Ouest* 39–53.

mentor led him to develop a network beyond France and even Europe. As professor and dean in Lyon, he actively promoted international exchanges, both through the study of comparative law, for which Lyon rapidly gained fame, and by helping to establish the École de Droit in Beirut, Lebanon, then a French protectorate. Under the leadership of a small cohort of similarly minded and creative scholars who were eager to look beyond the European continent, Lyon came to rival Paris, becoming one of the focal points of the global network of critical jurists.

As we know, the champions of modern *dominium* were keen to highlight the Roman pedigree of each of their reinvented doctrines; by the same token, Josserand was eager to present abuse of rights as more authentically Roman than the law of modern absolute *dominium*. Masterfully appropriating the liberal narrative of the *Roman* versus the *medieval*, Josserand questioned whether the absolutist conception of property was, in fact, truly Roman, and argued that the concept of abuse of rights originated in the "real" and "good" Roman law, that is, the jurisprudence of the Roman *praetor*, the magistrate charged with administering equity.

> The odious maxim *"dura lex sed lex,"* which does not seem to be truly Roman, is, in any event, completely false for the Roman law of the good epoch; it made way for its corrective and antagonist *"summum ius summa iniuria,"* and the praetorian right, in its admirable, harmonious development, is the shining illustration of and the triumphant march of abuse of rights. It is possible that this concept, so humane, lively and flexible, was temporarily overshadowed in medieval times with the advent of the cold Scholastic, but, in any case, it reappeared with the Renaissance of Roman law.[675]

The Roman law Josserand invoked hardly resembled that of his liberal adversaries: it was a social and equitable law, rather than a law that enabled and magnified the individual will. Unsurprisingly, the critics of abuse of rights vehemently rejected this characterization. Italian Romanist Vittorio Scialoja noted with irony and contempt: "This, in other words, is the doctrine of *aemulatio*, shaped in all its features by the medieval approach, and nevertheless pitched as Roman."[676] Scialoja declared that abuse of rights and the similar but more limited concept of

---

[675] L. Josserand, *De l'esprit des droits et de leur relativité: théorie dite de l'abus des droits*, 2nd ed. (Paris: Dalloz, 1939), 4.

[676] V. Scialoja, "Nota a Corte di Cassazione di Firenze del 13 dicembre 1877" (1878) III(1) *Foro Italiano* 481.

aemulatio were alien to Roman law and were instead a medieval invention of the fourteenth-century scholars known as the Commentators to reflect the new Christian ethic.[677] In classical Latin, the Italian Romanist claimed, the word *aemulatio* hardly meant acts lacking any utility and exclusively inspired by a malicious intent.[678] Further, Scialoja noted, the Roman sources offered as evidence of the existence of the doctrine of abuse of rights in Roman law were either too broad, and were therefore merely declamatory, bore no relation to the topic of *aemulatio*, or concerned public law and were hardly extensible to private law.[679] After rehearsing a variety of textual arguments, Scialoja called upon the core elements of the liberal, anti-medieval narrative and attributed to the doctrine the shortcomings of all things medieval: excessive complexity, oppression, uncertainty, and unpredictability. To give his readers a taste of the type of conceptual and moral hairsplitting that courts seeking to apply the doctrine would have to engage in, Scialoja noted:

> *Aemulatio* may be good or bad; the first is virtue, the second a vice. In the latter, however, one has to distinguish the *aemulatio* that is putatively licit, the one in which the owner harms another with the intent of gaining some benefit for himself, and the actually illcit *aemulatio*, in which the owner acts with the intent to harm, *animus nocendi*. *Aemulatio* is not presumed, the burden of proof is on the plaintiff but, if certain circumstances are present, there is an exception.[680]

Not only did the debate on abuse of rights involve opposite views of what authentic Roman law stood for, it also placed front and center the question of the essential nature of property and, relatedly, the methodology of property analysis. Josserand's essay, which went through several, expanded editions, was theoretically ambitious. Josserand viewed the doctrine of abuse of rights as the forebear of a larger transformation in the very imaginary of property. Abuse of rights promised to temper the liberal idea of rights "as powerful war-machines susceptible of being deployed against society at large or against single individuals."[681] Taking aim at the image of rights as spheres of liberty that harmoniously

---

[677] Id., 486. On Scialoja's critique of abuse of rights, see Giovanni Cazzetta, "Abuso del diritto e forma di unità del guiridico" (2017) 58 *Rivista di Diritto Civile* 559–581; Massimo Brutti, *Vittorio Scialoja, Emilio Betti: Due Visioni del Diritto Civile* (Turin: Giappichelli, 2013).

[678] Scialoja, "Nota a Corte di Cassazione di Firenze 13 dicembre 1877," 486.

[679] Scialoja, "Aemulatio," 428.

[680] Id., 436.

[681] Josserand, *De l'abus des droits*, 10.

coexist – a dear treasure of the German writers and omnipresent in the treatises of the great masters of modern *dominium* – Josserand reconceptualized rights and liberty. In any given society, Josserand wrote, rights clash and compete, and the task of the legislature is not to assign to each an inviolable sphere but to organize and coordinate wisely their inevitable conflicts.[682] Rights are indeed a guarantee of liberty, not of an abstract, egoistic, and anti-social liberty but of a social liberty embodying a higher ideal of solidarity and justice. In Josserand's words:

> the relativity of rights has long been postulated because of their origin: social products, rights are to serve a social purpose. Whatever idea one has regarding the origins of law, and even if one acknowledges the existence of some sort of natural law, prior and superior to positive law, one has to admit that our individual prerogatives presuppose the consent of the social community, whether emanating expressly from the public powers or coming directly from the collective consciousness .... In any way, individual prerogatives, even the most egoistic, are social products in form and in substance; it would be unconceivable that they could be exercised at the right holder's convenience, diverted from their original purpose and employed for any goal; it would be contrary to their origin as well as to the most urgent need of the social community which confers them.[683]

Having redefined rights and liberty, Josserand cleared the way for an objective, rather than purely subjective, doctrine of abuse of rights, one that took into account the purpose or function of the right.

> But this first limitation [quantitative, in intensity] is not sufficient. Our jurisprudence has established that rights need to have another limitation as well, more significant and more equitable .... This limitation is driven by the idea of the purpose of rights. When the legislature confers on us a prerogative, it is not for us to make whatever use of it: the legislature has in mind a specific goal. All institutions have a purpose that is their *raison d'être* and against which they cannot work. Each right is called to serve towards a certain goal and it is not for individuals to take the right in a different direction. That would be not use but abuse and may render its author liable.[684]

In juristic circles, many remained impervious to Josserand's idea of property rights as created by the legislature for a social purpose and continued to insist on the image of the natural, independent, and

---

[682] Id., 2.
[683] Josserand, *De l'esprit des droits et de leur relativité*, 320.
[684] Josserand, *De l'abus des droits*, 5.

absolute spheres of ownership that had punctuated the treatises of the masters of modern *dominium*. Vittorio Scialoja was among the stubborn defenders of the image of the spheres:

> In fact, law in an objective sense, traces the limits of the single individual liberties: but as we said above, these limits are traced according to necessity. The single liberties resemble polyhedra that touch each other in every point of their periphery, so that you cannot exit from one without invading the other; but, conversely, as far as you do not invade another's, you do not exit your own. Hence as long as there is not legal invasion of another's right, either that of single individuals or that of society, nobody can be said to have transgressed the limits of her right.[685]

Another vehement critic of abuse of rights was Georges Ripert (1880–1958), a member of the Paris old guard. Ripert published a review of Josserand's essay in the prestigious *Revue critique de législation et de jurisprudence*, which he directed. The review was a scathing critique of Josserand's essay, an indictment of the social pioneers of the law faculty of Lyon, and a bitter attack on Josserand's very character. Ripert saw abuse of rights as an aberration and the surest way to plunge society into anarchy and socialism. Ripert artfully evoked the specter of "Soviet materialism":

> The University of Lyon seems to have an inclination towards the Code Civil of the Soviet Socialist Republics. Its *Institut de Droit Comparé* has provided a translation presented by Mr. Lambert as a magic mirror refracting the guiding principles of a new legal regime. Mr. Josserand, in turn, seems to look at law through this mirror . . .. This book [Josserand's] which opens with an invocation of the principles of eternal justice against those of strict law, which on certain pages seems to be written by an unabashed idealist, ends, in a peculiar contradiction, by taking as a model the code of a purely materialist society lost in the absurd dream of an entirely rational economy.[686]

Despite Ripert's denunciation of abuse of rights as an instrument of socialism, writers with a radical redistributive agenda, such as the Italian proponents of the approach known as *socialismo giuridico* (legal socialism), barely mentioned abuse of rights, believing that its corrective impact was too limited. For instance, Giuseppe Vadalà-Papale (1854–1921), one of the most prominent figures in the movement,

---

[685] Scialoia, "Aemulatio," 440.
[686] Georges Ripert, "Abus ou relativité des droits" (1929) 49 *Revue critique de législation et de jurisprudence* 39.

advocated a complete overhaul of private law and a novel *codice privato-sociale* (private-social code) but largely ignored abuse of rights, always remaining at the margins of the debate over the doctrine.[687]

As the contrast between Josserand's image of property as social and relative and Scialoja's image of property rights as polyhedra with neat boundaries suggests, the debate over abuse of rights was closely tied to a larger methodological debate about the present and future, not only of property law but of private law more generally. Was private law an abstract, logical science akin to geometry or a purpose-oriented social science? Abuse of rights exemplified the new pragmatic and purposive understanding of private law that was increasingly gaining attention among jurists. The stakes were high and not purely intellectual. On the ultimate predominance of formalism or purposivism turned very real professional interests: what counted as "good scholarship"? Who should have access to the higher ranks of the profession? What type of training best equipped jurists to hold high-level positions in government or the judiciary? were all live questions. Formalism had, obviously, never been the only approach to the study of private law; as we have seen, some of the architects of modern *dominium* did in fact show unexpected openness to the "living law" of property. But sophisticated logical and systematic analysis of private law concepts had long been the hallmark of legal science. For members of the juristic profession who saw themselves as the custodians of this science, the new sociological and purpose-oriented approach was a threat. There were prominent converts too. The most illustrious among the converts was Rudolph von Jhering. Jhering's essay "Der Kampf ums Recht" ("The Struggle for Law")[688] made a big splash and was followed, in 1877 and 1888, by two volumes entitled *Der Zweck im Recht (Law as a Means to an End)*.[689] Jhering was a charismatic figure and a brilliant writer, whose work reached a wide audience of educated nonspecialists. As Albert Kocourek wrote in the introduction to the

---

[687] A. Loria, "Socialismo Giuridico" (1893) 1 *La Scienza del Diritto Privato* fascicle 8, page 819.

[688] Rudolf von Jhering, "Der Kampf um das Recht," in *Vortrag des Hofrates Professor Jhering Gehalten in der Wiener Juristischen Gesellschaft am 11. März 1872.* (Wien: Verlag der G. J. Manz'schen Buchhandlung, 1872); for an English translation, see Rudolf von Jhering, *The Struggle for Law* (John Lalor, trans.) (Chicago: Callaghan & Company, 1915).

[689] Rudolf von Jhering, *Der Zweck im Recht.* (Leipzig: Druck und Verlag von Breitkopf & Hartel, 1877); for an English translation, see Rudolf von Jhering, *Law as a Means to an End* (Isaac Husik, trans.) (New York: Macmillan, 1921).

English translation of "Der Kampf ums Recht," "the power of his personality is attested by the fact of his great popularity; his lectures were always crowded with listeners; and his home was the shrine at which the devoted from all quarters of the world worshipped."[690] For Jhering, legal science was to be concerned not with abstract rights but with "social mechanics," with the struggle between competing interests. Jhering's image was powerful:

> This is the picture of society as life presents it daily to our eyes. Thousands of rollers, wheels and knives, as in a mighty machine, move restlessly, some in one direction, some in another . . . . This social mechanics is identical with the principle of the levers of social motion. There are four such levers. Two of them have egoism as their motive and presupposition; I call them the lower of egoistic social levers . . . . Opposed to these are two other impulses which have not egoism as their motive or presupposition, but on the contrary the denial thereof; I call them the higher.[691]

Abuse of rights generated so much hostility among those who viewed private law as a matter of logical concepts and natural rights because it was one of the tools that could be used to control the levers of the "mighty machine."

Expanding the Roman Law of Things: Salvatore Pugliatti and the Image of Property as a Tree

Property scholars seem to have a particular taste for images drawn from nature. The concept of property developed by Wesley N. Hohfeld and the Realists in the United States is often described as a "bundle of sticks" to highlight that property is a set of entitlements, or sticks, variously shaped and variously bundled together, for the purpose of governing relations among individuals with regard to resources. At approximately the same time Hohfeld and the Realists were developing what came to be known as the "bundle of sticks" image, French and Italian jurists were also revolutionizing their understanding of the concept of property to openly reflect the relational and necessarily limited nature of property. Like their American colleagues, they too relied on an image drawn from nature. The Sicilian jurist Salvatore Pugliatti (1903–1976), in his *La Proprietà nel Nuovo Diritto*, compared property to a tree.[692] The trunk of the tree

---

[690] A. Kocourek, "Introduction," in Jhering, *The Struggle for Law*, x.

[691] Jhering, *Law as a Means to an End*, 71–72.

[692] S. Pugliatti, *La Proprietà nel Nuovo Diritto* (Milan: A. Giuffrè, 1964), 149.

represents the core, or the essence, of property, namely the right to control the use of the thing. The branches are the many different resource-specific ownership regimes, that is, combinations of proprietary entitlements that are specifically assembled and shaped to promote the individual and societal values and interests implicated by different types of "things," from agricultural land, to urban residential housing, water, minerals, commercial real estate, and things of historic value. Pugliatti's image of the property tree, and the efforts of contemporaries of Pugliatti like Josserand and the Italian Filippo Vassalli (1885–1955) to diversify property by grounding it in resources, was a dramatic expansion of the Roman "law of things" and may be the most cogent and inspirational of the ideas developed by the critics of absolute *dominium*.

The foundations of the tenet that property is a pluralistic institution, consisting of multiple, resource-based ownership regimes, were laid by French jurists, starting at the beginning of the twentieth century. Most of the refinement, however, was done in the 1930s in Italy.[693] The proving ground for the conceptualization of property as a tree was the debate on the new draft Italian Codice Civile, which would become law in 1942. The Italian civil code of 1865 largely followed the French Code Napoléon and thereby glorified the idea of absolute *dominium*.[694] The drafting of the new code was the occasion to outline a concept of property that would reflect the many ways in which, in real life, property law had changed. First, property was becoming increasingly "incorporeal." Patents, trademarks, and *fonds de commerce* were new, crucial, intangible forms of property.[695] Further, property rights were becoming limited and "specialized."[696] In both Italy and France, early twentieth-century legislative provisions limited the use rights and transfer rights of owners of

---

[693] The idea of property as a tree with a unitary trunk and many branches was Pugliatti's, but the intuition that property has many branches was first outlined by Josserand and Vassalli. See L. Josserand, "Configuration du droit de propriété dans l'ordre juridique nouveau," in *Mélanges juridiques, dédiés à M. le professeur Sugiyama* (Tokyo: Association japonaise des juristes de langue française, Maison France-Japon, 1940), 95–110. See also F. Vassalli, "Per una definizione legislativa del diritto di proprietà," in *Scritti Giuridici*, vol. II (Milan: Giuffrè, 1960), 329.

[694] D. Corradini, *Garantismo e statualismo: Le codificazioni civilistiche dell'Ottocento*. (Milan: Giuffrè, 1986), 125; C. Ghisalberti, *La codificazione del diritto in Italia, 1865–1942* (Rome: Laterza, 1985), 251; S. Rodotà, *Il terribile diritto. Studi sulla proprietà privata e i beni comuni* (Bologna: Il Mulino, 2013), chapter 2.

[695] Josserand, "Configuration," 104.

[696] See Pugliatti, *La Proprietà nel Nuovo Diritto*, 1–33, where he discussese the special rules for a variety of resources including mines, railways, water, and urban streets.

things of historical and artistic interest.[697] In Italy, starting in the 1920s, land reclamation laws imposed on owners duties to improve and to cultivate their land. The Italian government also subjected owners of utilities or industries of critical importance to the national economy, such as textile and manufacturing, to imposed obligations and limitations. Emergency legislation passed in the years of the First World War further limited the rights of owners of specific resources, in particular their right not to be expropriated. Military authorities could temporarily occupy or use resources important to national security, such as land, buildings, or means of transportation.[698] Finally, the boundaries between private property and public property were also changing, with the result that the inventory of resources subtracted from private property and held by the state in trust for the public expanded.

The effort to reconceptualize property to reflect these changes took place against the background of dramatic events: the crisis of liberalism and the rise of Fascism.[699] Italian Fascism was the outcome of the economic and social crisis of late nineteenth-century Italy, greatly exacerbated by the First World War.[700] Under the guidance of the liberal-constitutional monarchy that held power in Italy between 1861 and 1919, Italy enjoyed rapid but uneven economic development. The liberal monarchy failed to broaden its base and to respond to the working classes' demands for change. The First World War worsened the economic situation, exposing the incompetence of the liberal political class and radicalizing the masses. The years 1918–1920, the "Two Red Years," witnessed mass unrest and the paralysis of the parliamentary system. The Fascists' rise to power was extremely rapid. Fascism sought to

---

[697] Vassalli, "Per una definizione legislativa del diritto di proprietà," 333–337; Josserand, "Configuration," 105.

[698] Pugliatti, *La Proprietà nel Nuovo Diritto*, 23–24.

[699] On the rise of Italian Fascism, see generally, A. Lyttelton, *Italian Fascisms from Pareto to Gentile* (New York: Harper and Row, 1975); A. De Grand, *Italian Fascism: Its Origins and Development*, 3rd ed. (Lincoln: University of Nebraska Press, 2000); on the agrarian crisis, see generally, F. M. Snowden, *Violence and the Great Estates in the South of Italy: Apulia, 1900–1922* (Cambridge: Cambridge University Press, 1986), 175; M. Rossi-Doria, *Riforma Agraria e Azione Meridionalista* (Naples: L'ancora del Mediterraneo, 2003 [1948]).

[700] On the crisis of liberalism and the rise of fascism in Italy, see C. Seton-Watson, *Italy from Liberalism to Fascism, 1870–1925* (London: Methuen, 1967); M. De Cecco, "The Economy from Liberalism to Fascism," in A. Lyttelton (ed.), *Liberal and Fascist Italy, 1900–1945* (Oxford: Oxford University Press, 2002), 62–82; J. Pollard, *The Fascist Experience in Italy* (Milton Park: Routledge, 1998).

replace the weak liberal state with an authoritarian, corporatist state. Presented as an alternative to the evils of "individualistic liberalism" and Bolshevism, corporatism sought to overcome social conflict by organizing society and the economy into associations ("corporations") of workers and employers and by facilitating cooperation between them in the national interest.[701]

The new Codice Civile was one of the most publicized initiatives of the Fascists. The law of property was of critical importance in a corporatist system, as the new relations between groups of workers and employers needed to rest on new property relations. In 1935, the Fascist Confederation of Agricultural Workers convened in Rome the first national conference on agrarian law. The topic of the conference was "Il concetto fascista della proprietà privata."[702] The central theme of the writings of Fascist property scholars was the idea that the interest of the individual owner is subordinated to the larger interest of the Fascist state, identified as the expansion of national production. Mussolini's project of economic self-sufficiency made efficiency in production a priority, and the 1927 Carta del Lavoro exalted the theme of enterprise productivity and economic solidarity in the superior interest of the nation.[703]

Pugliatti developed his concept of property against this background. He was an eclectic intellectual, a jurist but also a literary and music critic, "a true Renaissance man," in the words of his contemporary Arturo Claro Jemolo (1891–1981). Culturally deeply rooted in his native Sicily, he was part of the Sicilian literary avant-garde and lifelong friend and soulmate of the poet Salvatore Quasimodo (1901–1968). Pugliatti's rise to academic power exemplifies the professional trajectory of many in the new generation of critics, who began as disruptive innovators and landed as power figures. He started at the margins of academia, as an assistant librarian, and rapidly gained a reputation for his novel blend of conceptualism and purpose-oriented jurisprudence. As he emerged as a leading intellectual innovator, Pugliatti went on to become dean of the law school of the University of Messina and to establish his own long-lived and highly influential academic network, known as La Scuola Messinese. Politically, Pugliatti was a social-democrat, secular but with

---

[701] P. Grossi, *A History of European Law* (L. Hooper, trans.) (Malden, MA: Wiley-Blackwell, 2010), 138.

[702] G. Arias, "La proprietà privata nel diritto fascista" (1935) 6 *Lo Stato* 333.

[703] G. Leibholz, "V. Carta del Lavoro 21 aprile 1927," in *Zu Den Problemen des fascistischen Verfassungrechts: Akademische Antrittsvorlesung* (Berlin: De Gruyter, 2019), 99–106.

an interest in Catholic thought, reflected in the many letters he exchanged with Giorgio La Pira, one of the most prominent figures in the Christian Democratic Party. As to his relationship to Fascism, Pugliatti was part of the large group of Italian intellectuals who did not actively support the regime and who privately expressed condemnation of it but who never openly disassociated from it.[704]

The image of the tree nicely captures the entwined tensions that pervaded Pugliatti's approach to property: his pragmatic attention to the real life of property but also his reluctance to dissolve the concept of property into a pure sociological description and his commitment to the liberal values of freedom and autonomy associated with property but also his focus on regulating and limiting property in the public interest. For Pugliatti, property, despite the dramatic legislative and regulatory transformations that were reshaping its scope, was, nevertheless, a concept with a coherent structure and one best illustrated by the image of a tree. The tree emphasized the fundamental, autonomous interests of the individual owner, while also recognizing that property regulation necessarily responds to the multifarious, real-life questions inherent in the governance of different resources.

Normatively, Fascist property was narrowly monistic, foregrounding one single value: the productive strength of the Fascist nation, which trumped the interest of the individual owner. By contrast, the trunk of Pugliatti's tree, that is, the core entitlement of property, was the owner's interest in controlling the use of the resource, the full range of possible alternative beneficial uses to which a resource may be put.[705] The trunk represented the autonomy and individualization of property that *la*

---

[704] Salvatore Pugliatti maintained an ambiguous relationship to the Fascist regime. A critic of the regime, he maintained formal relations of affiliation and collaboration with the GUF, the Fascist association of university students and faculty. This formal affiliation allowed him to launch a number of cultural projects, including the experimental theater project know as Teatro Sperimentale di Messina. His anti-Fascist sentiments are reflected in several anecdotes. Luigi Ferlazzo Natoli in his biography of Pugliatti tells that once Pugliatti arrived at a public event of the GUF wearing a white shirt rather than the black Fascist uniform. Ferlazzo Natoli also recounts that Pugliatti had been denounced as anti-Fascist and that the Fascist regime put him under surveillance. One day an employee of the postal office showed up at Pugliatti's home and handed him a letter. The letter was addressed to the Fascist authorities and was yet another denunciation of Pugliatti's anti-Fascism; it asked that Pugliatti be confined in one the Fascists' specialized locations. The postal employee had seen the content of the letter and took it out of the mailbag to protect Pugliatti. See Luigi Ferlazzo Natoli, *Letteratura e diritti. Scritti su Salvatore Pugliatti* (Milan: Giuffrè, 2002), 62, 69.

[705] Pugliatti, *La Proprietà nel Nuovo Diritto*, 159.

concezione fascista della proprietà privata (the Fascist conception of private property) sought to diminish or negate. References to the liberal language of individual "sovereignty" punctuated Pugliatti's property writings, because, as Ludovico Barassi (1873–1956), another liberal contemporary of Pugliatti, put it, "in times of fascist rule, we need not be afraid of words."[706]

If the trunk of the tree represented the right to the full beneficial use of the resource, the branches represented the many, differently shaped, resource-specific combinations of ownership entitlements: agrarian property, family property, affordable urban residential property, entrepreneurial property, and intellectual property. In their treatises, the nineteenth-century writers had centered the property system on one form of ownership, *dominium*, indifferent to context and resource type and had reduced the pluralistic and lively Roman law of things to an abstract and lifeless set of classifications. Josserand and Pugliatti breathed new life into the law of things. Property, Josserand wrote, being the law of things, is inevitably and intrinsically pluralistic.

> Because of the differences in its object, property takes on different shapes depending on the type of resource involved. Property is no longer uniform, rather it is multiform, infinitely diverse and varied. There is no longer one property but many properties, each with its own specialized regime.[707]

Josserand noted that land itself, the primary object of modern *dominium* and the almost exclusive focus of the nineteenth jurists, had hardly ever been governed through uniform rules and that this differentiation was destined to grow.

> Even if we limit our investigation to real property, we find that, within this genre there are multiple species. Agricultural land is treated differently than urban real estate. In France a rural code is being drafted that contains all the rules regulating agricultural life and, in most countries, most notably in Italy, an agrarian law is developing; [it is] a prominent legal innovation that is attracting the attention of lawmakers and law professors, in universities as well as in the official palaces. And other special regimes have developed within real property: family property has its own regime and so does low-income housing.[708]

---

[706] Id., 187.
[707] Josserand, "Configuration," 100.
[708] Id., 102.

That property is pluralistic and grounded in resources rapidly became a commonplace among jurists, nicely captured by Filippo Vassalli when he noted that, in order to accurately describe the real life of property, "we have to recognize that there is no longer one property, rather there are many properties. This is because the public interest demands that different resources be regulated differently to reflect the different policy objectives specific to those different resources."[709]

Pugliatti's branches, or Vassalli's properties, marked a qualitative shift in the jurists' conceptualization and normative analysis of property. Property, these jurists warned, is a pluralistic institution, both structurally and normatively. It consists of multiple ownership regimes and it serves different values and interests. Property's pluralism may seem obvious to today's readers, and it had certainly been evident to the Roman jurists. But well into the twentieth century, different generations of "modernizers" had obliterated and suppressed property's pluralism. For the nineteenth-century ideologues of absolute *dominium*, from the most pedestrian exegetists to the most sophisticated conceptualists, property law was to serve one goal: enabling the will of the individual. Later, Mussolini's militant jurists sought to transform the law of property to serve the needs of production and the oppression of the Fascist state. Reacting to this ideological monism, Josserand and Pugliatti foregrounded the many normative ambitions of a modern and liberal law of property: enabling autonomy, grounding personhood, promoting productive efficiency, and securing a modicum of equity in access to resources. These plural values and interests are often in conflict with each other, and courts and legislatures are inevitably called upon to weigh hard trade-offs. The legacy of our jurists was to show that these normative trade-offs appear less intractable when grounded in the actual context of specific resources. The characteristics of different resources narrow the scope of lawmakers' normative choices, suggesting what values and interests are particularly relevant in specific cases and what trade-offs are desirable. Freedom of action or privacy, equitable distribution, efficiency, and participatory management have different weight and meaning depending on whether the resource owned is an irrigation canal, a home, a parcel of agricultural land, or a manufacturing firm.

---

[709] Vassalli, "Per una definizione legislativa del diritto di proprietà," 331.

The Social Function of Property and the *Lex Agraria*

The idea that property has a "social function" was another critical contribution of the social jurists that has continued to inspire or enrage property writers to this day.[710] The theory of the "social function" of property resonated with jurists around the globe and energized a variety of local property agendas that, until then, had remained confined to small, and often marginal, circles. The "social function" rapidly became a rallying cry connecting jurists in different countries into a loose intellectual and political network that shared seemingly kindred goals and sensibilities. And yet, behind this unifying new motto, there lay a myriad of "social function" theories. Property's social function was endlessly reshaped and repurposed, proving to be a tool for emancipation as well as for oppression. It was the legal device used to enfranchise landless agrarian workers, to empower indigenous peoples in the struggle to recover ancestral lands, and to liberate the industrial working class. But, in the hands of Fascists and authoritarian regimes, it also functioned as an effective means of suppressing political rights and restricting market liberties. In the second half of the nineteenth century, for most German and French jurists, the social function meant merely the acknowledgment that property invariably and necessarily entails obligations on the part of the owner. A handful of Italian and French writers envisioned the social function as the lynchpin of a more ambitious *socialismo giuridico* or *socialism juridique*. At the turn of the century, revolutionary and reformist social movements in Mexico, Colombia, and Chile, supported by sympathetic academic jurists, dramatically expanded this "socialist" variant of the theory and deployed it to support ambitious agrarian reform agendas focused on the redistribution of land. For jurists in Nazi Germany, Fascist Italy, and Vichy France, the concept that property has a social function legitimized the effort to redirect individual economic rights toward the pursuit of the state's goal of a productive national economy.[711]

---

[710] G. S. Alexander, "The Social Obligation Norm in American Property Law" (2009) 94 *Cornell Law Review* 745; see also S. R. Foster and D. Bonilla (eds.), "The Social Function of Property: A Comparative Perspective" (2011) 80 *Fordham Law Review* 101.

[711] A. Somma, "I giuristi francesi e il diritto della 'grande trasformazione,'" in B. Durand, J.-P. Le Crom, and A. Somma (eds.), *Le droit sous Vichy* (Frankfurt am Main: Vittorio Klosterman, 2006), 437–452. See also A. De Vita, "Proprietà e persona nella strategia dell'esclusione. Rimeditare Vichy: tutto in ordine niente a posto," in *Le droit sous Vichy*, 11–50; P. G. Monateri and A. Somma, "The Fascist Theory of Contract," in C. Joerges

Today, the social function of property is most often equated with the more expansive formulations that undergirded the efforts of radical and progressive reformers around the globe. One of earliest discussions of the social function of property, however, is to be found in the pages of an essay that the German jurist Otto von Gierke, by no means a radical, presented on April 5, 1889, to the juristische Gesellschaft, the "Juristic Society," of Vienna. A prominent member of the Germanist school of law, Gierke opposed the reinvention of Roman *dominium* and believed that modern German law should reflect an ancient – and no less fictitious – Germanic legal tradition centered on the community rather than the individual. Entitled "Die soziale Aufgabe des Privatrechts" ("The Social Task of Private Law"), the essay argued that property law has a social *Aufgabe* (task) and that its doctrines should be reshaped to reflect this task. Interestingly, among the doctrines that Gierke would have adopted were some that attracted much anti-feudal or anti-medieval rhetoric.

> Here lie the roots of the need for a specific land law, where acquisition and forfeiture, alienation, encumbrance and indebtedness of ownership in land is regulated by provisions in harmony with its unique nature, and distinct from movable things .... A private law, which understands its social vocation, must understand the continuity of land. It must not let itself be distracted either by doctrinaire points of view, nor by the dominant capitalist view in the levelling of property rights. All recognition of free disposition must be founded on protection against self-destruction of land ownership through over-indebtedness and fragmentation .... Reform of the law for inheriting land, which has begun [intermittently], cannot stand [completed] until German farmers are guaranteed the strongest bulwark against external attack and internal subversion .... There is one of the most urgent roles for modern private law, to create the necessary boundaries for the [*fideicommissum*], but in those boundaries to protect the family form of property.[712]

The social task Gierke envisioned for the law of property was that of securing agrarian landownership, large and small, and protecting direct producers, whom he saw as the backbone of a robust community. To this end, Gierke was willing to support property doctrines such as the

---

and N. Singh Ghaleigh (eds.), *Darker Legacies of Law in Europe* (London: Bloomsbury, 2003), 55–70.

[712] Otto von Gierke, *Die soziale Aufgabe des Privatrechts* (Berlin: Springer, 1889); for the English translation, see Otto von Gierke, "The Social Role of Private Law" (E. McGaughey, trans.) (2018) 19(4) *German Law Journal* 1068–1072.

imposition of positive duties and restraints on alienation, doctrines that the advocates of modern *dominium* were dismissing as feudal remnants, inimical to the free circulation of property.

Three years before Gierke's essay was published, another jurist, this time an actual "radical," both politically and methodologically, had formulated an "organicist" version of the social function theory that today few outside of Italy remember. Enrico Cimbali (1855–1887) was a native of Bronte, a small Sicilian town, who rose to prominence in Italian juristic circles for his eclectic appropriation of images from organic biology and for popularizing, along with a small cohort of fellow socialists, the idea of *socialismo giuridico* (legal socialism). Cimbali encouraged Italian jurists to free themselves from their more established French and German colleagues and to find their own voice. To be sure, Cimbali's approach to property was methodologically eccentric. The son of a doctor, Cimbali, in his essay "La nuova fase del diritto civile" ("The New Phase of Civil Law"), described property as similar to a digestive organ in living beings:

> Hence, property, like any other organ for nutrition in living beings, is the productive system, in which the substances necessary for the sustenance of the social body are gathered and processed. Now, any productive system adapts constantly under the incessant pressure of two forces: the force of the body itself and the force of the surrounding environment from which the body derives its nutrients . . . . For this reason, as the social body progressively evolves, the form and content of property have always been mutable, depending on the needs of the body.[713]

Couched in this confusing language drawn from biology was a straight-forward notion: property serves the changing needs of society and, hence, it transforms continuously. As society had entered a new phase, with the dramatic expansion of industrial development and the emergence of a new social class, the working class, property was to transform accordingly and enter a "new phase," as the title of the essay suggested. The idea that property law is in continuous transformation was in itself far from novel or radical, but the specific transformations that Cimbali envisioned for the "new phase" did seem radical to many of his contemporaries: the expansion of public property alongside private property; a new govern-ance regime for "moveable property," that is, resources such as industrial

---

[713] Enrico Cimbali, *La nuova fase del diritto civile nei rapporti economici e sociali* (Turin: UTE, 1885), 173.

machinery and financial assets that were becoming increasingly more relevant in the rapidly transforming economy; and a more effective system of expropriation of private property "for reasons of agrarian improvement or industrial development."[714] Cimbali also had a more ambitious and long-term goal: drafting a Codice Privato-Sociale (Private-Social Code) containing a fundamentally revised set of legal rules governing private law. This Codice Privato-Sociale would be capable of mediating between the conflicting interests and needs of individuals and society, and of redressing the power asymmetries between owners of the means of production and the working class.[715]

Cimbali's work remained virtually unknown in juristic circles in Europe, and it was a French jurist, Léon Duguit (1859–1928), who was ultimately credited with coining the term "social function." Now celebrated as a "prodigy" and a "profound innovator," Duguit was brushed off as a social scientist rather than a jurist by many of his contemporaries in Europe. However, due to his tireless academic traveling, he forged strong ties with other social jurists around the globe. The social function of property was the topic of one of six lectures that Duguit delivered in Buenos Aires in 1911. The gist of his theory, Duguit announced, was that property had transformed: once a right of the individual, property had become a function.

> As to property, in modern law, property is no longer the sacred and absolute right that the holder of wealth has over [an object]. Property is, and must be, the indispensable condition for the prosperity and greatness of societies, and collectivist doctrines are a return to barbarity. However, property is no longer a right; rather, it is a social function. The owner, that is the holder of wealth, for the very fact of holding wealth, has a social function to accomplish. To the extent that he pursues this mission his proprietary prerogatives are protected. If he does not accomplish this mission or he does so poorly, for example if he leaves his land idle or lets his house fall into disrepair, the government can legitimately force him to accomplish his social function as owner, which is to deploy the wealth he owns in accordance with its purpose.[716]

While this passage came to be seen as a far-reaching normative statement and inspired generations of reformers around the world, Duguit meant it

---

[714] Id., 186ff.
[715] Id., 357.
[716] Léon Duguit, *Les transformations générals du droit privé depuis le Code Napoléon* (Paris: Libraire Felix Alcan, 1912), 21–22.

as purely descriptive. The point, Duguit clarified, was not that property should become collective, nor that individual property should disappear; all Duguit intended to show was that, as a matter or law, owners were, increasingly more often, protected only to the extent that they played the function expected of them as holders of capital, that is, expanding the wealth of society as a whole. Duguit did not wish "to waste time" addressing the inequitable distribution of wealth, which he took as a "fact." And certainly, Duguit did not intend to incite class struggle:

> I am also not going to inquire whether, as some schools of thought believe, there is an irremediable opposition between those who own wealth and those who do not, between the proprietary class and the proletarian class and whether the latter needs to expropriate and annihilate the former. Yet, I cannot restrain myself from saying that, in my opinion, these schools of thought have a completely mistaken appreciation of things: the structure of modern societies is much more complex. In particular, in France, a large number of individuals are both owners and workers. It is a crime to preach class struggle and I believe that we are moving not towards the annihilation of one class by the other but towards a regime of coordination and hierarchization of the classes.[717]

Duguit's call for a body of property law that would allow for greater coordination between the needs of capital and labor echoed a larger theme that, as we have seen, had long been dominant in utopian socialist writings: the   need   for   a   new   science   of   social   and productive organization.

Duguit was no political radical and, in Europe, his influence remained largely methodological and limited to politically moderate circles. Jurists cited his social function theory as evidence of a new sociological appreciation of the role of property law in governing social interdependence and facilitating uses of property that benefit society. It was in the formerly colonial periphery of Europe that jurists articulated a more expansive idea of social function, one that went well beyond the idea of social cooperation. In Egypt, Abd-el Razzak-el Sanhuri, the mastermind of the Egyptian Civil Code of 1949, sought but ultimately failed to include the concept of social function in the new Code. In his extensive commentary to the Code, the al-Wasit fi Sharh al-Qanun al-Madani al-Jadid, Sanhuri took great pains to explain that while the concept of social function had not been explicitly mentioned in the new Code, it clearly informed many of its rules. Yet, the actual scope of Sanhuri's idea of social function was

---

[717] Id., 161.

ambiguous. Sanhuri oscillated between the more limited notion of social function as social cooperation that dominated juristic debates on the European continent and a more far-reaching concept that legitimized significant redistribution and the nationalization of resources. It is certainly the more limited notion of social function that Sanhuri had in mind when discussing the Code's rules imposing duties of cooperation among owners of the upper floors and owners of the lower floors in apartment buildings.

> Positive actions from the owner: Here, the social function of the right to property reaches its ultimate goals by obliging the owner to preform position actions in the interest of third parties. The following are some examples: 1. In the ownership of floors, the owner of the lower floor has the obligation to perform the works and arrangements necessary to prevent the collapse of upper floors.[718]

As one scholar of Sanhuri recently argued, Sanhuri viewed the apartment building as a metaphor for society. Just as the owners of the upper floors and of the lower floors need to cooperate to secure the stability of the building and prevent its collapse, social actors need to collaborate in order to avert the disintegration of the social edifice.[719] However, as Sanhuri's delved deeper into his theory, moving from positive law examples to the normative foundations of the social function of property, the scope of his theory expanded. Sanhuri placed front and center owners' debt to society, paving the way for more incisive redistributive reforms. As Sanhuri explained:

> There is no doubt that property is both an individual and social right at the same time. That it is an individual right has been explained earlier. That it is a social right can be founded on two things: (1) the principle of social solidarity: this principle mandates cooperation in society. Property is the main pillar of this cooperation. The owner should always consider himself, as it is, in fact, his situation, a member in a society that he takes from and gives back to. (2) Although an owner has acquired his property through his work, as stated before, he is still indebted to society for what he had earned. His work alone does not earn him the property. Society has contributed considerably to his efforts until he acquired all that he owns. Society's contribution in the efforts of the owner is on the same level of the contribution of a family if not more. If the contribution of the

---

[718] Abd al-Razzāq Ahmad al-Sanhūrī, *al Waṣīt fī sharih al qanun al madanī*, vol. 8 (Beirut: dār 'ihya' al turath, 1967), §343, 559.

[719] G. Bechor, *The Sanhuri Code and the Emergence of Modern Arab Civil Law (1932 to 1949)* (Leiden: Brill, 2007), 106.

family's members is the main justification for inheritance, there is no doubt that the contribution of society justifies that property should have a social function.[720]

Sanhuri's broader understanding of social function also underscored a robust idea of public interest that could justify the nationalization of critical resources. Sanhuri did not shy away from recognizing that:

> The contradiction between public interest and the right of the owner may reach a point in which the former would prevail . . .. Public interest may require the nationalization of property and the transfer of ownership to the state like in the case of banks, insurance companies and industrial firms. The right of property should not be a barrier in these cases.[721]

A similarly expansive idea of property's social function dominated juristic debates in Latin America. Duguit's lectures in Argentina inspired Latin American jurists to outline ambitious conceptions of the social function of property, directly aimed at transformative redistributive action. In Argentina, Chile, and Mexico, the publication of Duguit's lectures reinvigorated local ideas about the social dimension of property, prompting a spate of creativity on the part of jurists who saw themselves as fighting for land redistribution alongside peasants and social reformers. Nowhere was this cross-pollination more fertile than in Mexico, where the revolution of 1910, the agrarian movement's struggle against the landowning *hacendados*, the agrarian law of 1915, and the constitution of 1917 created the unique conditions for a group of Mexican jurists, who had established close relationships with members of the Italian *socialismo giuridico* movement, to expand the notion of social function and to put into practice the latter's call for a *Codice Privato-Sociale*.

Francisco Ruiz and the Socialization of Property Law in the Mexican Civil Code of 1928

In Mexico, after the success of the struggles for independence (1810–1821), the agrarian class structure that had solidified during the colonial period – in which owners of the *haciendas* and the Church, the

---

[720] Abd al-Razzāq Ahmad al-Sanhūrī, al Waṣīt, *al Waṣīt fī sharih al qanun al madanī*, § 338, 554.
[721] Id., §339, 555.

single largest landowner, exploited the labor of a vast class of landless *peones* subject to servile coercion – hardly changed. If anything, legislation adopted over the course of the nineteenth century further reinforced the existing inequities in the distribution of land. The Ley de Desamortización, or the Ley Lerdo, after Miguel Lerdo de Tejada, Ministro de Hacienda when the law was passed in 1856, and the Ley de Nacionalización de Bienes Eclesiásticos of 1859 facilitated the transfer of Church land into the hands of large private owners.[722] Similarly, the Ley sobre Ocupación y Enajenación de Terrenos Baldíos passed by Porfirio Diaz in 1894 resulted in the large-scale appropriation of the lands of the indigenous population and the *pueblos* by the landowning class.[723] Further, during the thirty years of Porfirio Diaz's dictatorship, as the regime's efforts resulted in greater involvement in the global market economy, owners of *haciendas* further increased the servile exactions on the peasantry in an attempt to maximize their profits. Historians estimate that, during the so-called *Porfiriato*, 97 percent of the agricultural land was owned by less than one thousand families and only 2 percent and 1 percent respectively were owned by small owners and the *pueblos*.[724] Of the fifteen million inhabitants Mexico counted in 1910, over three million were subject to both direct coercion and economic exploitation.

To redress the dispossession of peasant and indigenous lands, Emiliano Zapata and Otilio Montaño drafted the incendiary Plan de Ayala in 1911.[725] Drafted when Francisco Madero, the leader and president who had successfully ousted Porfirio Diaz, failed to take decisive action on the agrarian question, the plan escalated the efforts of the Zapatistas. The central demand of the plan was the expropriation, subject to prior payment of compensation, of one-third of the *latifundia* and the transfer of the expropriated land to the *pueblos* and citizens of Mexico

---

[722] The Ley de Desamortización de Bienes de la Iglesia y de Corporaciones. Lerdo de Tejada, 25 de junio de 1856 is available at https://archivos.juridicas.unam.mx/www/bjv/libros/12/5625/17.pdf; the Ley de Nacionalización de los Bienes Eclesiásticos, 12 de julio de 1859 is available at https://archivos.juridicas.unam.mx/www/bjv/libros/12/5625/23.pdf.

[723] The Ley sobre Ocupación y Enajenación de Terrenos Baldíos de los Estados Unidos Mexicanos, 26 de marzo de 1894 is available at https://archivos.juridicas.unam.mx/www/bjv/libros/2/940/39.pdf.

[724] J. M. Magallón Ibarra, *Instituciones de Derecho Civil*, 2nd ed., vol. 1 (Mexico: El Porrua, 1987), 82–83.

[725] The Plan de Ayala, 28 de noviembre de 1911 is available at www.ordenjuridico.gob.mx/Constitucion/CH8.pdf.

under different ownership forms, including *ejidos, colonias,* and *fundos.* But the call for land redistribution came loud and clear not only from radical agrarian leaders but also from moderates. Already a couple of years earlier, in 1906, the Partido Liberal Mexicano had published a Programa y Manifiesto that sought to revive the spirit of the much-decried Roman *lex agraria,* aiming to cap the amount of land private individuals could own.[726]

It was against this background that a small but ideologically diverse cohort of prominent Mexican jurists took up the task of reenvisioning the law of property. The first step was to retrieve and repurpose the Roman *lex agraria.* Throughout the nineteenth century, liberal jurists had characterized the *lex agraria* as the ultimate instance of state oppression and an illustration of the futility of redistributive efforts. Not since the Abbé de Mably's essay *De la Législation* (1776) had an open and clear call for a modern *lex agraria* been heard in liberal circles. The mastermind of the Mexican Ley Agraria of January 6, 1915, was Luis Cabrera Lobato (1876–1954), a jurist, poet, journalist, and politician who played a critical role in revolutionary and postrevolutionary political life. The son of a small *pueblerino* baker, Cabrera rose to the top ranks of the juristic profession, becoming director of the Escuela de Jurisprudencia in the newly established Universidad Nacional de México. Cabrera is often remembered as the spokesman of the brand of revolutionary constitutional ideology known as *carrancismo,* after Venustiano Carranza (1859–1920), the leader of the northern revolutionary Constitutionalist Army and later president of Mexico. Considered "too radical" for a cabinet post by the moderate President Francisco I. Madero, whose timid approach to the agrarian question eventually led to his downfall, Cabrera had nuanced views about property. He was deeply committed to freeing the peasant class from the oppression of the *hacendados* but also to defending the liberal concept of property and protecting the proprietary rights of small owners.[727]

On December 31, 1912, Cabrera presented to the Camera de Diputados his project of agrarian law in a speech entitled "La reconstitución de los ejidos de los pueblos como medio de suprimir la

---

[726] The Programa del Partido Liberal Mexicano y Manifiesto a la Nacion, 1 de julio de 1906 is available at www.ordenjuridico.gob.mx/Constitucion/CH6.pdf.

[727] On Cabrera, see "Introducción Biográfica," in L. Cabrera, *Obras Completas. Volume 1: Obra Jurídica* (Mexico: Ediciones Oasis, 1972), viii–xix; see also *Luis Cabrera: Bibiliografía (Aspectos de su Vida, Paginas Escogidas)* (Mexico: Cultura, 1951).

esclavitud de los jornalero mexicano."[728] In his remarks, Cabrera went right into explaining the core causes of the agrarian question, the related phenomena of *peonismo* and *hacendismo*. The former is the "de-facto slavery, or feudal servitude" in which the day laborer (*el peón jornaliero*) finds himself, especially in the southeast of the country, which results from the economic, political, and legal privileges enjoyed by the land-owning class.[729] The latter, Cabrera explained, is the economic suppression and unfair competition that characterize the interactions between large landowners and small landowners in the shadow of the fiscal inequities and the many privileges from which the former benefit and that lead to absorption of small properties by large ones.[730] The objective of the proposal, Cabrera concluded, is to eradicate peonage and to combat *hacendismo*. While Cabrera's goals resonated with the root-and-branch ideas of the Plan de Ayala, the means he proposed were fully consistent with the ideas of the "constitutionalists," whose base consisted of liberal intellectuals and the middle class. Cabrera was adamant that the *ley agraria* was to be passed by the democratically elected legislature, "through constitutional means" and in full respect of private property.[731] By no means an enemy of private property, Cabrera was also under no illusion that one piece of legislation could solve the agrarian question. There are multiple agrarian questions and there need to be multiple agrarian laws, Cabrera warned his fellow *diputados*.[732]

Cabrera's proposal tackled one aspect of the agrarian question. Before taking steps to create and protect a class of small owners, Cabrera explained, a much greater problem needed to be solved: freeing the *pueblos* from the economic and political pressure that the *haciendas* exerted over them. Certainly, Cabrera's solution contradicted the orthodoxy of the modern liberal discourse of property. Every single element of his proposal belied the conventional wisdom of liberal jurists. Cabrera sought to empower communities first before empowering individuals, to do so by reconstituting the *ejidos*, a form of common ownership that had flourished during the colonial period and that closely resembled the much-derided medieval commons of Europe; to make the *ejidos*

---

[728] L. Cabrera, "La reconstitución de los ejidos de los pueblos como medio de suprimir la esclavitud de los jornalero mexicano," in *Obras Completas*, 137.
[729] Id., 139.
[730] Id.
[731] Id., 158.
[732] Id., 143.

inalienable in order to protect the long-term security of the *pueblos*; and to obtain the land needed through expropriation, rather than through the more palatable, but largely ineffective, action of *reivendicacion*. That groups were to be prioritized was Cabrera's firm conviction, repeated numerous times in the speech:

> Slowly, the other agrarian problem, the real one, became clear, which consists in the need to give land to the hundreds of thousands who do not have any. It is necessary to give land not to the individuals but to social groups.[733]

In explaining why reconstituting the *ejidos* and making them inalienable would be the most effective way to empower the *pueblos*, Cabrera painted a picture of the colonial era that bore little resemblance to the conventional accounts of the retrograde and feudal past of *Nueva España*, one in which the relationship between the local rural populations and the *haciendas* was not obviously tilted in favor of the latter.

> In the economic agrarian struggle of the colonial period between the *pueblos* and the *haciendas*, the *pueblos* had chances of prevailing because of their privileges, of their organization, and the effective cooperation that, over the centuries, the indigenous populations and the inhabitants of the *pueblos* had developed, and most importantly because of the enormous power that the possession of the *proprios* [i.e., communally owned parcels to be assigned to individual members of the *pueblos* for cultivation] as a source of wealth, and the *ejidos* as a means of security, gave to the *pueblos*.[734]

One would imagine that a jurist like Cabrera, considered too radical for a cabinet post by Francisco I. Madero's advisors, and with the guts to push forward a *ley agraria* that flew in the face of the prescriptions of his liberal colleagues, would also welcome *la socialización* of property law. And yet, a little over a decade later, as the debate over the new Código Civil of 1928 was raging, Cabrera vocally defended modern, liberal *dominium*. The draft code reflected the new idea of a "private-social code" advanced in the pages of Enrico Cimbali's essay, endorsed the social function theory, and adopted the doctrine of abuse of rights. As a member of the committee on legislative reform of the Barra Mexicana (the Mexican Bar Association), Cabrera encouraged the bar to repudiate the social conception of property embraced by the drafters and to

---

[733] Id., 143.
[734] Id., 145.

advocate for retaining *el sistema clasico de la propiedad.*[735] Cabrera's concise paragraph did little to illuminate the reasons for his stance. He expressed concern about imposing "vague" obligations on owners and invited the Barra Mexicana to reject the articles of the draft code that established positive duties, but he added that he saw no need for the committee to address the larger social and economic reasons why the social conception of property was misguided.[736]

While Cabrera was skeptical about the social function theory, the four members of the drafting commission, in spite of their ideological differences, resolutely stated their determination to depart from the "individualist tendency" that informed Roman property law and to adopt the "progressive" idea of property. The *Exposición de Motivos* that accompanied the code, penned by Francisco H. Ruiz (1872–1958), was an ambitious document that openly endorsed the ideas of the "legal socialism" movement. Ruiz was not a socialist and his moderate positions were considered "a fair compromise" between the views of two other members of the drafting commission, the radical Ignacio García Téllez and the conservative Rafael García Peña. Yet Ruiz had come to embrace the "socialization" of private law probably after reading the work of the Italian *émigré* Francesco Cosentini (1870–1944), whom he cited in the "Exposición." Cosentini was a member of the *socialismo giuridico* movement who traveled extensively, from Belgium, to Cuba, to Mexico, gaining scholarly prominence outside of his native Italy.[737] He was an eclectic scholar who restlessly sought to advance his own, more expansive, and substantive variant of the socialist agenda in widely different fields of law, from private law to international law. For Cosentini, *socialismo jurídico* meant more than the mere focus on social interdependence and the need for a greater interplay between the "social" and the "individual" element in private law, opinions which, by the beginning of the twentieth century, were relatively widely held in juristic circles. Remedying distributive inequities was the linchpin of Cosentini's agenda as scholar and as activist. In his proposal for a Código Civil Pan-Americano, he argued in favor of an *estado social democrático*, tasked with promoting substantive equality:

---

[735] L. Cabrera, "Los bienes y la propiedad conforme al nuevo Código Civil," in *Obras Completas*, 267.

[736] Id.

[737] J. R. Narváez Hernández, "El Código Privado-Social. Influencia de Francesco Cosentini en el Código Civil mexicano de 1928" (2004) 16 *Anuario Mexicano de Historia del Derecho* 201–226.

No other branch of human activity is positioned to pursue the principle of equality, the foundation of democracy, better than law. However it is necessary to specify that this equality here is formal equality (all are equal before the laws; the laws are the same for all, as is written in the temple of Themis) not real equality, because the same inequities persist due to natural differences, such as the difference in intellectual capacity, as well as in differences that are much more artificial . . .. The solution is the diffusion of education and the equitable distribution of wealth.[738]

A visiting professor at the Universidad Nacional Autónoma de México in the years in which the drafting commission for the new Código Civil was at work, Cosentini not only made it onto the reading list of Francisco Ruiz but also became close to the most progressive member of the commission, Ignacio García Téllez. The intellectual exchanges between these three jurists left an obvious imprint on the Código Civil. The understanding of property that emerged from these conversations went well beyond the social function theory articulated by Gierke or Duguit and also surpassed the notion of multiple, resource-specific properties, outlined by Josserand and Pugliatti; it was boldly and explicitly focused on wealth redistribution. As the *Exposición de Motivos* made clear:

> The necessity to distribute wealth, to protect the weak and the ones who lack knowledge against the powerful and the knowledgeable, the unrestrained competition generated by the introduction of machines and the phenomenal development of large-scale industry, which profoundly affects the working class, has made it imperative that the state regulate social and economic relations, relegating to a secondary role the principle that the will of the parties is the supreme law of contracts.[739]

Francisco Ruiz, the moderate voice on the drafting commission, did not fully embrace the new idea of property as a "function" *en vogue* in progressive circles and continued to conceptualize property as a right. Yet, the right to property outlined in Ruiz's pages bore little resemblance to *dominium*, which Cabrera had dubbed "el sistema clasico de la propiedad." For Ruiz, property was a "rational and necessary means" to satisfy the fundamental needs of all members of society and to facilitate their "full and harmonious" development.[740] The challenge for property

---

[738] F. Cosentini, *Código Civil Pan-Americano* (Havana: Vox Populorum, 1929), 17.
[739] *Exposición de Motivos del Código Civil para el Distrito y Territorios Federales de 1928*, 2nd ed. (Mexico: Edición Fundo de Cultura Económica, 1929), 3.
[740] F. Ruiz, "La socializacion del derecho privado y el Código Civil de 1928" (1946) 8(31) *Revista de la secuela nacional de jurisprudencia* 79

reformers, Ruiz suggested, was to transform property from a tool of oppression into a mechanism for human emancipation and dignity for all. As Ruiz wrote:

> The problem is to devise a property regime that secures to all men an entitlement to enjoy the resources offered by nature; [a property regime] that would not prevent resources from being distributed so that all men have, at a minimum, the ability to satisfy their fundamental needs.[741]

The notion of dignity and humanity that, for Ruiz, was the linchpin of a just property system was capacious and not exclusively linked to labor. By "all men," Ruiz meant not only productive members of society but also those unable to contribute their fair share through no fault of their own. While vulnerability had hardly entered the discourse of modern liberal property, it was a recurrent theme in Ruiz's writings.

> That labor is the only source, the only reason that justifies property is to be accepted with some reservations. There are individuals who have not realized any productive labor and yet, for the sole reason that they need to live, have a right to the means that allow them to satisfy their necessities, which is a duty. Children, the elderly, the disabled even though they are not producers – they cannot work – have a right to receive what is necessary for life, and not as a matter of charity or liberality but as an actual right that has as its sole foundation the necessity to live, which is a duty.[742]

The urgency that pervaded Ruiz's agenda for the socialization of property law, the weight that he placed on equity in the distribution of lands, and the recurrent appeal to dignity and emancipation for the most vulnerable were a legacy of the revolutionary decade of 1910–1920. The revolutionary leaders of 1910–1920 believed that there would be no lasting peace until the agrarian question was solved and, hence, they embarked on the task of undoing a past of peasant oppression and indigenous dispossession. As one scholar has put it, "after a century of experimentation with borrowed political and philosophical theories which did not fit [Mexico's] particular problem and therefore offered golden opportunities to demagogues, landgrabbers and exploiters,"[743] the

---

[741] Id., 80.
[742] Id., 81.
[743] H. Phipps, "The Agrarian Phase of the Mexican Revolution of 1910–1920" (March 1924) 39(1) *Political Science Quarterly* 1–18.

revolutionary leaders forged their own expansive property vocabulary and a new legal regime for landownership. The *Ley* of January 6, 1915, and the 1917 Constitution outlined and enshrined a far-reaching interpretation of the social function of property that provided for the restitution of indigenous lands; restored and expanded the *ejidos*; recognized the legal capacity of *muncipalidades* and *pueblos* to own real property; redistributed, through the use of eminent domain, the largest landed estates and *haciendas*; maintained public property by revoking concessions for the sale of public lands; and prohibited the Church from owning land and administering loans connected to real estate. These legal measures sought to transform the understanding and the discourse of modern property, and their echoes can be heard even in the writings of moderate jurists like Francisco Ruiz.

Conclusions

As the advancement of agrarian and industrial capitalism on the European continent deepened social and economic inequities, bringing exploitation and suffering for many and immense wealth for relatively few, reformist jurists sought to repurpose Roman doctrines in order to introduce social duties and purposes into the law of property. This reformist effort initially provoked alarm and vocal opposition in liberal juristic circles. Yet, rarely did courts or legislators apply or enact these doctrines in their broadest and potentially most effective formulations. The discourse of social property hardly went beyond vague acknowledgments that owners and nonowners are interdependent and that owners owe basic duties to each other and to the community. In fact, social doctrines did more to entrench modern *dominium* than to displace it or effectively correct it. The fictional legal concept of absolute *dominium*, reinvented by liberal jurists in the earlier part of the nineteenth century, conferred legitimacy to capitalist relations of production but as a legal framework proved inadequate to ensure the long-term stability of capitalism. The law of *dominium* lacked the flexibility needed for an increasingly diversified economy, the tools to effectively address social interdependence and negative externalities, and a menu of lesser property forms that would assist owners' efforts to generate new assets and forms of value. Further, the hyper-individualistic ideology that informed the law of modern *dominium* and the complete obliviousness to the fundamental needs of agrarian and industrial direct producers intensified class antagonism and thereby threatened social stability. Social property doctrines repurposed from Roman law addressed these obvious flaws. The multiplication of property frameworks via the Roman law of things, the doctrine of abuse of rights, and the theory that property has a social function made Romanist-bourgeois property a legal framework better able to facilitate the expansion of capitalist economies and to secure their long-term operation.

~

Conclusions

The Romanist-bourgeois property tradition that eased the advance of liberal capitalism in nineteenth-century Europe remained dominant throughout the twentieth century, despite its obvious shortcomings. Surprisingly, its influence seems only to be growing, even among the most sophisticated property theorists in the United States. Several of the centerpieces of Romanist-bourgeois property have made a spectacular comeback. Henry Smith and Thomas Merrill have repurposed the Roman conceptual architecture of property centered on *dominium* and the right to exclude. While the right to exclude by no means captures every relevant attribute of the institution of property, giving individuals the right to exclude others from particular resources is a cost-effective way of organizing the management and control of resources in society and one that also promotes a variety of other ends, including, willingness to share resources.[744] Novel theories of abuse of rights continue to resurface and to spark controversy. Larissa Katz has recently proposed a principle of abuse of rights focused on owners' reasons for action.[745] Because owners' power to make authoritative decisions about the use of resources inevitably threatens the autonomy interests of others, the exercise of this authority over others is legitimate only if owners have can present a worthwhile agenda for the resource. Critics have noted the limited use of this account of abuse of property rights that merely scrutinizes the owners' reasons and have proposed a more capacious, anti-domination principle of abuse of rights.[746] The social function of

---

[744] Thomas W. Merrill, "Property and the Right to Exclude II" (2014) 3 *Brigham-Kanner Property Rights Conference Journal* 1.

[745] Larissa Katz, "Spite and Extortion: A Jurisdictional Principle of Abuse of Property Right" (2013) 122 *Yale Law Journal* 100.

[746] Mitchell N. Berman, "Abuse of Rights without Political Foundations: A Response to Katz" (2014) 124 *Yale Law Journal Forum* 44.

property has also experienced a similar revival with Gregory Alexander, who, in a foundational essay, courageously implied a broad social obligation norm in US property law, one that is not limited to curbing owners' powers but goes as far as foregrounding the place of nonowners and requiring redistributive intervention.[747] Alexander's piece proved highly influential, sparking a rich conversation about the merits and limits of the social function of property in property circles in the United States.

These recent efforts at reviving the most well-known principles of the Romanist-bourgeois property tradition have certainly pushed the boundaries of property theory. Yet, historically, the legacy of these concepts appears to have been pernicious or, at best, shallow and ineffectual. As we have seen, *dominium* lent legitimacy to all forms of economic and racial domination and foregrounded a thin idea of individual autonomy, one that discounts the reality of dependency and entrenched societal hierarchies, as the lodestar of modern and contemporary property law. Furthermore, one wonders whether even recent, sophisticated, relational notions of autonomy and self-authorship should indeed be the *primary* forms of today's property law.[748] A growing chorus of economists and sociologists, activists, and policymakers compellingly argue that, in light of steadily rising economic inequality and formidable threats to the environment, it is imperative that our property system prioritize the collective over the individual. Further, while informed by sound sociological methodology and by important efficiency and equity goals, the doctrines of abuse of rights and the social function of property have proved largely inconsequential. The historically prevailing subjective formulations of abuse of rights hardly went beyond a recognition of the obvious fact of social interdependence. No less dubious is the bequest of the social function of property. As Duguit himself admitted, the aim of the social function of property was not "to waste time" addressing the inequitable distribution of wealth, which he took as a given, but rather to limit the protection of property, protecting owners only to the extent that they play the function expected of them as holders of capital.[749]

---

[747] Gregory S. Alexander, "The Social Obligation Norm in American Property Law" (2009) 94 *Cornell Law Review* 745.

[748] Rashmi Dyal-Chand, "Property, Collectivity and Restraint," blog post on Law & Political Economy, January 28, 2021, available at https://lpeproject.org/blog/property-collectivity-and-restraint/.

[749] Léon Duguit, *Les transformations générals du droit privé depuis le Code Napoléon* (Paris: Libraire Felix Alcan, 1912), 21–22.

And one should not forget that in Nazi Germany and Fascist Italy, the concept that property has a social function lent legitimacy to an authoritarian and murderous social order and to the regime's economic agenda.

Does this unimpressive legacy condemn the Romanist-bourgeois property tradition to the dustbin of history? Is there anything in this property tradition that is still of any use? Are there intuitions that elucidate and advance our understanding of what is property and how it works? And, most importantly, is there any tool in this tradition that holds promise for a transformative property agenda, in line with the values of democratic equality and sustainability? In this book, I argued that the crucial legacy of the Romanist-bourgeois property tradition is to be found not in its most well-know concepts but rather in two neglected concepts: the much decried, "feudal" concept of divided *dominium* and the Roman concept of property as a "law of things." In combination, these twin ideas provide explanatory and critical insights that are key premises of an agenda of democratic-egalitarian transformation. Divided *dominium* and the "law of things" make plain that property is, always and only, a social relation pertaining to how two or more persons are related with respect to a resource and structured around competing pairs of entitlements.[750]

Divided *dominium*, the rich inventory of real-life forms of ownership in which entitlements over land were split between two individuals with correlative rights and duties, placed in plain sight the intrinsically relational nature of property. The relation between owners with rights and nonowners with duties is *prior to*, that is, *constitutive*, of property. As Talha Syed put it "one simply cannot even have the concept 'right' without already having the concept 'duty,'" just as "for instance, one simply cannot even have the concept "teacher" without also already having the concept 'student.'" In other words, it is the relation that constitutes the "pair" of component parts and the parts do not exist outside of the relation.[751] Paradoxically, divided *dominium* makes plain an uncomfortable truth. The intellectual energy spent in the

---

[750] Anna di Robilant and Talha Syed, "Property's Building Blocks: Hohfeld in Europe and Beyond," in Wesley Hohfeld, *A Century Later. Edited Works, Select Personal Papers and Original Commentaries* (Shyamkrishna Balganesh, Ted M. Sichelman, and Henry E. Smith, eds.) (Cambridge: Cambridge University Press, 2022), 223–256.

[751] Id., 227.

century-long controversy between the liberal proponents of "absolute *dominium*" and the social jurists who called for relative and qualified property entitlements was, in a sense, wasted. Because property is inescapably a social relation, "absolute" *dominium* is impossible, not merely undesirable, and the claim that entitlements ought to be "relative" is nothing more than the explicit recognition of something that was always obvious.[752]

The Romanist-bourgeois "law of things" highlights the contextual and resource-specific nature of property. The anchoring of property in resources may well be the single most enduring theme in the history of European practices and theory around property law and one that was marginal to the Hohfeldian/Realist critical analysis of property and was intentionally dropped in recent accounts that seek to disintegrate property, making it virtually indistinguishable from human rights, or personal rights, or rights to life and liberty.[753] The Roman jurists were the first to see what is today obvious to an important strand of progressive property theory. Property is neither a formalistic architecture built around a single core value nor a fragmented set of discontinuous usages, such that lawyers could easily manipulate the legal structures of contemporary capitalist economies "without using the term property at all." Property is distinctively significant because it is how we structure social relations with respect to specific resources, to form persons and satisfy interests through the allocation, production, and distribution of goods. The "law of things" grounds property questions in the context of specific resources and requires us to engage in a purposive analysis of what matters, requiring external frames of positive (e.g., economic) and normative (e.g., political philosophical) analysis.

This unique legacy of the Romanist-bourgeois property tradition aids our explanatory understanding of the social structure of late capitalist relations and allows us to critically delimit the conceptual structure and political valence of neoliberal discourse.[754] But these are only preliminary steps for democratic-egalitarian transformation. The next, key, step is to articulate an actual program of institutional transformation. As Jed Purdy and David Grewal put it in a recent blog post, we need "to embed"

---

[752] Id., at 228.
[753] Thomas C. Grey, "The Disintegration of Property" (1980) 22 *Nomos* 69–85.
[754] Talha Syed, "Legal Realism and CLS from an LPE Perspective," unpublished manuscript, on file with author (2022).

a market in a web of legally specified relationships, expectations, and values that define and discipline the power exercised within property relations and link that power to a vision of a tolerably legitimate social order."[755] The Romanist-bourgeois tradition has little to offer in this crucial programmatic step.

---

[755] David Singh Grewal and Jedediah Britton-Purdy, "Liberalism, Property and the Means of Production," blog post on Law & Political Economy Project, January 25, 2021, available at https://lpeproject.org/blog/liberalism-property-and-the-means-of-production/.

REFERENCES

Abel, Wilhelm, *Geschichte der deutschen Landwirtschaft vom frühen Mittelalter bis zum 19. Jahrhundert* (Stuttgart: Verlag Eugen Ulmer, 1962).

Agamben, Giorgio, "Introduction," in Michele Spano (ed.). *Il valore delle cose* (Macerata: Quodlibet, 2015).

Akkermans, Bram, "The Numerus Clausus of Property Rights," in Michele Graziadei and Lionel Smith (eds.), *Comparative Property Law: Global Perspectives* (Cheltenham: Edward Elgar, 2017), 8-12.

Albano, Manuel Carrasco, *Comentarios sobre la Constitucion Politica de 1833*, 2nd ed. (Santiago: Imprenta de la Libraria del Mercurio, 1874).

Alexander, Gregory S., "Pluralism and Property" (2011) 80 *Fordham Law Review* 1017-1052.

Property and Human Flourishing (Oxford: Oxford University Press, 2018).

"The Social Obligation Norm in American Property Law" (2009) 94(4) *Cornell Law Review* 745-819.

Alibrandi, Ilario, *Teoria del Possesso Secondo il Diritto Romano* (Rome: G. Aurelj, 1871).

Amunátegui, Miguel Luis, *Introducción: Proyecto Inedito del Código Civil, Opuscolos Científicos, in Obras Completas de Don Andrés Bello*, vol. 13 (Santiago: Imprenta Ramirez, 1890).

Anderson, Perry, *Lineages of the Absolutist State* (London: Verso, 1979).

Passages from Antiquity to Feudalism (London: Verso, 1974).

Ando, Clifford, *Imperial Ideology and Provincial Loyalty in the Roman Empire* (Berkeley: University California Press, 2000).

Anguita, Leopoldo Urrutia, "Vulgarización sobre la posesión ante el Código Civil chileno" (1934) 31(1-2) *Revista de derecho y jurisprudencia* 5-13.

Anon. (A Barrister of the Inner Temple), *The Code Napoleon; or, the French Civil Code* (London: William Benning, 1827).

Appiani, *Bellorum civilium*, Emilio Gabba (ed.) (Firenze: La "Nuova Italia" Editrice 1958).

Arcieri, Gaetano, *Trattato dell'enfiteusi* (Naples: Morelli, 1864).

Arias, Gino, "La Proprietà Privata nel Diritto Fascista" (1935) 6(5) *Lo Stato: Lo Stato Rivista di Scienze Politiche e Giuridiche* 332-335.

Arnaud, André-Jean, *Les Juristes Face à la société du XIXe siècle à nos jours* (Paris: Presses Universitaires de France, 1975).

Les Origines Doctrinales du Code Civil Français (Paris: Librairie Générale de Droit et Jurisprudence, 1969).

Arndts, Karl Ludwig, *Lehrbuch der Pandekten*, vol. 1 (Munich: Cotta'sche Buchhandlung, 1865).

Lehrbuch der Pandekten, vol. 4 (Munich: J. G. Cotta'sche Buchhandlung, 1861).

Arndts, Lodovico, *Trattato delle Pandette*, Filippo Serafini (trans.) (Bologna: Tipi Fava & Gragnani, 1872).

Atkins, Jed W., *Roman Political Thought* (Cambridge: Cambridge University Press, 2018).

Atria, Fernando, "Derechos Reales" (2005) 2 *Revista de Derecho de la Universidad Adolfo Ibañez* 29–105.

"El sistema de acciones reales, parte especial: la acción de precario" (2017) 30 *Revista derecho Valdivia* 57– 86.

Audren, Frédéric, and Fillon, Catherine, "Louis Josserand ou la construction d'une autorité doctrinale" (2009) 1 *Revue trimestrielle de droit civil* 39–76.

Audren, Frédéric, and Halpérin, Jean Louis, *La Culture Juridique Française: Entre Mythes et Realités, XIX–XX Siècles* (Paris: CNRS Éditions, 2013).

Backhaus, Jürgen Georg, *Physiocracy, Antiphysiocracy and Pfeiffer* (New York: Springer-Verlag, 2011).

Badian, Ernst, "Tiberius Gracchus and the Beginning of the Roman Revolution" (1972) 1 *Aufstieg und Niedergang der römischen Welt* 668–731.

Baillon-Passe, Christian, "Réponse à Jean-Pascal Chazal: mission accomplie, on va relire Josserand" (2003) 32 *Dalloz* 2190–2191.

Barnave, Joseph, *Oeuvres Posthumes. Introduction à la Révolution Française* (Paris: Bérenger, 1842).

Barros, Lauro, *Ensayo sobre la condición de las clases rurales en Chile. Memoria presentada al Concurso de la Exposición Internacional de 1875* (Santiago: Imprenta Agricola de Enrique Ahrens, 1875).

Barthélemy, Dominique, "The Feudal Revolution: I" (1996) 152 *Past & Present* 196–205.

Bayly, Christopher A., *The Birth of the Modern World 1780–1914* (Malden, MA: Blackwell, 2004).

Bechor, Guy, *The Sanhuri Code and the Emergence of Modern Arab Civil Law (1932 to 1949)* (Leiden: Brill, 2008).

Bechtel, Heinrich, *Wirtschaftsgeschichte Deutschlands* (München: Callwey, 1956).

Belime, William, *Traité du droit de possession et des actions possessoires* (Paris: Joubert, 1842).

Bell, Abraham, and Parchomovsky, Gideon, "Reconfiguring Property in Three Dimensions" (2008) 75 *University of Chicago Law Review* 1015–1070.

Bell, Sinclair W., and Plessis, Paul Du (eds.), *Roman Law before the Twelve Tables: An Interdisciplinary Approach* (Edinburgh: Edinburgh University Press, 2020).

Belleau, Marie Claire, "Les Juristes Inquiets" (1999) 40 *Les Cahiers de Droit* 507–544.

Bello, Don Andrés, "La Agricultura de la Zona Tórrida (1826), Poesias," in *Obras Completas de Don Andrés Bello*, vol. 3 (Santiago: Imprenta Ramirez, 1883).

"Latín y Derecho Romano, Opuscolos Literarios," in *Obras Completas de Don Andrés Bello*, vol. 8 (Santiago: Imprenta Ramirez, 1885).

"Proemio del Derecho Romano, Opuscolos Jurídicos," in *Obras Completas de Don Andrés Bello*, vol. 9 (Santiago: Imprenta Ramirez, 1885).

"Proyecto de Código Civil," in *Obras Completas de Don Andrés Bello*, vol. 12 (Santiago: Imprenta Ramirez, 1887).

"Temas de Historia y Geografia," in *Obras Completas de Andrés Bello*, vol. 23 (Caracas: Fundación La Casa de Bello, 1981).

Belviso, Jacobus de, *Apparatus in Usus & Consuetudines Feudorum* (Heidelberg: Hans Kohl, 1559).

Berman, Marshall, *All That Is Solid Melts into Air: The Experience of Modernity* (New York: Penguin, 1982).

Beseler, Georg, *System Des Gemeinen Deutschen Privatrechts*, 4th ed. (Berlin: Weidmann, 1885).

Volksrecht und Juristenrecht (Leipzig: Weidmann, 1843).

Besnier, Bernard, "La conception stoïcienne de la matière" 2003 (1) *Revue de métaphysique et de morale* 51–64.

Bilbao, Fransico, "Revolución," in *Obras Completas de Francisco Bilbao*, vol. 1 (Buenos Aires: Imprenta de Buenos Aires, 1865), 7–42.

"Sociabilidad Chilena," in *Obras Completas*, 3–16.

Birks, Peter, and Nicholas, Barry (eds.), *New Perspectives in the Roman Law of Property: Essays for Barry Nicholas* (Oxford: Oxford University Press, 1989).

Bisson, Thomas N., "The Feudal Revolution" (1994) 142 *Past & Present* 6–42.

Blaufarb, Rafe, *The Great Demarcation: The French Revolution and the Invention of Modern Property* (Oxford: Oxford University Press, 2016).

Bleicken, Jochen "'In provinciali solo dominium populi Romani est vel Caesaris.' Zur Kolonisationspolitik der ausgehenden Republik und frühen Kaiserzeit" (1974) 4 *Chiron* 359–414.

Böcking, Eduard, *Institutionen*, vol. 2 (Bonn: Adolf Marcus/Georgi, 1843).

Bois, Guy, *La Mutation de l'An Mil: Lournand, Village Mâconnais de l'Antiquité au Féodalisme* (Paris: Fayard, 1994).

Bonfante, Pietro, *Corso di Diritto Romano: La Proprietà*, vol. 2 (Milan: Giuffrè, 1968) [reprint].

Corso di diritto romano: Diritti Reali, vol. 3 (Milan: Giuffrè, 1972) [reprint].

Istituzioni di diritto romano, 10th ed. (Turin: Giappichelli, 1946).

"La Catalogne du Milieu du Xe à la fin du XIe Siècle: Croissance et Mutations d'une Société" (1982) 98 *Cahier de Civilisation Médiévale* 143–147.

Scritti giuridici varii: Proprietà e servitù, vol. 2 (Turin: UTET, 1918).

Bonnecase, Julien, *L'École de l'Exégèse en Droit Civil: Les Traits Distinctifs de sa Doctrine et de ses Méthodes d'Après la Profession de Foi de ses Plus Illustres Représentants* (Paris: E. de Boccard, 1924).

Science du droit et romantisme: le conflit des conceptions juridiques en France de 1880 à l'heure actuelle (Paris: Librairie du Recueil Sirey, 1928)

Bourde, Andre J., *Agronomie et Agronomes en France au XVIIIe Siècle* (Paris: SEVPEN, 1967).

The Influence of England on the French Agronomists, 1750–1789 (Cambridge: Cambridge University Press, 1953).

Bourdieu, Pierre, *Homo Academicus*, Peter Collier (trans.) (Standford: Stanford University Press, 1988).

Bourgeois, Leon, *Solidarité* (Paris: Armand Colin, 1896).

Bowen, Edwin W., "The Relief Problem of Ancient Rome" (1942) 37 *The Classical Journal* 407–420.

Bowman, Alan, and Wilson, Andrew (eds.), *Quantifying the Roman Economy* (Oxford: Oxford University Press, 2009).

Brenner, Robert, "Agrarian Class Structure and Economic Development in Pre-Industrial Europe" (1976) 70(1) *Past & Present* 30.

"The Agrarian Roots of European Capitalism" (1982) 97(1) *Past & Present* 16.

"The Agrarian Roots of European Capitalism," in Trevor H. Aston and C. H. E. Philpin (eds.), *The Brenner Debate: Agrarian Class Structure and Economic Development in Pre-Industrial Europe* (Cambridge: Cambridge University Press, 1985), 10–63.

"Bourgeois Revolution and Transition to Capitalism," in A. L. Beier et al. (eds.), *The First Modern Society: Essays in English History in Honour of Lawrence Stone* (Cambridge: Cambridge University Press, 1989), 271–304.

Brett, Annabel, "Individual and Community in the 'Second Scholastic': Subjective Rights in Domingo de Soto and Francisco Suárez," in Constance Blackwell and Sachiko Kusukawa (eds.), *Philosophy in the Sixteenth and Seventeenth Centuries: Conversations with Aristotle* (London: Routledge, 1999), 146–168.

Brissot, Jacques-Pierre, *Un indépendant à l'ordre des Avocats: sur la décadence du barreau en France* (Berlin: 1781).

Bruns, Carl Georg, *Das Recht des Besitzes im Mittelalter und in der Gegenwart*, vol. 1 (Tübingen: H. Laupp'schen Buchhandlung, 1848).

Brutti, Massimo, *Vittorio Scialoja, Emilio Betti: Due Visioni del Diritto Civile* (Turin: Giappichelli, 2013).

Buckland, William W., and McNair, Arnold D., *Roman Law and Common Law: A Comparison in Outline*, 2nd ed. (Cambridge: Cambridge University Press, 1965).

Burdese, Alberto, *Studi sull'ager publicus* (Turin: Giappichelli, 1952).

Burns, Robert P., "Blackstone's Theory of the 'Absolute' Rights of Property" (1985) 54 *University of Cincinnati Law Review* 67–86.

Butler, Eliza Mariab, *The Tyranny of Greece over Germany: A Study of the Influence Exercised by Greek Art and Poetry over the Great Writers of the Eighteenth, Nineteenth and Twentieth Centuries* (Cambridge: Cambridge University Press, 1935).

Byers, Michael, "Abuse of Rights: An Old Principle, A New Age" (2002) 47 *McGill Law Journal* 389–434.

Cabanis, André, "Le Courant Néo-Monarchiste sous le Consulat" in J. Tulard (ed.), in *La Contre-Révolution. Origines, histoire, postérité* (Paris: Perrin, 1990), 313–324.

Cabrera, Luis, *Luis Cabrera: Bibiliografía: Aspectos de su Vida, Paginas Escogidas*, Mercedes Cabrera (ed.) (Mexico: Cultura, 1951).

"La reconstitución de los ejidos de los pueblos como medio de suprimir la esclavitud de los jornalero mexicano," in *Obras Completas*, vol. 1 (Mexico: Ediciones Oasis, 1972).

"Los Bienes y la Propiedad Conforme al Nuevo Codido Civil," in *Obras Completas*, vol. 1 (Mexico: Ediciones Oasis 1972), 258–321.

Cahan, Jean Axelrad, "The Concept of Property in Marx's Theory of History: A Defense of the Autonomy of the Socio-economic Base" (1994) 58(4) *Science & Society* 392–414.

Caldera, Hugo D., "La Garantía Constitucional del Derecho de Propiedad y la Expropiación" (1979) 6(1/4) *Revista Chilena De Derecho* 312–335.

Camara de Diputados, "Sesión 43 Ordinaria, 9/1/1864," in Sesiones de Congreso Nacional 1864 [Chile].

Capdequi, José Maria Ots, *España en América*, 2nd ed. (Bogota: Universidad Nacional de Colombia, 1952).

Capogrossi Colognesi, Luigi, "Alcuni problemi di storia romana arcaica: 'ager publicus,' 'gentes' e client," (1980) 22 *Bullettino dell'Istituto di Diritto Romano "Vittorio Scialoja"* 29–65.

"Ager publicus e ager privatus dall'età arcaica al compromesso patrizio-plebeo," in Jaime Roset (ed.), *Estudios en homenaje al Profesor Juan Iglesias*, vol. 2 (Madrid: Universidad Complutense de Madrid, 1988), 639–650.

Law and Power in the Making of the Roman Commonwealth, Laura Copp (trans.) (Cambridge: Cambridge University Press, 2014).

"Proprietà," *Enciclopedia del diritto 160–225*, vol. 37 (Milan: Giuffrè, 1988).

Carbonnier, Jean, *Flexible droit: Pour une sociologie du droit sans rigueur*, 10th ed. (Paris: LGDJ, 2001).

Carcaterra, Antonio, *Le definizioni dei giuristi romani: metodo, mezzi e fini* (Naples: Jovene, 1966).

[Bruno Schmidlin], "Horoi, pithana und regulae – Zum Einfluß der Rhetorik und Dialektik auf die juristische Regelbildung," in Hildegard Temporini (ed.), *Aufstieg und Niedergang der römischen Welt*, vol. 15 Recht (Methoden; Schulen: Einzelne Juristen, 1976), 101–130.

Carcopino, Jérôme, *Autour des Gracques: Etudes Critiques* (Paris: Les Belles Lettres, 1967).

Cazzetta, Giovanni "Abuso del diritto e forma di unità del guiridico" (2017) 58 *Rivista di Diritto Civile* 559–581.

Centeno, Miguel A., and Agustin E. Ferraro, "Republics of the Possible: State Building in Latin America and Spain," in Miguel A. Centeno and Agustin E. Ferraro (eds.), *State and Nation Making in Latin America and Spain: Republics of the Possible* (Cambridge: Cambridge University Press, 2013), 3–24.

Chacón, Jacinto, *Exposición Razonada y Estudio Comparativo del Código Civil Chileno*, vol. 2 (Valaparaiso: Imprenta de Mercurio 1878).

Chaimowicz, Thomas, *Antiquity as the Source of Modernity: Freedom and Balance in the Thought of Montesquieu and Burke* (Piscataway, NJ: Routledge, 2008).

Chazal, Jean-Pascal, "Relire Josserand', oui mais ... sans le trahir!" (2003) 27 *Recueil Dalloz Sirey de doctrine de jurisprudence et de législation* 1777–1781.

Christman, John, *The Myth of Property: Toward an Egalitarian Theory of Ownership* (Oxford: Oxford University Press, 1994).

Cicero. *Brutus. Orator*, G. L. Hendrickson (trans.) Loeb Classical Library 342 (Cambridge, MA: Harvard University Press, 1939).

    De Domo Sua, N. H. Watts (trans.) Leob Classical Library 158 (Cambridge, MA: Harvard University Press, 1923).

    De Finibus H. Rackham (trans.) Loeb Classical Library 40 (Cambridge, MA: Harvard University Press, 1931).

    De Lege Agraria, J. F. Freese (trans.) Loeb Classical Library 240 (Cambridge, MA: Harvard University Press, 1930).

    De Officiis, Walter Miller (trans.) Loeb Classical Library 30 (Cambridge, MA: Harvard University Press, 1913).

    De Oratore, E. W. Sutton (trans.) Loeb Classical Library 348 (Cambridge, MA: Harvard University Press, 1942).

    Topica, H. M. Hubbell (trans.) Loeb Classical Library 386 (Cambridge, MA: Harvard University Press, 1949).

    Tusculanae Disputationes, J. E. King (trans.) Loeb Classical Library 141 (Cambridge, MA: Harvard University Press, 1927).

Cimbali, Enrico, *La nouva fase del diritto civile nei rapporti economici e sociali con proposte di riforma della legislazione civile vigente*, 3rd ed. (Turin: Unione Tipografico-Editrice, 1885).

Codex Justinianus, Paulus, Krueger et al. (eds.), *Corpus Iuris Civis* (Berolina: Apud Weidmannos, 1900).

Codice per lo Regno delle Due Sicilie (Napoli: dalla stamperia reale della Real tip. del Ministero di Stato della cancelleria generale, 1854).

Cohen, Felix S., "The Pragmatic Meaning of Private Property Dialogue on Private Property" (1954) 9 *Rutgers University Law Review* 357–387.

Cohen, Morris R., "Property and Sovereignty" (1927) 13 *Cornell Law Quarterly* 8–30.

Conte, Emanuele, "Framing the Feudal Bond" (2012) 80 *Tijdschrift Voor Rechtsgeschiedenis* 481–495.

"Modena 1182, the Origins of a New Paradigm of Ownership: The Interface between Historical Contingency and Scholarly Invention of Legal Categories" (2018) 15 *Glossae European Journal of Legal History* 5–19.

"Pillio da Medicina," in Italo Birocchi, Ennio Cortese, Antonello Mattone, and Marco Nicola Milletti (eds.), *Dizionario Biografico dei Giuristi Italiani (XII–XX secolo)*, vol. 2 (Bologna: Il Mulino, 2013) 531–536.

Conze, Werner, "Nation und Gesellschaft – Zwei Grundbegriffe der revolutionären Epoche," in 198 *Historische Zeitschrift* (Oldenburg: Walter De Gruyter & Co, 1964), 1–43.

Cornell, Tim J., *The Beginnings of Rome: Italy and Rome from the Bronze Age to the Punic Wars (c. 1000–264 BC)* (London: Routledge, 1995).

Corradini, *Domenico Garantismo e statualismo: Le codificazioni civilistiche dell'Ottocento*, 3rd ed. (Milan: Giuffrè, 1986).

Cortese, Ennio (ed.), *La proprietà e le proprietà: Pontignano, 30 settembre – 3 ottobre 1985* (Milan: Giuffrè, 1988).

Cosentini, Francesco, *Código Civil Pan-Americano* (Havana: Vox Populorum, 1929).

Council of Europe, Colloquy on European Law, "Abuse of Rights and Equivalent Concepts: The Principle and Its Present Day Application," in *Proceedings of the Nineteenth Colloquy on European Law, Luxembourg, 6–9 November 1989* (Strasbourg: Council of Europe, 1990), 1–180.

Cruz, Feliú Guillermo, *La Abolicion de la Esclavitud en Chile*, 2nd ed. (Santiago: Editorial Universitaria, 1973).

Cuche, Paul, *A la recherche du fondement du droit: y a-t-il un romantisme juridique? Extrait de la Revue trimestrielle de droit civil 2* (Paris: Librairie du Recueil Sirey, 1929).

Dagan, Hanoch, "Markets for Self-Authorship" (2018) 27 *Cornell Journal of Law & Public Policy* 577–600.

Property: Values and Interests (Oxford: Oxford University Press, 2011).

"The Real Legacy of American Legal Realism" (2018) 38 *Oxford Journal of Legal Studies* 123.

Dann, Otto, "Gleichheit und Gleichberechtigung, " in Otto Brunner, Werner Conze, and Reinhart Koselleck (eds.), *Geschichtliche Grundbegriffe: Historisches Lexikon zur politisch-sozialen Sprache in Deutschland*, vol. 2 (Stuttgart: Klett-Cotta, 1972), 1006–1026.

Davidson, Nestor M., "Standardization and Pluralism in Property Law" (2008) 61 *Vanderbilt Law Review* 1597–1666.

De Cecco, Marcello, "The Economy from Liberalism to Fascism," in Adrian Lyttelton (ed.), *Liberal and Fascist Italy, 1900–1945* (Oxford: Oxford University Press, 2002), 62–73.

De Grand, Alexander J., *Italian Fascism: Its Origins and Development*, 3rd ed. (Lincoln: University of Nebraska Press, 2000).

Delalleau, Charles, *Traité de l'expropriation pour cause d'utilité publique*, vol. 1 (Paris: Cosse, Marchal et Compagnie, 1866).

Delvincourt, Claude-Étienne, *Cours de Code Civil*, vol. 3 (Paris: Fournier, 1819).

Demolombe, Charles, *Cours de Code Napoléon: Traité de la Distinction des Biens, de la Propriété, de l'Usufruit, de l'Usage et de l'Habitation*, 2nd ed., 2 vols. (Paris: Durand, 1861).

Deroussin, David, "Josserand, Le Code Civil et le Code Libanais des obligations et contrats," in *Le Code civil français et le dialogue des cultures juridiques* (Paris: Bruylant, 2007), 49–94.

de Saxoferrato, Bartolus, *In Primam Digesti Novi Partem Commentaria* (Torino: Augustae Taurinorum, 1589).

   In Primam Digesti Novi Partem (Venice: Giunti, 1585).

Desmoulins, Camille, *La France Libre*, 3rd ed. (1789).

Diezte, Gottfried, *In Defense of Property* (Baltimore: The Johns Hopkins Press, 1963).

D'Isernia, Andrea, *Libellus omnium legum allegatarum per Andream de Isernia in vsibus feudorum* (Venice, 1576).

Dominguez, Ramón, *Nuestro Sistema de Inquilinaje* (Santiago: Imprenta del Correo, 1867).

Donahue, Charles, "Private Law Without the State and During Its Formation" (2008) 56(3) *The American Journal of Comparative Law* 541–566.

Donahue, Charles Jr., "*Ius* in the Subjective Sense in Roman Law: Reflections on Villey and Tierney," in Domenico Maffei, Italo Birocchi, Mario Caravale, Emanuele Conte, and Ugo Petronio (eds.), *A Ennio Cortese*, vol. 1 (Rome: Il Cigno Edizioni, 2001), 506–535.

dos Santos Chuna, Alexandre, "The Social Function of Property in Brazilian Law" (2011) 80 *Fordham Law Review* 1171–1182.

Dross, M. William, and Favario, Thierry (eds.), *Un ordre juridique nouveau? Dialogues avec Louis Josserand* (Paris: Mare & Martin, 2014).

Duby, Georges, *La Société aux XIe et XIIe Siècles dans la Région Mâconnaise* (Paris: Ed. de l'Ecole des Hautes Etudes en Sciences Sociales, 1989).

Duguit, Léon, "Changes of Principle in the Field of Liberty, Contract, Liability and Property," in *The Progress of Continental Law in the Nineteenth Century*, The Continental Legal History Series, vol. 11 (Boston: Little, Brown, and Company, 1918), 65–146.

Le droit social, le droit individuel et la transformation de l'État: conférences faites à l'École des hautes études sociale (Paris: F. Alcan, 1908).

Les Transformations Generals du Droit Prive Depuis le Code Napoleon (Paris: Librarie Felix Alcan, 1912).

Dumas-Lavenac, Sophie, "Le Droit selon Louis Josserand" (2015) 2 *Revue juridique de l'Ouest* 39–53.

Dupin, Andre Marie Jean Jacques, *Dissertation sur la Vie et les Ouvrages de Pothier* (Paris: Béchet Aîné, 1825).

Duscio, Francesco, and Vecchio, Vincenzo, *Dell'enfiteusi, o commentario del tit. 9 nel libro 3 delle Leggi per lo Regno delle Due Sicilie*, vol. 1 (Catania: Pietro Giuntini, 1852).

Eberle, Lisa Pilar, "Law, Empire, and the Making of Roman Estates in the Provinces during the Late Republic" (2016) 3(1) *Critical Analysis of Law* 50–69.

Edict den erleichterten Besitz und den freien Gebrauch des Grundeigentums so wie die persönlichen Verhältnisse der Land-Bewohner betreffend (Memel: Königreich Preußen, 1807).

Egana, Juan, *Memoria Sobre Los Mayorazgos de Chile* (Santiago: Imprenta de R. Rengifo, 1828).

Fabres, José Clemente, *Instituciones de derecho civil chileno*, vol. 1 (Valparaíso: Imprenta del Universo, 1863).

Feenstra, Robert, *Fata Iuris Romani, Études d'Histoire du Droit* (Leyde: Presses Universitaires de Leyde, 1974).

Fenet, Pierre-Antoine (ed.), *Recueil complet des travaux préparatoires du Code civil*, 15 vols. (Paris: Videcoq, 1836).

Fenouillet, Dominique, "Étienne Louis Josserand (1868–1941)" (1996) 17 *Revue d'histoire des Facultés de droit et de la science juridique* 27–46.

Filangieri, Gaetano, *Scienza della Legislazione*, vol. 2 (Milan: Società Tipografica de' Classici Italiani, 1822).

Finley, Moses I., *The Ancient Economy* (Berkeley: University of California Press, 1999).

(ed.), *Studies in Roman Property* (Cambridge: Cambridge University Press, 1976).

Flower, Harriet I., *Roman Republics* (Princeton, NJ: Princeton University Press, 2010).

Foster, Sheila R., and Bonilla, Daniel, "The Social Function of Property: A Comparative Perspective" (2011) 80 *Fordham Law Review* 1003–1015.

Fox, Robert, *The Culture of Science in France, 1700–1900* (Aldershot: Ashgate, 1992).

Fox-Genovese, Elizabeth, *The Origins of Physiocracy* (Ithaca, NY: Cornell University Press, 1976).

Frank, Andre Gunder, *Capitalism and Underdevelopment in Latin America: Historical Studies of Chile and Brazil* (New York: Monthly Review Press, 1967).

Frémont, Auguste-Federic-Mathilde, *Recherches Historiques et Biographiques sur Pothier: Publiées à l'Occasion de l'Érection de sa Statue* (Orleans: Gatineau, 1859).

Frier, Bruce W., *The Rise of the Roman Jurists: Studies in Cicero's Pro Caecina* (Princeton, NJ: Princeton University Press, 1985)

Frontinus, Sextus Julius, *De Aquis Urbis Romae*, H. R. Rogers (ed.) (Cambridge: Cambridge University Press 2004).

Gagliardo, John G., *From Pariah to Patriot: The Changing Image of the German Peasant* (Lexington: University Press of Kentucky, 1969).

Gaius, *Institutiones or Institutes of Roman Law*, Edward Poste (trans.) (Oxford: Clarendon Press, 1904).

Gallo, Filippo, *Studi sulla distinzione fra "res mancipi" e "res nec mancipi"* (Turin: G. Giappichelli, 1958).

Gamauf, Richard, and Hausmaninger, Herbert (eds.), *A Casebook on Roman Property Law*, George A. Sheets (trans.) (Oxford: Oxford University Press, 2012).

Gans, Eduard, *System des Römischen Civilrechts im Grundrisse* (Berlin: Ferdinand Dümmler, 1827).

Garat, Dominique-Joseph, "Nouvelles Litteraires: Suite de l'Extrait des Loix Municipales de Langeudoc, Etc." (February 19, 1785) no. 8 *Mercure de France* 103–123.

Garaud, Marcel, *Histoire Générale du Droit Privé Français: de 1789 à 1804, La Révolution et la Propriété Foncière*, vol. 2 (Paris: Recueil Sirey, 1958).

Garnsey, Peter et al., *The Roman Empire: Economy, Society and Culture*, 2nd ed. (Oakland: University of California Press, 2015).

Gaudemet, Jean, "Tendances et Méthodes en Droit Romain" (1955) 145 *Revue Philosophique de la France et de l'Étranger* 140–179.

Ghisalberti, Carlo, *La Codificazione del Diritto in Italia, 1865–1942* (Rome: Laterza, 1985).

Giardina, Andrea, "The Transition to Late Antiquity," in Walter Scheidel, Ian Morris, and Richard P. Saller (eds.), *The Cambridge Economic History of the Greco-Roman World* (Cambridge: Cambridge University Press, 2007), 741–768.

Gierke, Otto Friedrich von, *Die soziale Aufgabe des Privatrechts* (Berlin: Springer, 1889).

Deutsches Privatrechts, vol. 2 (Leipzig: Duncker und Humblot, 1905).

"The Social Role of Private Law," Ewan McGaughey (trans.) (2018) 19(4) *German Law Journal* 1017–1116.

Goldhammer, Jesse, *The Headless Republic: Sacrificial Violence in Modern French Thought* (Ithaca, NY: Cornell University Press, 2005).

Goltz, Theodor von der, *Geschichte der deutschen Landwirtschaft* (Stuttgart: Cotta, 1902–1903).

Gooch, George Peabody, *Germany and the French Revolution* (London: Longmans, Green, and Co., 1920).

History and Historians in the Nineteenth Century (London: Longman, Green and Co, 1913).

Gongora, Mario, *Origen de los Inquilinos de Chile Central* (Santiago: Editorial Universitaria, 1960).

Gordley, James, and Mattei, Ugo, "Protecting Possession" (1996) 44(2) *The American Journal of Comparative Law* 293–334.

Gordley, James R., "Suárez and Natural Law," in Benjamin Hill and Henrik Lagerlund (eds.), *The Philosophy of Francisco Suárez* (Oxford: Oxford University Press, 2012), 209–229.

Gray, Marion W., *Prussia in Transition: Society and Politics under the Stein Reform Ministry of 1808* (Philadelphia: The American Philosophical Society, 1958)

Grossi, Paolo, *A History of European Law*, Lawrence Hooper (trans.) (Malden, MA: Wiley-Blackwell, 2010).

Il Dominio e le Cose: Percezioni Medievali e Moderne Dei Diritti Reali (Milano: Giuffrè Editore, 1992).

"Un Paradiso per Pothier, Robert-Joseph Pothier e la Proprietà Moderna" (1985) 14 *Quaderni Fiorentini per la Storia del Pensiero Giuridico Moderno* 401–456.

Gutteridge, H. C., "Abuse of Rights" (1933) 5 *Cambridge Law Journal* 22–45.

Haferkamp, Hans-Peter, "The Science of Private Law and the State in Nineteenth Century Germany" (2008) 56(3) *The American Journal of Comparative Law* 667–689.

Hahn, Henricus, *Dissertatio inauguralis de iure rerum et iuris in re speciebus harumque divisionibus in genere* (Helmstedt: Heredes Lucii, 1639).

Hakim, Nader, "La Contribution de l'Université à l'Élaboration de la Doctrine Civiliste au XIXe siècle," in Maryvonne Hecquard-Théron (ed.), *Les Facultés de Droit inspiratrices du droit?* (Toulouse: Presses de l'Université des Sciences Sociales, 2005), 15–33.

"Socialisation du droit et romantisme juridique: autour d'une controverse entre Julien Bonnecase et Paul Cuche," in Bernard Gallinato-Contino and Nader Hakim (eds.), *De la terre à l'usine: des hommes et du droit. Mélanges offerts à Gérard Aubin* (Bordeaux: Presses Universitaires de Bordeaux, 2014), 139–173.

Harries, Jill, and Wood, I. N., *The Theodosian Code* (Ithaca, NY: Cornell University Press, 1993).

Hawkins, Cameron, *Roman Artisans and the Urban Economy* (Cambridge: Cambridge University Press, 2016).

Hayem, Henri, "La Renaissance des Études Juridiques en France sous le Consulat" (1905) 29(3) *Nouvelle Revue Historique de Droit Français et Étranger* 96–122.

Henrion de Pansey, Pierre-Paul-Nicolas, "Justices de paix," *Ouvres Judiciaires du Président Henrion de Pansey* (Paris: Dussillon, 1843).

Hervé, Francois, *Théorie des Matières Féodales et Censuelles*, vol. 1 (Paris: Knapen and Sons, 1785).

Heyne, Christian Gottlob, *Opuscula Academica Collecta*, vol. 4 (Göttingen: Dieterich, 1796).

Higgs, Henry, *The Physiocrats: Six Lectures of the French Economistes of the Eighteenth Century* (London: MacMillan and Co., 1897).

Holbach, Paul-Henri-Dietrich d', *La Politique Naturelle, ou Discours sur les Vrais Principes du Gouvernement*, vol. 1 (London: Marc-Michel Rey, 1773).

Holden, Jane, and Harrison, Carolyn (eds.), *Law and Geography* (Oxford: Oxford University Press, 2003).

Hopkins, Keith, *Conquerors and Slaves* (Cambridge: Cambridge University Press, 1978).

Infante, José Miguel, *El Valdiviano Federal*, no. 75 (January 20, 1834).

Ipsen, Günther, "Staat aus dem Volk: Scheitern, Wollen, Vollbringen des Freiherrn vom Stein in der Preußischen Reform" (1973) 12 *Der Staat – Zeitschrift für Staatslehre* 147, 157.

Irti, Natalino, *L'età della decodificazione* (Milan: Giuffrè, 1999).

Israel, Jonathan I., *The Enlightenment That Failed: Ideas, Revolution, and Democratic Defeat* (Oxford: Oxford University Press, 2019).

 Radical Enlightenment: Philosophy and the Making of Modernity 1650–1750 (Oxford: Oxford University Press, 2002).

Jakab, Éva, "Property Rights in Ancient Rome," in Paul Erdkamp, Koenraad Verboven, and Arjan Zuiderhoek (eds.), *Ownership and Exploitation of Land and Natural Resources in the Roman World* (Oxford: Oxford University Press, 2015), 107–131.

Jaksić, Ivan, *Andrés Bello: Scholarship and Nation-Building in Nineteenth-Century Latin America* (Cambridge: Cambridge University Press, 2001).

Jara, A., *Ley de 10 de junio de 1823*, in *Legislación indigenista de Chile* (Mexico: Instituto Indigenista Interamericano, 1956).

Jaraquemada, Pedro José Prado, *Los Actuales Poseedores de Mayorazgos de Chile Apoyan la Justicia con que la Representacion Nacional ha Dercectado su Reduccion al Valor Primitivo en que se Fundaron* (Santiago: Imprenta de la Independencia, 1827).

Jestaz, Philippe, and Jamin, Christophe, *La Doctrine* (Paris: Dalloz, 2004).

Jhering, Rudolf von, *Der Kampf ums Recht, Vortrag des Hofrates Professor Jhering Gehalten in der Wiener Juristischen Gesellschaft am 11. März 1872* (Vienna: Manz'sche Buchhandlung, 1872).

Law as a Means to an End, Isaac Husik (trans.) (Boston: The Boston Book Company, 1913)

The Struggle for Law, John Lalor (trans.) (Chicago: Callaghan & Company, 1915).

Sul fondamento della protezione del possesso, Francesco Forlani (trans.) (Milan: Vallardi, 1872).

Über den Grund des Besitzschutzes (Jena: Maute's Verlag, 1869).

Der Zweck im Recht, vol. 1 (Leipzig: Breitkopf und Härtel, 1877).

Joerges, Christian, "Die Wissenschaft vom Privatrecht und der Nationalstaat," EUI Working Paper LAW no. 98/4, European University Institute, 1998.

Jolowicz, Herbert Felix, and Nicholas, Barry, *Historical Introduction to the Study of Roman Law*, 3rd ed. (Cambridge: Cambridge University Press, 1972).

Jones, Peter M., *The Peasantry in the French Revolution* (Cambridge: Cambridge University Press, 1988).

Jördens, Andrea, "Possession and Provincial Practice," in Paul J. du Plessis, Clifford Ando, and Kaius Touri (eds.), *The Oxford Handbook of Roman Law and Society* (Oxford: Oxford University Press, 2016), 553–568.

Josserand, Louis, "Configuration du droit de propriété dans l'ordre juridique nouveau," in *Mélanges juridiques, dédiés à M. le professeur Sugiyama* (Tokyo: Association Japonaise des Juristes de Langue Française; Maison Franco-Japonaise, 1940), 95–110.

De l'abus des droits (Paris: Arthur Rosseau Editeur, 1905).

De l'esprit des droits et de leur relativité: théorie dite de l'abus des droits, 2nd ed. (Paris: Dalloz, 1939).

Justi, Johann Heinrich Gottlob von, *Staatswirtschaft* (Leipzig: B. C. Breitkopf, 1758).

Kagan, K. Kahana, "*Res Corporalis and Res Incorporalis: A Comparison of Roman and English Law of Interests of Life*" (1945–1946) 20 *Tulane Law Review* 98–111.

Kantorowicz, Hermann, *Was ist uns Savigny?* (Berlin: C. Heymanns Verlag, 1912).

Kaplan, Steven L., and Reinert, Sophus A. (eds.), *The Economic Turn: Recasting Political Economy in Enlightenment Europe* (London: Anthem Press, 2019), 30–120.

Karlowa, Otto, *Römische Rechtsgeschichte*, vol. 2 (Leipzig: Metzger and Wittig, 1901).

Kaser, Max, *Eigentum und Besitz im älteren römischen Recht*, 2nd ed. (Cologne: Böhlau, 1956).

Das römische Privatrecht, 2 vols. (Munich: C. H. Beck, 1955) [reprint].

Katz, Larissa, "Spite and Extortion: A Jurisdictional Principle of Abuse of Property Right" (2013) 122 *Yale Law Journal* 1444–1483.

Kay, Philip, *Rome's Economic Revolution* (Oxford: Oxford University Press, 2014).

Kehoe, Dennis P., *Law and Rural Economy in the Roman Empire* (Ann Arbor: The University of Michigan Press, 2007).

"Property Rights over Land and Economic Growth in the Roman Empire," in Paul Erdkamp, Koenraad Verboven, and Arjan Zuiderhoek (eds.), *Ownership and Exploitation of Land and Natural Resources in the Roman World* (Oxford: Oxford University Press, 2015), 88–106.

Kehr, Eckart, "Zur Genesis der preußischen Bürokratie und des Rechtsstaats," in *Der Primat der Innenpolitik: Gesammelte Aufsätze zur Preussisch-Deutschen Sozialgeschichte im 19. und 20. Jahrhundert (Veröffentlichungen der Historischen Kommission zu Berlin)*, vol. 19 (1965), 31–52.

Kelley, Donald R., "Gaius Noster: Substructures of Western Social Thought" (1979) 84(3) *The American Historical Review* 619–648.

The Historians and the Law in Postrevolutionary France (Princeton, NJ: Princeton University Press, 1984).

"The Metaphysics of Law: An Essay on the Very Young Marx" (1978) 83(2) *American Historical Review* 350–367.

Kelley, Donald R., and Smith, Bonnie G., "What Was Property? Legal Dimensions of the Social Question in France (1789–1848)" (1984) 128(3) *Proceedings of the American Philosophical Society* 200–230.

Kennedy, Duncan, "A Semiotics of Critique" (1991) 42 *Syracuse Law Review* 75–116.

Kitchen, Martin, *The Political Economy of Germany 1815–1914* (Montreal: McGill-Queen's University Press, 1978).

Klubock, Thomas, "Ránquil: Violence and Peasant Politics on Chile's Southern Frontier" in Greg Grandin and Gilbert M. Joseph (eds.), *A Century of Revolution: Insurgent and Counterinsurgent Violence during Latin America's Long Cold War* (Durham, NC: Duke University Press, 2010), 121–159.

Knapp, Georg Friedrich, *Die Bauernbefreiung und der Ursprung der Landarbeiter in den älteren Teilen Preußens* (Leipzig: Duncker & Humblot, 1887).

Kocourek, Albert, "Introduction," in Rudolf von Jhering, *The Struggle for Law*, John Lalor (trans.) (Chicago: Callaghan and Company, 1915).

Koselleck, Reinhart, *Preußen zwischen Reform und Revolution: Allgemeines Landrecht, Verwaltung und soziale Bewegung von 1791 bis 1848* (Stuttgart: Ernst Klett Verlag, 1967).

Kraus, Christian Jacob, "Gutachten über die Aufhebung der Privatuntertänigkeit in Ost- und Westpreußen (1802)," in Werner Conze (ed.), *Quellen zur Geschichte der deutschen Bauernbefreiung* (Göttingen: Musterschmidt, 1957), 66–75.

Kunkel, Wolfgang, *An Introduction to Roman Legal and Constitutional History*, John M. Kelly (trans.), 2nd ed. (Oxford: Oxford University Press, 1973).

Laclau, Ernesto, "Feudalism and Capitalism in Latin America" (May/June 1971) I (67) *New Left Review* 19–38.

Lamennais, Félicite Robert de, *De l'esclavage moderne* (Paris: Pagnerre Editeur, 1840).

Larousse, Pierre, *Grand Dictionnaire Universel du XIXe Siècle*, 17 vols. (Paris, 1868).

Laurent, François, *Principes de droit civil Français*, vol. 6 (Brussels: Bruylant, 1871).

Lee, Daniel, "'Office Is a Thing Borrowed': Jean Bodin on Offices and Seigneurial Government" (2013) 41(3) *Political Theory* 409–440.

Popular Sovereignty in Early Modern Constitutional Thought (Oxford: Oxford University Press, 2016).

Lehman, Karl, *Das Langobardische Lehnrecht* (Gottingen: Dieterich, 1896).

"Lettres au Redacteur du Producteur sur le systeme de la cooperation mutuelle, et de la communaute de biens, d'apres le pla de M Owen" (4 Julliut 1826) 4 *Le Producteur: journal de l'industrie, des sciences et des beaux-arts* 526–544.

Leibholz, Gerhard, "Carta del Lavoro 21 aprile 1927," in *Zu Den Problemen des ascistischen Verfassungrechts: Akademische Antrittsvorlesung* (Berlin: De Gruyter, 2019 [1928]), 99–106.

Lemercier de la Riviere, Paul Pierre, *L'Ordre Naturel et Essentiel de Societes Politiques* (Paris: Desaint Libraire, 1767).

Lenaerts, Annekatrien, "The General Principle of the Prohibition of Abuse of Rights: A Critical Position on Its Role in a Codified European Contract Law" (2010) 18 *European Review of Private Law* 1121.

"Ley de Desamortización de Bienes de la Iglesia y de Corporaciones. Lerdo de Tejada, 25 de Junio de 1856," in *Derechos del pueblo mexicano. México a través de sus constituciones*, volumen II, sección segunda (Historia constitucional, 1831–1918), https://archivos.juridicas.unam.mx/www/bjv/libros/12/5625/17.pdf.

"Ley de Nacionalización de los Bienes Eclesiásticos, 12 de julio de 1859," in *Derechos del pueblo mexicano México a través de sus constituciones*, volumen II, sección segunda (Historia constitucional, 1831–1918), https://archivos.juridicas.unam.mx/www/bjv/libros/12/5625/23.pdf.

"Ley Sobre Ocupación y Enajenación de Terrenos Baldios de los Estados Unidos Mexicanos, 26 de marzo de 1894," in *Derechos del pueblo mexicano, México a través de sus constituciones*, volumen II, sección segunda (Historia constitucional,1831–1918), https://archivos.juridicas.unam.mx/www/bjv/libros/2/940/39.pdf.

Liberatore, Pasquale, *Trattato dell' Enfiteusi in Corso di diritto civile del Signor Delvincourt, novellamente tradotto dall'ultima edizione francese ed accompagnato dalla nuova giurisprudenza civile del Regno delle Due Sicilie*, vol. 10 (Naples: Nel Nuovo Gabinetto Letterario Largo Trinità Maggiore, 1841).

Lieber, Francis, *Reminiscences of an Intercourse with Mr. Niebuhr, the Historian During a Residence with Him in Rome, in the Years 1822 and 1823* (Philadelphia: Carey, Lea & Blanchard, 1835).

Lindenfeld, David F., *The Practical Imagination: The German Sciences of the State in the Nineteenth Century* (Chicago: University of Chicago Press, 1997).

Livy, *Ab Urbe Condita*, Robert Seymour Conway and C. Flamstead Walters (eds.) (Oxonii: E Typographeo Clarendoniano, 1914), 44–50.

Locré de Roissy, Jean Guillaume, *Esprit du Code Napoléo*, vol. 1 (Paris: Imprimerie Impériale,1805).

Loria, Achille, "Socialismo Giuridico" (1893) 1 *La Scienza del Diritto Privato* 419–527.

Loyseau, Charles, *Traité des Seigneuries* (Paris: Abel L'Angelier, 1608).

Luzzatto, Giuseppe, *Sul regime del suolo nelle province romane: spunti critici e problematica. in Atti del Convegno Internationale sul tema: I diritti locali nelle province romane con particolare riguardo alle condizioni giuridiche del suolo (Roma, 26–28 ottobre 1971)* (Rome: Accademia Nazionale dei Lincei, 1974).

Lyttelton, Adrian (ed.), *Italian Fascisms from Pareto to Gentile* (New York: Harper and Row, 1975).

Mackrell, John Q. C., *The Attack on "Feudalism" in Eighteenth Century France* (London: Routledge, 2013).

MacRae, Duncan, *Legible Religion: Books, Gods, and Rituals in Roman Culture* (Cambridge, MA: Harvard University Press, 2016).

Magallón Ibarra, Jose Mario, *Instituciones de Derecho Civil*, vol. 1 (Mexico: El Porrua, 1987).

Maleville, Jacques de, *Analyse Raisonnée de la Discussion du Code Civil au Conseil d'État*, vol. 2 (Paris, 1805).

Mann, Golo, *Deutsche Geschichte des 19. und 20. Jahrhunderts* (Frankfurt a.M.: Fischer, 1969).

Manning, Joseph G., *The Last Pharaohs: Egypt under the Ptolemies, 305–30 BC.* (Princeton, NJ: Princeton University Press, 2009).

Marcadé, Victor-Napoléon, *Élements du Droit Civil Français ou Explication Méthodique et Raisonée du Code Civil*, vol. 2 (Paris: Cotillon, 1842).

Markoff, John, *The Abolition of Feudalism: Peasants, Lords and the Legislators in the French Revolution* (University Park: Pennsylvania State University Press, 1996).

Martin, Xavier, "Nature humaine et Code Napoléon" (1985) 2 *Droits* 117–128.

Martini, Remo, *Le definizioni dei giuristi romani* (Milan: Giuffrè, 1966).

Marx, Karl, *1 Das Kapital*, 25 Karl Marx-Freiderich Engles Werke (Berlin: Dietz, 1972).

   3 Das Kapital, 25 Karl Marx-Freiderich Engles Werke (Berlin: Dietz, 1972).

   Einleitung, 13 Karl Marx and Friedrich Engels, Marx Engels Werke 615–641 (Berlin: Dietz, 1971).

Zur Kritik der Hegelschen Rechtsphilosophie, 1 Karl Marx and Friedrich Engels, Marx Engels Werke 203–333 (Berlin: Dietz, 1981).

"Zur Kritik der politischen Okonomie," in *A Contribution to the Critique of Political Economy*, S. W. Ryazanskaya (trans.), Maurice Dobb (ed.) (Moscow: Progress Publishers, 1970).

Marx, Karl, and Engels, Friedrich, "Manifest der Kommunistischen Partei," in *Manifesto of the Communist Party*, Karl Marx and Frederick Engels (trans.), Frederick Engels (ed.) (Chicago: Charles H. Kerr & Company, 1888).

Mauer, Hermann, *Das landschaftliche Kreditwesen Preußens agrargeschichtlich und volkwirtschaftlich betrachtet: Ein Beitrag zur Geschichte der Bodenkreditpolitik des Preußischen Staates* (Straßburg: Verlag von Karl F. Trübner, 1907).

Maupetit, Michel-René, *Lettres de Michel-René Maupetit: Député à l'Assemblée Nationale Constituante* (Charleston, SC: Nabu Press, 2010).

Maza, Sarah, *The Myth of the French Bourgeoisie: An Essay on the Social Imaginary 1750–1850* (Cambridge, MA: Harvard University Press, 2005).

"Mensaje con que el Presidente de la República, don Manuel Montt, y el Ministro de Justicia, don Francisco Javier Ovalle, remitieron al congreso de 22 de noviembre de 18 el proyecto de Código Civil," in Pedro L. Urquieta (ed.), *Obras Completas de Andres Bello* (Caracas: Fundacion la Casa de Bello, 1981), 87–106.

Merlin, Philippe-Antoine, *Rapport fait au comité des droits féodaux le 4 septembre 1789, sur l'objet et l'ordre du travail dont il est chargé* (Versailles: Baudouin, 1789).

Meyer, Eugenia, "Introducción Biográfica," in Luis Cabrera (ed.), *Obras Completas*, vol. 1 (Mexico: Ediciones Oasis, 1972), viii–xix.

Mirabeau, Victor R., *L'Ami des Hommes ou Traité de la Population*, vol. 1 (Avignon, 1756).

Mirow, M. C., *Latin American Law: A History of Private Law and Institutions in Spanish America* (Austin: University of Texas Press, 2004).

"Léon Duguit and the Social Function of Property in Argentina," in Paul Babie and Jessica Viven-Wilksch (eds.), *Léon Duguit and the Social Obligation Norm of Property: A Translation and Global Exploration* (Singapore: Springer Singapore, 2019), 267–285.

"Origins of the Social Function of Property in Chile" (2011) 80 *Fordham Law Review* 1183–1218.

Moatti, Claudia, *The Birth of Critical Thinking in Republican Rome*, Janet Lloyd (trans.) (Cambridge: Cambridge University Press, 2015).

Momigliano, Arnaldo, "Niebuhr and the Agrarian Problems of Rome" (1982) 21(4) *History and Theory* 3–15.

Mommsen, Theodor, "Nuovo esemplare dell'editto 'de accusationibus' di Costantino: Lettera del Prof. T. Mommsen al Prof. V. Scialoja" (1889) 2 *Bullettino dell'Istituto di Diritto Romano* 129–135.

Monateri, Pier Giuseppe, and Somma, Allesandro "The Fascist Theory of Contract," in Michael Stolleis et al. (eds.), *Darker Legacies of Law in Europe* (London: Bloomsbury, 2003), 55–70.

Monier, Raymond, "La date d'apparition du dominium et de la distinction juridique des res en corporales et incorporales," in *Studi in onore di Siro Solozzi* (Naples: Jovene, 1948), 357–374.

Monson, Andrew, Communal Agriculture in the Ptolemaic and Roman Fayyum Princeton/Stanford Working Papers in Classics Paper No. 100703 (2007), doi.org/10.2139/ssrn.1426939.

From the Ptolemies to the Romans: Political and Economic Change in Egypt (Cambridge: Cambridge University Press, 2012).

de Montmorency, J. E., "Robert Jospeh Pothier and French Law" (1914) 13 *Journal of the Society of Comparative Legislation and International Law* 265–287.

Mooers, Colin, *The Making of Bourgeois Europe: Absolutism, Revolution, and the Rise of Capitalism England, France and Germany* (London: Verso, 1991).

Moore, Barrington, *Social Origins of Dictatorship and Democracy: Lord and Peasant in the Making of the Modern World* (Boston: Beacon Press, 1966).

Motte, Olivier J., "Demolombe, Jean Charles Florent," in Michael Stolleis (ed.), *Juristen: ein biographisches Lexikon; von der Antike bis zum 20. Jahrhundert,* 2nd ed. (Munich: Beck, 2001).

Mottek, Hans, *Wirtschaftsgeschichte Deutschlands: Ein Grundriss* (Berlin: Deutscher Verlag der Wissenschaften, 1957).

Mourlon, Frédéric, *Répétitions Écrites sur le Code Civil,* 13th ed., vol. 1 (Paris: Garnier, 1896).

Moyn, Samuel, and Sartori, Andrew, "Approaches to Global Intellectual History," in *Global Intellectual History* (New York: Columbia University Press, 2013), 3–30.

Munzer, Stephen R., *A Theory of Property* (Cambridge: Cambridge University Press, 1990).

Narváez Hernández, José Ramón, "El Código Privado-Social: Influencia de Francesco Cosentini en el Código Civil Mexicano de 1928" (2004) 16 *Anuario Mexicano de Historia del Derecho* 201–226.

Natoli, Luigi Ferlazzo, *Letteratura e Diritti. Scritti su Salvatore Pugliatti* (Milan: Giuffrè, 2002).

Nicholas, Barry, *An Introduction to Roman Law* (Oxford: Claredon Press, 1962).

Niebuhr, Barthold Georg, *The History of Rome,* Julius Charles Hare and Connop Thirlwall (trans.), vol. 2 (Philadelphia: Thomas Wardle, 1835).

"Letter 213 to Savigny Venice 4th Sept., 1816," in Chevalier Bunsen, Brandis, and Lorbell (eds.), *The Life and Letters of Barthold George Niebuhr: With Essays on His Character and Influence* (New York: Harper and Brothers, 1852), 319–321.

Römische Geschichte, vol. 2 (Berlin: 1836).

Niort, Jean-François, "Le Code civil ou la réaction à l'œuvre en Métropole et aux Colonies," in Niort (ed.), *Du Code noir au Code Civil. Jalons pour l'Histoire du Droit à la Guadeloupe. Perspectives Comparées avec La Martinique, La Guyane et la République d'Haïti* (Paris: L'Harmattan, 2007), 59–86.

Nippel, Wilfried, *Ancient and Modern Democracy: Two Concepts of Liberty?*, Keith Tribe (trans.) (Cambridge: Cambridge University Press, 2015).

Obermann, Karl, "Bemerkungen über die soziale und nationale Bedeutung der preußischen Reformbewegung unter dem Ministerium des Freiherrn vom Stein," in *Die Volksmassen: Gestalter der Geschichte – Festgabe für Leo Stern* (Berlin: Rutten & Loening 1962), 127–153.

Olson, Richard G., *Science and Scientism in Nineteenth-Century Europe* (Urbana; Chicago: University of Illinois Press, 2008).

Ortolan, Joseph-Louis-Elzéar, *Explication Historique des Instituts de l'Empereur Justinien*, 6th ed., vol. 1 (Paris: H. Plon, 1857).

Ostrom, Elinor, "How Types of Goods and Property Rights Jointly Affect Collective Action" (2003) 15 *Journal of Theoretical Politics* 239–270.

Ouvry, Henry Aimé, *Stein and His Reformers in Prussia, with Reference to the Land Question in England: And an Appendix Containing the Views of Richard Cobden and J. S. Mill's Advice to Land Reformers* (London: Kerby and Endean, 1873).

Pardessus, Jean-Marie, "Rapport de la commission," in Charles Vanufel and Clément Felix Champion de Villeneuve (eds.), *Code des Colons de Saint-Domingue* (Paris: Vergne, 1826), 93–134.

Parker, Harold Talbot, *The Cult of Antiquity and the French Revolutionaries: A Study in the Development of the Revolutionary Spirit* (London: Octagon Books, 1965).

Paterculus, Velleius, *Compendium of Roman History Augusti*, Frederick W. Shipley (trans.) (Cambridge, MA: Harvard University Press, 1924).

Patetta, Friderico (ed.), "Excerpta Codicis Vaticani *Reg. 435*," in Antonio Gaudenzi and Giovanni Battista Palmerio (eds.), *Bibliotheca iuridica medii aevi*, vol. 2 (Bologna: Libreria Fratelli Treves di Pietro Virano, 1892), p. 135–136.

Peabody, Sue, *"There Are No Slaves in France": The Political Culture of Race and Slavery in the Ancien Régime* (Oxford: Oxford University Press, 1997).

Pereira, Juan de Solórzano, *Politica Indiana* (1647), https://rarebooks.library.nd.edu/exhibits/durand/indies/solorzano.html.

Perozzi, Silvio, *Sulla struttura delle servitù prediali in diritto romano* (Rome: Forzani, 1888).

Perry, Erskine, *Von Savigny's Treatise on Possession: Or the Jus Possessionis of the Civil Law*, 6th ed. (London: S. Sweet, 1848).

Phipps, Helen, "The Agrarian Phase of the Mexican Revolution of 1910–1920" (1924) 39(1) *Political Science Quarterly* 1–18.

Pinelo, Antonio De León, *Tratado de Confirmaciones Reales, Encomiendas, Oficios y Casos en que se Requieren para las Indias* (s.n., 1630).

"Plan de Ayala: Edicion Conmemorativa 93" (Camera de Disputados 2019) (original published in 1913), http://biblioteca.diputados.gob.mx/janium/bv/ce/lxiv/plan-ayala.pdf.

Planck, Gottlieb Jakob, *Leges agrariae pestiferae et execrabiles*, Opuscula Academica Collecta, vol. 4, Christian Gottlob Heyne (ed.) (Göttingen: Dieterich, 1796), 350–373.

Planiol, Marcel, *Traité élémentaire de droit civil*, 4th ed., vol. 2 (Paris: Librairie générale de droit et de jurisprudence, 1907).

Plessis, Paul Du, *Borkowski's Textbook on Roman Law*, 4th ed. (Oxford: Oxford University Press, 2010).

Plutarch, *Vitae Parallelae: Tiberius Gracchus*, vol. 2, E. G. H. Schaefer (ed.) (Leipzig: J. A. G. Weigelii, 1820–1822).

Pocock, J. G. A., *The Ancient Constitution and the Feudal Law: A Study of English Historical Thought in the Seventeenth Century* (Cambridge: Cambridge University Press, 1987).

Pollard, John F., *The Fascist Experience in Italy* (New York: Routledge, 1998).

Pollock, Federick, *The Law of Torts* (London: Stevens, 1890).

"Review of 'Property, Its Duties and Rights Historically, Philosophically and Religiously Regarded: Essays by Various Writers, with an Introduction by the Bishop of Oxford'" (1914) 30 *The Law Quarterly Review* 111–112.

Poly, Jean-Pierre, and Bournazel, Eric, *The Feudal Transformation, 900–1200*, Caroline Higgitt (trans.) (New York: Holmes & Meier, 1991).

La Mutation Féodale, Xe–XIIe Siècles (Paris: Presses Universitaires de France, 1980).

Portalis, Jean-Étienne-Marie, "Discours de rentrée à l'Académie de législation. Paris – 26 novembre 1803" (2014) *Les Cahiers Portalis* 31–34.

"Essai sur l'utlité de la codification," in *Discours, Rapport et Travaux inédits sur le Code Civil* (Paris: Joubert, 1844), 5–6.

"Exposé des motifs du projet de loi sur la propriété, titre II, livre II du *Code Civil*, présenté le 26 Nivôse an XII," in *Ecrits et discours juridiques et politiques* (Marseille: Presses Universitaires d'Aix, 1988), 111–127.

"Exposé general du système du Code Civil," in Jean Guillaume Locré de Roissy (ed.), *La législation civile, commerciale et criminelle de la France, ou Commentaire et complément des Code Français*, vol. 1 (Paris: Treuttel and Würtz, 1827), 316–336.

Pothier, Robert Joseph, *Oeuvres posthumes de M. Pothier*, vol. 1 (Paris: Guillaume Debure, 1777).

Traité du Droit de Domaine de Propriété, vol. 1 (Paris: Guillaume Debure, 1772).

Programa del Partido Liberal Mexicano y Manifiesto a la Nacion (Mexico: Archivo General de la Nación, July 1, 1906).

Proudhon, Jean-Baptiste-Victor, *Traité du Domaine de Propriété* (Brussels: Meline, Cans et compagnie, 1842).

Proudhon, Pierre-Joseph, "*Lettre à Karl Marx, Lyon, 17 mai 1846*," in J. A. L Langlois (ed.), *Correspondance de P.-J. Proudhon*, vol. 2 (Geneva: Slatkine Reprints, 1971), 198–202.

"Qu'est-ce que la propriété?," in Donald R. Kelley and Bonnie G. Smith (eds. and trans.), *Oeuvres completes de P.-J. Proudhon*, vol. 1 (Paris: Lacroix Editeurs, 1873), 200–230.

"Qu'est-ce que la propriété?," in Donald R. Kelley and Bonnie G. Smith (eds. and trans.), *What Is Property?* (Cambridge: Cambridge University Press, 1994), 200–230.

Théorie de la propriété (Paris: Flamarion, 1862).

Puchta, Georg Friedrich, *Corso delle Istituzioni di G. F. Puchta*, Antonio Turchiarulo (trans.) (Naples: Tipografia all'insegna del Diogene, 1854).

Cursus der Institutionen, vol. 3 (Leipzig: Breitkopf und Härtel, 1841–1847).

Pugliatti, Salvatore, *La Proprietà nel Nuovo Diritto* (Milan: Giuffrè, 1954).

Quesnay, Francois, "Maximes générales du gouvernement économique d'un royaume agricole et notes sur ces maximes," in Auguste Oncken (ed.), *Oeuvres économiques et philosophiques de F. Quesnay* (Paris: Jules Peelman, 1888), 330–336.

Quinzacara, Eduardo Cordero, "La Dogmática Constitucional de la Propiedad en el Derecho Chileno" (2006) 33 *Revista Chilena de Derecho* 125.

Raack, Richard C., *The Fall of Stein* (Cambridge, MA: Harvard University Press, 1965).

Ramirez Rondo, María Deborah, "Concepión del Estado Agrario en Andrés Bello" (2015) 41 *Revista de Derecho y Reforma Agraria* 91–96.

Rathbone, Dominic W., "The Control and Exploitation of *ager publicus* in Italy under the Roman Republic," in Jean-Jacques Aubert (ed.), *Tâches publiques en enterprise privée dans le monde romain* (Geneva: University of Neuchâtel, 2003), 135–178.

Economic Rationalism and Rural Society in Third-Century A.D. Egypt: The Heroninos Archive and the Appianus Estate (Cambridge: Cambridge University Press, 1991).

Reimann, Mathias, "Nineteenth Century German Legal Science" (1990) 31(4) *Boston College Law Review* 837–897.

Reinert, Sophus A., "Another Grand Tour: Cameralism and Antiphysiocracy in Baden, Tuscany and Denmark-Norway," in Jurgen Backhaus (ed.), *Physiocracy, Antiphysiocracy and Pfeiffer* (New York: Springer, 2011), 39–96.

Rémy, Philippe, "Le Rôle de l'Exégèse dans l'Enseignement du Droit au XIXe Siècle" (1985) *Revue d'Histoire des Facultés de Droit et de la Culture Juridique, du Monde des Juristes et du Livre Juridique* 91–105.

Renauldon, Joseph, *Traité Historique et Pratique des Droits Seigneuriaux* (Paris: Despilly, 1765).

Renner, Karl, *The Institutions of Private Law and Their Social Functions*, Agnes Zchwarzschild (trans.) (London: Routledge, 1949).

Die Rechtinstitute des Privatrechts und ihre sozial Function: Ein Beitrag zur Kritik des bürgerlichen Rechts (Tübingen: J. C. B. Mohr, 1929).

Rescigno, Pietro, *L'Abuso del Diritto* (Bologna: Il Mulino, 1998).

Reuter, Timothy, "Debate: The Feudal Revolution: III" (1997) 155 *Past & Present* 177–195.

Reynolds, Susan, "Fiefs and Vassals: Fiefs and Vassals after Twelve Years," in Sverre Bagge, Michael H. Gelting, and Thomas Lindkvist (eds.), *Feudalism: New Landscapes of Debate* (Turnhout: Brepols, 2011), 15–26.

Ripert, Georges, "Abus ou relativité des droitsin" (1929) 49 *Revue critique de législation et de jurisprudence* 33–63.

Ritter, Gerhard, *Stein – Eine politische Biographie*, 3rd ed. (Stuttgart: Deutsche Verlagsanstalt, 1958).

di Robilant, Anna, and Syed, Talha, "Property's Building Blocks: Hohfeld in Europe and Beyond," in Shyamkrishna Balganesh, Ted Sichelman, and Henry E. Smith (eds.), *Wesley Hohfeld a Century Later Edited Work, Select Personal Papers, and Original Commentaries* (Cambridge: Cambridge University Press, 2022), 223–257.

Rodger, Alan, *Owners and Neighbours in Roman Law* (Oxford: Clarendon Press, 1972).

Rodotà, Stefano, *Il terribile diritto. Studi sulla proprietà privata e i beni comuni* (Bologna: Il Mulino, 2013).

Roederer, Pierre-Louis, *De la Propriété Considérée dans ses rapports avec les droits politiques*, 3rd ed. (Paris: Hector Bossange, 1830).

Rosanvallon, Pierre, *The Society of Equals*, Arthur Goldhammer, trans. (Cambridge, MA: Harvard University Press, 2013).

Rose, Carol M., "Canons of Property Talk, or Blackstone's Anxiety" (1998) 108 *Yale Law Journal* 601–632.

Rose, R. B., "The Red Scare of the 1790s: The French Revolution and the Agrarian Law" (1984) 103(1) *Past & Present* 113–130.

Roselaar, Saskia, *Public Land in the Roman Republic: A Social and Economic History of Ager Publicus in Italy, 396–89 BC* (Oxford: Oxford University Press, 2010).

Rosenberg, Hans, *Bureaucracy, Aristocracy and Autocracy: The Prussian Experience 1660–1815* (Boston: Beacon Press, 1968).

Rossi-Doria, Malio, *Riforma Agraria e Azione Meridionalista* (Naples: L'ancora del Mediterraneo, 2003 [1948]).

Rota, Antonio, "L'apparato di Pillio alle Consuetudines feudorum e il Ms. 1004 dell'Archivo di Stato di Roma" (1938) 14 *Studi e Memorie per la storia dell'Università di Bologna* 112–113.

Rudorff, Adolf August Friedrich, "Ueber den Rechtsgrund der possessorischen Interdicte" (1831) 7 *Zeitschrift für geschichtliche Rechtswissenschaften* 90–114.

Ruefner, Thomas, "The Roman Concept of Ownership and the Medieval Doctrine of Dominium Utile," in John W. Cairns and Paul J. du Plessis (eds.), *The Creation of Ius Commune: From Casus to Regula* (Edinburgh: Edinburgh University Press, 2010), 127–142.

Ruiz, Francisco H., "La Socialization del Derecho Privado y el Codigo Civil de 1928" (July–December 1946) 8 *Revista de la Escuela Nacional de Jurisprudencia* 45–88.

Sala-Molins, Louis, *Les Miseres des Lumieres* (Paris: Editions Robert Laffont, 1992).

Saleilles, Raymond, *Étude sur la théorie générale de l'obligation d'après le premier projet de code civil pour l'Empire allemand*, 2nd ed. (Paris: F. Pichon, 1901).

Samburski, Samuel, *Physics of the Stoics* (Princeton, NJ: Princeton University Press, 1959).

Samuels, Warren J., "The Physiocratic Theory of Property and the State" (1961) 75 *The Quarterly Journal of Economics* 96–111.

Sanders, James E., *The Vanguard of the Atlantic World. Creating Modernity, Nation and Democracy in Nineteenth-Century Latin America* (Durham, NC: Duke University Press, 2014).

Santamaria, Fransisco, *Nuevo código civil para el Distrito y territorios federales : expedido en 30 de agosto de 1928; exposición de motivos, de la Comisión autora del Proyecto* (Mexico: Ediciones Botas, 1933).

Sarmiento, D. F., *Facundo* (Buenos Aires: Librería la Facultad, 1921).

Sarris, Peter, "The Eastern Empire from Constantine to Heraclius (306–641)," in Cyril Mango (ed.), *The Oxford History of Byzantium* (Oxford: Oxford University Press, 2002), 19–70.

Savigny, Friedrich Karl von, *Vom Beruf unserer Zeit für Gesetzgebung und Rechtswissenschaft* (Heidelberg: Mohr und Zimmer, 1814).

Geschichte des römischen Rechts im Mittelalter, vol. 1 (Heidelberg: Mohr und Zimmer, 1826)

The History of the Roman Law During the Middle Ages, Elias Cathcart (trans.), vol. 1 (London: Adam Black, 1829).

Das Recht des Besitzes (Giessen: Heyer, 1837).

Das Recht des Besitzes. Eine civilistische Abhandlung (Giessen: Heyer, 1803).

System des heutigen römischen Rechts, vol. 1 (Berlin: Veit, 1840).

System of Modern Roman Law, William Holloway (trans.), vol. 1 (Madras: J. Higginbotham, 1867).

Of the Vocation of Our Age for Legislation and Jurisprudence, Abraham Hayward (trans.) (London: Littlewood & Co., 1831).

Von Savigny's Treatise on Possession: Or, the Jus Possessionis of the Civil Law, Erskine Perry (trans.) (London: S. Sweet, 1848).

Scheidel, Walter (ed.), *The Cambridge Companion to the Roman Economy* (Cambridge: Cambridge University Press, 2012).

Schiavone, Aldo, *Alle Origini del Diritto Romano Rorghese: Hegel Contro Savigny* (Rome: Laterza, 1984).

The End of the Past: Ancient Rome and the Modern West, Margery H. Schneider (trans.) (Cambridge, MA: Harvard University Press, 2000).

The Invention of Law in the West, Jeremy Carden and Antony Shugar (trans.) (Cambridge, MA: Harvard University Press, 2011).

Progresso (Bologna: Il Mulino, 2020).

La storia spezzata. Roma antica e Occidente moderno (Rome: Laterza, 1996).

Schissler, Hanna, *Preußische Agrargesellschaft im Wandel – Wirtschaftliche, gesellschaftliche und politische Transformationsprozesse von 1763–1847* (Göttingen: Vandenhoek und Ruprecht, 1978).

Schlumbohm, Jürgen, *Freiheit: Die Anfänge der bürgerlichen in Deutschland im Spiegel ihres Leitwortes* (Düsseldorf: Pädagogischer Verlag Schwann, 1975).

Schmidlin, Bruno, *Die römischen Rechtsregeln* (Cologne: Böhlau, 1970).

Schmidt, Walter, "Marx und Engels über den historischen Platz der preußischen Reformen," in *Preußische Reformen – Wirkungen und Grenzen. Aus Anlass des 150. Todestages des Freiherrn vom und zum Stein* (Berlin: Akademie-Verlag, 1982), 54–74.

Schorr, David B., "How Blackstone Became a Blackstonian" (2009) 10 *Theoretical Inquiries in Law* 103–126.

Schulz, Fritz, *Classical Roman Law* (Oxford: Clarendon Press, 1951).

History of Roman Legal Science (Oxford: Clarendon Press, 1946).

Scialoja, Vittorio, "Aemulatio," in *Enciclopedia Giuridica Italiana*, vol. 1 (Milan: Società Editrice Libraria, 1910), 426–452.

"Nota a Corte di Cassazione di Firenze del 13 dicembre 1877" (1878) III(1) *Il Foro Italiano* 481–493.

Teoria della proprietà nel diritto romano, Pietro Bonfante (ed.), vol. 1 (Rome: Sampaolesi, 1928).

Scozzafava, Oberdan Tommaso, "La Soluzione Proprietaria di Robert-Joseph Pothier" (1980) 9 *Rivista Diritto Commerciale* 327–344.

Seneca, Lucius Annaeus, De beneficiis: Opera Quae Supersunt, Friedrich Haase (ed.), vol. 2 (Leipzig: De Gruyter, 1884).

Seppel, Marten and Tribe, Keith (eds.), *Cameralism in Practice: State Administration and Economy in Early Modern Europe* (Woodbridge: Boydell Press, 2017).

Servant, Hélène, "Les registres d'état civil en Guadeloupe: le reflet d'une histoire mouvementée" (2007) 146–147 *Bulletin de la Société d'Histoire de la Guadeloupe* 93–111.

"Sesión del Congreso Nacional 66, en 21 de marzo de 1825, número 151, por Frai Matías Fuenzalida," in Valentín Letelier (ed.), *Sesiones de los Cuerpos Lejislativos de la República de Chile (1810–1845)*, vol. 11 (Valparaíso: Biblioteca del Congreso Nacional de Chile, 1886–1908), p. 476–477.

Seton-Watson, Christopher, *Italy from Liberalism to Fascism, 1870–1925* (London: Methuen, 1967).

Shartel, Burke, "Meanings of Possession" (1931) 6 *Minnesota Law Review* 611–637.

Sheehan, James, *German Liberalism in the Nineteenth Century* (Chicago: University of Chicago Press, 1979).

Sherwin-White, Adrian Nicholas, *The Roman Citizenship* (Oxford: Clarendon Press, 1973).

Shovlin, John, *The Political Economy of Virtue: Luxury, Patriotism, and the Origins of the French Revolution* (Ithaca, NY: Cornell University Press, 2006).

Sieyes, Emmanuel-Joseph, *Qu'est-ce que le tiers état?* (Paris: Correard, 1822).

Simon, Walter M., *The Failure of the Prussian Reform Movement 1807–1919* (Ithaca, NY: Cornell University Press, 1955).

Simonde de Sismondi, J.-C.-L., *Nouveaux principes d'économie politique ou De la richesse dans ses rapports avec la population* (Paris: Delaunay Libraire, 1819).

Singer, Joseph W., "Property as the Law of Democracy" (2014) 63 *Duke Law Journal* 1287–1336.

Skocpol, Theda, *States and Social Revolutions* (Cambridge: Cambridge University Press, 1979).

Smith, Henry E., "Property as the Law of Things" (2012) 125 *Harvard Law Review* 1691–1726.

Smith, Vanessa, "Joseph Banks's Intermediaries: Rethinking Global Cultural Exchange," in Samuel Moyn and Andrew Sartori (eds.), *Global Intellectual History* (New York: Columbia University Press, 2013), 81–109.

Snowden, Frank M., *Violence and the Great Estates in the South of Italy: Apulia, 1900–1922* (Cambridge: Cambridge University Press, 1986).

Soboul, Albert, *La France Napoléonienne* (Paris: Arthaud, 1983).

Solar, Luis Claro, *De los Bienes, in 4 Explicaciones de Derecho Civil y Comparado 8* (Santiago: Jurídica de Chile, 1992).

"Nota a sentencia" (1905) 3 *Revista de derecho y jurisprudencia* 294–301.

Somma, Allesandro "I Giuristi Francesi e il Diritto della 'Grande Trasformazione,'" in Bernard Durand, Jean Pierre Le Crom, and Allesandro Somma (eds.), *Le droit sous Vichy* (Frankfurt am Main: Vittorio Klosterman, 2006), 437–452.

Şotropa, Valeriu, *Le droit romain en Dacie* (Amsterdam: J. C. Gieben, 1990).

Steel, Catherine, "Introduction: The Legacy of the Roman Republican Senate" (2015) 7(1) *Classical Receptions Journal* 1–10.

Steenland, Kyle, "Notes on Feudalism and Capitalism in Latin America" (1975) 2(1) *Latin American Perspectives* 49–58.

Stein, Peter, *Regulae Iuris: From Juristic Rules to Legal Maxims* (Edinburgh: Edinburgh University Press, 1966).

Roman Law in European History (Cambridge: Cambridge University Press, 1999).

Steinlechner, Paul, *Das Wesen der iuris communio und iuris quasi communio* (Innsbruck: Wagner, 1876).

Stella, Attilio, "Bringing the Feudal Law Back Home: Social Practice and the Law of Fiefs in Italy and Provence (1100–1250)" (2020) 46(4) *Journal of Medieval History* 396–418.

Stewart, John Hall, *A Documentary Survey of the French Revolution* (New York: Macmillan, 1951).

Stockton, David L., *The Gracchi* (Oxford: Clarendon Press, 1979).

Strahilewitz, Lior J., "The Right to Destroy" (2005) 114 *Yale Law Journal* 781–854.

Summenhart, Konrad, *De contractibus* (Hagenaw: Heinrich Gran for Johannes Rynman, 1500).

Taine, Hippolyte, *Les Origines de la France Contemporaine: La Révolution* (Paris: Hachette and Co., 1882).

Talamanca, Mario, "Gli ordinamenti provinciali nella prospettiva dei giuristi tardoclassici," in Gian Gualberto Archi (ed.), *Istituzioni giuridiche e realtà politiche nel tardo impero (III–V sec. d.C.)* (Milan: Giuffrè, 1976), 95–246.

Tchernia, André, *The Romans and Trade* (Oxford: Oxford University Press, 2016).

Temin, Peter, *The Roman Market Economy* (Princeton, NJ: Princeton University Press, 2013).

Thiers, Adolphe, *De la Propriété* (Paris: Paulin, l'Heureux et Cie, 1848).

Thomas, Yan, "Le valeur des choses: Le droit romain hors la religion" (2002) 57(6) *Annales: Histoire, Sciences Sociales* 1431–1462.

Tibiletti, Gianfranco, "Il possesso dell'*ager publicus* e le norme *de modo agrorum* sino ai Gracchi" (1948) 26 *Athenaeum* 173–236.

"Il possesso dell'*ager publicus* e le norme *de modo agrorum* sino ai Gracchi" (1949) 27 *Athenaeum* 3–42.

Tierney, Brian, *The Idea of Natural Rights* (Atlanta: Scholars Press, 1997).

Liberty and Law: The Idea of Permissive Natural Law, 1100–1800 (Washington, DC: Catholic University of America Press, 2014).

Toews, John Edward, *Becoming Historical: Cultural Reformation and Public Memory in Early Nineteenth-Century Berlin* (Cambridge: Cambridge University Press, 2004).

Toullier, Charles-Bonaventure-Marie, *Le Droit Civil Français Suivant l'Ordre du Code*, 6th ed., vols. 1–3 (Paris: Cotillon, 1846).

Toynbee, Arnold, *Hannibal's Legacy: The Hannibalic War's Effects on Roman Life* (London: Oxford University Press, 1965).

Troplong, Raymond Theodore, *Commentaire sur la prescription* (Brussels: Meline, Cans et Compagnie, 1843).

De la propriété d'après le Code civil (Paris: Pagnerre, 1848).

Trosne, Guillaume-François Le, *De l'Ordre Social: Ouvrage Suivi d'un Traité Élémentaire sur la Valeur, l'Argent, la Circulation, l'Industrie et le Commerce Intérieur et Extérieur* (Paris: Guillaume Debure, 1777).

Éloge Historique de M. Pothier (Orleans: Vve Rouzeau-Montaut, 1773).

Trucco, Humberto, "Teoría de la posesión inscrita dentro del Código Civil chileno" (August 1910) 7(6) *Rvista de derecho y jurisprudencia* 132–150.

Tuck, Richard, *The Sleeping Sovereign: The Invention of Modern Democracy* (Cambridge: Cambridge University Press, 2015).

Tuori, Kaius, "The Myth of Quintus Mucius Scaevola: Founding Father of Legal Science?" (2004) 72(3–4) *Tijdschrift voor Rechtsgeschiedenis* 243–262.

Tuori, Kaius, and Björklund, Heta (eds.), *Roman Law and the Idea of Europe* (London: Bloomsbury, 2019).

Ulpian, *Liber singularis regularum*, Paulus Krueger (ed.) (Berolini: Apud Weidmannos, 1878).

Vardi, Liana, *The Physiocrats and the World of the Enlightenment* (Cambridge: Cambridge University Press, 2012).

Vargas, Victorio Pescio, *Manual de derecho civil*, vol. 9 (Santiago: Jurídica de Chile, 1978).

Vassalli, Fillippo E., *Scritti Giuridici: Contributi alla teoria dei beni pubblici*, vol. 2 (Milan: Giuffrè, 1960).

Vicuna, Félix Vicuña, *El Porvenir del Hombre* (Valparaiso: Imprenta del Comercio, 1858).

Vidal, Michel, "La Propriété dans l'école de l'exégèse en France" (1976–1977) 5–6 *Quaderni Fioreninti per la Storia del Pensiero Giuridico Moderno* 7–40.

Villata, Maria Di Renzi "La Formazione dei Libri Feudorum, tra Pratica di Giudici e Scienza di Dottori," in *Il Feudalesimo nell'Alto Medioevo* (Spoleto: Preso de SEDE del Centro, 2000), 651–720.

Villey, Michel, *Le droit et les droits de l'homme* (Paris: Presses Universitaires de France, 1983).

La formation de la pensee juridique moderne, 4th ed. (Paris: Montchretien, 1975).

Vinogradoff, Paul, "Introduction," in Rudolf Huebner (ed.), *A History of Germanic Private Law*, Francis S. Philbrick (trans.) (Boston: Little, Brown & Company, 1918).

Visscher, Fernand de, *Mancipium et res mancipi* (Rome: Apollinaris, 1936).

Nouvelles études de droit romain: public et privé (Milan: Giuffrè, 1949).

Vita, Anna de, "Proprietà e Persona nella Strategia dell'Esclusione. Rimeditare Vichy: Tutto in Ordine Niente a Posto," in *Le droit sous Vichy* (Frankfort am Main: Klosterman, 2006), 11–50.

Wächter, Carl Georg von, *Handbuch des im Königreiche Württemberg geltenden Privatrechts* (Stuttgart: Metzler, 1842).

"Ueber Theilung und Theilbarkeit der Sachen und Rechte" (1844) 27 *Archiv für die civilistische Praxis* 155.

Wakefield, Andre, *The Disordered Police State: German Cameralism as Science and Practice* (Chicago: University of Chicago Press, 2009).

Warmelo, Paul van, "Aspects of Joint Ownership in Roman Law" (1957) 25(2) *Tijdschrift voor Rechtsgeschiedenis* 125–195.

Watkins, Thomas H., "Vespasian and the Italic Right" (1988) 84(2) *The Classical Journal* 117–136.

Watson, Alan, "The Birth of the Legal Profession" (1987) 85 *Michigan Law Review* 1071–1082.

The Law of Property in the Later Roman Republic (Oxford: Clarendon Press, 1968).

Weimar, Peter, "Die Handschriften des Liber Feudorum und seiner Glossen" (1990) 1 *Rivista Intenrazionale di Diritto Comune* 31–98.

Wesenbeck, Matthaeus, "ad Digest 41.1," in *Pandectas Iuris Civilis* (Basel: Eusebius Episcopius, 1566).

White, Steven D., "The Feudal Revolution: II" (1996) 152 *Past & Present* 205–223.

Whitman, James Q., *The Legacy of Roman Law in the German Romantic Era* (Princeton, NJ: Princeton University Press, 2014).

Wichmann, Christian August, *Über die natürlichsten Mittel die Frohn-Dienste bey Kammer- und Ritter-Güthern ohne Nachtheil der Grundherren aufzuheben* (Leipzig: J. G. I. Breitkopf, Sohn und Comp, 1795).

Wickham, Chris, "Debate: The Feudal Revolution: IV" (1997) 155 *Past & Present* 196–208.

Wieacker, Franz, "Cicero und die Fachjurisprudenz seiner Zeit" (1978) 3 *Ciceroniana* 69–77.

History of Private Law in Europe: With Particular Reference to Germany, Tony Weir (trans.) (Oxford: Clarendon Press, 1995).

"Über das Verhältnis der römishen Fachjurisprudenz zur griechisch-hellenistischen Theorie" (1969) 20 *Iura: rivista internazionale di diritto romano e antico* 448–477.

Windscheid, Bernardo, *Diritto delle Pandette: con note e riferimenti al diritto civile italiano*, vol. I, Carlo Fadda and Paolo Emilio Bensa (trans.) (Turin: Unione Tipografico-Editrice, 1930).

Lehrbuch des Pandektenrechts, 6th ed., vol. 1 (Frankfurt: Rütten & Loening, 1887).

Wolfe, Martin, "Jean Bodin on Taxes: The Sovereignty-Taxes Paradox" (1968) 83(2) *Political Science Quarterly* 268–284.

Wolff, Hans Julius, *Roman Law. An Historical Introduction* (Norman: University of Oklahoma Press, 1951).

Wood, Ellen Meiksins, *Liberty and Property: A Social History of Western Political Thought from the Renaissance to Enlightenment* (London: Verso, 2012).

The Origin of Capitalism. A Longer View (London: Verso, 2017).

The Pristine Culture of Capitalism: A Historical Essay on Old Regimes and Modern States (London: Verso, 1991).

Xifaras, Mikhail, "L'École de l'Exégèse: Est Elle Historique? Le Cas de Raymond-Théodore Troplong (1795–1869), Lecteur de Friedrich Carl von Savigny," in Mohnhaupt Heinz and Kervégan Jean-François (eds.), *Influences et Réceptions Mutuelles du Droit et de la Philosophie en France et en Allemagne* (Frankfurt: Klostermann, 2001), 177–209.

"Ya-t-il une théorie de la propriété chez Pierre-Joseph Proudhon" (2004) 47 *Corpus, Revue de philosophie* 229–282.

Yavetz, Zvi, "Why Rome?: Zeitgeist and Ancient Historians in Early 19th Century Germany" (1976) 97(3) *American Journal of Philology* 276–296.

Zuiderhoek, Arjan, "Introduction: Land and Natural Resources in the Roman World in Historiographical and Theoretical Perspective," in Paul Erdkamp, Koenraad Verboven, and Arjan Zuiderhoek (eds.), *Ownership and Exploitation of Land and Natural Resources in the Roman World 1–18* (Oxford: Oxford University Press, 2015).

INDEX